R. Gupta's®

Objective

PHYSICAL EDUCATION

Study Material with Highly Useful Questions
for Competitive & Entrance Exams

By
RPH EDITORIAL BOARD

RAMESH PUBLISHING HOUSE, New Delhi

Published by
O.P. Gupta *for* Ramesh Publishing House

Admin. Office
12-H, New Daryaganj Road, Opp. Officers' Mess,
New Delhi-110002 ✆ 23261567, 23275224, 23275124

E-mail: info@rameshpublishinghouse.com
Website: www.rameshpublishinghouse.com

Showroom
● Balaji Market, Nai Sarak, Delhi-6 ✆ 23253720, 23282525
● 4457, Nai Sarak, Delhi-6, ✆ 23918938

Book Code: R-1915

ISBN: 978-93-86845-26-9

2nd Edition: 1905

HSN Code: 49011010

CONTENTS

Physical Education

1. AIMS OF PHYSICAL EDUCATION

INTRODUCTION

In order to properly understand the meaning of physical education It is essential for us to understand the meaning of general education. Physical education is after all part of general education. Both are complementary to each other. They are like two faces of the same coin.

Ordinarily we consider all activities which make the body healthy and active as physical conditions. This interpretation however is wrong. Physical education goes beyond that. Its true scope is related to all those activities which build up human physique so that they impart knowledge of human and social behaviour and in turn help all in an all round development. In short it means that physical education helps not only in physical development of the body but also in all round development of human personality. It is wrong therefore to consider sports as same thing as physical education : it is not Similarly, games too do not constitute physical education, though games are part and parcel of physical education. Again, activities of entertainment too are not to be considered as physical education. Physical education is the education of both mind and body which help in an all-round growth of human personality.

DEFINITION OF PHYSICAL EDUCATION

Different scholars have given different definitions of Physical education. While some have only put emphasis on the physical activities others give greater importance to the growth and development of mental faculties.

H.C.Buck has given the following definition of Physical education. According to him Physical education as part of general education educates the boys and girls about the physical activities and through these exercises develop the human body.'

According to Voltmer and Esslinger, "Physical education is that part of education which takes place through physical activity."

Again, J.B.Nash defines Physical education as follows:

"Physical education is that part of education which is related to activities of the major human muscles."

Physical education is an education through human movement where many of the educational objectives are achieved by means of big muscle activities involving sport, games, gymnastics, dance and exercises. *– Harold M. Barrow.*

Physical education, an integral part of the total education process, is a field of endeavour that has as its aim the improvement of human performance through the medium of physical activities that have been selected with a view to realizing this outcome.

– Charles A Bucher.

Physical education is the sum of those experiences which come to the individual through movement. *– Delbert Oberteuffer.*

Physical education is the sum of man's physical activities selected as a kind and conducted as to outcomes. *– Jesse Feiring Williams.*

Physical education is that phase of the whole field of education that deals with big muscle activities and their related responses.

– Jay B Nash.

We can clearly observe that none of the definitions given above meets the objectives fully so that we can comprehend the meaning and significance of Physical education It is clear that the scholars have given interpretation of physical education in their own way. Undoubtedly we all have to agree that physical education is basically and essentially physical activity of the human body.

The following definitions given by the author himself should seem more appropriate and comprehensive. 'Physical education is an essential part of education which, by developing a balanced growth of body, mind and intellect imparts knowledge of social attitudes and behaviour and help all members of society in effecting an all-round development.'

AIMS OF PHYSICAL EDUCATION

We all agree that the various kinds of education have some objective or the other. The different kinds of education encourage the children, adults and elder people to achieve the definite objective. Now, physical education too has a definite objective. It caters to all age-groups, be it children, or youth or elderly people. We all must accept the view that an activity which is undertaken without a set objective goes waste, both in matter of time and money. The paramount objective of physical education is an all-round development of personality. The following is a detailed account of the objectives of Physical education :

1. **Complete Physical Development**

   Physical education aims at a complete development of physical human body. It enlightens us about all aspects of human body which ultimately go to develop it. Physical education develops all the processes and organs of the body simultaneously. These days physical education has acquired an added popularity and more and more people are beginning to understand its proper importance. In this respect TV., Radio and other similar governmental agencies have played a significant role, because they have helped its message reach every home in every nook and corner.

2. **Sufficient Increase in Skill**

   Every individual has certain physical efficiency in his body. Physical education helps the Individual to increase his efficiency. When an individual has learnt about the basic knowledge of how his body works, he is likely to use is to acquire greater efficiency. He becomes skilled in physical activities which he may undertake.

3. **Making Ideal Life**

   Physical education goes a long way in teaching an individual how to lead an ideal life. The successful and intelligent men of the world were able to lead their lives and left behind an imprint because they were well-versed in physical education. Apart from being helpful to an individual to lead a successful life, it also helps a nation to form able and good citizens. All capable players and physical instructors everywhere are leading a successful life.

4. **Making Body immune and Healthy**

   The chief aim of physical education is always to make a person develop a healthy body immune to diseases through relevant exercises of all organs of the body. All those who undertake exercises everyday can keep the body fit and the various organs of the body develop immunity to diseases and disorders. Not only that, they can assist others to keep body healthy and fit by imparting to him knowledge about the working of human body and its various organs.

5. **Feeling of Integration & Patriotism**

   When individuals play in a team they always develop a team-spirit. This spirit is always above all consideration of caste or nationality of other players in the team. A team has only one over-riding aim and that is to play the game. Here individual interests do not enter the minds of the players. All those nations whose players play a game single- mindedly are always able to do better than those teams who play for themselves. All institutions as NCC, NSS. Scouting /Guides are sending out the messages of national integration and patriotism.

6. **Development of Qualities of Good Behaviour**

   Physical education develops qualities of good behaviour among all. In physical education the students are taught lessons of duties towards others. They also learn how to keep themselves healthy and fit. Physical education also imparts love, compassion, brotherhood and discipline, co-operation and humility. The students also learn to respect their elders. It is easier to impart lessons in good behaviour among children, and in turn they too learn them easily in tender age.

7. Development of Feelings of Tolerance and Courage

Physical education develops tolerance and courage. While playing, the children are often made to face defeat in the field. Even the spectators may speak hundred ill things about the players and their performance. In the face of it the players have to, and they must, display complete equanimity (tolerance). It is equally necessary that the players on the field must not let their courage and enthusiasm flag. All such situations are bound to inculcate spirit of tolerance and of courage. Physical education develops courage in the face of defeat and tolerance in the face of victory.

OBJECTIVES OF PHYSICAL EDUCATION

Every kind of education must have two objectives before it, one that is its major objective and the *other* minor or subsidiary objectives

While the minor objectives of different kinds of education can be the same but the major objective of each kind is always different and exclusive. There are always, different steps prescribed through which we may achieve those objectives. The objective of any kind of education is the highest point of achievement, and there Is nothing beyond it worth achieving. In certain cases we may choose to substitute some minor objective for the major objective, and then efforts are made to achieve it. It is right to say then that without objective or a definite target the labour put in is always more and efforts are also more labourious,

The following are the objectives of physical education :

1. To prepare healthy and able-bodied citizens for a country.
2. To constitute an unparalleled and ideal society.
3. To impart education and to arouse interest in education through games.
4. To be able to use leisure (spare time).
5. To determine an objective keeping in view time, place and circumstances.

Besides, the objectives mentioned above there are other minor objectives too. Though the objectives of physical education are significant, it is said to note that it has not acquired the status of an elite occupation. The reason is that it lacks any technical objective as such which may remain the same everywhere and at all times. There are comparatively other occupations which suit every place and society. One naturally considers them important. Physical education has not been given as great an importance as to other occupations and so it has not become an organised and high class occupations. As it is, physical education serves the role of subsidiary to general education almost in the fashion of a manager serving his master.

PHYSICAL EDUCATION IN INDIA

History of Physical Education in India started from the Indus valley Civilization when most nations of the Europe had not even opened their eyes. The greatest drawback in our civilization, without doubt, has been that the people never kept the written records of their cultural and political adventures. Whatever we have received from our ancient people that is our heritage based' on traditions and customs, hearsays or legends. Whether they are really reliable, cannot be said with certainty, but excavations at prehistoric sites like Mohenjodaro and Harappa etc. that remind us of the existence of a great civilization about 3000 years ago. Excavation reveals that there were gigantic public baths as we find in later Roman period, where people used to do some exercise to keep themselves physically fit.

Oil-massaging seems to be widely known to ancient people. **Gambling** was one of the most popular sports in this period of pre-historic reckoning. Children mostly played with birds and beast made of clay. They had pet animals also. When the Aryan occupied Sapta Sindhu, they pushed down the Dravidians—the aboriginal tribes of India. Certain facts connected with such a transitional period show that dancing was a very vigorous and very popular activity among the inhabitants of Indian sub-continent. That is why people of Indus Valley Civilization were physically very strong.

In fact, the History of Physical Education in India can be studied along with the classification of various periods of political history of India, which is divided into the following ages:

1. Vedic Age (2000—1000 B.C.)
2. Epic Age (1000—600 B.C.)
3. Historical Age (600 B.C.)
4. Nalandine Period (300 A.D.)
5. Rajput Period (300 to 1200 A.D.)
6. Muslim Period (1200 to 1750 A.D.)
7. British Period (upto 1947 A.D.)
8. Post Independence Development (1947-till date)

MODERN VIEW OF PHYSICAL EDUCATION

The concept of Physical Education has changed considerably in the modern period. Today it is being taught as a specialised subject and a lot of value is being included in the subject matter of the Physical Education. There was a time, when playful activities as a separate profession was simply treated as wastage of time. But in the modern times sports and physical activities are treated as inseparable part of human life as well as dignity and prestige of a nation. For example, America is a super power, not only in terms of economic and technological advaueer, but also in the sports arena. In all International events the performance of American athletes and sports person is incomparable. On the other side, while we are talking about Indian as emerging world power, but its recognition at International level as a super power is always doubtful. The performance of Indians at regional and International level does not reflect, the character of a super power.

The modern concept of Physical Education is now being well understood by Indian policy-makers, that is why, Physical Education has been introduced now as a subject in schools from secondary level onwards. Physical Education cannot be treated in isolation, it is very much part of general education curriculum. There is great concern among intellectuals and decision makers about the well being of our children, who are heavily loaded with three R's oriented concept of

education. The lifestyle of the students have been affected by academic burden, long hours of school, career competitions and stress of modern living conditions especially in metropolitan and cosmopolitan cities. Moreover, students are mentally occupied but their physical movements are restricted, and this has put limitations on free time at their disposal which made them just passive learners.

In the light of the above cited facts, physical education is now most sought after subject in the educational curriculum in the new millennium. Modern concept of physical education has attached broader and wider meaning to the term *physical education* as compared to the traditional concept of physical education which was narrowly conceived by the educationist in particular and society as a whole, particularly in India.

SCOPE OF PHYSICAL EDUCATION

In modern age, in the sphere of Physical Education, not only physical activities, gymnastics, drill and marching are included, but, for the development of human personality, emphasis is on his mental, physical, social and moral sides also. These aspects of human life are developed through participating in physical activities. This shows that the scope of Physical is now vast, which can cover almost all the requirements of an individual.

Physical Education is multifaceted and multidimensional activities and process which contributes to the growth and development of the student as well as helps in all round development of the personality. Although the scope of physical development is vast, inexhaustible and endless, according to Boudhard, McPherson and Taylor, the scope of physical education could be understood in the following four parts:

1. Physical Education as a Discipline : Day by day new advancement is taking place in the strategy and field work of Physical Education. Recently physical education has been recognised as a discipline because it is a scientific study of human body in action. Physical education has been taught in the school both theoretically and practically. Although the base of theory subject remains to be in applied sciences and other disciplines, yet it makes physical education a unique subject in its own technical way. A number of research have been conducted on people involved in physical activities and sports. Various kinds of physical therapy is a contribution of Physical Education.

2. Physical Education as a Subject Matter: In modern society, the concept of Physical Education has changed vastly. Today it is being treated as a specialized subject having deep relation with other subjects of humanities and sciences. Physical education derives principles from various science and art subjects. It makes physical education a worthwhile subject matter within the educational process. The relationship between Physical Education and other subjects can be elaborated as below:

- Physiology combined with Physical Education and sports becomes Exercise Physiology.
- Sociology combined with Physical Education and sports becomes Sports Sociology.
- Bio and Physical combined with Physical Education and sports becomes Biomechanics.
- Psychology combined with Physical Education and sports becomes Sports Psychology.

Physical Education is a dynamic profession. It covers all aspect of individuals needs and interests e.g., from simple play to competitive sports are covered under Physical Education program. In Physical Education, there is sincere desire on the part of practioners to have public recognition and acceptance. They wanted their field to have professional status.

Physical Education also derives certain important philosophies from humanities and arts such as aesthetic, appreciation, fine movements, methodologies, profession, code of conduct and techniques of teaching.

Although the theoretical principles of physical education originally come from other disciplines but implications of these science or areas become more fruitful for human beings when they are combined with physical education and sports.

3. Physical Education as a Field of Activity: The prime concern of Physical Education as a subject is its association with field activities. Right from the beginning various physical activities, which were performed by individual, are treated today as beginning of playful activities. Physical Education is multifacet and multi-dimension activity which includes games, recreation, fitness programmes, yoga, adventure sports etc.

In this category following may be studied:
- (a) Yoga
- (b) Rhythmics
- (c) Games and Sports
- (d) Gymnastics
- (e) Recreation
- (f) Self Defence Activities.

4. Physical Education as a Service: The service concept of Physical Education has been an integral part of education since ages. Teaching as profession is based on scientific facts obtained through scholarly endeavors. It differs from the trade in several aspects. The principles and practices of Physical Education come from a wide area of learning such as Biology, Physiology, Anatomy, Psychology, Sociology, Zoology, etc. However, principles should not be framed at the cost of humanity. Physical education is considered as a professional field of study and provides opportunities to students to undergo the teacher training program in order to prepare them to be prospective teachers of Physical Education.

This field of study also ensures adequate provision of facilities and programmes to be implemented as compulsory and elective courses in educational institutions. This professional service area also provides avenues for general public to follow a programme of one's choice and interest in order to maintain fitness. It also facilitates in the weight management and rehabilitation of injuries and various ailments. All principles must take into account the need of the society and must reflect the social purposes. If a man is to survive he must know how to adjust socially with others. This aspect of behaviour is best obtained from humanities. Thus, Physical Education is both an Art, and a Science, but it is the science which makes a profession in the realm of reference of humanities.

Games, sports and physical activities learnt through physical education programme enable a person to wisely utilise the leisure time through participation and also provide the scope to attain high performance for participation at different levels of competitions. As a specialized subject of Physical Education, the following activities can be included under the scope of Physical Education :

    (i) *Corrective Exercises:* Through these the deformities in the body of the students are removed. Sometimes these defects are because of the defects in muscles and for these no use light corrective exercises.

    (ii) Games, Sport and swimming: This include athletics, Table-Tennis, Hockey, foot ball, basket ball, Swimming etc.

    (iii) *Self Defence Activities* :This includes *Dunds,* Boxing, *Lathi Gathka* and Pulls ups.

    (iv) *Fundamental Gymnastics :* Through these activities the balance of the body is maintained. For this, running, walking, climbing like activities are recommended.

    (v) *Rhythmics* : In this Lezium, Tipri and Dances are included.

    (vi) *Recreation* : This includes the following activities like Camping, Hiking, Fishing and Nature study.

    (vii) *Yoga* : This includes Asanas, Pranayamas and other yogic exercises.

Thus, we can clearly say that the field and scope of Physical Education is very vast. With the increasing tension and hectic schedule in modern life, the requirement of various types of physical activities has grown up considerably.

IMPORTANCE OF PHYSICAL EDUCATION

Physical education contributes to the over all development of the child especially in the new millennium. Because of the advanced technology, the lifestyle of the people changing very fast. Physical activity in daily life will be limited to switching on and off of the remote controls of every instrument and electronic devices, for example : operating of computer, television, telephone, music system and other household gaggets etc. People have become more passive than ever before because of satellite transmitted programs run by cable operators almost all over the country, school going population like to watch such programs to satisfy their feelings of thrill and excitement by passive participation instead of active participation in physical activity.

Inactivity will have implication on the health of child to a great extent. To keep oneself physically fit and healthy, minimum activities are required at every stage of human life. For example,

    (i) During childhood, physical activities are required for somato-psychic-development i.e., proper growth and development.

    (ii) During adulthood, physical activities are required to maintain good health and fitness.

    (iii) During old age, physical activities are required to prevent and treat any possible physical ailment in vital organs and keep oneself independent and physically fit.

As the saying goes "physical exercise not only add years to life, but life to years". It means physical activities give life to the person till one survives and it helps one to live healthy without any disease or ailment.

MISCONCEPTION ABOUT PHYSICAL EDUCATION

There are few misconceptions in the mind of the people with regard to the physical education, especially those who are related with education and do not try to understand physical education in the right perspective.

Some of the misconceptions are as follows:

1. Physical education is not necessary for school children, especially during school hours.

2. Physical education does not have academic values.

3. The objectives of physical education are merely related with the development of physical fitness, and does not contribute towards intellectual development.

4. Some people still think that physical education is just doing physical training.
5. In many institutions physical education is the rest period between academic classes.

CONTROVERSIES ON THE NAME OF PHYSICAL EDUCATION

Physical education uses physical activity to produce holistic improvements in a person's physical, mental, and emotional qualities. It treats each person as a unit, a whole being, rather than as having separate physical and mental qualities that bear no relation to and have no effect on each other. Physical education is in reality a broad field of interests. Its basic concern is the improvement of human movement. More specifically, it deals with the relationship between human movement and other areas of education: the relationship of the body's physical development to its mind and soul as they are being developed. This focus on the effect of physical development on other areas of human growth and development contributes to the uniquely broad scope of physical education. No other single field is concerned with the total development of the human.

As the varying definitions show, the basic points that define the field are named consistently by different scholars;

1. Physical education is conducted through physical means; that is some sort of physical activity or some type of movement is involved.
2. Physical activity is usually (though not always) moderately vigorous, it is concerned with gross motor movements, and the skills involved do not have to be very finely developed or of high quality for benefits to be gained.
3. Although the student gains these benefits by a physical process, the educational benefits for the student include improvements in non-physical areas such as intellectual, social, and aesthetic growth; that is, the cognitive and affective domains.

There has been long standing controversy among educators of Physical Education, regarding its name and usages. Some of the proposed names are:

Movement Arts: It is a slightly less broad version of the movement arts and sciences label. This title eliminates some of the overlap of study within the sciences that are concerned with certain aspects of human movement, but it might create the problem of disregarding the precision of science within the field.

Movement Education: Movement Education refers to the broader meaning of physical education, but there can be confusion over the use of the term. Many educators interpret the term as referring primarily to dance activities, which is only a narrow part of physical education, while others have confused it with the movement education from England that developed at the elementary school level.

Developmental Motor: Developmental motor performance expresses physical education's concern with motor performance and its development. The problem with this label lies in both its breadth and its lack of clarity: Does it describe the whole work of physical education? Would a typical educator in another field know what physical educators do according to this title?

Exercise Science: It became widely used in the 1990s. It has the advantage of defining a wider area of emphasis than simply sport. Another of its strengths is that it is easier for people outside the field to recognize its focus. This trait is valuable when a major driving force for a new name is to improve the reputation (and name recognition) of the field both among the public and among scholars in other fields.

Kinesiology : Kinesiology is a title that some departments began using as early as 1960s. Primarily research-oriented, the term refers to the study of human movement or, more recently, physical activity. However, in the sense that it refers to a particular study, it gives no indication of the breadth of what is taught. A student in physical education does not necessarily study movement. Teaching the strategy involved in playing a team game, Physical Education Manual for example, is definitely a part of physical education, but it is not kinesiology, or the study of movement skill. As practitioners are not always involved in studying the movement itself, kinesiology is too narrow in scope to define the whole field.

Human Physical Sciences: Human physical sciences points out some of the characteristics of the field, because it is concerned with studying the areas of the physical sciences (such as physics and the laws of mechanics) as they relate to people. However, to understand its use as a descriptive title for physical education, people must know exactly what the physical sciences are, as well as the difference between physical education and the overlapping areas within the sciences.

Physical Fitness or Simply Fitness: It refers primarily to the bodily aspects of fitness, which makes it simply a more modern version of the older title of physical training. Physical fitness is a state of health or of the body's ability to withstand the stresses of daily life. Because programs of physical fitness concentrate primarily on physical goals, the term is too narrow to include the broader goals of physical education.

Athletics, Sport Sciences: Athletics, Sport Sciences or simply sport are too narrow to represent the whole field of physical education. We know sport and what it represents. Athletics is essentially the same thing, although scholars will debate this statement at the philosophical level. Athletics refers to competitive activities, organized games, and sports, on either a team or an individual basis. Competitive activities are only one phase of physical education, and, as mentioned, they are not always educational.

Physical education and sport is becoming a more common title. That title extends the concerns of physical education by making it clear that it is a concern of the field, but at the same time, it shows that sport is not the only concern. This title has two inherent benefits:

It retains the traditional designation, which is familiar to the public, yet it includes sport, which is vitally involved in physical education and is seen by many scholars as the primary area of physical education's concern.

Some people prefer to keep the title physical education. Although many physical educators are not satisfied with this title, they realize that the public at least has some idea of what it means. They believe that developing a new image for the old term may be easier than trying to teach the public to recognise a new, unfamiliar title.

No agreement has been reached, but perhaps the most common recent replacement has been the label of physical education and sport. The largest movement away from the physical education designation at this time is towards the use of names that include the word exercise.

No matter what the final designation, we should keep in mind that each of the proposals depends heavily on individual interpretations of the focus within the field. Perhaps that diversity of opinion is a virtue in itself, because it echoes the earlier definition of physical education as a very broad area of work and study that includes many people who seem to have little relationship to each other in their interests and tasks.

PHYSICAL EDUCATION AS A PART OF EDUCATION PROCESS

"Sound body keeps sound mind" explains the place of physical education in education process. Mind and body cannot be separated. They are in one entity. Without body, mind can not be educated and in the same way without mind, body cannot be trained. The only difference is that in education process, "mind" is the point of concentration, whereas in physical education, body is considered media to educate through big muscle activity, There has to be balance between teaching and learning process so that there is an equal development of both mind and body of the child.

The definition of education as well as physical education concentrate on equal opportunity to all for maximum development of the potential of the child to draw out the best, The education and physical education when combined together contributes in the harmonious development of the personality.

During recent times even the education is also in the process of modification where in learning by doing is once again emphasised by educationist. On the other side, the aims and objectives of physical education also have been set to achieve the goal of education through these activities which contribute to the total development of the individual.

The contribution of physical activity towards achieving objectives of education has been justified by many concrete examples. While involving in any type of activity, child learns simultaneously more than one thing at a time. For example, the skill, the technique, and also the tactics and strategies to win over the opponents in the playing situation. Moreover, there are certain rules and regulations which are to be followed by them and also to control over one's own emotions, accepting of defeats, maintaining balance at the time of winning. There are numerous situations created wherein an individual has to make adjustments with many. These types of situations cannot be created in the class rooms. Hence for the allround development of the personality, education through physical education contributes to a great extent.

Keeping in view, the contributions of physical education in the education process, physical education has been accepted as an integral part of general education, Although the place of physical education in the educational process is still in its infancy in India, but gradually picking up its roots and serving the needs of the students and also of the society. In other words, physical education is not only an integral part of general education but also an essential part of the total education of the child for overall development of the personality.

CONTRIBUTION OF PHYSICAL EDUCATION

As mentioned earlier, Physical Education has been accepted as an integral part of Education. The Physical Education teachers work for the ultimate purpose of general education. The approach in case of class room teacher and that of Physical Education may be different, but the ultimate goals are the same. Let us now examine as to how far has Physical Education teacher can help in achieving the objectives of general education which may be classified according to C.A. Bucher under four heads:

1. The Objectives of Self Realization : These objectives, in short, aim at developing the individual by making him realise his potentialities and discovering his own abilities. Physical Education contributes to these objectives in the following ways:

(i) *An Inquiring Mind:* Physical Education develops an inquiring mind which tries to see his environment, examine his own ability, and stimulate his curiosity. These qualities are essential to an educated figure.

(ii) *Knowledge of Diseases and Health:* Happiness and success in life, to a great extent, are dependent upon health. One can't maintain one's health without the knowledge of health and disease. Physical Education contributes to this knowledge by giving instructions on the **3**R's of health— *Refreshment, Relaxation* and *Recreation.*

(iii) *Family and Community Health :* An Educated person maintains his own health and helps in maintaining the health of his family members and community. Without community health, it is difficult to maintain one's own health. Physical Education provides in-depth information regarding school health and community health, in all its physical, mental and social aspects.

(iv) *Skill as a Participant and Spectator in Sports* : Physical Education develops in the participants, the skills of performance and observation. Through the program of Physical Education activities one develops keen and probing eyes for understanding them.

(v) *Resources of Utilizing Leisure Hours in Mental Pursuits:* An educated person uses his leisure time properly. Physical Education makes a man resourceful in various activities. It teaches many recreational activities which can be used at leisure time for getting mental poise.

(vi) *Appreciation of Beauty:* An educated person uses his finer senses in the appreciation of beauty around him. He must have aesthetics sense. Physical Education provides innumerable opportunities for the development of this sense in man. The human body, if developed proportionally, is one of the most beautiful creation in the universe. Physical Education is the key to a *'beautiful'* body.

(vii) *Directing One's Life towards Worthwhile Goals* : An educated person guides his life as a captain guides his ship in the right direction. Physical Education can help in guidance program, so that the individual can set right his moral code and aim of life.

2. The Objectives of Human Realization :

Human relationship is key to happiness and successful life. An educated person is very much expected to have good relations with his fellow beings. *Physical Education contributes to the establishment of human relations in the following ways:*

(i) Ideal Physical Education program places human relationship and human welfare first. In planning a program in Physical Education consideration is to be given to the welfare of the participants. Even while framing a rule, human welfare or the welfare of the participants. Even while framing a rule, human welfare or the welfare of the participant is kept first of all. In a skill or a technique or a game sports, welfare of others is protected. Here nothing injurious or harmful act is encouraged.

(ii) Ideal Physical Education program enables each individual to enjoy a rich social experience through play. Play offers opportunity rich social experiences whenever one is indulged in. Educated persons ensures social qualities. These can be gained through play activity, games and sports. Hence Physical Education activities provide unlimited opportunities of socialization.

(iii) Ideal Physical Education program helps the individual to play co-operatively with others as co-operation is key to success. Without co-operation there is no play. Physical Education through team game play enhances the spirit of co-operation.

(iv) Ideal Physical Education program teaches courtesy, fair play and sportsmanship. Courtesy and politeness are the bases of citizenship training with the result there is a lot of changes in the behaviour of the person.

(v) Ideal Physical Education program contributes to family and home living. Some Physical Education generates all the good qualities for the proper understanding of the fellow being and making good adjustment in the society. A better family environment and home life is ensured.

3. The Objectives of Economic Efficiency :

Physical Education can achieve these objectives through the following:

(i) *Education for Good Workmanship:* Work is essential for all and workmanship is essential for a successful life. Physical Education instills in a child a habit to work by developing his Physical qualities.

(ii) *Education for Vocational Placement:* Physical Educator is the best suitable person for guiding the students properly for choosing their vocations in the course of their life.

(iii) *Education for Successful Work :* Success of a work depends to a great extent, on the health of a worker. Physical Education's main objective is the health and its problems. Hence good health ensures better work.

(iv) *Education for Professional Growth:* Physical Education caters to this need by guiding the student properly in the direction of adopting the right profession. Right type of selection and guidance definitely helps the people to embrace this profession.

(v) *Education for Wise Consumption of Goods and Services :* Educated person brings and uses his goods with wisdom. Physical Education teaches us the utility of different types of clothes, values of goods and art of selection of goods.

4. The Objectives of Civil Responsibility : These objectives are achieved through the following:

(i) *Education for Humanitarianism :* Physical Education teaches all to be human and sympathetic to all, to be friendly and social with all.

(ii) *Education for Tolerance :* Quality which is of paramount importance in a human being is the spirit and power of tolerance, so that one could adjust in the group living. Physical Education teaches this quality through the medium of activity.

(iii) *Education for Conformance with Laws:* Participants in Physical Education activities are to obey laws of games and sports. Through these activities one learns not only to be obedient to rules in games but also in social circles.

(iv) *Education for Civic Responsibility:* Physical Education develops responsibility

in an individual by giving him responsibility in various situations. When a person learns to shoulder the responsibility in game situations, he then enables himself to bear the work in his life situations, who there favourable or adverse.

(v) *Education for Democratic Living:* Democracy has a fake play in Physical Education. Hence it is an ideal field for learning *democracy* practically.

CONCLUSION

Physical Education, of late has been introduced as a subject in a number of states all over the country. This has been made compulsory as a part of new sports policy of the Government of India. On the recommendations of warriors commissions and committees, pertaining to sports, health and Physical activities oriented programs, the Government of India launched an ambitious program to *"catch them early"* with an objective to achieve some place at International sports arena by Indian sports men. The introduction of Physical Education will also make people aware about their health, physical fitness and discipline, which are an integral part of Physical Education. Physical Education, of taught properly can help in the regeneration of the sense of patriotism and National integration.

OBJECTIVE QUESTIONS

1. Physical Education helps us to build:
(*a*) Good health   (*b*) Good character
(*c*) Both (a) and (b)   (*d*) None of these

2. The World Health Organisation (WHO) had set a target that every person in the world should become health conscious by:
(*a*) 1994 A.D.   (*b*) 1998 A.D.
(*c*) 2000 A.D.   (*d*) 2006 A.D.

3. With whom the International Olympic Committee had signed an agreement for furthering the course of health for all and sports for all by 2000 A.D. :
(*a*) Government of India
(*b*) All the developed countries

(*c*) All the developing countries
(*d*) The World Health Organisation

4. 'Sound mind in a sound body' should be achieved by:
(*a*) taking proper diets
(*b*) taking proper medicines
(*c*) taking proper care of environments
(*d*) taking proper exercise in a routine way

5. What can be earned through regular and systematic fitness programme and positive lifestyle habits:
(*a*) Sound mind
(*b*) Sound wealth
(*c*) Healthy body
(*d*) Physical fitness and wellness

6. The capacity to carry out reasonably well various forms of physical activities without being unduly tired and includes qualities important to the individuals health and well being is considered as:
    (*a*) Physical fitness   (*b*) Modern life style
    (*c*) Both the above   (*d*) None of these

7. Which of the following is the quality that enables one to continue engaging in reasonably vigorous physical activities for extended periods of time:
    (*a*) Muscular Endurance
    (*b*) Cardio-respiratory Endurance
    (*c*) Agelity
    (*d*) Flexibility

8. Which of the following is the amount of muscular force one is capable of exerting in a single muscular contraction:
    (*a*) Agility   (*b*) Power
    (*c*) Speed   (*d*) Strength

9. Which of the following is the quality that enables a person to sustain localised muscle group activities for extended periods of time:
    (*a*) Flexibility
    (*b*) Strength
    (*c*) Muscular endurance
    (*d*) None of these

10. Which of the following is the ability of the human body to change direction quickly and effectively:
    (*a*) Cardio-respiratory endurance
    (*b*) Muscular endurance
    (*c*) Flexibility
    (*d*) Agility

11. Which of the following refers to the functional capacity of a joint to move through a normal range of motion:
    (*a*) Agility   (*b*) Power
    (*c*) Flexibility   (*d*) None of these

12. Which of the following is the quality of a muscle to contract forcefully in the quickest possible time:
    (*a*) Power   (*b*) Speed
    (*c*) Strength   (*d*) None of these

13. How many categories can physical fitness be classified into:
    (*a*) Four   (*b*) Five
    (*c*) Two   (*d*) Three

14. Which one of the following is not a component of health related physical fitness:
    (*a*) Cardio-respiratory endurance
    (*b*) Muscular strength & endurance
    (*c*) Body composition
    (*d*) Coordination

15. Which one of the following is not a component of Motor Skill related physical fitness:
    (*a*) Endurance   (*b*) Balance
    (*c*) Flexibility   (*d*) Agility

16. Which of the following is considered as the constant and deliberate effort to remain healthy and attain highest potential for well being:
    (*a*) Fitness   (*b*) Wellness
    (*c*) Coordination   (*d*) Endurance

17. Which of the following is the first demand of the fitness program:
    (*a*) Regularity   (*b*) Tolerance
    (*c*) Progression   (*d*) Specificity

18. The level at which the human body favourably responds to an exercise is called:
    (*a*) Progression
    (*b*) Total Body Involvement
    (*c*) Tolerance
    (*d*) Exercise Tolerance

19. What adversely affects regularity and progression of physical fitness programme:
    (*a*) Over exercise
    (*b*) Adequate amount of rest & sleep
    (*c*) Insufficient rest and sleep
    (*d*) None of them

20. Which one is not an advantage of fitness program:
    (*a*) It relieves tension and stress of life
    (*b*) It fasts up the aging process
    (*c*) It regulates and improves overall body functions
    (*d*) It decreases the risk of cronic heart diseases and illness

21. Choose the correct statement regarding physical fitness:
    (*a*) It motivates toward negative life style
    (*b*) It increases the risk of chronic heart diseases and illness
    (*c*) It decreases level of energy and productivity
    (*d*) It improves posture and physical appearance

22. Which of the following is required for an individual to develop and maintain fitness:
    (*a*) Early to bed
    (*b*) Early to rise
    (*c*) Regular physical activity
    (*d*) None of the above

23. The concept of wellness goes beyond:
    (*a*) Absence of mere disease
    (*b*) Optimal physical fitness
    (*c*) Both the above
    (*d*) None of the above

24. In which year the new concept called 'Wellness' was developed?
    (*a*) 1980   (*b*) 1985
    (*c*) 1990   (*d*) 1999

25. Which of the following is/are basic functions for which the human organism was created?
    (*a*) Movement
    (*b*) Physical activity
    (*c*) Both the above
    (*d*) None of the above

26. Which of the following is/are demand(s) a deeper understanding of the various principles that control the development of different components of physical fitness:
    (*a*) Proper development of physical fitness
    (*b*) Proper maintenance of physical fitness
    (*c*) Both the above
    (*d*) None of the above

27. The dosage of exercise should be—— to guarantee the improvement of physical fitness level of an individual.
    (*a*) Progressively increased
    (*b*) Rapidly increased
    (*c*) Randomly increased
    (*d*) None of the above

28. Cardiovascular risk factors can also be reduced through a systematic and well developed programme of:
    (*a*) Sports   (*b*) Fitness activities
    (*c*) Healthy lifestyle (*d*) All the above

29. Lowering of high density lipoprotein (HDL) is harmful effect of:
    (*a*) Consumption of alcohol
    (*b*) Consumption of hard drug
    (*c*) Cigarette smoking
    (*d*) Tobacco chewing

30. Which of the following are decisive factors to assess dietary requirements of an individual
    (*a*) Age and sex
    (*b*) Age, sex and height
    (*c*) Age, sex, height and activity level
    (*d*) None of the above

31. Which of the following is/are not managed properly, can become a serious hazard and put constant strain on the cardiovascular system which may in turn lead to heart disease:
    (*a*) Tension
    (*b*) Stress
    (*c*) Both the above
    (*d*) None of the above

32. About which of the following it is said, "no doubt it enhance sports performance but lead to very serious long term effects on the sports persons. —
    (*a*) Alcohol   (*b*) Drugs
    (*c*) Smoking   (*d*) Tobacco chewing

33. H.D.L. stands for:
    (*a*) Highly Diluted Liquor
    (*b*) Hard Drugs and Liquors
    (*c*) High Density Lipoprotein
    (*d*) Highest Drug Level

34. Food that contain a low or moderate amount of calories but are packed with nutrients are called:
    (*a*) High nutrient density foods
    (*b*) Low nutrient density foods
    (*c*) Balanced food
    (*d*) None of the above

35. In order to guarantee a better, healthier, happier and more productive life each individual to be taught to control:
  (*a*) his bad habits
  (*b*) his over dreaming habits
  (*c*) his sleeping sickness
  (*d*) his personal health habits

36. Regarding advantages of wellness, which of the following statement is incorrect:
  (*a*) It improves of efficiency of cardio-vascular system
  (*b*) It helps in better management of stress and tension
  (*c*) It increases recovery time after strenuous activity
  (*d*) It delays the aging process

37. Which one of the following is not a benefit of aerobic activities:
  (*a*) It lowers resting heart rate
  (*b*) It decreases stroke volume and cardiac output
  (*c*) It prevents coronary heart disease
  (*d*) It helps in maintaining ideal body weight

38. Which one of the following is not associated with 'Free hand exercises'?
  (*a*) Body stretch
  (*b*) Knee bends
  (*c*) Jogging
  (*d*) Spot running

39. The purpose of which of the following is to develop various muscles or muscle groups besides affecting other systems of the body:
  (*a*) Walking
  (*b*) Jogging
  (*c*) Skipping
  (*d*) Calisthenics

40. Which of the following exercises maintains natural elasticity of blood vessels and helps in maintenance of blood pressure in normal limits
  (*a*) Regular brisk walking
  (*b*) Trunk twisting
  (*c*) Alternate step skipping
  (*d*) Rocker step skipping

41. Which of the following exercise is considered as the easy running and an elementary economical and personally geared exercise programme to develop general physical fitness:
  (*a*) Spot running
  (*b*) Jogging
  (*c*) Regular brisk walking
  (*d*) Skipping

42. Through, which of the following exercise, gross muscle groups and ankle knee joints can be exercised:
  (*a*) Jogging
  (*b*) Skipping
  (*c*) Spot running
  (*d*) Regular brisk walking

43. Choose the correct statement regarding jogging:
  (*a*) Early morning hours are suitable for jogging
  (*b*) Late evening hours are suitable for jogging
  (*c*) Both the above
  (*d*) None of the above

44. What precautions should be taken in jogging:
  (*a*) It should be done on softer grass or surface rather than harder surfaces like roads and pavements
  (*b*) It should not be done 2 to 3 hours after a meal
  (*c*) It should not be done during extreme heat and humid conditions
  (*d*) All the above

45. During jogging, stitch is commonly occured. It may be relieved by:
  (*a*) Deep breathing
  (*b*) Change of posture
  (*c*) Hand pressure over the site of pain
  (*d*) All the above

46. Which of the following exercise is good for improving and maintaining overall physical fitness, particularly fitness on the heart, lungs and circulation:
  (*a*) Swimming   (*b*) Cycling
  (*c*) Skipping   (*d*) None of these

47. Which of the following develops on one side of the abdomen or lower chest with the jolting action of jogging?
(*a*) A stitch
(*b*) A cramp
(*c*) Both the above
(*d*) None of the above

48. Tightening of muscles causing spasms which are painful is called:
(*a*) A stitch
(*b*) A cramp
(*c*) Stretch
(*d*) None of the above

49. How many types can skipping be performed?
(*a*) Two   (*b*) Three
(*c*) Four   (*d*) Five

50. Which one of the following is not a type of skipping exercises?
(*a*) Two foot basic step
(*b*) Alternate step
(*c*) Spread leg raise
(*d*) Alternate toe touching

51. Which of the following exercise involves a jump over the rope with the right foot (jump), a second hop on the same foot (rebound), then a jump over the rope with the left foot (jump) and another hop on the same foot (rebound)—
(*a*) Two foot basic step
(*b*) Spread leg raise
(*c*) Alternate step
(*d*) None of the above

52. Which of the following exercise includes two jumps for each complete turn of the rope—
(*a*) Rocker step
(*b*) Two foot basic step
(*c*) Alternate step
(*d*) None of the above

53. In which of the following exercise as the rope passes under the front foot, the- weight is transformed forward allowing the back foot to rise and the rope to pass under it.
(*a*) Rocker step

(*b*) Two foot basic step
(*c*) Spread leg raise
(*d*) None of the above

54. To start, in which of the following exercise, the rope is kept at the back, maintaining stride position with legs?
(*a*) Rocker step
(*b*) Alternate step
(*c*) Spread leg raise
(*d*) None of the above

55. Choose the correct statement.
(*a*) The effects produced by skipping on the body are similar to that of jogging and swimming
(*b*) One should avoid skipping if he is over weight
(*c*) Skipping should be avoided on the hard surface to prevent impact injuries
(*d*) All the above

56. Regarding cycling choose the correct statement—
(*a*) It is an aerobic exercise
(*b*) It should be avoided on busy and crowded roads
(*c*) It gives all the benefits of jogging and swimming
(*d*) All the above

57. New policy on education and extra curricular activities has highlighted
(*a*) The need of physical activities
(*b*) The need of healthful atmosphere
(*c*) Both the above
(*d*) None of the above

58. Among the following which is the commonly used weight training exercise?
(*a*) Two arms press   (*b*) Steps ups
(*c*) Prone lateral raise (*d*) All the above

59. Among the followings which is a training method by which exercises of various kinds are performed in sequence with or without apparatus after having given a dosage?
(*a*) Half squat
(*b*) Arm curl
(*c*) Circuit training
(*d*) None of the above

60. Unlike developing countries, which of the following country focuses more and more on the building up healthy and social nation?
 (*a*) Germany
 (*b*) U.S.A.
 (*c*) United Kingdom
 (*d*) All the above

61. While setting up a circuit which of the following point(s) should be kept in mind?
 (*a*) Exercises must be simple to perform at a predetermined work rate
 (*b*) Exercise load must be on an individual basis
 (*c*) The selected exercises must be strenuous, loading the individual within his exercise tolerance level
 (*d*) All the above

62. Among the following exercises which one cannot be included in a circuit?
 (*a*) Agility runs
 (*b*) Squat thrust
 (*c*) Cycling
 (*d*) Rope climbing

63. Among the following exercises which can be included in a circuit?
 (*a*) Step ups
 (*b*) Stair running
 (*c*) Standing long jump
 (*d*) All the above

64. In context of the nature of sports training, choose the correct statement(s).
 (*a*) It is referred to individual high performance in one particular game or sport or an event
 (*b*) It is systematic and well planned
 (*c*) It requires a sports life corresponding to the demands of competition
 (*d*) All the above

65. A good warm up session increases the body and muscle temperature which help in—
 (*a*) Increasing enzyme activity and also improves metabolic reaction associated with production of energy
 (*b*) Enhances blood flow and availability of oxygen
 (*c*) Lowers contraction and reflex time of muscles
 (*d*) All the above

66. During warm up which of the following sequence of exercise are recommended?
 (*a*) Stretching exercises, Calisthenics and Formal activity
 (*b*) Calisthenics, Formal activity and Stretching exercises
 (*c*) Formal activity, Stretching exercises and Calisthenics
 (*d*) None of the above

67. Research studies reveal that heart rate and consumption of oxygen during maximal exercise are directly related to—
 (*a*) Body temperature
 (*b*) Room temperature
 (*c*) Muscle temperature
 (*d*) All the above

68. The actual duration of warming up depends upon—
 (*a*) The nature of activity
 (*b*) The climate
 (*c*) The time of the day
 (*d*) All the above

69. The warming up session is divided into—
 (*a*) Three parts (*b*) Two parts
 (*c*) Four parts (*d*) One part

70. One should warm up for about—
 (*a*) 10 minutes
 (*b*) 20 minutes
 (*c*) 30 minutes
 (*d*) 45 minutes

71. During limbering or cooling down which of the following sequence of exercises is performed?
 (*a*) Formal activity, Stretching exercises and Calisthenics
 (*b*) Calisthenics, Formal activity and Stretching exercises
 (*c*) Stretching exercises and Formal activity
 (*d*) Formal activity, Calisthenics and Stretching exercises

72. Which of the following reduces pains and aches which are a normal part of competition or training programme?
  (*a*) Formal activity   (*b*) Stretching exercises
  (*c*) Calisthenics   (*d*) None of the above

73. The duration of cooling down may range from
  (*a*) 0 to 10 minutes   (*b*) 0 to 15 minutes
  (*c*) 10 to 20 minutes   (*d*) 20 to 30 minutes

74. The method of sports training should be
  (*a*) Planned for years together
  (*b*) Purposeful
  (*c*) Effective for the development of performance
  (*d*) All the above

75. Strength is an important component of
  (*a*) Various conditional abilities
  (*b*) Skills
  (*c*) Tactical actions
  (*d*) All the above

76. In context of strength, choose the correct statement(s)—
  (*a*) It has been considered as the most important conditional ability
  (*b*) It has been the most significant factor to enhance skill and capacity
  (*c*) It is the ability of a muscle to get over resistance
  (*d*) All the above

77. How many types of resistance is overcome by the sports person in games and sports?
  (*a*) Two   (*b*) Three
  (*c*) Four   (*d*) Five

78. Which of the following event can not be included in Frictional resistance?
  (*a*) Wrestling   (*b*) Swimming
  (*c*) Cycling   (*d*) Rowing

79. Which one of the following is an example of Resistance of opponent?
  (*a*) Swimming   (*b*) Boxing
  (*c*) Skiing   (*d*) Jumping

80. Strength depends upon—
  (*a*) Physiological cross-section of the muscle
  (*b*) Morphology of the muscle
  (*c*) Coordination of muscles that participate in the movement

  (*d*) All the above

81. Greater the phosphorous store in the body—
  (*a*) Lower will be the production of energy for contraction of muscles
  (*b*) Higher will be the production of energy for contraction of muscles
  (*c*) Lower will be the production of energy for expansion of muscles
  (*d*) Higher will be the production expansion of muscles

82. The people of South-East Asia are—
  (*a*) Heavier in weight and strong in muscle power
  (*b*) Heavier in weight but weak in muscle power
  (*c*) Lighter in weight but strong in muscle power
  (*d*) Lighter in weight and weak in muscle power

83. Strength ability can be classified into—
  (*a*) Two types   (*b*) Three types
  (*c*) Four types   (*d*) Five types

84. The ability of a muscle to get over resistance of maximum intensity of stimulus in a single muscular contraction is known as—
  (*a*) Strength endurance
  (*b*) Explosive strength
  (*c*) Maximum strength
  (*d*) Body weight

85. Which of the following is important in heavy resistance, i.e., weightlifting and throwing events
  (*a*) Strength endurance
  (*b*) Explosive strength
  (*c*) Maximum strength
  (*d*) Body weight

86. Strength endurance can be of—
  (*a*) Static (Isometric)
  (*b*) Dynamic (Isotonic)
  (*c*) Both the above
  (*d*) None of the above

87. Among the following which one is a combination of strength and speed abilities?
  (*a*) Explosive strength
  (*b*) Strength endurance
  (*c*) Maximum strength
  (*d*) None of the above

88. Which of the following is the ability of a muscle to get over resistance of medium intensity of stimulus for as long time as possible?
(a) Explosive strength
(b) Strength endurance
(c) Maximum strength
(d) Body weight

89. Which of the following is the ability of a muscle to get over resistance of sub-maximum intensity of stimulus as fast as possible?
(a) Explosive strength
(b) Strength endurance
(c) Maximum strength
(d) None of the above

90. The best example of strength endurance is—
(a) Sprints   (b) Wrestling
(c) Discuss throws   (d) All the above

91. Which one of the following is the best example of explosive strength?
(a) Sprints   (b) Wrestling
(c) Discuss throws   (d) All the above

92. Which one of the following is the best example of maximum strength?
(a) Weight lifting   (b) Distance cycling
(c) Hitting in hockey (d) All the above

93. Which of the following exercises is/are used for developing strength?
(a) Exercises in which one's own body weight is overcome
(b) Exercises with loading apparatus
(c) Exercises involving competitive movement and done with additional weights
(d) All the above

94. The tension produced in the muscle as it shortens is affected by—
(a) The initial length of the muscle fibers
(b) The angle of pull of the muscle
(c) The speed of contraction
(d) All the above

95. The strength training exercises can be classified into—
(a) Four categories   (b) Six categories
(c) Three categories   (d) Five categories

96. Which of the following exercises aim at strengthening the total muscular system of the body for the purpose of general athletic development?
(a) General strength exercises
(b) Specific strength exercises
(c) Competitive exercises
(d) None of the above

97. Which of the following exercises lay down the base for specific muscular strength training?
(a) Specific strength exercises
(b) General strength exercises
(c) Competitive exercises
(d) None of the above

98. Which of the following exercises aim at strenghening those muscles which perform active role in the competitive sports ?
(a) Specific strength exercises
(b) General strength exercises
(c) Competitive exercises
(d) None of the above

ANSWERS

1.	(c)	2.	(c)	3.	(d)	4.	(d)	5.	(d)	6.	(a)	7.	(b)	8.	(d)
9.	(c)	10.	(d)	11.	(c)	12.	(a)	13.	(c)	14.	(d)	15.	(c)	16.	(b)
17.	(c)	18.	(d)	19.	(c)	20.	(b)	21.	(d)	22.	(c)	23.	(c)	24.	(a)
25.	(c)	26.	(c)	27.	(a)	28.	(d)	29.	(c)	30.	(c)	31.	(c)	32.	(b)
33.	(c)	34.	(a)	35.	(d)	36.	(c)	37.	(b)	38.	(c)	39.	(d)	40.	(a)
41.	(b)	42.	(a)	43.	(c)	44.	(d)	45.	(d)	46.	(a)	47.	(a)	48.	(b)
49.	(c)	50.	(d)	51.	(c)	52.	(b)	53.	(a)	54.	(c)	55.	(d)	56.	(d)
57.	(c)	58.	(d)	59.	(c)	60.	(d)	61.	(d)	62.	(c)	63.	(d)	64.	(d)
65.	(d)	66.	(a)	67.	(c)	68.	(d)	69.	(b)	70.	(c)	71.	(d)	72.	(b)
73.	(c)	74.	(d)	75.	(d)	76.	(d)	77.	(c)	78.	(a)	79.	(b)	80.	(d)
81.	(b)	82.	(c)	83.	(b)	84.	(c)	85.	(c)	86.	(c)	87.	(a)	88.	(b)
89.	(a)	90.	(b)	91.	(a)	92.	(a)	93.	(d)	94.	(d)	95.	(c)	96.	(a)
97.	(b)	98.	(a)												

2. SPORTS PSYCHOLOGY

MEANING OF SPORTS PSYCHOLOGY

Psychology is a very wide subject. It can be applied to all branches of human knowledge and activities. It also deals with fitness of human mind and body. But Sports Psychology for Physical Education largely deals with fitness of human body. It lays stress on the fact that physical as well as mental development of human beings depends upon their physical fitness through games and sports. Hence Sports Psychology for Physical Education has great significance in the all—round development of an individual. Therefore, it is essential that we should know the exact meaning of Sports Psychology for Physical Education.

According to Mr. **K.M. Burns,** *'Sports Psychology for Physical Education is that branch of Psychology which deals with physical fitness of an individual through his participation in games and sports."*

AIMS OF SPORTS PSYCHOLOGY

Sports Psychology for Physical Education is an integral part of Psychology. Hence its aims are a kin to those of Psychology. Besides this, it has some particular aims also. Hence the aims of Sports Psychology for Physical Education can be studied in three forms, as follows :

1. General Aims
2. Social Aims
3. Particular Aims

Details of above-mentioned aims are given below:

1. General Aims : Sports Psychology for Physical Education has the same general aims as those of Educational Psychology. These aims revolve round the balanced and all-round development of child. It means that in general terms Sports Psychology for Physical Education aims at physical, mental, intellectual, moral and spiritual development of the child. With this purpose in view, Sports Psychology for Physical Education has the general aim of education before it. The general aim of education, as described by T P. Nunn is as follows

"Education should give rise to such situations as aim at all round or perfect development of the child, so that he may contribute his full share to the progress of mankind when he grows up."

2. Social Aims : Physical and Sports Psychology has the same social aims as those of Educational Psychology. The social aims of Educational Psychology lead towards the socialisation of the child. It means that there should be provision for such a type of education as enables the child to become a useful member of society when he grows up. John Dewey has very aptly remarked about it, *"Education does the same work for social life of the individual as food for the body."*

Hamayun Kabir has also said the same thing in a different way, *"If a person has' to become a useful member of society, he has not only to aim at individual development, but also at the development of society."* We should not forget that man is a social being. He grows up in society and develops in society. Hence Education as well as Sports Education should aim at making the child a useful member of society when he grows up.

Thus we come to realize that Sports Education or Physical Education plays a significant role in all-round development of the child through games and sports. This all-round development includes perfect socialisation of the child. The name "Physical Education or Sports Education" should not mislead us to think that it aims at mere physical development of the child. He has to live in society. So his development is complete only when he is perfectly at ease with the society in which he lives. However, Sports Education does not fulfill this aim through text book studies, but through games and sports.

3. **Particular Aims :** Sports Psychology for Physical Education has its particular aims also. One of these particular aims is to improve the physical health of the students through games and sports. Its another allied particular aim is to prepare the students for various sports and games competitions.

In tact, proficiency in games and sports competitions is the most important particular aim of Physical Education. Hence Sports Psychology for Physical Education deals with physical activities and competitions in games and sports from a psychological angle in order to bring about perfection in them.

SPORTS PSYCHOLOGY AND PSYCHOLOGY

1. **Healthy Behaviour**

   Both Psychology and Sports Psychology work for the behaviour modification in the behaviour of the individual. It is essential for the balanced development of the individual so that through sublimation of instincts, he should be led towards healthy behaviour under all circumstances. Hence healthy behaviour of the individual, through sublimation of instincts, is the common link between Psychology and Sports Psychology for Physical Education.

   Sports Psychology for Physical Education lays stress on the fact that the players should show balanced behaviour in games even if it is difficult to keep such a balance in certain instigating and provocating situations. Hence Sports Psychology for Physical Education has to probe into the causes and sources of human behaviour as much as Psychology. It has also to utilize the methods of sublimation of instincts for the modification of human behaviour as much as Psychology has to it.

2. **Relationship of providing Stimulus**

   It is essential for every kind of work that it should be done properly with full energy of the individual. Psychology reveals that this kind of energy is mostly the outcome of some stimulus. Every one requires some stimulus for filling energy in his work. The labourer can work with full energy only if there is some stimulus for his work. A student busy in studies requires this stimulus for filling energy in his pursuit for studies. Similarly, a player requires this stimulus for filling energy in his sports activities and performance at games. This stimulus may be some attractive prize for outstanding performance in games and sports or it may he enhancement of public honour of the player or of the school for which he is playing. Hence the study of proper stimulus for a particular kind of work or a particular game is the object of common relationship between Psychology and Sports Psychology for Physical Education.

3. **Relationship in Preparation for Work**

   Every kind of work can be done best if the worker is fully prepared for it. This holds good for a labourer, a businessman, a student as well as a player. Hence Psychology and Sports Psychology both try to prepare a worker or a player for the work or game in which he is going to take part. There are certain conditions for every kind of work or activity. Both Psychology and Sports Psychology for Physical Education have to study these conditions. They lay stress on the fulfillment of these conditions before the commencement of the work or the game.

   Hence we come to the conclusion that there is a close relationship between Psychology and Sports Psychology for Physical Education.

USES AND SCOPE OF SPORTS PSYCHOLOGY

Sports Psychology for Physical Education has many uses. Hence its scope is very wide. Following are the uses of Sports Psychology for Physical Education :

1. Reveals Sources of Physical Development: Sports Psychology for Physical Education deals with all kinds of physical activities, games and sports. Thus it reveals real sources of physical development for all students and individuals. For instance, in playing games the players have to undergo a great deal of physical labour for a certain period of time. This affords simple exercise for all limbs of the body. It improves the general health of players. It develops their body as regards energy as well as beauty. More over, it increases their stamina for sustained physical activity.

2. Co-ordination of Body and Mind: Sports Psychology for Physical Education deals with the co-ordination of body and mind through all kinds of physical activities and games. We see that all physical activities, games and sports bring about co-ordination of body and mind, because in all of them body and mind are at work simultaneously and they work in proper co-ordination. Sports Psychology for Physical Education studies the process of co-ordination of body and mind and tries to increase this co-ordination at every step. This use of Sports Psychology for Physical Education widens its scope in all spheres of life.

3. Means of Teaching Lessons of Life: Sports Psychology for Physical Education explores the means, which teach lessons of life. Given ahead are some of these lessons :

(i) *Lesson of Good Citizenship:* Sports Psychology for Physical Education deals with the lesson of good citizenship, because all physical activities, games and sports teach the lesson of good citizenship to the students. In fact, play-field can prove more important than classroom in teaching this lesson. This lesson plays a very important part in the formation of necessary qualities for ideal citizenship of a country.

(ii) *Lesson of Discipline:* Sports Psychology for Physical Education teaches the lesson of discipline. Every physical activity or every game has its rules and they have to be obeyed. Moreover, all players are required to play in perfect discipline. They have to obey the orders of their captain. They have to accept all the decisions of the referee even if they think that some of his decisions are quite wrong. Thus they form the habit of observing strict discipline throughout their life.

(iii) *Lesson of Balanced Life:* Sports Psychology for Physical Education teaches the lesson of balanced life to all those persons who take part in physical activities, games and sports of any kind. Players and Sportsmen are expected to have a balanced state of mind under all circumstances and all situations. They are expected not to be overjoyed at their victory in a match. Similarly, they are expected not to be frustrated or disappointed at their defeat They learn the lesson of having a balanced state of mind in all situations of life. In fact, children learn at the playground "how to win and how to lose in life".

(iv) *Lesson of Sociability :* Sports Psychology for Physical Education teaches the lesson of sociability. All physical activities, games and sports have a great value as a medium of social interaction. The players get ample opportunities for mixing up with one another and overcoming mutual differences of many kinds. In this way, they learn the lesson of making up with other people in society. Thus all players become sociable in life.

(v) *Lesson of Healthy Competition:* Sports Psychology for Physical Education teaches the lesson of healthy competition. It lays stress on fair competition without any foul play. This lesson has a very wide scope in life, because it can be applied to the whole life. When a player enters real life and has to face competition with others, he indulges in fair competition, without employing any unfair means for achieving personal gain at the cost of others.

(vi) *Lesson of Self-denial and Sacrifice:* Sports Psychology for Physical Education plays a significant role in teaching lesson of self denial and sacrifice through games and sports. In fact, games and sports teach the students to work with un-selfish motives. The players are not expected to play for their personal honour and personal fame when they play a match. They, on the other hand, play for the good name and honour of the team or the school for which they play. They learn the lesson of self-denial at every inch of a game. For example, while taking part in a hockey or foot-ball match, each player shows self—denial when he passes the ball to another player of his team instead of trying to take the ball to the goal-area himself and usurp all the glory of scoring a goal and winning the match.

(vii) *Lesson of Appreciation for Opponents :* Sports Psychology for Physical Education teaches the lesson of appreciation for opponents. It teaches a player to respect the players of opposite side. It also teaches him to appreciate the merits of the players of the opposite team, whether they win or lose the match. Sports Psychology for Physical Education expects all players to apply this lesson to real life and appreciate the merits of opponents even enemies in life.

(viii) *Lesson of Adjustment and Team Spirit:* Sports Psychology for Physical Education teaches the lesson of adjustment and team spirit to all players. It teaches every player to adjust himself with other players and allow them their due share in the game. Every player is expected to subordinate himself to fit into the team and to co-operate with other players for the common benefit of the team. Experiences of a joint effort in a team when all its players work together towards a common goal are a great source of training in team spirit. This teaching helps a player in real life also. He tries to adjust himself in real life, so as to co-operate with others and work for a common goal through team spirit.

(ix) *Lesson of Responsibility and Leadership:* Sports Psychology for Physical Education teaches the lesson of responsibility and leadership to the players. Although the players are expected to show self-denial and to work in the team spirit, yet there are several critical occasions in a game, when every player has to depend entirely upon himself and make very quick decisions to act promptly. It is a very valuable training in life. It trains a player for taking initiative in real life and realizing responsibility during every critical situation in life.

Thus we see that Sports Psychology for Physical Education has many uses for a career in sports as well as for real life. In fact, Sports Psychology has a very wide scope because of its manifold uses and multiple lesson for life.

CONCLUSION

We can say in conclusion that Sports Psychology for Physical Education has become very popular among students. It is a boon for those students, who want to improve their physical health, become good players and grow into the successful citizens of their country.

CAUSES OF POPULARITY OF SPORTS PSYCHOLOGY

Sports Psychology for Physical Education has become very popular in schools. It is popular among the students as well as among the teachers and parents of the students. Following are the main causes of popularity of Sports Psychology for Physical Education :

1. Means of Improving Health: Sports Psychology for Physical Education deals with means of improving health. All the students want to improve their health. Their parents also want to see their sons and daughters in good health. Hence Sports Psychology for physical Education has become very popular among the students and their parents, because it deals with all aspect of games and sports, which are good means of improving health.

2. Making Students Skilful and Intelligent: All sorts of physical activities, games and sports make the students skilful and intelligent if they take part in them in a proper way. Sports Psychology in Physical Education teaches the students how to take part in all physical activities, games and sports in a proper way. It makes the players understand that they can win a match only if they play carefully, skillfully and intelligently. Thus games and sports are very helpful for increasing the skill and intelligence of players. Sports Psychology in Physical Education lets the players know the psychological methods of improving skill and intelligence required for playing the games in the best possible way. This adds to the popularity of Sports Psychology in schools.

3. Means of Recreation: All physical activities, sports and games are very good means of recreation. It is an admitted fact that recreation is an essential factor for happy and successful life of students. They have to pass through a laborious course of studies for getting through their examinations. They are busy for most part of their life with their studies. Hence, it is very difficult for them to feel happy and cheerful without recreation. Games and Sports have a great receptive value. Sports Psychology for Physical Education reveals many good methods of making games and sports as recreative as possible. With the help of Sports Psychology the students get very good recreation through games and sports. It tells them how to forget all their anxieties, worries and strains of studies while playing a game. It tells them that even indoor games, such as Ludo, Carrom and Table Tennis provide them with great recreation. In fact, Sports Psychology for Physical Education makes all games a great source of recreation and enjoyment. Hence it has become very popular with students, who want recreation everyday after their studies.

4. Training for Leadership: Sports Psychology for Physical education helps the players in getting training for leadership through games. It reveals such psychological methods of getting maximum benefit from games that when a student becomes a good player, he acquires most of the qualities of a good leader, such as getting full co-operation from all his playmates and achieving success even in most difficult circumstances. It was for this reason that Duke of Wellington had remarked, "I have won the battle of Waterloo at the play-fields of Eton." He was the student and a player of Football at Public School, Eton in England, where games and sports were conducted with the help of Sports Psychology. Duke of Wellington had the firm belief that he had defeated Napoleon at the battle-field of Waterloo, because he had learnt all the qualities of a good Army Officer and a successful general by taking part in games at Eton.

Sports Psychology offers a full training course to those good players who aspire to become a captain or get a chance of becoming the captain of a game. It gives them full training of how to become successful captains of games as well as successful leaders of people in actual life. It trains them in the right way of commanding others and giving them the right lead in games as well as in real life. Hence Sports Psychology for Physical Education has become very popular with those players who aspire to become captains of one game or the other and who subsequently aim at becoming leaders of people in actual life.

5. Getting Preference Over others: Sports Psychology for Physical Education brings home to all good players in schools and colleges the fact that being good players they have a right for getting preference over other students in the matter of fee concession, admissions to educational institutes for higher studies and many other facilities. It also reveals to them the fact that they have the right for getting preference over other candidates, when they compete with them for securing a good post in public or private sector, because good sports qualifications are in no way less than good academic qualifications. All this makes Sports Psychology for Physical Education very popular with all good players.

6. Useful for Teachers: Sports Psychology for Physical Education is very popular among the teachers because it lets them know how to learn and study the nature and character of their students in the play-field. Sports Psychology reveals that a teacher can learn more of his students in the play-field than he can do so in the class room, because the students express themselves freely in the play-field. With the full knowledge of the nature and character of his students, the teacher can make his work easy and effective. Hence Sports Psychology for Physical Education is very popular among the teachers.

7. Helpful to parents: Sports Psychology for Physical Education is very helpful to the parents of the students. It reveals to the parents the fact that if their sons and daughters are good players, they are sure to pass their leisure time gainfully and they will not fall into bad company. Sports Psychology also reveals to the parents of good players that they should not worry about the future careers of their sons or daughters, because being good players they are sure to get preference over others everywhere in life. They are sure to get well-settled in life because their good sports qualifications will surely help them in being fixed up in good posts. Sports Psychology for Physical Education makes the parents wise enough to encourage their sons and daughters to take active part in games and become good players during student life, so that they become successful individuals in every walk of life.

CONCLUSION

We can conclude that Sports Psychology for Physical Education is very popular among students, teachers and parents of the students because it lets them know the manifold uses and advantages of being good in games and sports. In advanced and developed countries of the world, Sports Psychology for Physical Education has reached very advanced stages and wide research work has been done in it. But in India a great deal of research work is required to be done in it in order to make it an advanced subject.

SUGGESTIONS

It is suggested that, keeping in view the growing popularity of Sports Psychology for Physical Education, advanced researches in this subject should be conducted not only in Colleges for Sports and Physical Education, but also in all Colleges and Colleges of Education in India, so that our country may be able to keep her pace with all developed countries of the world in producing good players and athletes, who can win laurels in Olympic and other International Tournaments in games and sports.

NEED OF PSYCHOLOGY IN EDUCATION

The need of Psychology in Education can be best understood in the light of the purpose of the two subjects. By Psychology we mean the study of behaviour and by Education we mean the modification of behaviour. Hence it is quite clear that there is great need of psychology in education, because we cannot bring about modification in behaviour without the study of behaviour. Moreover, how far behaviour can be modified or how much successfully can changes in behaviour be brought about, requires the knowledge of Psychology. Hence, the teacher who is concerned with modification of behaviour finds Psychology of great help to him.

It is worth noting here that Psychology does not suggest or formulate aims of education. It is the job of Philosophy to define or formulate aims. However, it is Psychology which points out the practicability of an aim. Ross has very aptly remarked about it, *"Although Psychology cannot formulate the aims of education, a reliable Psychology will tell us at once whether an aim of education is hopelessly in the clouds or whether it is possible of achievement.*

Not only does Psychology tell whether a particular aim is possible or not, but it also points out whether we have succeeded in it or not. In the words of Drever, "the bearing of Psychology on the aim of education does not end with deciding whether it is possible or impossible but it also tells the educator whether he has succeeded in his aim or not."

Next important task of education is to promote the learning behaviour. Learning involves the following three functions

  (a) to elicit the desired response

  (b) to strengthen the responses and thereby decrease the reaction time between the stimulus and the response.

  (c) to do away with all the undesired responses. All these functions of learning involve the study of Psychology of learning as essential for the teacher.

Next important task of education is that of evaluation. Evaluation of learning of the child and also the efficiency of the teacher require very sensitive and standardized tests of evaluation. Psychology in this context has done a wonderful job in devising various kinds of new type objective test, achievement test and intelligence tests etc. These tests are of great importance for the mental measurement of students.

We can say that Psychology has its bearing on the following three main aspects of education:

1. The understanding of the child, his instincts, habits, abilities and character.
2. The proper selection of the material, intellectual or otherwise, which is required for the education of the child at different stages of his mental development.
3. In the selection of right methods of teaching and the proper organisation of school management.

Ryburn has suggested the following three main directions in which the knowledge of Psychology helps us in the process of education:

(a) To understand children and their nature.
(b) To understand ourselves.
(c) To determine what methods we should use in teaching and in our general dealings with the children.

Ryburn has further pointed out that there are three relationships. First is the child-teacher relationship, second is the child-society relationship and the third in the child-subject relationship. The ideal education grows out of the harmonious interaction of the three. It is here that Psychology renders help to us. We follow these lines, so as to develop these relationships.

Campbell has suggested the following aims of Psychology of education:

1. To outline the various aspects of learning process.
2. To outline the main phases in psychological growth from infancy to maturity.
3. To match subject matter and process to be learnt to levels of development and psychological principles.
4. To give some training in assessing the learning standard of the child.
5. To give the teacher an insight into his own psychological processes and his own role as a teacher.

RELATIONSHIP BETWEEN PSYCHOLOGY AND SPORTS PSYCHOLOGY

There is a close relationship between Psychology and Sports Psychology for Physical Education on the following lines :

1. This relationship centers round the behaviour of the individual or the player. It is necessary for the all round development of the individual or the player that modification of his behaviour should be brought about with the help of Psychology, A player should have balanced development of his personality. It is necessary for this purpose that there should be sublimation of his instincts. It is possible only with the help of Psychology.
2. A player should be a useful member of society. It is possible only when he takes an active part in all the activities of the society and does not keep himself aloof for society. This leads to relationship between Psychology and Sports Psychology for Physical Education because both aim at socialization of the individual's or the player.
3. The players have to pass through certain such instigating and provocating situations in which it is difficult for them to keep their behaviour in a balanced form but it **is** expected of them to show balanced behaviour in all situations and under all circumstances. Hence it becomes necessary to bring about modification of their behaviour. Thus modification of behaviour is a common link between Psychology and Sports Psychology for Physical Education. Psychology studies all kinds of human behaviour. Hence modification of behaviour is possible only through the relationship and help of Psychology. According to Campbell, *Sports Psychology takes the help of Psychology at every step while giving training to the players for showing them right type of behavious in various games and physical activities."*

RELATIONSHIP OF SPORTS PSYCHOLOGY WITH VARIOUS BRANCHES OF PSYCHOLOGY

Sports Psychology has close relationship with many branches of Psychology. Here we deal with such a relationship with some branches of Psychology :

1. **Relationship with Individual Psychology**

   Every player and athlete is an individual in himself. He possesses his individual personality. He has some personal or individual habits. He has his individual tendencies and personal mental problems. We cannot give him training in sports without studying all those tendencies and mental problems. All these studies are possible only through Individual Psychology. Thus Sports Psychology takes free help from Individual Psychology. This shows that there is a close relationship between them

2. **Relationship with Educational Psychology**

   Sports Psychology is fundamentally a part of education. At school and college standard, the students are required to take part in games, sports and physical activities. Schools and colleges play a significant role in preparing students for competitions in games and sports at various levels. Thus sports are an integral part of education and Sports Psychology is an integral part of Educational Psychology.

3. **Relationship with Developmental Psychology**

   Man is undergoing constant development. He has to go through various stages of development. His behaviour also undergoes changes according to the change in the standard of development. Developmental Psychology studies the behaviour of man in different stages of his development. Sports Education or Physical Education has to give training to various players of different stages of development. Hence it has to take help from Developmental Psychology in some way or the other. While giving training to small children in Sports and Physical activities, we have to take help from Child Psychology. While giving training to adolescents in Sports and Physical activities, we have to take help from Adolescent Psychology. Similarly, while giving training to adults in Sports and Physical activities, we have to take help from Adult Psychology.

4. **Relationship with Physical Psychology**

   Sports Psychology mainly deals with physical activities involved in games. Hence there is a natural relationship between Sports Psychology and Physical Psychology. It studies in details the physical structures of human body and various physical system working in it.

5. **Relationship with Social or Group Psychology**

   The player or the athlete is an individual as well as a social being. His behaviour is influenced by social powers and social tendencies. He has also to adjust himself with other members of the team or his playmates. Hence, Sports Psychology has to take the help of Social or Group Psychology, because it is only through Social or Group Psychology that behaviour of an individual in society or group can be studied.

6. **Relationship with Clinical or Medical Psychology**

   The minds of players are put under many mental pressures and mental fears during completion in games. This has a bad influence upon their performance in games. Hence Sports Psychology takes the help of Clinical or Medical Psychology to control all such mental pressures and fears and fill encouragement in the minds of players.

PSYCHOLOGICAL TOPICS FOR STUDY IN SPORTS PSYCHOLOGY

Sports Psychology has to deal with many mental processes having influence upon the performance of players and athletes in games and sports.

The following psychological items can be studied in Sports Psychology :

1. **Behaviour**

   Sport Psychology has to study the behaviour of players and athletes while they are playing or performing physical activities. It has to take help from Psychology for studying such a behaviour. In fact, the behaviour involved in sports has two sources—mental and physical.

The mental source of behaviour includes various sentiments, instincts, mental situations, attitudes, sympathies etc. The physical source includes nervous systems and glands. Instincts and feelings are the basis for behaviour. An individual expresses his behaviour physically through motor skills. All the physical activities are the sum total of motor skills of an individual. Thus Sports Psychology studies the relationship between mental activities and physical activities of the players and athletes with the help of Psychology.

2. **Heredity and Environment**

Heredity and Environment play an important part in the growth and dedevelopment of an individual. There is a great influence of heredity and environment upon the behaviour and efficiency of players and athletes. Hence, it is necessary to study through the help of Psychology the heredity and environment of the players and athletes before imparting them training in games and sports.

3. **Individual Differences**

There are individual differences in all persons. In fact no two persons can be alike. Individual differences can be in the form of physical and mental differences. The capabilities, interests, aptitudes, habits, feelings, activities and tendencies of every individual differ from other individuals. There are individual differences from the view point of sex also. Training in games and sports cannot be imparted to players and athletes without the study of these individual differences. Sports Psychology has to take help from Psychology for such a study.

4. **Personality and Intelligence**

Sports Psychology deals with the development of the personality and intelligence of the players and athletes. Hence, it has to conduct a thorough study of their personality and intelligence with the help of Psychology. The standard of sports training or Physical Education depends upon the personality and intelligence of the trainee. The motor skills to be used in sports training are to be kept within the standard of the Personality of the player or athlete. For this purpose full help is to be sought from Psychology.

5. **Stages of Development**

Sports training or Physical education cannot be imparted properly without the knowledge of the stages of development of players and athletes. Psychology studies the various stages of development in Infancy, Childhood, Adolescence and Adulthood. Hence Sports Psychology has to take the help of Psychology for this kind of knowledge.

6. **Learning**

The process of learning is closely connected with Psychology. Sports Psychology has to take the help of Psychology for employing proper methods of training and learning. It also has to take the help of Psychology for creating proper environment for learning.

7. **Measurement and Evaluation**

Sports Training requires the use of the latest methods of measurement and evaluation. Hence Sports Psychology has to take the help of Psychology for knowing the latest methods of the measurement of intelligence, personality, interests and aptitudes.

PROFESSIONAL NEED OF PSYCHOLOGY IN SPORTS EDUCATION

Sports Education or Physical Education has the following constituents just like the constituents of Education

1. Learner
2. Coach
3. Learning Material
4. Learning Process
5. Learning Situation.

All the above mentioned constituents of Sports Education require the help of Psychology in one way or the other. It is necessary to discuss the extent of the help of Psychology in all these constituents of Sports Education :

1. Learner: Learner is the most important constituent of Sports Education. The person who receives Education or Sports Education is called learner, whether he be a student or a player. In General Education as well as Sports Education the personality of the learner is developed through modification of his behaviour. For this purpose the behaviour of the student or the player is observed thoroughly with the help of Psychology. Sports deal mainly with playing games or indulging in physical activities, but these activities depend upon behaviour-pattern of the individual player. The behaviour-pattern has to be studied thoroughly with the help of Psychology. If the coach studies thoroughly the natural or main instincts of the player or the athlete, he can bring about great improvement in the quality of his playing capabilities or physical activities.

Moreover, the coach has also to take into account the age of the learner. The behaviour pattern of the child can easily be molded, but it takes a lot of effort to mould the behaviour pattern of an adolescent or an adult learner. The coach has to take the help of Psychology at every step in molding the behaviour pattern of the child player, adolescent player and adult player. The coach cannot understand the change in behaviour pattern at different stages of the development of the learner, without the help of Psychology. Moreover, the coach has to take exact measurements of the intelligence and other capabilities of the player or the athlete in order to give him the right type of training in the development of his capabilities.

2. Coach or Physical Director: The Coach or Physical Director plays a very important part in Sports Education or Physical Education. First of all, he has to create a suitable atmosphere for the right type of training or coaching. He has to make the players familiar with the latest techniques of playing a game or performing physical activities. He has also to improve their stamina in the long process of playing. He can perform all these duties well only with the help of Psychology.

The coach has not only to know thoroughly the learners or players, but he should also try to know himself thoroughly. Sometimes his own behaviour becomes a hurdle in the proper development of the learners or players while he blames them for their poor performance. Hence the coach should study himself through 'Self Introspection' He should then get rid of the drawbacks or weaknesses in his behaviour, which put a hurdle in the proper development and proper performance of the players or athletes. He can do so only with the help of Psychology at every step.

3. Learning Material: There is a great diversity in the learning material of Sports Education at the various stages of the development of the learners. The players and athletes have to take part in various competitions in games and sports. The programme of training for them depends upon their particular stage of development. The learning material required for the training depends entirely upon the stage of development of the players and athletes. This stage of development can be known only with the help of Psychology.

4. Learning Process: The success in Sports Education, as in General Education, depends, to a great extent, upon the proper learning process. The teaching process as well as the learning process adopted should be according to the interests, aptitudes and capabilities of the learners. This can be done only with the help of Psychology. Moreover, the coach should be fully conversant with the various laws and principles of learning, rules of perception and transfer of learning. He should also keep in view individual differences of the learner. In all these things he has to take the help of Psychology.

5. Learning Situations: Good, teaching and good learing is possible only in congenial situations. In order to make Sports Education most effective, the coach should create such a good atmosphere, as is free from any kind of strain, repression And averse criticism. Besides this, the place where Sports Education is imparted should be free from dust, dirt and smoke. It should be protected from the sun and rain. The personal behaviour of the coach also has great effect upon creating good learning situations. In all basic things Psychology plays a very significant role.

From the above discussion it is quite clear that good Sports Education is possible only with the proper knowledge and full help of Psychology at every step of giving training to players or athletes.

OBJECTIVE QUESTIONS

1. According to ancient Greek philosophers, philosophy means:
   (*a*) Love of wisdom
   (*b*) A subject matter
   (*c*) A method
   (*d*) None of the above

2. The most important characteristic of philosophical method is:
   (*a*) Analysis   (*b*) Synthesis
   (*c*) Both   (*d*) Neither

3. The relation between philosophy and science is:
   (*a*) Contradictory   (*b*) Complimentary
   (*c*) Both   (*d*) Neither

4. The philosophical problems include:
   (*a*) Epistemological problems
   (*b*) Metaphysical problems
   (*c*) Axiological problems
   (*d*) All the above

5. The problems of philosophy are concerned with:
   (*a*) Knowledge and experience
   (*b*) Reality or existence
   (*c*) Values and ideals
   (*d*) All the above

6. The important aspects of philosohpical problems are :
   (*a*) Critical   (*b*) Synthetic
   (*c*) Both   (*d*) Neither

7. The philosophical attitude includes :
   (*a*) Wonder   (*b*) Doubt
   (*c*) Criticism   (*d*) All the above

8. The philosophical methods includes:
   (*a*) Induction   (*b*) Deduction
   (*c*) Dialectical   (*d*) All the above

9. Philosophising requires the process of:
   (*a*) Analysis   (*b*) Synthesis
   (*c*) Criticism   (*d*) All the above

10. The term *induction* means:
   (*a*) General to particular
   (*b*) Particular to general
   (*c*) Both
   (*d*) Neither

11. The philosopher is more concerned with:
   (*a*) Induction
   (*b*) Deduction
   (*c*) Dialectics
   (*d*) None of the above

12. The contemporary trend in philosophical method is:
   (*a*) Analysis
   (*b*) Synthesis
   (*c*) Dialectics
   (*d*) None of the above

13. Philosophical activity is concerned with:
   (*a*) Thinking   (*b*) Synthesising
   (*c*) Criticising   (*d*) All the above

14. Philosophical thinking is characterised by:
   (*a*) Philosophical effect
   (*b*) Philosophical conclusion
   (*c*) Philosophical results
   (*d*) All the above

15. The philosophical effect can be seen upon:
   (*a*) The Philosopher   (*b*) The group life
   (*c*) The culture   (*d*) All the above

16. Philosophical conclusions are concerned with:
   (*a*) Knowledge   (*b*) Reality
   (*c*) Values   (*d*) All the above

17. The relation of philosophy with human knowledge is:
   (*a*) Necessary
   (*b*) Not necessary
   (*c*) indifferent
   (*d*) None of the above

18. The philosophical conclusions in different times and places are:
   (*a*) Similar   (*b*) Dissimilar
   (*c*) Both   (*d*) Neither

19. The chief differences among thinking being are:
- (*a*) Physical
- (*b*) Biological
- (*c*) Philosophical
- (*d*) None of the above

20. A bad philosophy can be substituted by:
- (*a*) Science
- (*b*) Religion
- (*c*) Better philosophy
- (*d*) None of the above

21. The mean score of any class test is the result of:
- (*a*) Dividing the sum of all scores by the number of scores
- (*b*) Determining the middle score when all the scores have been listed from the highest to the lowest
- (*c*) Determining the most frequent score
- (*d*) Adding all the scores and dividing by the most frequent score
- (*e*) Adding the highest and lowest scores and dividing by two

22. The least justifiable use of the results of a standardized reading test is to:
- (*a*) Identify areas of pupil deficiency
- (*b*) Evaluate the reading instruction programme
- (*c*) Serve as a basis for report card marks
- (*d*) Serve as the basis for class groupings

23. Fifteen-year-old Kavita has taken to wearing the same style sweaters that her teacher wears. This form of behaviour is known as:
- (*a*) Compensation   (*b*) Transference
- (*c*) Identification   (*d*) Regression
- (*e*) Egocentrism

24. At least one third of the learning that will determine later levels of school achievement has already taken place by age of six. This is a statement most closely associated with the writings of:
- (*a*) Benjamin Bloom   (*b*) Margaret Mead
- (*c*) Martin Mayer   (*d*) Fritz Red
- (*e*) Nathan Glazer

25. Of the following, the one situation that will cause the greatest difficulty for a child in the initial stages of reading instruction is:
- (*a*) Confusion of left and right directionality
- (*b*) Possessing an 9 Q of 90
- (*c*) Having older sibling who are successful readers
- (*d*) Never having attended kindergarten
- (*e*) Being an avid television watcher

26. In preparing a fifth-grade class to take a standardized reading test, the teacher is best advised to:
- (*a*) Tell the children that the test is very important and they should do the best they can
- (*b*) Ditto key questions from a previous test and allow the pupils to answer them
- (*c*) Do nothing
- (*d*) Coach the below-grade-level readers, as the rest of the class will do well anyway
- (*e*) Give the pupils practice in answering questions similar to the type that will appear on the test.

27. All of the following are acceptable goals for dealing with behaviour problems in the classroom, except:
- (*a*) Helping the child to improve his/her self-control
- (*b*) Being impersonal and objective
- (*c*) Understanding the offence
- (*d*) Utilizing appeals to children that have personal implications
- (*e*) Punishing when necessary, in private

28. Of the following, the most unreliable predicator of educational achievement is:
- (*a*) Inherited biological potential for learning
- (*b*) Ethnic origin of parents
- (*c*) Family background and training
- (*d*) Classroom experiences
- (*e*) Self-concept

29. When a test has a high degree of reliability, one can conclude that:
- (*a*) There is the likelihood that a pupil will maintain his/her position among the

same group of test-takers when he/she takes an equivalent test

(*b*) There is a likelihood that a pupil will get a high in score when he/she takes an equivalent lest

(*c*) The test is measuring what it intends to measure

(*d*) The test is highly objective

(*e*) The test is for prognostic purposes

30. The likelihood that a pupil will maintain his her position among the same group of test takers when he/she takes an equivalent test is a measure of the test's:

(*a*) Objectivity   (*b*) Validity

(*c*) Reliability   (*d*) Construction

(*e*) Prognostic ability

31. The child who trips over a desk and the kicks the desk is exhibiting the behaviour mechanism known is:

(*a*) Conversion   (*b*) Identification

(*c*) Projection   (*d*) Attention-getting

(*e*) Negativism

32. Most useful for studying pupil inter-relationship is the:

(*a*) Anecdotal record (*b*) Case study

(*c*) Rorschach Test (*d*) Sociogram

(*e*) Kuder Preference Test

33. The best argument for a group intelligence test is that it:

(*a*) Treats all children equally

(*b*) Provides the teacher with diagnostic information

(*c*) Is less tension producing that an individual test

(*d*) Is the least expensive way to attain an IQ

(*e*) Serves as the basis for assigning basal readers

34. Of the following essentials of learning, the one that takes precedence over the other has:

(*a*) Average intelligence

(*b*) Ability to read

(*c*) An intact home

(*d*) Desire to learn

(*e*) A good teacher

35. A child from a disorganized home will experience the greatest difficulty with:

(*a*) Well-structured lessons

(*b*) Independent study

(*c*) Programmed instruction

(*d*) Work books

(*e*) Short-answer tests

36. The child with locomotors problems should be seated in the right-hand corner of the classroom, because:

(*a*) He can better interact with the teacher

(*b*) Movement of other children does not interfere

(*c*) He can see the blackboard properly

(*d*) He can go out of the classroom easily

37. The first step in dealing with a disabled child in the classroom is:

(*a*) His referring to him to appropriate agencies

(*b*) Diagnosis of his learning problems

(*c*) Identification of the disability

(*d*) Making special arrangements in the classroom

38. Impairment refers to:

(*a*) Any form of organic disorder of dysfunction

(*b*) Loss or reduction of function

(*c*) Difficulty in performing activity

(*d*) A restriction imposed upon an individual which affects his functioning

39. Disability refers to:

(*a*) Abnormality of some part of the body

(*b*) Loss or reduction of functional activity resulting from impairment

(*c*) Loss of body part resulting from an accident

(*d*) Dysfunction of some body parts

40. Parent involvement in meeting educational needs of the disabled child is essential because:

(*a*) They require special attention

(*b*) They have to manage disability at house

(*c*) They have to arrange for medical help

(*d*) They provide support to educational efforts at school.

41. Emotion is defined as -
(*a*) Feeling   (*b*) Disturbed
(*c*) Fear of future   (*d*) State of Organism

42. A reliable psychological test means-
(*a*) Accuracy of measurement
(*b*) Forecasting behaviour
(*c*) Consistency of measurement
(*d*) None of the above

43. The first test intelligence was developed by
(*a*) Binet and Simon
(*b*) Pavlov and Watson
(*c*) Terman and Merril
(*d*) Maslow and McDougall

44. In developmental process the terms "gang-age" occurs during -
(*a*) Early childhood   (*b*) Puberty
(*c*) Infancy   (*d*) Later Childhood

45. Cognition deals with -
(*a*) Learning   (*b*) Memory
(*c*) Creativity   (*d*) All of the above

46. Which is not a primary motive -
(*a*) Affection   (*b*) Hunger
(*c*) Sex   (*d*) Thirst

47. What processes are part of classical conditioning?
(*a*) Generalization   (*b*) Discrimination
(*c*) Extinction   (*d*) All the above.

48. Psychology is taught to the student of physical education because -
(*a*) It enhances performance
(*b*) It is related to behaviour
(*c*) It helps in learning
(*d*) It motivates athletes

49. In psychological testing, norm is defined as -
(*a*) Record of performance
(*b*) Unique performance of a team
(*c*) Average performance of the team
(*d*) Highest performance of athlete

50. What level of stress may enhance performance of athletes?
(*a*) Heightened
(*b*) Moderate
(*c*) Optimal
(*d*) None of the above.

51. Outstanding athletes usually posses certain personality characteristics, such as -
(*a*) Aggressiveness
(*b*) Neurotic
(*c*) Ambivalence
(*d*) Submissiveness

52. Psycho-Sexual development takes place during-
(*a*) Later childhood
(*b*) Adolescence
(*c*) Young Age
(*d*) Adulthood

53. The psychologist who has been most closely related with the study of achievement motivation is-
(*a*) Eclelland   (*b*) Maslow
(*c*) Croom   (*d*) Mc Gregor

54. The concept of mental age was given by -
(*a*) Stern   (*b*) Galton
(*c*) Binet   (*d*) Watson

55. The impulses that travel from CNS to muscle are called-
(*a*) Efferent   (*b*) Afferent
(*c*) Sensation   (*d*) All the above

56. Which one is the simplest form of Cognition-
(*a*) Conception   (*b*) Perception
(*c*) Sensation   (*d*) Affection

57. The functional division of spinal cord are
(*a*) Somatic motor   (*b*) Somatic Sensory
(*c*) Visceral motor   (*d*) None of the above

58. The response defined as a result of training is called -
(*a*) Conditioned stimulus
(*b*) Unconditioned reflex
(*c*) Conditioned reflex
(*d*) Conation

59. Sports performance is the bi-product of -
(*a*) Skill
(*b*) Conditional ability
(*c*) Total personality
(*d*) Tactical ability

60. The first metamorphosis falls between the age of
(a) 7-10 years   (b) 3-5 years
(c) 11-14 years   (d) 2-4 years

61. Which is the most effective method for encouraging self learning -
(a) Demonstration method
(b) Lecture method
(c) Observation method
(d) Task method

62. Body mind relationship was first promulgated by?
(a) Socrates   (b) Plato
(c) Hitler   (d) Homer.

63. Who said, 'I think therefore I am?'
(a) Discartes   (b) Plato
(c) Aristotle   (d) Rousseau

64. Who said, 'sound mind in a sound body?'
(a) Discartes   (b) Rousseau
(c) Aristotle   (d) Plato.

65. The hereditary factors of learning are -
(a) Height and weight
(b) Physical structure
(c) Body composition
(d) All of the above.

66. Autogenic training is a technique
(a) To bring about relaxation in body
(b) To increase anxiety level
(c) To counter avoidance syndrome
(d) None of the above.

67. The stress condition is -
(a) Advantageous to the performer
(b) Detrimental to the performer
(c) Neither (a) nor (b)
(d) Helpful in the development of strength

68. Violence associated with the competition sport is mainly due to -
(a) The very nature of the competitive sport
(b) The social tensions within the society
(c) The social backwardness
(d) Identity of spectators with teams on racial, religious or national considerations.

69. The personal factors in learning are -
(a) Heredity factors
(b) Fitness factors
(c) Psychological factors
(d) All of the above

70. Gestalt has propounded -
(a) Theory of trial and error
(b) Theory of conditioning
(c) Theory of learning
(d) Nione of the above.

71. Feedback method -
(a) is helpful to the learner
(b) is detrimental to the learner
(c) is neither helpful nor detrimental
(d) none of the above

72. Learning of physical skills is concerned with-
(a) Cognitive learning
(b) Affective learning
(c) Motor learning
(d) All of the above

73. Natural motivation is also known as -
(a) Intrinsic   (b) Self assertion
(c) Self actualization (d) Extrinsic.

74. Human psychology is confined to the study of-
(a) Behaviour   (b) Mind
(c) Soul   (d) Relationship

75. Which of the following is a law of learning?
(a) Law of readiness
(b) Law of exercise
(c) Law of effect
(d) All of the above

76. Mental development includes -
(a) External and internal organs
(b) Reasoning and thinking
(c) Ethical and moral
(d) Emotional maturity

77. Through which of the following methods, desirable channels are provided for the release of emotional energy
(a) Inhibition   (b) Sublimation
(c) Catharsis   (d) Repression

78. The rate of progress in learning slows down and reaches a limit beyond which further improvement seems impossible. It is known as-
(*a*) Plateau
(*b*) Loss of interest
(*c*) Boredom
(*d*) Difficult stage

79. The therapy of psychoanalysis was developed by-
(*a*) Skinner   (*b*) Sigmund Freud
(*c*) Plato   (*d*) Darwin

80. Which is the description of the methods of personality measurements?
(*a*) Rating scale.
(*b*) Interviews &observations
(*c*) Paper & pencil test
(*d*) All of the above

81. Eros refers to
(*a*) Life instincts
(*b*) Energy
(*c*) Aggressive and destructive urges
(*d*) Judge for thought of ego

82. According to Frieud's psychoanalytic theory, internalized parent is
(*a*) Ego   (*b*) Superego
(*c*) Conscience   (*d*) Ego ideal

83. Which level of consciousness contains material that can be easily brought to awareness?
(*a*) Unconscious
(*b*) Conscious
(*c*) Preconscious
(*d*) Conscious and preconscious

84. The conflict where the boy feels rivalry with his father for the affection of the mother is
(*a*) Oedipus conflict (*b*) Electra conflict
(*c*) Both   (*d*) None

85. Which leadership style takes full charge of his team?
(*a*) Permissive   (*b*) Autocratic
(*c*) Directive   (*d*) Democratic

86. Encouragement by spectators is a
(*a*) Social incentive
(*b*) Monetary incentive
(*c*) Reward incentive
(*d*) Social competitive incentive

87. Cognitive evaluation theory of motivation was propounded by
(*a*) Thorndike   (*b*) Kohler
(*c*) Pavlov   (*d*) Deci

88. Behaviour carried out with the intention of harming another person is called
(*a*) Stress   (*b*) Tension
(*c*) Aggression   (*d*) Anxiety

89. According to Frieud, the typical moral arm of the personality is
(*a*) ID
(*b*) Ego
(*c*) Super Ego
(*d*) Both ego and superego

90. The leader who allows complete freedom in decision making and does not participate in the group activities
(*a*) Autocratic
(*b*) Democratic
(*c*) Lassez fair
(*d*) None of the above

91. Stress is
(*a*) Advantageous to the player
(*b*) Detrimental to his abilities
(*c*) Both advantageous and detrimental as per the situation
(*d*) None

92. Maslow places _______ needs at the bottom of hierarchy
(*a*) Esteem   (*b*) Belongingness
(*c*) Safety   (*d*) Physiological

93. Which need is on top of the Maslow's hierarchy of needs?
(*a*) Self-actualization
(*b*) Esteem
(*c*) Belongingness
(*d*) Safety

94. ERG theory was given by
(*a*) Maslow   (*b*) Alderfer
(*c*) Jung   (*d*) Mcclellan

95. Alderfer's theory categorizes needs into three categories. The most important is
(*a*) Growth needs   (*b*) Relatedness need
(*c*) Existence need   (*d*) None

96. Which of the following is an intrinsic motivator?
(*a*) Pay   (*b*) Promotion
(*c*) Feed back   (*d*) Interest of play

97. The two factor theory of motivation is given by
(*a*) Maslow   (*b*) Jung
(*c*) Alderfer   (*d*) Herzberg

98. Reinforcement theory of motivation is given by
(*a*) Jung   (*b*) Hezberg
(*c*) Skinner   (*d*) Maslow

99. Which law of learning states that things most often repeated are best retained?
(*a*) Law of readiness
(*b*) Law of exercise
(*c*) Law of effect
(*d*) Law of recency

100. The state of being first creates a strong almost unusable impression. This is
(*a*) Law of primacy   (*b*) law of intensity
(*c*) Law of recency   (*d*) Law of effect

ANSWERS

1. (*b*)	2. (*c*)	3. (*b*)	4. (*a*)	5. (*d*)	6. (*c*)	7. (*d*)	8. (*d*)
9. (*d*)	10. (*b*)	11. (*c*)	12. (*a*)	13. (*d*)	14. (*d*)	15. (*d*)	16. (*d*)
17. (*a*)	18. (*c*)	19. (*c*)	20. (*c*)	21. (*a*)	22. (*c*)	23. (*c*)	24. (*a*)
25. (*a*)	26. (*e*)	27. (*d*)	28. (*b*)	29. (*a*)	30. (*c*)	31. (*c*)	32. (*c*)
33. (*d*)	34. (*d*)	35. (*d*)	36. (*b*)	37. (*c*)	38. (*a*)	39. (*b*)	40. (*d*)
41. (*b*)	42. (*c*)	43. (*a*)	44. (*b*)	45. (*d*)	46. (*a*)	47. (*d*)	48. (*b*)
49. (*c*)	50. (*c*)	51. (*a*)	52. (*b*)	53. (*a*)	54. (*c*)	55. (*a*)	56. (*c*)
57. (*b*)	58. (*c*)	59. (*c*)	60. (*a*)	61. (*c*)	62. (*b*)	63. (*a*)	64. (*d*)
65. (*d*)	66. (*a*)	67. (*b*)	68. (*d*)	69. (*d*)	70. (*c*)	71. (*a*)	72. (*c*)
73. (*a*)	74. (*a*)	75. (*d*)	76. (*b*)	77. (*c*)	78. (*a*)	79. (*b*)	80. (*d*)
81. (*a*)	82. (*b*)	83. (*c*)	84. (*a*)	85. (*c*)	86. (*a*)	87. (*d*)	88. (*c*)
89. (*c*)	90. (*c*)	91. (*c*)	92. (*d*)	93. (*a*)	94. (*b*)	95. (*c*)	96. (*d*)
97. (*d*)	98. (*c*)	99. (*b*)	100. (*a*)				

3. EMOTIONS IN GAMES AND SPORTS

IMPORTANCE OF EMOTIONS IN GAMES AND SPORTS

There is a great importance of emotions in games and sports. The physical activities of players and athletes are very much influenced by emotions. The emotions of fear and anger, for instance, have a negative effect upon their physical activities and movements of muscles. The coach should advise the players and athletes to keep their emotions under control, so that their physical activities and movements of muscles are not affected in a negative way.

As far as mild emotions are concerned, they are not harmful in any way for good performance in games and athletes. But these emotions are harmful to a great extent in this field of activities. Hence, the players and athlete should be trained in such a way that they do not allow their emotions to become tense.

THEORIES OF EMOTIONS

Various theories have been put forward to explain occurrence of emotion. They are as follows :

1. **Cannon—Bard Emergency Theory of Emotions**

    According to Cannon and Bard, sympathetic action in the nervous system occurs not only in emergencies of violence but bodily results of such action also place the individual in a state of preparedness to meet the threat of all such emergencies. Sympathetic action is useful in emergency of violence. For example, digestive functions are stopped voluntary muscles get more blood, adrenalin is discharged, blood sugar is released, heart beats become rapid, dilation of the muscles of lungs makes the individual easy to breathe as there is greater supply of oxygen. So all these functions are useful to meet arty kind of emergency as the individual gets more energy and he indulges in violent activities.

2. **James-Lange Theory of Emotion**

    An American psychologist, W. James and C.G. Lange, a Danish psychologist have given their own theory of emotions. According to their view points, the conscious emotions consist of a man's awareness of his bodily changes as they occur in his emotions. There is a stimulus to an emotion. The organism responds reflexively and then the conscious awareness of these reflex changes give the man his feeling of emotion. According to James, "The bodily changes follow directly the perception of the exciting fact and our feeling of the same changes as they occur in the emotion." It means that we do not cry because we feel sorry, but we feel sorry because we cry.

Conclusion drawn from the Theories: Both the above theories agree upon the fact that the seat of emotions is the thalamus or hypothalamus, receiving stimuli from the receptors. But further, James-Lange has stated that first these sensations come to the affectors, then through thalamus they go again to the higher centres of the brain, where the individual becomes conscious of the bodily changes and has various emotions.

Cannos and Bard have stated occurrence of emotion a bit differently. According to them, sensations received from receptors go to the centre or higher centre of the brain through thalamus i.e. lower centre of the brain and then come back again to the effectors. The resulting activity is the emotion.

EFFECTS OF EMOTION ON HUMAN LIFE

As already started mild emotions are not harmful for human life, but tense emotions have a negative effect upon human beings.

1. Tense emotions interfere with the physical growth and development of human beings. Their nerves get tense, digestion is disrupted and endocrine glands produce poisonous hormones. Sometimes, the strain is so tense that they cause danger to the life of the individual. They also cause nervousness and confusion.

2. Investigation have revealed that prolonged emotional strain causes stuttering and stammering.

3. Children adopt timid or aggressive attitude in the face of emotions and they suffer from frustration.

4. Learning suffers due to tense emotions. Learning of the skill of a game or the skill of an athletic event is prolonged due to the constant interference of emotions because emotional distress and frustration proves a great obstacle for learning in sports.

5. Pleasant emotions, such as joy, pleasure and delight promote learning. Hope, encouragement, affection and satisfaction are the psychological factors motivating learning ability. Hence it is essential that players and sportsmen are helped to experience pleasant emotions under all circumstances.

6. Emotionally disturbed persons are socially maladjusted and disapproved. Human beings learn through social interaction. But emotionality stands in the way of social interaction. Temper outbursts are never appreciated by the members of society. To win friends and social applause one has to be emotionally balanced and mature.

7. Sometimes children become problematic and delinquent when they are unable to adjust themselves to the environment due to their emotional nature. It has been found out that 66% children coming from unusual environment, broken homes and tense emotional atmosphere are delinquent, and problematic children.

8. Emotions disrupt mental health. Too much worry, frustration, anxiety, rage and fear interfere with normal mental health. Such individuals begin suffering from various mental diseases, morbid fears, complexes and other mental abnormalities.

CONCLUSION

In short, tense emotion always brings forth frustration, conflicts and dissatisfactions thereby shaking the, physical health of the individual.

Educational Implications: Educational psychology is concerned mainly with young children and pupils. These children possess emotions in crude and natural form. Education aims at utilizing these emotions into proper channels. It also aims at control and maturity of emotions. The teacher should see that all children possess consistency of emotions in face', of any difficulty or strain. Similarly the Coach or Physical Director should help the players and sportsmen in achieving consistency of emotions in all the situations and under all circumstances.

EMOTIONS AND PHYSICAL EDUCATION

From the point of view of psychology, it is not at all wise and advisable to study emotions independently and separately. Their form is very complicated. Sometimes various emotions are joined together, as anger, jealousy, pain, etc. Sometimes, under the influence of certain circumstances, only one emotion is aroused while at the other occasion it is possible that under the same circumstances more than one emotion may be aroused. Therefore, it is very difficult to describe emotions in their original form.

In popular language the word 'emotion' covers such experiences as fear, anger, joy, love, sorrow, etc. means usually a feeling which has specially become intense joy, say, intense pleasure. Further, emotions more than feeling are pure and simple, it is rather a drive to do something. The word 'emotion' has originated from a Greek word *'emovere' which* means movement. It is, of course, apart from being a feeling, an agitational, psychological and physiological state of the body when the whole organism is set on the war footing. In reality, emotion is an ecitation approach, Says Youngs, 'Emotions are actually disturbed effective states or processes which originate in psychological situations and which are revealed by marked bodily change in the glands and smooth muscles "Emotions", thinks Sandiford are innate responses heredity pattern reactions essentially chaotic in nature involving the whole body in their expression but particularly the glandular and visceral systems and their nervous connections and having intimate relationship with the preservation of the individual or the species.

Emotions are not foreign instructions, they are part and parcel of the unitary action system. The teacher must try to understand the maturation of these and do something constructive and educational about the environment.

Unpleasant feelings such as hate, fear and anger can lead to avoidance action or to form of behaviour that are negative and destructive in nature. Pleasant feelings like love, affection and sympathy can lead to ongoing practices and forms of behaviour that are both constructive and sociable.

The physical educationist has many opportunities for exercising his influence in such inflammable field as the emotion. The conception of the whole child is never more justified than when dealing with his emotional life.

If education is to be prevented from becoming sterile, it must draw upon the enormous potential of the child's emotional reservoirs. The fundamental elements in the development of emotional life is the training of this capacity to live in the sense, to become more and more delicately and completely aware of the world around us, because it is a good half of the meaning of life to be so. Animosity and tensions in the young child are not altogether under his control and play acts as a safety valve through Which he can pass without fear of any punitive action.

In Physical education weaknesses and strengths are readily spotted. Physical cowardice, fearfulness or nervousness become evident. Here the teacher gets a much more adequate view of personality in action than can be obtained from the narrow confines of the clinical laboratory—the class room. Play is basically a creative activity of child behaviour, that must be kept in mind.

INTEREST AND ATTITUDE

Interest

Interest has been defined as a *"favourable attitude towards object"*. Thus, interest is positive in nature. A high level of interest in a given area means a positive acceptance and perhaps an energetic attitude towards it. A low level of interest leads to passive and listless attitude towards a given goal or object.

Interest plays an important role in a directing and controlling human behaviour. It is the interest which is responsible for the persistent and constant quest, in the behaviour of an individual, to achieve some goal or earn a point of distinction. Interest is of great significance in education and sports, as all these activities are based upon interest. It is the human tendency to do the activity which is pleasure giving and not to do the activity which is pain giving. Most of the physical activities are pain giving wherein, a lot of discomfort is experienced by the athlete. If the teacher/coach is able to inculcate interest among the students/athletes, they will respond positively and withstand the laborious, activity. It is the interest which is helpful in maintaining discipline and order in the class. Most certainly the child, student or athlete should be allowed and encouraged to develop information and skill in the area of his special interest. Certainly any good teaching-learning procedure will attempt to develop more interest. Satisfying experience in learning process will motivate the students and in turn the students will take interest to repeat it. The efforts of the teacher will be useless unless he motivates the students in arousing their interest.

Attitude

Attitude plays an important role in learning and teaching because they form the basic part of an individual's readiness to learn. The acquisition of attitude itself constitutes a learning process which in physical education may be known as attainment of the motor skills or academic knowledge.

Interest and attitude are closely related to each other. Interest is nothing else but attitude which causes an individual to seek various activities in a given area. Both interest and attitude indicate a state of readiness to participate in or avoid a particular behaviour pattern.

Interest and attitude are like the two faces of a coin. Interest is a mental trait and attitude is mental process. Interest is reflected in attitude guided by it. Thus we see that interest and attitude are complimentary to each other.

TEACHER-STUDENT RELATIONSHIP

It is not the teacher who should decide what to teach and how to teach. But he should know what our schools exist for and what aims he is supposed to achieve. He must know why a particular experience or activity is being offered and what shall be the outcome of it. It is true that an ordinary teacher cannot be entrusted with the task of deciding what to teach or how to teach, yet he should know, the aims and objectives which are to be achieved through educational program.

In teaching-learning process, interaction is between the two individuals that is teacher and learner. Teacher is the one who is imparting some kind of knowledge to the other. The individual who is receiving knowledge is known as learner or pupil. For effective learning process, there has to be a very cordial relation between them. It is a known fact that a person learns from the individual whom he respects most. The effectiveness of teaching and learning is based on the degree of cordial relation between the teacher and the pupil.

In Physical education, teacher faces a some what different situation than other subject teachers. The teacher of physical education is the next important teacher in an institution, who has to be in constant touch with all the students. He has to maintain very close interaction with the pupil. His self is very easily exposed to his students. He has to be very open person to whom students can approach and talk without any hesitation. This is possible only if he understands the student as a whole. The teacher should be able to unfold the total self of the pupil. His dealing and behaviour is frank and fair.

The physical education teacher is to understand the behaviour and attitude of the pupil not only when he is within the four walls of the school, rather he should have thorough knowledge about his life, attitude, and behaviour outside the school premises. He should fully know about the social background of the pupil. The teacher should not have thorough knowledge only about the pupil but his/her parents and other family members also. All this will facilitate the teacher to modify his behaviour from student to student. The teacher must have faith and confidence in student that whatever he is teaching to the student it is not going waste and being assimilated by them. Similarly students should also have full faith and confidence in the teacher so that his teachings are well received and followed by them.

Unfortunately, in this materialistic world, teacher has lost the feeling of sacrifice and selflessness, dedication, devotion in the art of teaching. Similarly students have also developed the feeling that the teacher is just being paid for his teaching. Both teacher and the students have forgotten the Indian traditions of *"Guru-Shishya Parampara" when* teacher and the students were whole heartedly devoted to each other in *"Gurukul"* For effective teaching, the teacher has to be a model for the students so that students may follow his foot prints and the teaching-learning becomes an ideal and fruitful process.

SPORTSMANSHIP AND SPORTS ETHICS

"Sportsmanship" is a comprehensive term. It is applied not only to athletes but to non-athletes also. Sportsmanship is a symbol of tolerance, honesty, fairness, truthfulness, friendliness, patience and self-discipline. A true sportsman applies all these principles in true spirit on and off the field. Physical Education includes every thing which is important for the organisation and smooth conduct of sports competition. Every sportsman is expected to be very fair and honest in the play. He should not apply any unfair means, which may erode the very spirit of the competition. The athlete must show tolerance and respect towards every individual who is directly or indirectly connected with conduct

of sports competition. He must take care of self respect and also respect the dignity of others. He is friendly not only towards the members of the other team, coach, umpire, referee but also all other tournament officials and spectators. His behaviour on and off the field must be appreciable. The sportsman must be humble, obedient, and sincere in obeying all the rules and laws of the competition. He never gets irritated or loses temper in any case during competition against his own players, opponents, officials or spectators; Sportsman-like qualities will not only earn a good image for him in the sports world but will also be helpful in improving his performance. A true sportsman will neither be overjoyed on his victory nor be disheartened on his defeat. He shows a very rational behaviour in all the circumstances he is in.

ETHICS OF SPORTS COMPETITION

Ethics is concerned with morals and conduct; that is, with determining proper rules of behaviour. It is a study of ideal conduct and of the knowledge of right and wrong. It examines which actions are right and which are wrong, and what people should and should not do. It is an important concern for our field because we deal in human behaviour—with how it is shaped, how it shows itself, with all the shades of good and bad conduct that appear. The concept of ethics is very much related to the morality. Ethics is related to the moral values of the sports competition. Sportsmanship and ethics are deeply connected to each other. In sports world ethics is product of sports traditions, values and rituals which are, sometime, not covered under the laws of the games or sports. Some time their strength is more prominent than even laws and rules of the games or sports.

In sports competitions, the ethical values cannot be undermined. In certain cases they turn to be deciding factors in earning victory, or defeat. For example ethics demand that, player or athlete should never chide any of his team mate during competition for his silly mistakes rather he should always boost the morale of such player failing which the affected player will feel discouraged and performance will further go down. Sometime non-

ethical behaviour irritates the officials and crowd also. He will lose moral support from all quarters which is one of the important contributing factors for earning victory. Ethics, most fundamentally, is about seeking and promoting the good life—about finding out what it is, celebrating it, and keeping it in focus. It is about preserving values like truth, knowledge, excellence, friendship, excitement, and any number of other good things, virtues.

Ethics is also about compassion and sympathy—about making sure that the good life is shared with others who inhabit this planet with us. It is about caring for others, particularly those who do not have the position or power necessary to protect themselves or have their say or way.

It describe character in terms of four virtues that a person of good character displays: compassion, fairness, sportsmanship, and integrity. With compassion, *"players can be encouraged to see competitors as coparticipants, equally valuable, equally deserving of regard.... Fairness involves evenhandedness, equal consideration."* Sportsmanship *"involves an intense striving to succeed, tempered by commitment to a 'play spirit,' such that ethical standards will take precedence over strategic gain when the two conflict. "Finally, "integrity enables one to act on one's convictions, even if such action is negatively received by coach, team mates, or fans."*

No field is without problems. But the problems encountered in physical education and sports can be seen as particularly difficult. In many cases people find themselves caught in ethical dilemmas, unsure as to what is the best or most proper thing to do.

PROBLEMS IN PHYSICAL EDUCATION AND SPORTS

Problems in sports affect physical education. The public views the two areas as one, and many coaches work in physical education departments. Sport has changed considerably over the years. Both media coverage and financial investments have risen sharply. At the highest levels of competition, athletics can become almost a full-time job. Are such requirements by coaches or colleges ethical, even with scholarships?

Abuses of Sports

The first area of concern centers around the abuses in sports. These can be listed as : direct or indirect payments to students for athletic services; encouragement of students to move from college to college for athletic purposes; lack of faculty control in games and grounds; coaches of questionable morals and influence; 'and bad moral effects of games when rules are broken or evaded.

Overemphasis on School Sports

A second concern is the overemphasis on sports in the schools. If educators believe that sports make a genuine contribution to the educational process, then they should expect them to be important. In many cases, though, sports are overemphasized, that is, not used for lessons, but promoted simply for the victories and fame that can be gained. This problem needs to be considered seriously, because it reflects on physical education programs as well.

Overemphasis on Competitive Sports in Physical Education

A third concern is whether competitive sports are overemphasized in the physical education program. Although competitive sports may be overemphasized by less skilled teachers. A good teacher will prepare a well-balanced program that exposes students to all areas of physical activity. Physical educators need to evaluate their programs constantly to ensure that they are providing physical education, not simply promoting physical competition.

Relationship Between Physical Education and Sport

The fourth concern is still controversial—What is the relationship between physical education and sports? In public eyes, the two areas are one. The need to share facilities, equipment, and even budgets and faculty, causes conflict. Each area is affected by the public reputation of the other. Whether or not physical education and athletics wish to be a single area, they are often forced together by the public. This often situation cause unfortunate effects.

HOW DOES ETHICS RELATE TO PHYSICAL EDUCATION AND SPORTS?

Ethics is vital to the successful functioning of any society; that is, people must have standards of value by which they live. The development of ethical standards has long been a prominent part of the educational process. The Greeks spoke of the development of character as one of the most vital concerns, if not the most vital concern, of education.

If we agree that we need to develop character, of ethical standards, what does that need have to do with sports and physical education? Sports and physical education often are referred to as a laboratory of human experience, there for, more than in any other organized area, of the educational process, students are likely to show their inner selves. Sports and physical education challenge the students both physically and intellectually, and in the heat of intense competition, a person's true values often shows up. One person may be more concerned with fair play, while other may try to win in any possible way. This is the ultimate test of ethical standards, and no *other area of educational endeavor is so likely* to put the students to the test.

A major difference between physical education and sports is that physical education is concerned with personal outcomes, with learning, with development. Thus its ethic is different from that of sports, which is concerned with competitive success, rather than the Improvement of the individual. In physical education, ethical learning has to do with learning what is right, how to interact and co-operate with others, how to make decisions. In sports, ethics deal with the concept of fair play.

Originally sports was for competitors, but in modern times the influence of television has vastly increased the problem of the entertainment dilemma. When sport is still purely for the athlete, however, it is an excellent test of ethical behaviour.

SHOULD ETHICS AND VALUES BE TAUGHT?

If physical education and sport really are a "laboratory of human experience" as is claimed, what better place could be found to try to teach ethics and values to the future leaders of the world? Whenever lists of objectives for physical education have been prepared, the development of social and moral qualities are included.

It would be more accurate to suggest that sport provides the opportunity to display character rather than to develop it, but the ties between ethical character and sport and physical education are strong and of an ancient heritage.

Today the concern over ethical behaviour is rising as society becomes more aware of the need for ethical character of its members. The increasing consciousness of the need for the development of the older concept of ethical character is reflected by the appearance of texts specifically related to ethics, character development and sport. Programs need to stress character, ethics, and sportsmanship a new.

WHY SPORT HAS A POOR REPUTATION?

Sport has earned a poor reputation for many reasons. Which philosophies and practices have given sport this questionable reputation? One reason is the fact that coaches and athletes at lower levels of competition try to imitate the practices they see in the big-time sports programs. However, practices that might seem acceptable in professional athletics (which is essentially entertainment) often are inappropriate in amateur athletics. Unfortunately, we see many of the ideas of professional athletics at the lowest levels of competition. That such ideas reach lower levels of sport and remain there is the responsibility of the teacher-coach. Unless the teacher-coach opposes those practices, they will continue to spread.

The Supreme Importance of Victory

Two aspects of the overemphasis on victory might be called the "winning is the only motto" ethic and the "agony of defeat" syndrome. The *"winning is the only motto"* ethic comes from the popular coaches saying that *"Winning isn't everything, it's the only motto."*

The basic idea expressed here is that the only point of athletics is victory, so that the end justifies the means. At best, this is a gross abuse of the idea of sport as a contributor to the educational process.

If this philosophy is the philosophy of a school's coach or teacher, the school should have no sports program, because this motto does not have the slightest pretence of moral or educational values or ethics.

The "agony of defeat" syndrome covers the total range of sports, which according to television is *"the thrill of victory the agony of defeat."* One small question arises in response to this view: Why should we think that defeat must result in agony?

Sport is called a *"training ground for life"* by many coaches, but if agony is a person's response to every defeat in life, would that person be considered well adjusted? Defeat is a disappointment, sometimes an intense one, but the idea that it should be agony is another abuse of the place of sport in education and in life.

People who coach or compete in sports want to win. Winning, or trying to win, is a natural desire of the human race. Life is like a competition, but if we make victory with no holds barred the goal of life, we have removed most of the potential quality of that life. If victory is the ultimate lesson in school athletics, there is no lesson worth teaching, because the desire to win is inherent. No one wants to lose. The value of sport in the school curriculum lies in the other values that are taught or promoted during teaching, training, and competing. Victory is neither the only goal nor the highest goal in educational sport and physical education.

Poor Sportsmanship

Sportsmanship has been used for many years as an example of the best trait that athletics can develop. Unfortunately, there is no evidence that participating in competitive sports really does develop sportsmanship. We do have some evidence that sports competition can bring out sportsmanship or can inhibit or lessen it. Poor sportsmanship may be primarily a result of the examples given by coaches and teachers (and some parents) to their teams and to other student as they pursue victory and fame. Because of this influence, schools are looking increasingly for ways an means to teach sportsmanship.

The proverb that *"nice guys finish last"* is a good example of what is wrong with educational sport. Too many coaches and athletes have tried to live up to this motto. The idea is that decency is a sign of weakness, that a person who shows signs of character probably does not have the force of will to become a champion. The result is coaches who abuse their athletes and any ethical standards to pursue victory, because they do not think they can win if they play by the rules.

The other aspect of poor sportsmanship is the idea that "the coach loves a poor loser." We are increasingly treated to the spectacle of athletes who throw temper tantrums whenever they lose. This action is then cited by the coach or sports announcer as a sign of competitiveness or spirit. To be honest, it is nothing more than a sign of childish immaturity.

Lack of Joy in Sport

Traditionally sports are thought of as activities that people enjoy or that are fun to do. One aspect of contemporary sport seems to be the idea that sport should not be treated as fun, because winning or losing is too serious an issue to permit enjoyment. One example is similar to the last point made under poor sportsmanship. "Show me a good loser, and I'll show you a loser," as some coaches put it, is another example of an immature approach to sport.

Another view of the no-joy-in-sport philosophy is expressed by the coach who says, 'We're here to win, not to have a good time." If that is the coach's philosophy, the team has already lost, because the education of such a program will produce an entirely negative outcome.

The Place of Education in Sport

Actually, it would be more appropriate to refer to the place of the educator in sport because the concern here is with the coach's dedication to this teaching. Most coaches will say that sport is an important part of the educational process. The question is whether their practices uphold their claim of believing the statement. An example could be the "not so-dedicated teacher" syndrome, or the coach whose educational approach is best reflected in his defensive statement, "I get paid to win, not to teach". The most obvious fact in the statement is that this coach is not a teacher and does not consider himself a teacher. Moreover, the statement makes the observer suspect that the coach has never been interested in being a teacher.

Sports as Money

Money is the greatest force affecting athletics today because it lies at the heart of so many abuses of the educational goals of sports. The problem is form of the Midas touch: Athletes hope that everything they touch will pay off in dollars and cents.

Many of today's high school athletes are about as interested in the ethics of scholarships and fringe benefits as a professional athlete: Too often, we see the picture of functionally illiterate all-star high school athlete from a poor family who, after barely skipping high school, suddenly acquires a car, an improved wardrobe, perhaps a well-paid summer job, and the status of "amateur" college athlete. Too many coaches and athletes today believe that the cardinal rule of athletics is ''money making drive."

OBJECTIVE QUESTIONS

1. America is a Super Power in the field of:
   (*a*) Economic Arena
   (*b*) Technological Arena
   (*c*) Sports Arena
   (*d*) All of the above

2. Physical Education should be treated:
   (*a*) In isolation
   (*b*) A part of general curriculum
   (*c*) As a alien subject
   (*d*) Nothing can be said

3. Which among the following is not the repurcusion of the 'Rs' oriented concept of Education:
   (*a*) Heavy academic burden
   (*b*) Long hours of school
   (*c*) Stress of competition for high scoring
   (*d*) Relaxed atmosphere in the schools

4. Traditional concept of Physical Education was:
 (*a*) A narrow concept
 (*b*) A broader concept
 (*c*) Technological concept
 (*d*) Highly competitive concept

5. The modern concept of Physical Education stresses on:
 (*a*) Mental and physical development
 (*b*) Social and moral development
 (*c*) Mental and moral development
 (*d*) Mental, physical, social and moral development

6. One who looks after the physical fitness of the players is known as:
 (*a*) Physical Education Teacher
 (*b*) Bio-mechanic
 (*c*) Sports Psychologist
 (*d*) Physiologist

7. Which among the following is not included as an activity under physical education?
 (*a*) Games and sports (*b*) Gymnastics
 (*c*) Teaching   (*d*) Recreation

8. Which among the following is not included under the scope of Physical Education?
 (*a*) Yoga
 (*b*) Sports and swimming
 (*c*) Criminal investigation
 (*d*) Corrective exercises

9. The National Rifle Association was founded in:
 (*a*) 1937 A.D.   (*b*) 1946 A.D.
 (*c*) 1958 AD.   (*d*) 1969 A.D.

10. Sports Authority of India has its headquarter at:
 (*a*) Kolkata   (*b*) Mumbai
 (*c*) New Delhi   (*d*) Patiala

11. Which among the following is not included in Recreation activities?
 (*a*) Camping   (*b*) Fishing
 (*c*) Nature study   (*c*) Dances

12. Which among the following is not included in the Self-defence activities:
 (*a*) Dundo   (*b*) Lezium

 (*c*) Boxing   (*d*) Gathka

13. During Childhood Physical Activities are required for:
 (*a*) Somato-psychic development
 (*b*) Growth and development
 (*c*) Good health and fitness
 (*d*) Prevent and treat any possible physical ailment

14. Which is not the misconception about Physical Education?
 (*a*) Physical Education is not necessary for school children
 (*b*) Physical Education has not Academic value
 (*c*) Physical Education enhances muscular strength
 (*d*) Physical Education means doing physical training

15. Which among the following is not a proposed name for Physical Education:
 (*a*) Movement Arts
 (*b*) Movement Education
 (*c*) Kinesiology
 (*d*) Recreation Science

16. In which country movement education has been developed at the elementary school level?
 (*a*) Denmark
 (*b*) England
 (*c*) America
 (*d*) Japan

17. During adulthood physical activities required for:
 (*a*) Making skin beautiful
 (*b*) Maintaining good health and fitness
 (*c*) Proper growth and development
 (*d*) Treatment of possible ailments

18. Physical education is not:
 (*a*) An essential part of education
 (*b*) An integral part of education
 (*c*) An undesired physical science
 (*d*) Total education of the child for over development

19. Which among the following is not part of self realization as classified by C.A. Bucher?
 (*a*) An inquiring mind
 (*b*) Knowledge of diseases and health
 (*c*) Priority to human relationship and human welfare
 (*d*) Family and community health

20. Which does not fall under the objectives of Civil Responsibility?
 (*a*) Education for tolerance
 (*b*) Education for conformance with laws
 (*c*) Education for good workmanship
 (*d*) Education for democratic living

21. 'Catch them early' is a program for:
 (*a*) preparing international level sports persons
 (*b*) catching the tax evaders
 (*c*) training the coaches in right manner
 (*d*) All of these

22. Which among the following does not come under the objectives of Self-Realization:
 (*a*) Utilisation of leisure hours in mental pursuits
 (*b*) Appreciation of beauty
 (*c*) Contribution in family and community health
 (*d*) Education for social growth

23. Physical activities are the result of:
 (*a*) Neuro-muscular coordination
 (*b*) Muscular and body coordination
 (*c*) Recreational and auto-muscular co-ordination
 (*d*) None of these

24. The life process of human being developed with the:
 (*a*) Muscular activities
 (*b*) Respiratory system
 (*c*) Digestive system
 (*d*) Excretory system

25. What cover the bony framework below the skin?
 (*a*) White skin (*b*) Muscle fibres
 (*c*) Red blood cells (*d*) White blood cells

26. What is the approximate number of muscles in human body?
 (*a*) Four thousand (*b*) Six thousand

(*c*) Eight thousand (*d*) Five hundred

27. Which among the following is not a kind of muscle cells?
 (*a*) Voluntary (*b*) Non voluntary
 (*c*) Cardio (*d*) Extra cardio

28. The shortening of muscles is called:
 (*a*) Shrinking (*b*) Relaxation
 (*c*) Contraction (*d*) None of these

29. All the body movements are performed with the help of:
 (*a*) Skeletal muscles
 (*b*) Backbone muscles
 (*c*) Voluntary muscle cells
 (*d*) Cardio muscle cells

30. The quick source of fuel in the body is:
 (*a*) Milk (*b*) Water
 (*c*) Fats (*d*) Glycogen

31. How the thickening of the connective tissue within the muscle can be ensured?
 (*a*) Light exercise
 (*b*) Irregular exercise
 (*c*) Prolonged exercise
 (*d*) Morning exercise

32. The other name of circulatory system is:
 (*a*) Regulatory system
 (*b*) Transportation system
 (*c*) Complex system
 (*d*) None of these

33. Which among the following does under the category of blood vessels?
 (*a*) Capillaries (*b*) Artery
 (*c*) Vein (*d*) Heart

34. How many chambers are there in human heart?
 (*a*) Two (*b*) Three
 (*c*) Four (*d*) Five

35. The deoxy-generated blood comes to heart from:
 (*a*) Lungs (*b*) Whole body
 (*c*) Kidney (*d*) Brain

36. How much blood is pumped out by a normal heart in a minute?
 (*a*) 5 litres (*b*) 7 litres
 (*c*) 10.2 litres (*d*) 14.8 litres

37. How much blood is pumped out by the heart of an athlete?
  (*a*) 12.6 litres   (*b*) 15.6 litres
  (*c*) 19.4 litres   (*d*) 22 litres

38. As a regular exercise new capillaries are formed within the muscle fibres, which facilitates:
  (*a*) Strong muscle power
  (*b*) Quick removal of waste products from the body
  (*c*) Beauty of the skin
  (*d*) Strong heart and muscles

39. Which among the following is not an organ of respiratory system?
  (*a*) Trachea
  (*b*) Lungs
  (*c*) Bronchilus
  (*d*) Pulmonary artery

40. Which is called the 'Supreme Controller' of the Nervous System?
  (*a*) Autonomic nervous system
  (*b*) Central nervous system
  (*c*) Peripheral nervous system
  (*d*) Relay sensory system

41. What control the movements of the muscles :
  (*a*) Pancreas   (*b*) Nerves
  (*c*) Spinal cord   (*d*) Medulla

42. Animals derive organic food materials by consuming:
  (*a*) Plants products   (*b*) Humans product
  (*c*) Glycogen product (*d*) None of these

43. Removal of undigested food is known as:
  (*a*) Ingestion   (*b*) Digestion
  (*c*) Egestion   (*d*) Conversion

44. Which is the largest digestive gland in the body:
  (*a*) Liver   (*b*) Smal intestine
  (*c*) Large intestine   (*d*) Pancreas

45. Which function is not performed by liver:
  (*a*) Secretion of bile
  (*b*) Secretion of enzymes
  (*c*) Transportation of blood
  (*d*) Formation of Glycogenolysis

46. What is second wind?
  (*a*) When some tires
  (*b*) When one refreshes oneself
  (*c*) When an athlete is given extra energy
  (*d*) None of these

47. Which among the following is not a symptoms of second wind?
  (*a*) Lethargio movement
  (*b*) Nausea
  (*c*) Fast finishing
  (*d*) Breathlessness

48. What does not happen after second wind:
  (*a*) Removal of waste products from the body
  (*b*) Better association of neuromuscular structure
  (*c*) Increased metabolic activity of the body
  (*d*) Sensation of pain in the abdominal

49. Who was the first cricketer to receive Padam Bhushan Award?
  (*a*) C.K.Naidu   (*c*) Maharaj Kumar
  (*b*) S.M.Gavaskar   (*d*) Lala Amarnath

50. Who was the first to receive Rajiv Gandhi Khel Ratna Award?
  (*a*) S.R.Tendulkar   (*b*) Liander Paes
  (*c*) P. Gopichand   (*d*) D.P Azad

51. The primary function of sarcoplasmic reticulum is to
  (*a*) Store Calcium ions
  (*b*) help in contraction
  (*c*) store Mg^{2+} ions
  (*d*) its empty with no functions.

52. In skeletal mucles, the light areas are called
  (*a*) I-bands   (*b*) A-bands
  (*c*) T-tubules   (*d*) Z-line

53. A sacromere is an area
  (*a*) between two I-bands
  (*b*) between two Z-lines
  (*c*) between two A-bands
  (*d*) between I and A bands

54. Myosin heads are called
  (*a*) A-bands   (*b*) I-bands
  (*c*) Cross bridges   (*d*) Z-lines

55. Thin myofilament do not compose of which one of the following proteins?
(*a*) Actin (*b*) Troponin
(*c*) Tropomyosin (*d*) Myosin

56. Calcium from sacroplasmic reticulum fill the binding sets of which protein molecules?
(*a*) Troponin (*b*) Tropomyosin
(*c*) Actin (*d*) Myosin

57. Which element acts as the "on and off' switch of skeletal muscle?
(*a*) Mg^{2+} (*b*) Ca^{2+}
(*c*) Na^{+} (*d*) Cl^{-}

58. If a muscle fibre is stimulated so rapidly that it does not relax at all between stimuli, a small sustained contraction occurs called
(*a*) ischemia (*b*) fatigue
(*c*) tetanus (*d*) exhausion

59. Calcium in smooth muscles attaches to which protein?
(*a*) Actin (*b*) Troponin
(*c*) Tropomyosin (*d*) Calmodulin

60. Which smooth muscle is stimulated by nervous stimulation?
(*a*) Visceral smooth muscle
(*b*) Unitary smooth muscle
(*c*) Multiunit smooth muscle
(*d*) All

61. Which of the following is not a pathway of air during respiration?
(*a*) Pharynax (*b*) Trachea
(*c*) Diaphragm (*d*) Bronchi

62. Mark the correct passage of air during respiration.
(*a*) nasal cavity $\rightarrow$ pharynx $\rightarrow$ trachea $\rightarrow$ bronchi $\rightarrow$ alveoli
(*b*) nasal cavity $\rightarrow$ trachea $\rightarrow$ pharynx $\rightarrow$ bronchi $\rightarrow$ alveoli
(*c*) nasal cavity $\rightarrow$ trachea $\rightarrow$ pharynx $\rightarrow$ alveoli $\rightarrow$ bronchi
(*d*) trachea $\rightarrow$ pharynx $\rightarrow$ bronchi $\rightarrow$ alveoli $\rightarrow$ nasal cavity

63. The substance which reduces surface tension in alveoli in order to avoid the collapse
(*a*) blood (*b*) oxygen
(*c*) surfactant (*d*) alkali

64. What is the average total surface area of our lungs
(*a*) 65 sq. mt (*b*) 72 sq. mt
(*c*) 75 sq. mt (*d*) 79 sq. mt

65. What is the percentage of oxygen bound to haemoglobin in blood?
(*a*) 90.8% (*b*) 92.5%
(*c*) 95% (*d*) 98.5%

66. Apneustic and Oneumotoxic centres of respiration are located in which area of brain?
(*a*) Medulla (*b*) Cerebrum
(*c*) Cerebellum (*d*) Pons

67. Rhythmicity centre of respiration are located in
(*a*) Medulla (*b*) Cerebrum
(*c*) Cerebellum (*d*) Pons

68. Which of the following mechanisms are not responsible for increased respiratory rate during heavy exercise?
(*a*) increased CO_2
(*b*) increase in body temperature
(*c*) epinephrine release
(*d*) impulses from the cerebral cortex

69. Muscles at the back of the humerus are
(*a*) Quadriceps (*b*) Biceps
(*c*) Triceps (*d*) Intecostals

70. The muscle which is the strongest in human body is
(*a*) Quadriceps (*b*) Rectus femoris
(*c*) Sternomustoid (*d*) Triceps

71. In which type of fracture does the bone split along its length?
(*a*) Impacted (*b*) Depressed
(*c*) Green stick (*d*) Longitudinal

72. Which muscle is located on the upper back?
(*a*) Brachioradialis (*b*) pectineus
(*c*) Soleus (*d*) Trapezius

73. Soleus muscle is located in
    (*a*) Lower leg   (*b*) Forearm
    (*c*) Trunk   (*d*) Upper leg

74. Mark out the correct pair
    (*a*) Study of cells   I.   Osteology
    (*b*) Study of muscles II. Cytology
    (*c*) Study of bones   III. Myology
    (*d*) Study of organs IV. Splanchnology
                               of Viscera

75. Which of the following is not an electrical modality?
    (*a*) Ultraviolet light   (*b*) Lasers
    (*c*) TENS   (*d*) Ultrasound

76. Light energy having a wavelength greater than 730mm is termed
    (*a*) Infrared energy   (*b*) Ultra sound
    (*c*) Ultraviolet   (*d*) TENS

77. Which of the following ergogenic aids is not a stimulant?
    (*a*) Amphetamines   (*b*) Caeffine
    (*c*) Cocaine   (*d*) Morphine

78. Match the cause of fracture with their correct examples
    (*a*) Direct Blow   I.   Person falling and landing on hands suffering a broken arm
    (*b*) Indirect blow   II. Person playing football or skiing is susceptible to this injury
    (*c*) Twisting Forces III. Person who receives an electric shock can suffer fracture
    (*d*) Muscle Contractions IV. Person hit by a piece of flying rock and bone is broken at the point of impact.

79. Fractures where small fragments of bones are detached at the sites of muscle insertions are
    (*a*) Avulsion fractures
    (*b*) March fractures
    (*c*) Segmental fractures
    (*d*) Communicated fractures

80. Fractures where the bone is broken in two or more places and may heal slowly, due to the poor blood supply of smaller fragments is
    (*a*) Epiphyseal fractures
    (*b*) Greenstick fracture
    (*c*) Segmental fracture
    (*d*) Stress fracture

81. The anterior ten pair of ribs joint to a bony plate called:
    (*a*) Diaphragm   (*b*) Intercoastals
    (*c*) Sternum   (*d*) Trachea

82. What is the total number of rules surrounding and protecting the lungs and heart in the thoracic cavity?
    (*a*) Ten   (*b*) Twelve
    (*c*) Thirteen   (*d*) Fourteen

83. Trachea splits into two bronchi. The right bronchus divides again into
    (*a*) two bronchi   (*b*) two alveoli
    (*c*) three bronchi   (*d*) four alveoli

84. Left lung has
    (*a*) One lobe   (*b*) two lobes
    (*c*) three lobes   (*d*) four lobes

85. The total surface area covered by alveoli in lungs of man are
    (*a*) 80-90 m^2 (*b*) 70-90 m^2
    (*c*) 120-180 m^2 (*d*) 150-170 m^2

86. Breathing centre is located in
    (*a*) Cerebrum   (*b*) Cerebellum
    (*c*) Spine   (*d*) Medulla

87. The lung capacity of an average man is
    (*a*) 3 dm^3 (*b*) 4 dm^3
    (*c*) 5 dm^3 (*d*) 6 dm^3

88. What is the tidal volume of air a man can breathe in or out?
    (*a*) 400 cm^3 (*b*) 450 cm^3
    (*c*) 500 cm^3 (*d*) 550 cm^3

89. Even after forced expiration the air which remains in lungs and cannot be expelled is called
    (*a*) Vital capacity
    (*b*) Residual air
    (*c*) Expiratory reserve volume
    (*d*) Tidal volume

90. The air which is expelled from body as unchanged room air is called
(*a*) dead space air (*b*) residual air
(*c*) vital capacity (*d*) tidal volume

91. Which is the major inhibitory (neurotransmitter) in brain?
(*a*) GABA (*b*) Serotonin
(*c*) Acetylcholine (*d*) Dopamine

92. Which chemical mimics action of acetylcholine?
(*a*) Curare (*b*) Botulinum toxin
(*c*) Nicotine (*d*) Atropine

93. Which of the following neurotransmitters blocks action of acetylcholine?
(*a*) Atropine (*b*) Muscarine
(*c*) Nicotine (*d*) Eserine

94. Which major neurotransmitter is synthesized from choline and mitochiondrially derived acetyl co-enzyme A?
(*a*) GABA (*b*) Acetylcholine
(*c*) Dopamine (*d*) Norepinephrine

95. The function of Achilles Tendon is
(*a*) to flex foot towards knee
(*b*) to connect gastroenemius muscle to heel
(*c*) to raise leg
(*d*) to bend knee

96. The heart is surrounded by a sac like
(*a*) endosarc (*b*) perisac
(*c*) pericardium (*d*) endocardium

97. Which enzyme facilitates the conversion of glucose to Glucose 5 phosphate?
(*a*) Aldolase (*b*) Enolase
(*c*) Glucokinase (*d*) Pyruvate Kinase

98. Which of the enzymes is not present in mitochondrial matrix?
(*a*) Enzymes of TCAcycle
(*b*) Pyruvate dehydrogenase
(*c*) Adenylate Kinase
(*d*) Oxidative enzymes

99. The number of ATP generated through Kreb's cycle is
(*a*) 28 ATP (*b*) 24 ATP
(*c*) 22 ATP (*d*) 26 ATP

100. The number of ATP generated through glycolysis is:
(*a*) 6 ATP (*b*) 8 ATP
(*c*) 4 ATP (*d*) 10 ATP

ANSWERS

1. (*b*)	2. (*d*)	3. (*c*)	4. (*a*)	5. (*d*)	6. (*c*)	7. (*b*)	8. (*d*)
9. (*c*)	10. (*b*)	11. (*c*)	12. (*d*)	13. (*b*)	14. (*d*)	15. (*b*)	16. (*b*)
17. (*a*)	18. (*c*)	19. (*a*)	20. (*c*)	21. (*b*)	22. (*c*)	23. (*d*)	24. (*a*)
25. (*b*)	26. (*d*)	27. (*b*)	28. (*c*)	29. (*a*)	30. (*d*)	31. (*b*)	32. (*c*)
33. (*c*)	34. (*c*)	35. (*c*)	36. (*d*)	37. (*b*)	38. (*a*)	39. (*c*)	40. (*d*)
41. (*b*)	42. (*b*)	43. (*c*)	44. (*c*)	45. (*c*)	46. (*a*)	47. (*d*)	48. (*a*)
49. (*a*)	50. (*b*)	51. (*a*)	52. (*a*)	53. (*b*)	54. (*c*)	55. (*d*)	56. (*a*)
57. (*b*)	58. (*c*)	59. (*d*)	60. (*c*)	61. (*c*)	62. (*a*)	63. (*c*)	64. (*c*)
65. (*d*)	66. (*d*)	67. (*a*)	68. (*a*)	69. (*b*)	70. (*b*)	71. (*c*)	72. (*d*)
73. (*d*)	74. (*b*)	75. (*d*)	76. (*a*)	77. (*d*)	78. (*d*)	79. (*a*)	80. (*c*)
81. (*c*)	82. (*b*)	83. (*c*)	84. (*b*)	85. (*a*)	86. (*d*)	87. (*c*)	88. (*b*)
89. (*b*)	90. (*a*)	91. (*a*)	92. (*c*)	93. (*a*)	94. (*b*)	95. (*b*)	96. (*c*)
97. (*c*)	98. (*c*)	99. (*b*)	100. (*b*)				

4. ORGANISATION & ADMINISTRATION

MEANING OF ORGANISATION

It takes both time and organisation to run any institution. Before an institution comes into operation it passes through various stages. In Physical education we call these steps as organisation. No 'institution or group can attain its objectives unless it is run systematically. It is essential to organise an institution and to administer it well in order to run it and to achieve definite prescribed objectives. If the chief organiser lacks administrative capability the institution will be running at a loss and will fail to come up to an ideal state. In a school or a college there is need for an efficient administrator whether as a headmaster or a principal. He must understand well at what time which game is played and accordingly should be able to arrange and organise the game and thus help the children in their all round development.

MEANING OF ADMINISTRATION

In Physical education often people confuse between organisation and administration They consider them as one and the same. In fact there is a lot of difference between the two. We all know that in any institution it is essential to have many constituents working. When the constituents or parts are not working to the full there can be no administration. When the parts are working and are in order, it is only then that we shall need an administrator whose job it is to supervise the parts. In order that the meaning may be properly understood let us take an illustration. In a TV for example it is only when its parts are in order and working well that the TV will work. Their orderly working is organisation. Other things like control of sound, electricity choice of place where it is working and such other allied questions together fall under administration.

Basic Principles and Elements of Organisation and Administration

In any school or college efficient organisation of physical education depends upon the place (country), circumstances and time. It is necessary to keep time in view whether in the evening or in the morning. Some of the basic principles of organisation and administration are as follows :

1. Humanitarian Principles: It is but natural that the children participating in games may make mistakes, because it is human to err the physical instructor should be tactful in his approach. He should never commit the mistake of showing anger or rashness. It is better to first praise and take care to point out the flaws or drawbacks by taking the child away. He should not reprimand or try to pull down the child before others The children are often all humans and not animals. The trainer or instructor must display a human and warm attitude. Surely the child will respond better and display better performance.

2. Principle of Allied Elements: The success of a physical instructor directly depends upon the available human material. It is his job to use the available resources well. He must himself be well trained and should know his job well. In a school or college, the boys and girls are the raw material which the instructor should put to use usefully. He must learn to draw benefit from a lowly neon to the hitches official. The instructor should be able to excite the interest of the children and only then he can expect desired results.

3. Principle of Local Conservation: The instructor cannot achieve desired results without the co-operation of the patrons of the children getting training under him. The patrons (parents or spectators when they watch their children participating feel happy and proud at their performance. It is then that they will perhaps decide whether they shall permit their wards (children) to continue to get training or not. An instructor should take care to invite parents and other respected people to watch performances of the children off and on. At time they may even be invited to important meetings. It will encourage the children too. Surcly there will be good response and co-operation from the parents.

4. Principle of Harmony and Thoughtfulness: For the success of a physical education programme harmony must be cultivated with all those who are associated with the programme. There may be workers at different levels. They should be given responsibilities of the programme. If there is no harmony the entire programme will flop and others will have the occassion to make fun of it.

It is essential to call a meeting before the programme gets going. All possible problems can be sorted out there. If need be, an expert on any particular subject or department can be invited and his opinion taken. It is necessary to bear in mind that no single person or any single opinion should be given prominence. By doing so there is a likelihood that others may misunderstand and withdraw their co-operation. When taking any important decision due weight and importance should be shown to the opinion of others.

5. Principle of Clear Laws: It is necessary to let everyone know clearly all the rules and laws pertaining to the programme of physical education. It is advised that the copies of Rules etc may be put up on the Notice boards, in canteens, Panchayatghar and such places where everybody gets a chance to read. By doing so we not only draw the co-operation of all those participating, but there is an added benefit.

The students who are participating shall know the Rules and there will be no chance of the blame that they are being prejudiced against They will be able to participate enthusiastically and a healthy spirit of competition shall prevail.

6. Principle of Classification: It is necessary to divide children into different age-groups. Then a certain age-group at boys or girls will complete among their own age-group. That will generate a healthy and intense spirit of competition. There is

another benefit as well. The children watching outside shall have their interest aroused in the game. Surely they would also like to participate

Alongside it is necessary to divide all the boys or girls in a school into different groups or houses. There can be certain programmes where different groups may participate. Care should be taken not to ignore daily practice The different groups can have group-leaders. That in turn shall generate a spirit of leadership.

7. Principle of Correlation: The physical education programme will succed better through the principle of correlation. The children can be attracted to the subject of Physical education through corelated dramas declamations, essay competitions and also by arranging races among them or even by organising other interesting features. Such features are able to remove their fears and apprehensions and they are encouraged to participate.

8. Principle of Encouragement and Reward: It helps to reward suitably those children who have displayed good performance They may be given medals and other awards to boost their interest in Physical education and its programmes. The children fully understand the significance of awards They value it in terms of achievement and not in terms of its money value. Even a small item like a pencil can have an effect on the mind of the child who receives it. The reward may be in the form of an item or a shield, testimonial cup, trophy, medal or even cash

IMPORTANCE OF ORGANISATION AND ADMINISTRATION IN PHYSICAL EDUCATION

In the present times Physical Education is coming up as a regular career. It is becoming popular in schools and colleges for that reason. When the children watch a spectacle of games it is then that they are fascinated by the game and are then slowly drawn towards the game. Those children who enter a playfield with interest are sure to make a mark and earn distinctions.

In schools now there are regular games being played. Side by side it has become necessary to organise physical education programmes. Besides the country needs healthy citizens Physical education has a greater role to play in that direction and under the circumstances. When Physical education programmes are undertaken it is but natural that the need for instructors shall also grow. Without either of these the desired objectives are bound to remain a far cry.

PRINCIPLE OF ORGANISING FOR THE SUCCESS OF ADMINISTRATION IN PHYSICAL EDUCATION

In order that a Physical education programme may succeed well it is necessary to see how the various constituents act and interact. Sometimes the managers will find it difficult to manage a programme even though they have all kinds of facilities at their disposal. That happens when some flaw or drawback remains within the organisation. It is like the smaller parts of an engine. In order that the engine may perform well all its parts should be in order and also working well with the other parts. If one small part of an engine is out of order and not working well it is sure to disturb the working of other parts and of the entire engine. In this context we shall do well to study Luther Gullick's formula of seven important points. He has prescribed a formula which runs as POSDCRB. Let us see what do the different letters denote.

1. Planning
2. Organisation
3. Staff
4. Direction
5. Co-ordination
6. Reporting
7. Budgeting.

The formula or seven points indicate the importance of different aspects of organisation. No man can succeed well if he ignores any single aspect: all these aspects must coordinate well. Any organiser must take care to look after each different aspect in order that the programme undertaken by him may succeed.

DIVISION OF ACTIVITIES IN PHYSICAL EDUCATION

Any person who undertakes some physical activity does it within the bounds of his physical endurance. Each physical activity needs its own kind of skill and each one brings about a definite change and improvement in the human body. Generally speaking, physical activities make the body active, agile and physically strong and all these together develop an all round personality. Physical activities are of two kinds, one which are to be undertaken individually by a person all by himself. Then there are activities in which an individual takes part as part of the team. Again, there are some activities which an individual can undertake with ease while some other activities are not as easy. In certain physical activities an individual has to join hands with others and such activities call for participation by all.

There are certain governmental agencies in a State and in the country which supervise physical activities and programmes. Besides there are voluntary organisations too. But both of such agencies have but one common aim, viz social welfare of the citizens.

On the basis of individual, two some or dual and team Activities, we can divide physical activities as follows :

1. Team Activities: As the name shows, in team activities a person or participant takes part in co-operation with others who are also members of the team. Here co-operation of each member is necessary. There may be one or may be two persons managing the working of the team and the team members have to go by the instructions issued or given by them. At the same time the leader of the team has also the responsibility to look after individual interests. The choice of members and their number participating in an event or match is determined by the leader. In a team activity though the emphasis is always on the performance of the team but surely the overall results are always due to individual efforts. Such team activities encourage team-spirit which is in essence total co-operation with the other members of the team. An individual must work hard and put in his best performance even though the credit may go to the team. Such activities are sure to activities the body of an individual. Today TV and other mass media are playing a positive role in activating interest in team games by broadcasting important events. There are commercial concerns as well showing active interest in promoting team games by patronising them with money and in other ways. Hockey, football, volleyball, Cricket, Kabaddi, Kho-Kho. Handball, Softball, Basket Ball are all team activities.

2. Individual Activities: It is a natural instinct in all human beings that we desire to get results of our individual efforts, labour and technique. There are two kinds of benefits which accrue directly from the physical activities, one by way of entertainment, the other by way of physical well being. Both are important in their own ways. A person achieves success by putting to use his skill, strength and technique. In an individual activity a person learns the skill to safeguard himself. Here the need of co-operation from the other individuals is obliterated (not necessary). There are also far more opportunities to excel and display excellence. There are always meets and matches being arranged at different levels. In a school or college for example youth festivals or Games are regularly held. By taking part an individual can display his or her talent and ability. Such activities include track events, Throw events, Jump events, Tennis, Wrestling, Judo-Karate, Parallel-bars etc. Such events require talent as also continuous and hard practice. To some extent success is proportional to an individual physical capability also. A trainer should also make the choice of a participant keeping in view his or her physical ability in mind and then impart training accordingly.

3. Rhythmical Activities: All rhythmical activities are always accompanied by the rhythm of a drum, harmonium and such musical instrument. The participant undertake movements of their hands, limbs and body in tune with the sound of instruments. Such activities are enjoyed more by children. The sound of the instruments surely sends enthusiastic waves into their bodies and they respond. The children are more prone to physical activities than the elders and are more easily drawn to them. The children find it easier to grasp the various movements. In certain cases popular tunes or folk music or even folk lores may be drawn in for greater effect and joy. All such activities should

be presented gracefully and in an environment of discipline and decorum. Games like laziums, Dumbell, Mass P.T. are the living examples.

4. Gymnastics: All those physical activities which are performed inside a gymnasium or an amphitheatre with the help of instruments or devices are called Gymnastics. All gymnastics activities activate human body and strengthen muscles. Among the children these activities set up harmony between physical or muscular strength and the mental strength. There are some activities which are exclusively meant for males, others for females. The following six items are included among Gymnastics — Parellel-bar, Horizontal bar, Vaulting horse, Pommel horse, Roman Ring and ground work activities.

The activities meant for females are ground work, Balancing beam, vaulting horse and Uneven bar.

It is not necessary to undertake only above activities inside a gymnasium. There are others too, like wall bar, walk diving box and Roman ring etc. While participating in Gymnastics activities the presence of a coach or trainer is absolutely essential. Such activities should be taken around the age of eleven or so

5. Combatives: All those activities which are related to personal defence are known as Combative activities. It naturally includes activities related to evading a sudden attack from any predator. The essential fact to be borne in mind is the strength or challenge is to be met with skill and not necessarily with strength. Such activities need to be taught and practice from early age. It is but natural that during attack we instinctively throw up our hands and limbs while trying to save ourselves. Men have been busy devising combative activities since very early times. Today several definite techniques have evolved such combative activities are sure to cultivate spirit of fearlessness and courage among the children. These activities are useful in life, apart from their chief uses as games. Such activities as pushing the shoulders or shoulder push, pushing with hands or hand-push, Ateniwaza and Nage waza in Judo karate and similar activities. It is necessary for a trainer to bear in mind the height and age of a child participating. It is better for him to prepare himself and then instruct the child to emulate. There is no gainsaying the fact that such combative activities are absolutely essential, particularly for women who are always open to violent or passive attacks. All women (and men) must learn to defeat the nefarious and unwanted designs of bad elements in society.

6. Calisthenics: There are certain activities which are exclusively meant to beautiful human body through physical activities. Such activities are undertaken after body exercises and physical work. Such activities are called calisthenics. It is a Latin word composed of kallos and steno which mean beauty and strength. Literally thus calisthenics shall mean those activities which impart beauty and strength to human body. Such activities may or may not call for expenses, but surely these call for physical agility. They can go a long way in enhancing mental and physical energies of the body. Speed and agility are the basic essentials and they in turn make the body elastic and balanced. The muscles and joints gain in elasticity and mobility which in turn is sure to affect the entire human body. They should be undertaken not haphazardly, but in a definite order. A circus is sure to show us what wonders can be achieved in calisthenics. Girls and boys can be seen there displaying superbly the elasticity, agility and balance of their beautiful bodies.

It is clear then that calisthenics shall develop strength, tensility, agility and mobility in the human body. A trainer should be careful enough to display these activities correctly. He may use photographs and charts and such relevant material freely, during training.

OBJECTIVE QUESTIONS

1. Who founded Sri Hanuman Vyayam Prasarak Mandal Amravati in 1914 A.D.?
   (*a*) Krishna Brothers   (*b*) Vaidya Brothers
   (*c*) Keshav Brothers   (*d*) P Jha & Brothers

2. In which year Central Advisory Board of Physical Education and Recreation was set up?
   (*a*) 1936 A.D.   (*b*) 1950 A.D.
   (*c*) 1954 A.D.   (*d*) 1963 A.D.

3. In which year India participated in the Olympic games for the first time?
   (*a*) 1896 A.D.   (*b*) 1900 A.D.
   (*c*) 1904 A.D.   (*d*) 1907 A.D.

4. Who was the first President of Indian Olympic Association?
   (*a*) H.C Buck   (*b*) Dr. A.G. Nochren
   (*c*) Dorabji Tata   (*d*) G.D. Sondhi

5. The N.C.C. was introduced in the year 1948 by the:
   (*a*) President of India
   (*b*) The Act of Parliament
   (*c*) Help of voluntary organization
   (*d*) Ministry of Defence

6. Who introduced the Raj Kumari Coaching Scheme in 1953 A.D.?
   (*a*) Government of India
   (*b*) Punjab Government
   (*c*) Delhi Government
   (*d*) Uttar Pradesh Government

7. In which year Raj Kumari Coaching Scheme ceased to function?
   (*a*) 1961 A.D.   (*b*) 1965 A.D.
   (*c*) 1973 A.D.   (*d*) 1984 A.D.

8. The National Discipline Scheme took birth in the year:
   (*a*) 1948 A.D.   (*b*) 1954 A.D.
   (*c*) 1963 A.D.   (*d*) 1972 A.D.

9. What was the objective of Central Training Institute Sariska and Barwala?
   (*a*) Training for coaches
   (*b*) Training for National Discipline Scheme
   (*c*) Training for Physical Fitness
   (*d*) Training for self-defence

10. Who was the first chairman of All India Council of Sports?
    (*a*) Pt. J.L. Nehru
    (*b*) Gen. K.M. Kariappa
    (*c*) A. Jha
    (*d*) Dhyan Chand

11. In which year Maulana Abul Kalam Azad Trophy was instituted?
(*a*) 1951-52   (*b*) 1953-54
(*c*) 1956-57   (*d*) 1960-61

12. Lakshmibai National Institute of Physical Education is located at:
(*a*) Lucknow
(*b*) Hyderabad
(*c*) Gwalior
(*d*) Kurukshetra

13. In which year Lakshmibai National Institute of Physical Education was given the status of Deemed University?
(*a*) 1973 A.D.   (*b*) 1981 A.D.
(*c*) 1985 A.D.   (*d*) 1995 A.D.

14. What was the main objective of Kunzru Committee 1959?
(*a*) To study the problems of sportmen
(*b*) Create atmosphere in favour of Olympic movement
(*c*) Co-ordinate various schemes of physical education and sports
(*d*) Sports in schools

15. Which committee recommended the National Fitness corps programme for all students of the age group of 9-16 years?
(*a*) Kunzru committee
(*b*) B.R. Mehta committee
(*c*) Gen. K.M. Kariappa committee
(*d*) Asian Games Committee

16. Who launched the National Physical Efficiency Drive in the year 1959-60 A.D.?
(*a*) Union Ministry of Youth and Sports
(*b*) Union Ministry of Education
(*c*) University Grants Commission
(*d*) None of these

17. In which year Kaul-Kapoor Committee was setup?
(*a*) 1952 A.D.   (*b*) 1956 A.D.
(*c*) 1960 A.D.   (*d*) 1972 A.D.

18. Who appointed Kaul-Kapoor Committee to look into the improvement at sports?
(*a*) Government of India
(*b*) Punjab Government

(*c*) Maharashtra Government
(*d*) Indian Olympic Association

19. In which year Netaji Subhash National Institute of Sports was set up?
(*a*) 1956 A.D.   (*b*) 1961 A.D.
(*c*) 1964 A.D.   (*d*) 1972 A.D.

20. Who set up NIS Patiala?
(*a*) Punjab Government
(*b*) Indian Olympic Association
(*c*) Government of India
(*d*) None of these

21. On the recommendation of which committee, an integrated program of Physical Education and National Discipline was formulated in 1963?
(*a*) Kaul-Kapoor Committee
(*b*) Kunzru Committee
(*c*) National Physical Efficiency Drive
(*d*) SAI Committee Report

22. In which year National Sports Festival for women launched?
(*a*) 1963 A.D.   (*b*) 1970 A.D.
(*c*) 1975 A.D.   (*d*) 1980 A.D.

23. In which year National Welfare Fund for Sport persons set up?
(*a*) 1972 A.D.   (*b*) 1980 A.D.
(*c*) 1982 A.D.   (*d*) 1990 A.D.

24. What is the objective of National Welfare Fund for Sports persons?
(*a*) Help the young sports persons
(*b*) Help women athletes to compete at National level
(*c*) To assist sports persons of the yesteryears to live better life
(*d*) To assist schools to develop better sports facilities

25. In which year the first sports policy was formulated in India?
(*a*) 1951 A.D.   (*b*) 1965 A.D.
(*c*) 1976 A.D.   (*d*) 1982 A.D.

26. Sports Authority of India was set up in the year:
(*a*) 1964 A.D.   (*b*) 1972 A.D.
(*c*) 1980 A.D.   (*d*) 1984 A.D.

27. In which year National Institute of Physical Education and sports was merged with SAI?
(*a*) 1984 A.D.   (*b*) 1987 A.D.
(*c*) 1992 A.D.   (*d*) 1996 A.D.

28. High Altitude Training Centre is located at:
(*a*) Monsoorie (Uttarakhand)
(*b*) Shilong (Meghalaya)
(*c*) Shillaroo (Himachal Pradesh)
(*d*) Mount Abu (Rajasthan)

29. In which year the Indian Hockey Federation was founded?
(*a*) 1928 A.D.   (*b*) 1932 A.D.
(*c*) 1940 A.D.   (*d*) 1951 A.D.

30. The Board of Control for Cricket in India was set up in the year:
(*a*) 1905 A.D.   (*b*) 1921 A.D.
(*c*) 1928 A.D.   (*d*) 1936 A.D.

31. Which among the following was established after Independence of India?
(*a*) The Indian Hockey Federation
(*b*) All India Football Federation
(*c*) The National Cycling Federation
(*d*) The Hand-ball Association

32. In which year School Games Federation of India was set up?
(*a*) 1950 A.D.   (*b*) 1954 A.D.
(*c*) 1960 A.D.   (*d*) 1963 A.D.

33. The most important motto of Physical Education is:
(*a*) Healthy mind
(*b*) Healthy body
(*c*) Healthy Society and Nation
(*d*) Healthy body and healthy mind

34. Which among the following was not cited as objective of Physical Education by D.A. Sergent?
(*a*) Educative   (*b*) Recreative
(*c*) Reproductive   (*d*) Remedial

35. Which among the following was not listed the objective of Physical Education by Book Walter?
(*a*) Health
(*b*) Worthy use of Leisure time

(*c*) National integration
(*d*) Ethical character

36. Effective communication is essential in sports management to keep alive its-
(*a*) Dynamics   (*b*) Characteristics
(*c*) Principles   (*d*) Foundation

37. Blue Print of the competition plan is called-
(*a*) Technique   (*b*) Tactics
(*c*) Strategy   (*d*) Skill.

38. The first step in planning process is -
(*a*) Identification of target group
(*b*) Determination of goals
(*c*) Mobilization of resources
(*d*) Provision of facilities

39. Which of the following is against the principles of Organisation-
(*a*) Proper decentralization
(*b*) Proper communication
(*c*) Overlapping of authority
(*d*) Delegation of power

40. Intramural programme creates in students the sense of-
(*a*) Achievement   (*b*) Involvement
(*c*) Humor   (*d*) enjoyment

41. A leader must posses the following except-
(*a*) Missionary Zeal (*b*) Commitment
(*c*) Persuasiveness (*d*) Selfishness

42. The basic functions of management are-
(*a*) Planning and organisation
(*b*) Directing and programme development
(*c*) Personal management and financial management
(*d*) All of the above

43. Ambit within which the sports management must perform is generally referred to as
(*a*) Leadership in sports
(*b*) Sphere of sports management
(*c*) Evaluation in sports
(*d*) Innovation in sports

44. Which of the following is the first step in a sports programme?
(*a*) Directing   (*b*) Staffing
(*c*) Planning   (*d*) Budgeting

45. Terms Administration and Management are
(*a*) Synonymous to each other
(*b*) Entirely different from each other
(*c*) Somewhat similar to each other
(*d*) All of the above

46. Sports management is-
(*a*) An art
(*b*) A science
(*c*) Both a & b
(*d*) None of the above.

47. The first step in planning process is-
(*a*) Determination of objectives
(*b*) Resource mobilisation
(*c*) Constraints identification
(*d*) Evaluation of alternatives

48. Which of the following does not come under the purview of constraint identification in sports management?
(*a*) Geographical   (*b*) Physiological
(*c*) Economical   (*d*) Social

49. Which of the following is the prime objective of planning in sports?
(*a*) Entertainment
(*b*) For physical fitness
(*c*) Development of oneness
(*d*) All of the above

50. The plan in which only the chief executive dictates, initiates and monitors is called-
(*a*) Democratic plan
(*b*) Participative plan
(*c*) Authoritarian plan
(*d*) None of the above.

51. 'Getting the right facts to the right people at the right time in the right way' is called-
(*a*) Game management
(*b*) Public relations in sports
(*c*) Motivation for sports
(*d*) Leadership in sports

52. The last link of the sports management chain is-
(*a*) Control and evaluation
(*b*) Finance and budget
(*c*) Public relations

(*d*) None of the above

53. Funds for the sports programmes can be collected through-
(*a*) Alumni associations
(*b*) Donations/ gifts
(*c*) Funds from public sector undertakings
(*d*) All of the above

54. Objectives of a national sports organisation may be-
(*a*) To encourage the development of sports in the country
(*b*) To organize the championships at national and regional level
(*c*) To participate in international events from time to time be decided
(*d*) All of the above.

55. The ability to see the enterprise/ sports organisation as a whole is called-
(*a*) Human skill
(*b*) Conceptual skill
(*c*) Mechanical skill
(*d*) None of the above

56. The use of a particular method of teaching depends upon-
(*a*) Skill of the teacher
(*b*) Sex of the teacher
(*c*) Age of the teacher
(*d*) None of the above

57. Biological sciences suggest-
(*a*) Physical exercises and balanced nutrition are interrelated
(*b*) Variety of activity sustains interest
(*c*) Games and sports are great social experience
(*d*) Playfield does not recognize and distinction of cast, language, creed, colour etc.

58. Freehand activity generally done in group is called-
(*a*) Plyometrics
(*b*) Callisthenics
(*c*) Drill and marching
(*d*) Weight training

59. Which of the following is not a principle of lesson planning?
(*a*) Age and sex
(*b*) Progression
(*c*) Warming up
(*d*) Teachers experience

60. Which of the following is a method for the classification of pupil?
(*a*) Cozen method
(*b*) YMCA method
(*c*) Atlanta city method
(*d*) All of the above

61. The Rajiv Khel Ratna Award Scheme was launched in
(*a*) 1991-92 (*b*) 1992-93
(*c*) 1993-94 (*d*) 1994-95

62. The fund constituted to assist sports persons of yester years living in indigent circumstances is
(*a*) Rural Sports Programme
(*b*) National Welfare Fund
(*c*) National Sport Development fund
(*d*) National Service Volunteer Scheme

63. The award given to coaches who have trained sports persons or teams making outstanding achievements in the year is
(*a*) Arjuna Award
(*b*) Rajiv Gandhi Khel Ratna Award
(*c*) Dronacharya Award
(*d*) None

64. The Arjuna Award was instituted in
(*a*) 1960 (*b*) 1961
(*c*) 1962 (*d*) 1963

65. The National Sports Festival for Women was started in
(*a*) 1970 (*b*) 1974
(*c*) 1975 (*d*) 1976

66. Sports Talent Search Scholarship scheme was launched in
(*a*) 1970-71 (*b*) 1975-76
(*c*) 1977-78 (*d*) 1980-81

67. Ex-Officio president of SAI is
(*a*) President of India
(*b*) Prime Minister of India
(*c*) Union Minister of Youth Affairs & Sports
(*d*) Director General

68. Army Boys Sports Company (ABSC) scouts talent in the age group of
(*a*) 12-18 years (*b*) 8-14 years
(*c*) 10-14 years (*d*) 14-18 years

69. The Society for National Institute of Physical Education and Sports (SNIPES) merged with SAI in
(*a*) 1982 (*b*) 1983
(*c*) 1985 (*d*) 1987

70. SAI was established in
(*a*) 1985 (*b*) 1984
(*c*) 1983 (*d*) 1982

ANSWERS

1. (*b*)	2. (*b*)	3. (*d*)	4. (*c*)	5. (*b*)	6. (*a*)	7. (*a*)	8. (*b*)
9. (*b*)	10. (*b*)	11. (*c*)	12. (*c*)	13. (*d*)	14. (*c*)	15. (*a*)	16. (*b*)
17. (*c*)	18 (*a*)	19. (*b*)	20. (*c*)	21. (*b*)	22. (?)	23. (*c*)	24. (*c*)
25. (*d*)	26. (*d*)	27. (*b*)	28. (*c*)	29. (*a*)	30. (*c*)	31. (*d*)	32. (*b*)
33. (*d*)	34. (*c*)	35. (*c*)	36. (*a*)	37. (*c*)	38. (*b*)	39. (*c*)	40. (*b*)
41. (*d*)	42. (*d*)	43. (*d*)	44. (*c*)	45. (*a*)	46. (*c*)	47. (*a*)	48. (*d*)
49. (*d*)	50. (*c*)	51. (*b*)	52. (*a*)	53. (*d*)	54. (*d*)	55. (*b*)	56. (*a*)
57. (*a*)	58. (*a*)	59. (*d*)	60. (*d*)	61. (*a*)	62. (*b*)	63. (*c*)	64. (*b*)
65. (*c*)	66. (*a*)	67. (*b*)	68. (*b*)	69. (*d*)	70. (*a*)		

5. TEACHING TECHNIQUES

INTRODUCTION

The methods which a teacher adopts in order to teach any subject is called the Teaching method. No teacher can succeed without adopting the right method. Of course it is the teacher himself who decides what method to adopt. The idea always is that the students should be able to follow whatever he is teaching. He decides his own method which is based upon his past experience and knowledge of the subject. He must always keep in mind the mental standard of his students and accordingly choose the right method of teaching. In case his method fails to suit the capabilities of the students, surely they will not show interest in his lectures. The teacher who knows his subject well also should know that each chapter has to be taught in a different way. However the basic idea is to make education interesting and his methods such that he is able to catch the fancy of his pupils. Whatever be the method of teaching, the following will always remain as its chief characteristics.

CHARACTERISTICS OF TEACHING METHOD

The teachers adopt different methods to impart teaching to the students. All such methods have their own advantages, though some may be easier and more interesting than the others. Any good method of teaching must have the following characteristics in it :

1. A teacher's language should be easy, preferably regional.
2. A teacher should have the ability to make his subject understood properly by the students.
3. The method should be according to the mental ability of the students.

4. The teaching method should not lead to any tension of any kind.
5. The method should lead the students forward.
6. The teaching method should have the ability to draw out the inner capabilities of a student.
7. As far as possible, it should incorporate the latest skills and techniques evolved.
8. It should slowly and gradually lead students to greater knowledge.
9. It should bring out a subject and its importance properly.
10. It should arouse interest of the students.
11. There should be scope for entertainment.
12. It should be useful in every way.

These are the points or characteristics without which no education is possible at all. These characteristics apply to all kinds of education and without these there can be no education worth its name.

Teaching or Training Methods or Systems of Physical Education : There are several methods of teaching Physical Education. Some of these methods of teaching are as given below:

1. Lecture Method: Here, under this method, a teacher stands before a class and delivers a lecture in order to explain his subject. This method however cannot be very useful in teaching the subject of physical education since it is necessary here to demonstrate, mere lecturing is not sufficient. So, in Physical Education, a teacher must resort to other methods also. Physical Education is chiefly a practical subject and so there is less significance of theory. Here, it is necessary to divide a subject and impart training in parts. The teacher can and should resort to lecturing in between in order to explain a point, or even a subject. Without practical demonstrations the student is likely to lose interest in physical education.

2. Imitation Method: It is natural for any infant, and child to imitate (copy others). Some children are quick to copy and will easily pick up the ways their elders do, act and speak. A good teacher should draw benefit from this natural tendency of the children to imitate others. A good teacher should himself perform an activity and then encourage his students to copy him. They may not do well, but after some practice they will surely come up to the expected standard. Of course, the interest of the students is directly proportional to .the interest and keenness displayed by the teacher.

3. Demonstration Method: The Demonstration method of teaching is the most effective way of teaching physical education. Under this method a teacher may deliver a short lecture and then demonstrate himself to the students. The students will be impressed just as the demonstration (by the teacher) is done well. The demonstration should always be neat and not tardy. The students follow its various steps and so it should be the one which they can understand. A teacher should be ready to demonstrate several times, if necessary. The difficult parts or movements may be demonstrated separately and many times. The teacher may then ask a student to come forward and demonstrate. If necessary, they may be asked to come one by one and demonstrate. If the teacher finds any drawback he should point it out and ask others to avoid the drawback.

4. Command Method: Once the students have been able to grasp the way to do a particular activity, then the command method takes over. Here the teacher simply sends out commands or orders or signals and the students go over the activity as many times as the teacher asks them to do. The signals or commands may be many. It is also called Rhythm method.

5. Discussion Method: In this method the students are encouraged to discuss the subject among themselves. Here a teacher may ask the students either with himself, or among themselves. In a way Discussion method is a subsidiary of Lecture method. A teacher may broadly explain the subject and then ask questions from his students.

If any part is left out, the teacher can take it up and, through questions answers, make them all fully understand. It is a very effective method of teaching because there is a free discussion. The teacher learns about the mental ability of the students and the students too get to know their teacher better.

6. Dramatic Method: As the name shows, this teaching method has been borrowed from the drama. Just as history or some character can be understood when presented in a drama, similarly the physical activities and dance songs can be dramatised. It is always an easily understandable method. Frog..., Back Kicking and skipping are best understood with the help of dramatic method. Children take immense interest in it and never get tired. Of course, it will mean that new entertainment part has overtaken the theory part. It is particularly useful while teaching small children.

7. Whole Method: Here the subject is not divided up into smaller parts or units, but is taken up whole. The method includes lecture and demonstration methods. In this method a teacher has to do work continuously. There is a probability that the interest of a student may begin to flag, and that is why this method is employed for students above 18.

8. Part Method: In physical Education it is difficult to impart understanding of any one subject in one go, and so the activities have to be divided into smaller units. The teacher then takes up each part one by one. This method, viz part method is particularly useful in physical education. It appeals to children at all levels. Take an illustration. If the teacher has to teach three different words and their meanings, as On your marks', 'Set', Go' Now if he takes up one at a time, the students will understand better

9. At Will Method: There are many things which the children would like to self learn i.e learn by themselves. In this method, the children are given the equipment and are asked to go on play. There is no training or coaching given. The children learn to use the equipment all by themselves. It is likely to raise difficulties, no doubt. The child can go and consult the teacher, but generally speaking he learns by himself.

10. Mixed Method: The Mixed Method is indeed a composite for mixture of all the methods discussed earlier. At present this method is quite popular. In this method, the teacher comes and delivers a lecture, then demonstrates and later asks each one to copy and also demonstrate. He goes on advising and correcting. We can see that the mixed method is a combination of all the well known methods.

11. Inspection Method: This method is used for the purpose of familiarising the children by taking them on an inspection round of places. For example, the teacher may take them along to witness a competition. He can give his comments side by side. This method is very practical. The children can learn much about the techniques, the finer points of the game and even about the players. The same job can be done with the help of video cassettes also.

12. Whole Part Whole Method: This method is similar to the part method. In this method the teacher will do first part of an exercise as a unit. Then the other chief parts are also demonstrated. At the end the teacher will present the entire exercise by linking together all parts into one. The children are asked to practice each part separately and only at the end the whole exercise.

All methods discussed above have been adopted by the teachers, though not one of them wholly by any one teacher. But then we cannot tell any teacher which method to choose. It depends upon his convenience, wisdom, experience and knowledge. The basic principle is only one, viz that the student should be able to learn and show excellent results.

IMPORTANCE OF TEACHING METHOD OF PHYSICAL EDUCATION

Each method of teaching is good in its own way, and therefore has its own significance. Some methods are easier than the others. The following points can determine the real importance of any one method.

1. Whether a method has really brought about a real change in students.
2. Whether a method brings out the inner capabilities of a student.
3. Whether it has helped to improve discipline among students.
4. Whether it has added significantly to the level of knowledge of the students.
5. A real good method must improve the efficiency of the students.
6. A rcal good method acquaints the students with techniques.
7. A real good method should not tire a student easily.
8. By adopting an entertainment method students will enjoy while learning.
9. Without teaching method no training can be systematic.
10. All students should be taught similarly, otherwise there will be jealousy generated among them.
11. A real good method imparts quickest in the shortest time.
12. The best method is when the students are enthused to evolve techniques themselves.

We can say that methods of teaching have an important role to play. A teacher is always needed, though not all teachers are equally efficient.

PHYSICAL EDUCATION TEACHER AND PROBLEMS

Likewise other teachers in different subjects a Physical Teacher also has to acquire qualifications necessary for the profession of Physical Education. It is our view that a physical teacher has to do harder labour comparatively. That is because his education and knowledge are two directional-acquiring Education and also training as a physical teacher. In comparison with ordinary teachers teaching languages etc. a physical teacher has to spend more, because for playing any game he must buy all the accessories whether it is a pair of socks and shoes or buying equipment of the game, like a hockey or tennis balls. Then he may also have to move away from home daily or while taking part in matches and tournaments. He will also have to spend more to keep fit and for taking proper diet which is always better than what common boys at this age take. A physical teacher is expected to possess the following characteristics in him :

 (a) Personality
 (b) Healthy body
 (c) Young and active
 (d) sportsmanship
 (e) Intelligence
 (f) Coordination Power
 (g) Attractive work
 (h) Leadership
 (i) Tactful
 (j) Educated
 (k) Attentive
 (l) Capacity to lead others
 (m) Helpful
 (n) Escort and endure
 (o) Recreative

Besides, his body must be active, elastic and able to endure hard work. He should also be patient and full of courage and able to take risks

Educational Qualifications of Physical Education Teacher

The Physical Education Teacher should possess the following educational qualifications :

 1. High School/Matriculation or Equivalent
 2. Intermediate or Equivalent
 3. Graduate or Equivalent
 4. CPEd, DPEd, BPEd ; MPEd or equivalent

Problems of Physical Education Teacher

The biggest handicap in Physical Education, at least in India, is that parents do not feel attracted towards this career. That is because people on day-to-day life do not take part in games. It is limited to boys and girl and school and colleges. Games are not considered essential at all. They do not understand that our body which is a kind of machine needs active movements to keep it fit and active. There is no age-limit for exercising the body. A physical teacher or any person taking part in games is sure to lead a healthier life than those who do not take exercises regularly.

At the same time a physical teacher has a special role reserved for him for all important occasions and functions. He also has to keep his equipment ready and in a state of use. All this is not an easy job. A Physical teacher usually has to face the following kinds of problems

1. Problems of Suitable Fields: Without a proper playfield it is not possible to play a game. A playground or some kind of piece of land is essential. Where there is no open ground it is not possible to train oneself in fields games like athletics or hockey etc. Even at other times when the open grounds are available often these are unprotected and so again serve as a big problem. It is difficult to give training or to train oneself under these circumstances.

2. Problems of Large No. of Students and Selection: These days the number of students is going up. Those who fail have to seek admission. The rush is increasing year by year. In a class today, it is common sight to see more than 100 boys. Often there is one physical teacher appointed against about 250 boys. Invariably there is a single physical teacher even when there is need for more than one.

A teacher finds if difficult to choose the right kind of students who are really keen to take up physical education.

3. Problem of standard & Latest Equipment: The supply and lack of proper equipment is a big problem. Often one may see old and rickety and disshaped equipment lying in the schools and colleges. No coach can impart proper training without good equipment. Some Institutions either have no money to spend, or consider it a waste. Most of the institutions lack funds to buy the latest equipments. So this is a great problem.

4. Problem of maintenance of Equipment: Even when institutions have somehow managed to purchase equipment, it is said to see that they do not look after it when once it has been installed. The equipment and their upkeep is therefore a big problem in itself.

5. Problem of literature pertaining to physical education: Like other subjects, Physical Education too is a subject of study. Often the students take the subject lightly. One reason is that literature on the subject is insufficient. Mostly teachers are themselves ignorant of the developments having taken place in the various games and skills. It is essential to go in for the latest literature on the subject of physical education. Almost every other day there is some change occurring in Rules or in the matter of techniques and equipments. It is difficult to know if there is no provision for buying journals and books. Sometime some men consider it a waste of time and money to buy literature pertaining to Physical Education. It is a big problem today.

6. Problem of More Overload: Often it is noticed that in the institutions the Heads ask Physical Education teachers to teach other subjects besides physical education or even sometimes at the cost of Physical education itself. Physical teachers are assigned all kinds of duties which have no relevance to their own subject, Viz Physical education. Others too sometimes look down upon the physical teachers and their kind of work. Sometimes they are paid lesser than the other teachers. All this only brings down the status of Physical Education, and is thus a problem.

7. Problem of Student Control and Discipline: It is often seen that physical teachers are given the job of cultivating discipline among the students. On the national festivals etc. also this job falls upon the shoulders of physical teachers. Of course they do their duty on all such occasions.

8. Problems of Social Allowance: A physical teacher has no other ways of earning extra income. Each one of us are in need of many things in life. A physical teacher has to content himself within his means. Besides he needs extra diet as well. His life calls for hard labour for which he require, nourishment. In fact he should be given extra allowance further.

9. Problems of Residence near the Place of work: Often a physical teacher is called upon to be present in the playfield. He may have to go at all odd hours. The playfields are now-a-days often located out side the city. That will mean that he will have to cover distances between his residence, college or school and the playgrounds. It will be better if a physical teacher is given accommodation nearer the place of work. Where cities are congested these problems have become more acute.

10. Problem of Promotion: A physical teacher has to look after his regular teaching work, practice sessions on the playgrounds and besides all kinds of extra work, like the problem of discipline etc. It is often thought that physical teachers know beyond their games and so do not deserve any promotion while others may be given some incentives, physical teachers stay put where they are.

There are many problems facing the physical Education teachers. There is long struggle ahead before they can acquire status. However there are new avenues opening up. Better times lie before them.

QUALIFICATIONS FOR PHYSICAL EDUCATORS

Some special qualifications of the physical educator are as follows:

- The physical educator should be a graduate of an approved teacher training institution preparing teachers for physical education. The college or university should be selected with care.
- Since physical educations is based upon the foundational sciences of anatomy, physiology, biology, kinesiology, sociology, and psychology, the leader in this field should be well versed in these areas.
- The general education of physical educators is under continuous scrutiny and criticism. Such things as speech knowledge of world affairs, mastery of the arts, and other aspects of this area should be an important part of the physical educator. Since the nature of positions in this area requires frequent appearances in public, adequate knowledge and skill in this area are essential.

Physical education work is strenuous and therefore demands that members of the profession be in a state of buoyant, robust health in order that they may carry out their duties with efficiency and regularity. It should also be remembered that physical educators are supposed to build healthy. Therefore, they should be a good testimonial for their preachments.

Many moral and spiritual values are developed through participation in games and other physical education activities. It is essential, therefore, that the teacher of physical education have a proper background and possess such values that he or she will stress fair play, good sportsmanship, and a sound standard of values. The nature of his or her leadership should be such that the highest standards of moral and spiritual values are developed.

The physical educator should have a sincere interest in the teaching of physical education. Unless the individual has a form belief in the value of his work and a desire to help extend the benefits of such an endeavour to others, he will not be an asset to the profession. A sincere interest in the teaching of physical education means that one enjoys teaching individuals, participating in the gamut of activities incorporated in such programmes, helping others to realize the happiness and thrilling experiences of participation that he himself enjoys, and helping to develop citizenship traits conductive to democratic living. One must have a sincere love of the out-of-doors and of all the activities that make up the physical education programmes either indoors or out in the open. This means that anyone interested in physical education should enjoy sports and other activities. If there is not a liking for these activities the individual is in the wrong profession.

The physical educator should possess an acceptable standard of motor ability. Physical skills are basic to the physical education profession. If the physical educator is to reach various games and activities to others, it is necessary that he or she have skill in many of them.

The physical educator must enjoy working with people, as he is continually required to associate with human beings in an informal atmosphere when teaching physical education activities. The values of such a programme will be greatly increased of the physical educator teaches in a manner conductive to happiness, cooperation, and a spirit of friendship.

Mr. Emil Nyman, Principal of Lafayette School in Salt Lake City. Utah Lists the following items in respect to what he, as an administrator, expects of his physical education teachers. They are worthy of study:

1. Intelligent enough to talk about sex problems objectively.
2. Tactful enough to referee disputes fairly.
3. Altruistic enough to want to do some social service.
4. Trained enough in psychology to counsel young people.
5. Professional enough to serve his fellow workers in their improvement.
6. Kind enough to win young folks to his leadership.
7. Big enough to distinguish trifles from giants.
8. Doctor enough to heal the heartbreaks and soul injuries common to a big school.
9. Cultivated enough to be a model in taste and language.
10. Creative enough to be able to put art into physical education activities and to appreciate originality in others.
11 Vision enough to tolerate the antics of young folk and to make the most of them.
12. Big enough to overflow into the lives of other teachers in the school to keep them balanced and encouraged.
13. Funny enough to be the clown of organization if no one else turns up.
14. Wholesome enough to set the mental health climate of the school.
15. Religious enough to be secure, clean, optimistic, and courageous.
16. Skilful enough to provide practices in wholesome, constructive group living.
17. Moral enough to provide practices in wholesome, constructive group living.
18. Adaptable enough to make a physical education health programme in spite of weather, interferences, and lack of equipment.
19. Young enough to catch new ideas.

The American Association makes the following general recommendations for administrators interested in hiring physical education personnel:

1. Select physical education teachers from among the graduates of institutions which

offer outstanding professional physical education programmes.

2. Select physical education teachers who display a real enthusiasm for teaching as a life profession.
3. Select physical education teachers who have demonstrated outstanding ability in some field in addition to athletic coaching.
4. Select physical education teachers who are strongly recommended by qualified professional persons in addition to college athletic coaches.
5. Select physical education teachers who possess qualities with which young people can identify themselves.

The Need for a Cultural Background

This country is experiencing an age of specialization, and the prospective teacher must have training in all phases of his or her particular field. However, there is still a genuine need for a broad background of knowledge in all areas of learning. In order that an individual may assume duties and responsibilities as a good teacher and also as a good citizen, he should be able to understand, think, and talk intelligently about not only the profession but also the complexities of life as a whole.

The need for a broad cultural background seems to be especially applicable to teachers of health and physical education. Such specialists hold strategic positions. The nature of their work, close personal contact with students, place of leadership in the community, and the necessity for the coordination of their fields with other phases of the school and community programmes have implications which in many ways do not exist for the general classroom or academic teacher or leader in other areas.

Teachers of health and physical education possess many commendable qualities which make them stand out in the field of education. However, many members can be found occupying positions throughout the country who do not have a broad cultural background. These individuals use crude and careless language expressions, promote health and physical education as ends in themselves, fail to plan and organize their work in the light of sound educational principles, and are unable to converse or write in an intelligent manner. These judgments have received support, in various studies that have been conducted over the years. W.E. Perk and G.B. Fitzgerald reported on a survey many years ago conducted by the United States Office of Education in twenty-one universities and six colleges. This report pointed out that majors in the special fields were at the bottom of the teaching fields studied in respect to their cultural backgrounds. The study previously reported by Educational Testing Service of Princeton, New Jersey, shows that the situation has not changed.

Teacher Training Institutions must recognize the need for a general education that exists among leaders in these special fields and make the necessary provisions in their training programmes. In such a job cannot be done in four years, perhaps a five-year programme may be the solution.

This extended training period would not only make it possible to obtain greater training in the general cultural area, but also would eliminate many of the undesirable features of the present "four plus one" concept, where the student shops around and takes his master's degree, many times in an area totally unrelated to his needs. The five-year programme also provides students with the opportunity to pursue a second field or interest which could also result in broader cultural training.

Teacher training institutions should be concerned with establishing in each prospective teacher and leader a broad educational base. This broad base should include such things as English, history, psychology, economics, sociology, human growth and development, and the art of communication. It is also felt that there should be an intermingling of general and specialized elements of the curriculum throughout the training period. This special and general education should be woven into the fabric of the entire training period and should not be confined within certain limited compartments.

A broad background in all areas of knowledge is needed by leaders in these specialized fields. The curriculum should be flexible enough to insure that deficiencies in such important academic subjects as English, social studies, and science be made up whenever necessary to insure adequate preparation for the profession. If cultural training is part of the training of all leaders it will gain them the respect of the students, faculty, and the community. The individual who has secured his position primarily because he was an outstanding athlete on some causing will despite the fact that he may have language difficulties and lack breadth of knowledge, must become a thing of the past. Future training should guarantee health and physical education leaders who are enlightened and productive of good results. This is an age of specialization where the individual must be an expert in some particular vocation and also in the performance of his duties as an intelligent citizen.

TEACHING TECHNIQUES FOR PHYSICAL EDUCATION

This may be summarized for important aspects of teaching, not only physical education, but other subjects as well. Translating these terms into more theoretical language we find that explanation, demonstration, participation, and evaluation fit the topics to be covered in the teaching-learning situation. They will be considered separately with the hope that specific suggestions may be offered to make each more meaningful and to show how they interrelate.

A teacher will find it advisable to explain a new activity prior to demonstrating or playing it. This may be done in the classroom, before going to the playground or gymnasium, or when the children are assembled at the play area.

Before explaining the activity certain factors should be considered: Are the children comfortable, seated or standing where all can see and hear? Are they located so that the light is not shining in their eyes? Are they paying attendant, with no bouncing of balls or whispering while explanations are being made?

In presenting certain games, dances, or other activities it is important for the teacher to know something about the background or history of the respective activities. Children will enjoy the activity more if they know its origin, the reason for its invention, other countries in which it is played, and possible variations.

The teacher must be familiar with the games and dances to be taught; the fundamentals, formations, strategy, rules, and scoring. He also should have a knowledge of the play area or court to be used and whether there is adequate space in which one, two, or more groups may play. A knowledge of the equipment and supplies to be used is also important.

In the actual presentation of the game or dance the following suggestions may help the beginning teacher :

1. Arouse children's curiosity by means of interesting, colourful and unusual presentations.
2. Use auditory and visual aids in making presentations. These may be in the form of movies, film strips, slides, pictures, diagrams, charts, models, phonograph records, or tape recordings.
3. Keep explanations brief and simple. When teaching a complex activity, do not review all the rules before starting to play. Begin the activity and introduce pertinent rules as necessary.
4. The vocabulary used should be at one proper pupil level.
5. Opportunity should be provided for a limited number of questions. An excessive number will restrict the time for activity, and many of the questions will be answered by playing the activity. After the game or dance has been played for a short while, more question may be asked.
6. Present activities that are challenging but not overwhelming. Provide for "success" activities—those in which all may be successful—and then lead up to more difficult activities.
7. Try different methods of presenting activities. Remember that there is no "best" method.

Demonstration

In teaching many activities there should be no clear cut line of demarcation between the presentation and the demonstration phases. Often while the activity is being demonstrated, the necessary explanations of fundamentals, rules, formations, and skills may be made. It is important to consider the purpose of the demonstration. Is it to motivate, to show the activity as a whole, or to illustrate a detailed skill, step, or pattern?

Whenever the teacher demonstrates a skill or techniques, care should be taken to do the performance well; in so doing good pupil-teacher rapport may be built. If the teacher desires to demonstrate how to stand and how to make a foul shot in basketball, he should not aim toward the basket but should shoot toward an imaginary one. In so doing emphasis is placed on the method and technique of shooting rather than upon the success or failure of the ball to go through the basket.

For the most part it is advisable to have students demonstrate the activities. Demonstrations may be practiced before being show to the class, or children may be called upon to demonstrate without practice. Sometimes it is wise to have boys and girls give their own interpretation of the skills or dance steps without preliminary advice from the teacher.

At times an incorrect performance may be used to advantage in showing how not to do an activity, but it is extremely important that the correct technique be demonstrated immediately thereafter so that false impressions will not be left with the pupils.

Other suggestions to be considered when conducting the demonstration phase of the lesson include:

1. Keep at the pupil level.
2. Do not talk too much.
3. Allow for a limited number of questions.
4. Have supplies and equipment on hand and ready.
5. Show how apparatus and equipment should be moved and used.
6. Stress safety precautions.

Participation

The greatest amount of time in a physical education period should be devoted to the participation phase. In planning the programme consideration should be given to providing for maximum pupil and minimum teacher participation. This does not mean that the teacher should not participate, but that he should not have the major role in the activity. For example, many times the teacher feels that he should pitch in a softball game, "in order to speed up the game". How much better it would be to teach a boy or girl how to throw the ball so that it could be easily hit, or to use a batting tee. Then the teacher could devote time to teaching children how to bat, field and pitch.

For maximum pupil participation in certain activities the class should be divided into several groups. Each group will then play a game by itself. For relay races, skill drills and similar activities no more than six to eight players should assigned to groups or squad. Provision for minimum participation will reduce disciplinary problems.

Further suggestion regarding the participation phase of the lesson include the following:

1. Provide for a warm-up period prior to strenuous activities.
2. Adjust the rules, size of play areas, length of periods, and other conditions to the age, size, maturity, and skill of the group participating. Adapt games to weather conditions, i.e., if it is cold, use activities in which many or all children participate.
3. Remember that enjoyment and satisfaction are objectives to be attained in games, skills and dances.
4. Try to arrange children into homogeneous groups when teaching skills or playing games. Analyze difficulties and provide opportunities for remedial teaching.
5. Provide for leading and following opportunities during the participation phase. Other social characteristics should be observed and emphasized during the activity programme.
6. Occasionally the whole-part-whole method of teaching may be used. For example, the children first play the game as a whole, then encourage them to practice its separate parts or skills, after which they may return to playing the whole game.

7. Provide for frequent rest periods during the participation phase of the programme.
8. With younger children, change the activity frequently to maintain interest.
9. Use praise in preference to censure.
10. Close the activity phase of the period with the children wanting to continue, rather than being pleased that it is over.

Evaluation

When considering evaluation, it is necessary to look at the objectives of physical education to determine whether or not they are being realized.

The first objective is the physical one, which is divided into three parts. The appraisal of physical fitness should be both technical and formal, by those who administer the medical and health examinations, and non-technical, and informal, conducted by the classroom teachers. The latter observe the children daily and may recognize changes in their health status.

Secondly, the recognition of individual differences in children because of growth and development factors and physical, social, and emotional handicaps will require systematic evaluation. For example, is consideration given to the individual needs of pupils? Are activities provided for handicapped pupils?

The third part of the physical objective is skill development. If skills are to be learned, evaluation of progress is essential. The methods, types, and techniques of testing skills vary greatly in the elementary school. In the lower grades the measurement of skills is done almost entirely by subjective means; careful observation, judgment, and interpretation. The teacher observes the ability of children to throw, catch tag, skip, and do many other skills included in the programme of physical education. As a result of her observations, individual help may be given children who do not, in her opinion, measure up to their potential. If failures continue, the causes should be analysed and steps taken to remedy the failures.

In the upper grades the evaluation of skills becomes more objective. Objective measurement provides a score which does not depend upon the judgment of the tester. Results of skill tests are in units of distance, height, time, or number of successful performances. Older children are interested in their own progress, how they compare to others in their class, and how they rate with established standards. Many skills that are taught in the physical education classes lend themselves to objective measurement and should be included. There is probably no greater motivation for boys and girls learning sport skills, than to be able to see improvement through rest results. Objective skill testing many also be used to evaluate teaching and the programme. Stunts and tumbling in themselves are a series of evaluations. They can be presented in order of difficulty, and each child receive a check or rating on a chart, "Stunts and Tumbling." All of these activities have been classified according to physical factors involved: agility, flexibility, strength, and balance; inability to perform one or more activities may help the teacher to identify who are weak in these respective areas.

Many skills involving form, more than one player, and team play cannot be objectively tested. Therefore the subjective evaluation of skills has a place. Attention is called to the fact that many skills which should be taught do not necessarily need to be tested.

No objective tests are given in the dance section. Although many skills are involved, it would seem that the ultimate evaluation of dance is concerned with the attitudes of the children. If they enjoy dancing, have fun dancing with others, and learn the social amenities involved, the objective of dance will have been realized. A child lacking rhythm, coordination, or self-confidence will be obvious to everyone including the teacher and rather than highlight his inadequacies by tests, help should be given him.

The second major objective in physical education is the social-emotional objective. Evaluation of the various traits and characteristics that make up this objective may best be accomplished by subjective means. The teacher should observe situations in which the children show traits such as leadership, cooperation, and honesty, and attempt to evaluate changes in behaviour. Many times the emphasise, from an appraisal point of view, is not the negative aspects, and demerits are registered against students who trip, cheat, swear, or are unco-operative. Although these attitudes should be corrected, greater emphasise should be placed on the positive side, with frequent attention and merits given to favourable attitudes and signs of social growth of students.

The intellectual objective may be evaluated by both subjective and objective means. In the lower grades informal questioning about games, dances, or stunts will be adequate. With children in the upper grades it is also advisable to ask questions informally but it is recommended that simple objective type tests be constructed and used. The subject matter of the tests would include questions on the background or history of games and dances, the number of players on a team, the position names, simple rules and scoring.

PLANNING THE PROGRAMME

Introduction

In the elementary school the physical education programme should be planned around the growth and development of the children. The characteristics and needs peculiar to the various ages, and the physical, social, emotional, and intellectual objectives should form the basis of all activity curriculum planning. This chapter considers the planning of the instructional phase of the programme in the lower and upper grades and the extra-class programme.

Factors such as personnel, time allotments, available facilities, equipment, and supplies must be considered when planning the programme. Adaptations and adjustments may be, made to offset the lack of facilities and supplies, but it must be realized that to conduct a successful programme in physical education provision should be made for proper and adequate tools; space, equipment, and supplies.

Balance is a term that is constantly being used in programme planning. It implies a wide range of activities consistent with the specific grade level, the number of pupils, and the other factors mentioned previously. To help plan and attain balance in the programme, the following table, showing the types of activities and the suggested time percentages, is presented. Trends in percentages rather than specific amounts of time should be considered.

Some of the activities should be given when the programme is conducted outside on the play fields; others should be taught in the gymnasium. Some activities, such as body mechanics, should be included as a part of each daily programme whereas others are seasonal or offered intermittently throughout the year.

Note in the table that in the upper grades the boys and girls' programmes have been listed separately. Certain activities lend themselves better to teaching when the class in divided, with the boys participating in one activity and the girls in another. However, it should be realised that many of the activities can be taught to co-educational classes, and some definitely should be taught with both boys and girls in the class.

Although a knowledge and understanding is necessary to proper programme planning, the teacher must also know how to specifically prepare and use seasonal, weekly and daily programmes. Suggested programmes of these types are included, but it should be clearly understood that they are merely the framework or outline around which to build the school or class programme.

Lower Grades

Suggested seasonal programmes:

Fall

1. Class organization, forming lines, making circles, spacing, numbering, etc.
2. Warm-up activities, running and hoping, bending and stretching, etc.
3. Low organization activities; running and tag-games, simple ball skills and games, relays.
4. Playground apparatus; jungle gym, slides, etc.
5. Individual and couple activities: rope skipping, marbles, etc.
6. Rhythmic activities: basic rhythms, singing games.

Winter

1. Warm-up activities stretching, bending, walking, skipping, etc.
2. Rhythmic activities; basic rhythms, singing games, simple folk dance.

3. Low organization activities; skills, games relays.
4. Tumbling, apparatus, and stunts; mats, balance beam, self testing activities.

Spring
1. Warm-up activities; stretching, bending, running, hopping, skipping, etc.
2. Low organization activities; running and tag games, simple ball skills and games, relays.
3. Playground apparatus; jungle gym, seesaws, etc.
4. Individual and couple activities; rope skipping, tether ball, etc.
5. Singing games and simple fold dances.

Notes to Suggested Seasonal Programmes
1. Several types of activities may be included during each class period.
2. The general types of activities should be varied from day to day.
3. Progression and evaluation in the teaching of the activities are assumed.
4. The programme should be integrated with academic subject units.
5. Special days, such as holiday, should be observed with programmes appropriate to the occasion.

Suggested daily Programmes
Dressing Period, 2-3 minutes
1. Change to play clothes
2. Change to sneakers

Warm-up Period 3-5 minutes
1. Running, hopping, skipping
2. Bending and stretching
3. Mimetics—toys or animals

New Activity 8-12 minutes
1. Ball skills
2. Games; ball or running and tag
3. Dances
4. Apparatus, tumbling, stunts

Old Activity, 8-12 minutes
1. Game
2. Dance
3. Free play

Dress and Wash-up Period, 3-5 minutes
1. Change play clothes if worn
2. Change sneakers
3. Wash up, comb hair, drinks, etc.
    Total, 24-37 minutes.

Suggested seasonal programmes
Fall
1. Class organization; forming lines, squads, etc., attendance taking, numbering.
2. Warm-up activities; spot mimetics, calisthenics, running.
3. Team sports; skill drills, lead-up games, athletic team games.
4. Low organization activities; games, relays.
5. Individual and couple activities; rope skipping, couple games.

Winter
1. Warm-up activities, sport mimetics, calisthenics, free play, basket shooting.
2. Team sports; drills, lead up games, athletic team games.
3. Low organization activities; games, relays.
4. Rhythms; basic rhythms, folk, square, and social dancing.
5. Apparatus, tumbling, and stunts; ropes vaulting box, mats.
6. Individual and couple activities; shuffleboard, rope skipping.

Spring
1. Warm-up activities; spot mimetics, calisthenics, running.
2. Team sorts, skill drills, lead up games, athletic events.
3. Low organization activities, games, relays.
4. Individual and couple activities; rope skipping, couple games.

Suggested daily programmes
Dressing Period, 3-5 minutes.
1. Changes clothes; gym suits
2. Change sneakers

Warm-up Period, 3-5 minutes.
1. Spot mimetics
2. Calisthenics
3. Running

Fundamentals and Skill Drills, 20-25 minutes.
1. Sport skills
2. Dance steps and patterns
3. Apparatus, trundling, stunts

Play Period, 5-20 minutes.
1. Lead up games
2. Athletic team games

3. Dances
4. Free play
Dress and Wash-up Period, 5-10 minutes.
1. Changes clothes; if gym suits are worn
2. Changes sneakers
3. Wash-up, comb hair, drinks, etc.
   Total, 36-45 minutes

EXTRA-CLASS PROGRAMME

Introduction

To be considered well rounded and complete, the curriculum of physical education in the elementary school also include an extra-class programme. It may be conducted during the noon recess or in after-school hours. The term "extra-class is used in preference to extracurricular" because it should be considered within the total curriculum of the school and an addition to the "instructional class" period. Activities included in the extra-class programme should be an outgrowth or extension of those taught in the regular physical education class period.

The extra-class programme should be open to all children in the upper grades who want to play. Opportunities should be provided for children to participate and enjoy the activities with they have learned in the instructional period.

Children in the lower grades are usually not encouraged to attend the extra-class programme. The regular school day is sufficiently long for the to be away from home, and they are able to play many of the activities learned in school at home with neighborhood playmates.

In the upper grades, the extra-class programme is not only justified but necessary to meet the need of both boys and girls. Among these needs the following are included:

1. The need for more physical activity than children receive in the regular physical education classes.
2. The opportunity to play with other children. In certain communities, school facilities, either inside, outside, or both, are the only places in which children may play safety, or the school may be the only place in the neighbourhood where a sufficient number of children can get together to assure enough players to form terms.
3. The need to play games in their total form of regular number of innings or periods. This is made possible in the extra-class period because of the greater amount of time available for the game, dance, or contest.
4. The need for cooperation and competition.
5. The need for opportunities to develop leadership with children serving as captains of teams, officials scorers, timers, and in other capacities promoting leadership.

The extent of the extra-class programme depends on the facilities personnel available. Elementary schools with an outdoor play area that can accommodate two or more team sports, and one or more playrooms or a divided gymnasium, with personnel to cover these areas are able to offer a far more extensive programme to greater number of children than a school having only one playroom or field.

Much of the success and value of the programme depends on planning; the needs and interests of children should be met through a varied programme activities taken from the instructional phase of the programme.

Selling the programme is not difficult. The number of children wanting to participate usually far exceeds the programme's capacity to handle them effectively. However, attendance and interest will drop off if:

1. Too many children participate at once in too small an area.
2. Equal amounts of time are not provided for all children.
3. The activities offered are not adjusted to the children's interests.
4. The children are not given a voice in the planning and choice of activities.

Personnel

In the extra-class programme women teachers should supervise the girls, and men teachers the boys. The teachers need not be physical education specialists or coaches, but they must have an understanding of the characteristics and interests of children and at least a basic knowledge of the rules and fundamentals of the activities being played. They should also have organizational ability, *i.e.,* be able to set up tournaments, sports, or play-days, prepare forms for reporting scores, keep team and individual records, stimulate and maintain interest in the programme by means of bulletins, posters, and other media of publicity. Teachers who accept responsibility for the programme should enlist the help of student leaders within the school and/or interest students from the secondary school. These students may help by serving as officials team coaches, and assistants in charge of marking fields and taking care of equipment and supplies.

It is generally agreed that teachers serving in the extra class programme should be paid for their services above their regular salary. To assign teachers arbitrarily to "cover" certain days, whether or not they are trained, capable, or interested, benefits neither the programme nor the children.

OBJECTIVE QUESTIONS

1. The existence of soul in Indian philosophy has not been accepted by the schools known as:
   (*a*) The Charvakas   (*b*) The Buddhist
   (*c*) Both   (*d*) Neither

2. Man according to Charvaka Philosophy is:
   (*a*) The physical body
   (*b*) The self
   (*c*) The consciousness
   (*d*) None of the above

3. Human consciousness, according to Charvaka philosophy is:
   (*a*) Combination of five elements
   (*b*) Self
   (*c*) Body
   (*d*) None of the above

4. Happiness and sorrow and other mental activities, according to Charvaka are the attributes of:
   (*a*) Body
   (*b*) Self
   (*c*) Consciousness
   (*d*) None of the above

5. The relationship of consciousness and body according to Charvaka Philosophy is:
   (*a*) Consciousness is the product of body
   (*b*) Body is the product of consciousness
   (*c*) Both
   (*d*) Neither

6. Charvaka philosophers have been classified into:
   (*a*) Dhurta   (*b*) Susikshit
   (*c*) Both   (*d*) Neither

7. The age of Vatsyayan belongs to the Charvaka school of:
   (*a*) Dhurta   (*b*) Susikshit
   (*c*) Both   (*d*) Neither

8. On the question of nature of self the Charvaka philosophers can be classified as:
   (*a*) Dehatmavadin   (*b*) Indiriyatmavadin
   (*c*) Pranvadin   (*d*) All of above

9. According to Dehatmavadin Charvakas self is:
   (*a*) Body   (*b*) Sense organs
   (*c*) Vital Principle   (*d*) Mind

10. According to Indriyatmavadin Charvakas self is:
    (*a*) Body   (*b*) Sense organs
    (*c*) Vital principal   (*d*) Mind

11. According to Pranvadin Charvakas the nature of self is:
    (*a*) Body   (*b*) Sense organs
    (*c*) Vital principle   (*d*) Mind

12. According to Atma Manovadin, Charvakas self is:
    (*a*) Body   (*b*) Sense organ
    (*c*) Vital principle   (*d*) Mind

13. The Charvakas deny the existence of:
    (*a*) Self
    (*b*) Merit and Demerit
    (*c*) Heaven and Hell
    (*d*) All of the above

14. The Charvaka theory of self can be termed as:
(*a*) Materialist   (*b*) Vitalist
(*c*) Mentalist   (*d*) All of the above

15. The Jaina's proofs for the existence of self include:
(*a*) Direct proofs   (*b*) Indirect proof
(*c*) Both   (*d*) Neither

16. The indirect proofs for the existence of self according to the Jam philosophers are:
(*a*) Sole is mover   (*b*) Co-ordinator
(*c*) Efficient cause   (*d*) All of the above

17. The Jains have refuted the Charvaka view of self on the basis of:
(*a*) No evidence   (*b*) Against causation
(*c*) Illogical   (*d*) All the above

18. Buddhas theory of self is known as
(*a*) Theory of no-soul (*b*) Immutable self
(*c*) Eternal self   (*d*) None of the above

19. Buddha's theory of self is similar to the theory propounded in the West by:
(*a*) William James   (*b*) David Hume
(*c*) Bertrand Russel   (*d*) All of the above

20. Self according to Buddha is:
(*a*) Flow of consciousness
(*b*) Eternal
(*c*) Unchanging
(*d*) None of the above

21. The disadvantaged child's chances for success in school will be maximized when:
(*a*) He/she is given a high concentration of skills subjects
(*b*) He/she is provided with vocational training earlier than other children
(*c*) He/she is treated like any other child
(*d*) His/her intellectual potential is discovered and his/her education deficiencies are overcome
(*e*) it is realized that he/she needs a separate class to meet his/her needs.

22. "The individual develops through the head, the heart, and the hand." This was the educational philosophy of:
(*a*) Herbart   (*b*) Comenius
(*c*) Pestalozzi   (*d*) Froebel
(*e*) Rousseau

23. Martin Luther's greatest contribution to education was his:
(*a*) Ninety-Five Thesis
(*b*) Translation of the Bible into German
(*c*) Advocacy of a science curriculum for the universities
(*d*) Concept of justification by good works
(*e*) Advocacy of church control of schools

24. Of the following, the statement that is least educationally valid is that:
(*a*) Heterogeneous grouping is undemocratic
(*b*) Drill periods should be brief
(*c*) Study habits should be taught
(*d*) Overlearning constitutes a waste of time
(*e*) The quality of a student's notebook should be a factor in formulating the student's mark

25. To be successful with an over active child, the teacher should:
(*a*) Give the child extra written work so he/she will have a reason for remaining in his/her seat
(*b*) Allow the child to leave his/her seat whenever he/she becomes restless
(*c*) Provide the child with purposeful activities that legitimize the need for movement
(*d*) Isolate the child from the class
(*e*) Give the child a pass to the lavatory every half hour

26. Of the following bits of advice given by an experienced teacher to a new colleague, it would be better to ignore the one that states:
(*a*) If you have a very shy child, don't call on the child: wait until the child volunteers
(*b*) Give praise to even the poorest achiever: you can always find something worthwhile to praise
(*c*) When a child misbehaves, first look for the reason
(*d*) Write an interesting question on the board for the pupils to answer as soon as they enter the room
(*e*) Ask more 'how' and 'why' questions and not too many 'what' and 'who' question

27. Career education should begin:
 (*a*) In kindergarten
 (*b*) In the third or fourth grades
 (*c*) When the child enters junior high school
 (*d*) In high school economics classes
 (*e*) When the child begins to ask questions about jobs

28. During the first parent-teacher conference of the year, the teacher should do all of the following except:
 (*a*) Take notes
 (*b*) Include the child, when appropriate
 (*c*) Encourage the parent to talk about her child
 (*d*) Disagree with the parent's philosophy of childrearing
 (*e*) Offer a cup of coffee or tea

29. When the majority of pupils in science class is well below the grade level in reading, the teacher should:
 (*a*) Read to the class from the textbook
 (*b*) Plan many hands-on activities
 (*c*) Show many filmstrips
 (*d*) Prepare many dittoed sheets for the pupils to use
 (*e*) Lecture to the class, using simple language

30. A teacher notes poor attendance in class on Fridays, the day weekly tests are given.The teacher should:
 (*a*) Call the parents of the absentees
 (*b*) Schedule tests throughout the week
 (*c*) Do nothing
 (*d*) Tell the pupils that missing two test will result in a failing mark
 (*e*) Schedule all tests for Monday, after the children have had a restful weekend

31. In comparing the lecture and develop-mental lessons, all of the following are true except that:
 (*a*) There is more pupils activity in the developmental lesson
 (*b*) It is more difficult to ascertain pupils learning in a lecture lesson
 (*c*) The lecture method is more conducive to larger classes
 (*d*) Slow children derive more benefit from a lecture than brighter children do
 (*e*) Motivation and summary are necessary in both lessons

32. Group tests that have norms for each grade and that are administered in accordance with uniform procedure listed in a manual of instruction are called:
 (*a*) School-wide finals
 (*b*) Quizzes
 (*c*) Standardized tests
 (*d*) Class tests
 (*e*) The WAIS

33. All of the following are appropriate areas for pupil-teacher planning except:
 (*a*) The day's schedule
 (*b*) The selection of committees
 (*c*) The sequence in a skills programme
 (*d*) A class party
 (*e*) The selection of recreational reading

34. All of the following are examples of intrinsic motivation except:
 (*a*) Encouraging pupils to help develop the aim of a lesson
 (*b*) Permitting pupils to evaluate each other's answers
 (*c*) Utilizing pupil's backgrounds abd experiences
 (*d*) Giving short quizzes at the beginning of a lesson
 (*e*) Asking pupils to contribute to a class resource file

35. The most Important objective of committee work is to make children:
 (*a*) Practice parliamentary procedure
 (*b*) Develop the leadership skills of the high achievers
 (*c*) Develop skills of cooperative learning and problem-solving
 (*d*) Acquire factual information efficiently
 (*e*) Learn socialization skills

36. If on a fine day student refuse to have class study, what will you do?
(*a*) Will declare holiday
(*b*) Ask them to sit quietly in the class on that day
(*c*) Will engage them in some constructive activity
(*d*) Will engage them in gossiping on that day

37. If a student is given hard punishment, it may result into:
(*a*) The student may assault his teacher physically
(*b*) The student may leave the school and join some other institute
(*c*) His parents, may have bout with the teacher
(*d*) The student may develop disinterest in study, school and teacher in the form of disgusting

38. What a teacher should do if students do not take interest in lesson learning?
(*a*) He should tell it to them that how beneficial is it to learn it
(*b*) Should ask the reason of them not being taking interest
(*c*) Should himself try to know the reason and remove that
(*d*) Should complaint to the principal

39. The aim of a teacher should be:
(*a*) To make students to pass examination
(*b*) To discipline the student
(*c*) To polish the natural skill of the students
(*d*) To develop the social sense among them

40. Which is the best teaching method
(*a*) Iner-action method
(*b*) Reading book method
(*c*) Project method
(*d*) Audio-visual method

41. Fracture Means
(*a*) Broken bone
(*b*) Bone ends out of the place
(*c*) Stretching of tendons
(*d*) None of the above

42. Cryotherapy is also known as
(*a*) Ice therapy
(*b*) Hydrotherapy
(*c*) Electrotherapy
(*d*) None of the above

43. Lumbargo is also called
(*a*) Pain in the Head
(*b*) Pain in the abdomen
(*c*) Pain in the low-back
(*d*) All of the above

44. Contrast bath is recommended for
(*a*) Reducing a dislocated joint
(*b*) Reducing swelling
(*c*) Treatment of wound
(*d*) None of the above

45. The common injury in Basketball is
(*a*) Medial maniscus damage
(*b*) Damage medial ligament of the ankle
(*c*) Damage lateral ligament of the ankle
(*d*) All of the above

46. Electrical gadgets used for treating immediate sports injuries
(*a*) Ultra-violet rays
(*b*) Ultra sound
(*c*) Shortwavediathermy
(*d*) Infra-red rays

47. During training the sensation of vomiting is caused due to
(*a*) Accumulation of lactic acid
(*b*) Adrenaline
(*c*) Carbon dioxide
(*d*) All of the above

48. The first-aid treatment recommended for long distance exhausted athlete is
(*a*) Artificial respiration
(*b*) Massage
(*c*) Cryotherapy
(*d*) All of the above

49. Effleurage is always done
(*a*) From distal to proximal ends
(*b*) Across the muscles
(*c*) From proximal to distal ends
(*d*) Around joints

50. How do sports injuries occur?
  (*a*) Lack of knowledge
  (*b*) Inadequate training, technique and equipment
  (*c*) Carelessness
  (*d*) All the above

51. A work in which the amount of Oxygen taken in and used by the body is sufficient to provide the energy necessary for the performance of task is called as
  (*a*) Aerobic work
  (*b*) Anaerobic work
  (*c*) Full work
  (*d*) None of the above

52. A work in which the amount of oxygen that the body can supply is less than the amount necessary to perform the task is known as
  (*a*) Anaerobic work   (*b*) Aerobic work
  (*c*) Half work   (*d*) None

53. The ability of the total body to use oxygen for energy is called
  (*a*) Oxygen Consumption
  (*b*) Tidal volume
  (*c*) Both
  (*d*) None of the above

54. Which measurement is recognized as the best measurement of a person's cardio-vascular fitness
  (*a*) Body weight   (*b*) Pulse rate
  (*c*) Vo2 max   (*d*) None

55. How can the maximal Oxygen consumption increase
  (*a*) An increase in the amount of hemoglobin in the blood
  (*b*) An increase in the maximal cardiac output
  (*c*) An increase in amount and/or size of capillaries
  (*d*) All of the above

56. The target Zone heart rate ranges from 70 to 85% of individual's maximal heart rate, it is
  (*b*) True   (*c*) False
  (*d*) Both   (*e*) None of these

57. Formula for calculating Critical Heart Rate is
  (*a*) Resting heart rate + 09.60 (Maximal heart rate-Resting heart rate)

  (*b*) Resting heart rate –0.80 (Maximal heart rate-resting heart rate
  (*c*) Resting heart rate –0.60 (Maximal heart rate + resting heart rate)
  (*d*) None of the above

58. Why does muscle pull occur?
  (*a*) Insufficient warm up before game
  (*b*) Mineral deficiency
  (*c*) Muscle imbalance
  (*d*) All of the above

59. What should be applied when muscle pull occur?
  (*a*) Ice   (*b*) Warm water
  (*c*) Infrared Lamp   (*d*) None

60. Tennis elbows can be developed by
  (*a*) Only Tennis players
  (*b*) Only Badminton players
  (*c*) Both
  (*d*) None

61. What would you do when Tennis elbow is developed?
  (*a*) Stop playing game
  (*b*) Use crepe bandage
  (*c*) Use of Wrist band
  (*d*) None

62. What are the causes of muscle cramp?
  (*a*) Salt deficiency
  (*b*) Any injury to muscle
  (*c*) Hyper ventilation
  (*d*) All of the above

63. What do you understand by the word tendinities?
  (*a*) Fracture
  (*b*) An inflammation of the tendon
  (*c*) Both
  (*d*) Tiredness

64. What is the immediate management for sprain, strain and tendon injuries?
  (*a*) Using Ice packs   (*b*) Use of hot water
  (*c*) Infrared Lamp   (*d*) None of these

65. Cryo-therapy means
  (*a*) Cold-therapy
  (*b*) Heat application
  (*c*) Infrared
  (*d*) None

66. The word "Effleurage" is related with
(*a*) Massage
(*b*) Weight Training
(*c*) Sprint Training
(*d*) Endurance Training

67. The movement performed by the trainee with no aid on the body part of the subject may be termed as
(*a*) Passive manipulation
(*b*) Active manipulation
(*c*) Resistive manipulation
(*d*) None of these

68. The movement performed by the individual with the help of weight acting against the direction of movement may be termed as
(*a*) Resistive manipulation
(*b*) Assistive manipulation
(*c*) Passive manipulation
(*d*) None of these

69. Ethyl chloride is used in athletics as a means of treatment in
(*a*) Cryo-therapy   (*b*) Thermo-therapy
(*c*) Electro-therapy   (*d*) None of these

70. Diathermy and ultra-sound methods are used for the treatment of injuries in
(*a*) Cryo-therapy   (*b*) Thermo-therapy
(*c*) Electro-therapy   (*d*) None of these

71. A normal human body has
(*a*) One Kidney   (*b*) Two Kidneys
(*c*) Three Kidneys   (*d*) None of these

72. Human kidneys are situated at
(*a*) 12th thorasic to 3rd lumber segment
(*b*) 8th thorasic to 2nd lumber segment
(*c*) 10th thorasic to 3rd lumber segment
(*d*) None of these

73. The chief excretory organs of human body are
(*a*) Lungs   (*b*) Skin
(*c*) Two Kidneys   (*d*) None of these

74. Proximal convoluted tubule (PCT) or Pars comoluta is about
(*a*) 20 mm long   (*b*) 35 mm long
(*c*) 14 mm long   (*d*) None of these

75. Henless loop (pass recta) is
(*a*) V Shaped loop   (*b*) U shaped loop
(*c*) A shaped loop   (*d*) None of these

ANSWERS

1. (*c*)	2. (*a*)	3. (*a*)	4. (*a*)	5. (*a*)	6. (*c*)	7. (*b*)	8. (*d*)
9. (*a*)	10. (*b*)	11. (*c*)	12. (*d*)	13. (*d*)	14. (*c*)	15. (*d*)	16. (*d*)
17. (*a*)	18. (*d*)	19. (*a*)	20. (*b*)	21. (*d*)	22. (*c*)	23. (*b*)	24. (*d=*)
25. (*c*)	26. (*a*)	27. (*a*)	28. (*d*)	29. (*b*)	30. (*b*)	31. (*d*)	32. (*c*)
33. (*c*)	34. (*d*)	35. (*c*)	36. (*c*)	37. (*d*)	38. (*c*)	39. (*c*)	40. (*c*)
41. (*a*)	42. (*a*)	43. (*c*)	44. (*b*)	45. (*d*)	46. (*d*)	47. (*a*)	48. (*a*)
49. (*a*)	50. (*d*)	51. (*a*)	52. (*a*)	53. (*a*)	54. (*c*)	55. (*d*)	56. (*a*)
57. (*a*)	58. (*d*)	59. (*b*)	60. (*c*)	61. (*a*)	62. (*d*)	63. (*b*)	64. (*a*)
65. (*a*)	66. (*a*)	67. (*b*)	68. (*a*)	69. (*a*)	70. (*c*)	71. (*b*)	72. (*a*)
73. (*c*)	74. (*c*)	75. (*b*)					

6. OBJECTIVES OF HEALTH EDUCATION

INTRODUCTION

The World Health Organization defines health as "a state of complete physical, mental and social well-being, not merely the absence of disease or infirmity". On the other hand, it may also be defined as a condition in which the individual is able to mobilize all of his resources—intellectual, emotional, and physical-for optimum living. In these and other definitions, health is a highly valued asset, but one that is often taken for granted and some times not fully appreciated until it is lost. Health influences one's way of life, it improves personal efficiency and facilitates the attainment of personal goals.

Good teachers are sincerely and enthusiastically interested in children and youth, and want to see them grow and develop into healthy, well-adjusted men and women. This interest, coupled with knowledge of health problems and with ability and skill in helping pupils to understand themselves and to learn ways of solving health problems, can be a vital force in improving the health of present and future generations. Different people have defined health differently. For some, it is Physical health and for others social and mental health. But for the student of Physical Education, the concept of health is not a narrow one, but a wider concept, which covers physical, mental and social health of an individual. The most accepted definition of health education can be put in the following words:

"Health Education is a process which brings about changes in the knowledge and attitude of people and thereby effects the changes in health practices." From this definition we can conclude that health education aims to make individuals realize the importance of health and inculcate in them the habits conducive to the attainment of health. It also aims to impart complete knowledge that may help in developing good health and habits in maintaining optimum health. The objectives that help in realizing the aim of health education can be listed as under:

1. Educate people to make proper use of available health services.
2. Develop interest, attitude and skill in health matters conducive to healthful behaviour.
3. Spread knowledge regarding health matters and make people aware of health problems.
4. Help individuals realize that health is the most available asset.
5. Develop a sense of responsibility for the improvement of individual and community health.

Most people are not able to see through their actions beyond immediate pleasures. Some of their actions, and lifestyles create a mirage like situation which allures them towards their doom. Do you feel people who can afford all possible luxuries and comforts of life, and who can live a life practically without any physical work or those who can mask their sorrows, frustrations and tensions behind their acts of drinking, smoking or having a playboy image, are the happiest people on earth without any health problems? You are perhaps mistaken. Many such people who do not take timely preventive measures may suffer from one or more of such diseases like insomnia, low-back pain, hypertension (high blood pressure), heart problems, HIV OR HB-V infections. Some of their lifestyles, like habit of drinking or smoking are actually the result of their inadequacy to face realities of life which in-turn may even attack them by one or other kind of cancers.

NATURE AND SCOPE OF HEALTH EDUCATION

The strength and future upon of any nation depends on the health of its citizens and likewise their happiness also depends upon solely on their health. This means that both the strength and happiness are the direct outcomes of good health. If the people are not strong physically, they cannot defend their country and if their health is poor, they cannot enjoy the happiness of life to the maximum. This concept of greatest happiness out of life, automatically increases the scope and area of health education. Health education is multidisciplinary in nature because it largely draws its content from different fields of study like 1. Biological Sciences, 2. Medical Sciences, 3. Public Health, 4. Physical Sciences, and 5. Behavioral Science. The relevant subject areas from where health education draws its content under the sciences, include botany, zoology, anatomy, physiology, bacteriology, epidemiology, chemistry, physics, psychology and sociology.

Health education content is not the sum total of content of these subjects but it is content taken from those subjects which are relevant to the promotion of physical health and social effectiveness. It is then organised into broad areas of study which determine the scope of health education and then interpreted in a unique manner to achieve the goals of health education. The broad areas of health education include:

- Family life education;
- Prevention and control of communicable and non communicable diseases;
- Prevention of accidents (safety education), first aid, treatment of minor ailments associated with various body systems, and home nursing of sick;
- Consumer health;
- Occupational health;
- International heath;
- Personal health care and grooming;
- Healthful environment;
- Food and nutrition;
- Growth, development and care of sense organs;
- Rest, sleep, exercise and posture;
- Mental health;
- Study of mind altering substances alcohol, tobacco and drugs.

Physical Education and Health Education, though very often used together, are not synonymous. They are closely related to each other and not interchangeable. Health education and physical education are two separate disciplines. However, both share the common goal of development of high quality of physical, mental and social health in each individual enabling him or her to lead a personally satisfying and socially useful life. Each is a separate area of study with distinct content and area of activity and requires special and unique professional preparation which deals with ways of achieving the common goal of health and education which are specific and different for each discipline.

OBJECTIVES OF HEALTH EDUCATION

Everyone desires to live. Living alone is not sufficient. To live most is the doctrine of health. Living most aids in serving best. To live most indicates to raise up to the maximum standard of living, with a body possessing physique to discharge its optimum, deriving cent percent efficiency, with strength to do heavy work, with least fatigue, with skill, stamina and speed to do things with ease, with a mind not susceptible to minor irritation but can maintain equilibrium under all circumstances and with a capacity of mind and body to resist diseases and thus enable the individual to enjoy the essence of everything with confidence and courage. The long range objectives of health education are:

- to acquire relevant health knowledge, develop positive attitudes and practices necessary to stay healthy;
- to do what he or she can, individually and collectively, seeking help from concerned professionals, to promote (a) his or her own health, (*b*) health of his or her family members, and (*c*) health of others in the community;
- to promote improved preventive and promotive health behaviour in families

and in the community. These long range objectives lead to the ultimate goal of health education to live a personally satisfying and socially useful life.

- to develop a desire to be healthy;
- to become aware of meaning and concept of health;
- -to become familiar with factors and conditions that promote or adversely affect health.

HEALTH EDUCATION MEANING AND CONCEPT

Health Education is a way through which we can keep ourselves "fit and healthy". It is defined as "state of live most and save least". If an individual is healthy, he will be able to work nicely and can guide the fellows in other walks of life. Health Education is knowledge about good health, sleep, rest and keeping the body away from attack of deadly diseases. Healthy Education is an integral part of physical education since an unhealthy person cannot think of his total development. According to WHO, asquoled earlier, health has been defined as *"a state of complete physical, mental and social well being, and not merely absence of disease or infirmity"*. But to achieve this level of health is an ideal, which perhaps no one can attain.

However, a person can aspire to have a minimum level of health which will enable one to live a personally satisfying and socially useful life. To achieve this, a desired change in his existing health knowledge, his existing health related attitudes and his current health practices would have to be made. This will enable him to have a reasonable level of physical, mental and social well being, so that, he may be free from preventable diseases, disorders or infirmities

According to this, health education brings about desired change in knowledge, attitudes and practices which will ensure him this minimum level of health. But health education is not simple 'content', comprising of desired change in knowledge, attitudes and practices, it is also a process that empowers people to develop a capability (knowledge, attitudes and practices), of self-health-care (physical, mental and social health) through self-reliance (using available resources) and social responsibility (safe guarding health of community members)," Thus health education is both content and as well as a process. The main steps of this process are:

1. Helps the person to recognise his need (health problem). This comprises of his health problem and also the gap between existing knowledge, attitudes and practices and what this knowledge, attitudes and practices ought to be, to prevent the problem.

   [Need = what ought to be - what exists]

2. Setting goals (targets) to be achieved in affecting a change in knowledge, attitudes and practices through health education within a given time frame, along with helping the person to take steps to solve his health problem through treatment.

3. Assessing health education resources like reading material, counsellors, films, etc., and facility for treatment, Help in securing treatment will enhance your acceptance as a health educator to listen to your advice.

4. Helping the person to achieve the goals that is to bring about change in knowledge, attitudes and practices about the perceived health problem and advice of the medical expert entirely with his own efforts, and without causing any problem(s) for the community in the form of spreading the disease.

FACTORS AFFECTING AN INDIVIDUAL'S HEALTH

The three aspects—physical, social and mental are foundations of health and are interdependent. A person who does not enjoy healthful living, is a liability and a burden not only on himself but on his nation and on the human society as well whereas a person who has a good health is an asset. He works more and contribute much to the welfare of human race. To understand fully the environment of health and healthful living of an individual, we should study the factors, responsible for affecting the health of an individual. These can be listed as below:

1. Heredity: We inherit our physical structure and physiological functioning and even the humour and temperaments as a matter of inheritance. Some people are hereditarily phlegmatic while others are sanguine or choleric. There is ample evidence to prove that many diseases such as colour blindness, feeblemindedness, etc., are transmitted from one generation to the other. No medicine nor any other biological device has been able to change this natural process. Some people have weak lungs right from their birth. It is very difficult to cure them though prevention of certain kind and to help them to live for some time. Of course, this is nothing but dragging one's life. In such cases exercise can only be useful for the purpose of giving modalities to those limbs which have been either crippled or deformed due to birth traumas or accidents. Exercise only serves as a corrective measure here and not as a cure. A person generally weak derives least benefit from vigorous exercise.

2. Environment: Environment denotes two things, i.e. Physical environment objects around us and social environment—people and their ideas, customs, traditions, beliefs, etc. Scientific investigations have revealed that almost all the diseases are caused by the deadly minute organisms present in the environment, is neither congenial nor clean, no amount of physical exercise can do any good to the humans. Therefore, a good environment—physical and social, may include the following:

(a) Balanced and rich nutrition,

(b) Sensitivity,

(c) Cleanliness of the home and surroundings,

(d) Personal cleanliness,

(e) Pure air and pure water,

(f) Healthy traditions and customs, and

(g) Health knowledge.

3. Exercise: Exercise alone, if other factors directly concerned with the survival of the individual, are not sufficiently present, cannot make the person grow in 'quality' and efficiency. Rather it will deteriorate the organs, because due to

vigorous exercise there will be an increased load on the organism whereas it would not be getting sufficient nutrition to meet out the increasing demand and hence be in debt. Exercise is only a crowning factor for health.

4. Rest and Relaxation: The modern age is an age of tension stresses and strains arising out of the unceasing pursuit of materialistic goals. Even if so much industrialization has taken place on account of which man actually should have maximum rest and relaxation from corking cares and corroding anxieties of life but this is not the case. Rather the anxieties have considerably increased. Man has fallen prey to innumerable psychosomatic diseases due to the lack of proper rest and relaxation. In the promotion of health and happiness, rest and relaxation play a very important part. It is during the resting period that the body rebuilds the worn and torn tissues out of the food that we eat. During exercise the catabolic processes (wear and tear) are predominant while during rest anabolic (rebuilding) processes are more predominant. There should be a perfect balance between rest and work.

There are two aspects of rest and relaxation, i.e., physical and mental. Physical rest is required when the body has been exercised and mental rest, when mental fatigue has set in due to rigorous studies or thinking. It is the best method to change over from physical to mental and vice-versa. This keeps an ideal balance between the two aspects of rest and relaxation.

A balanced type of recreative activity is a panacea for all the ills leading to mental disturbance, i.e., in which more than 80% of our energy is wasted unnecessary. In the matter of work and rest the principle of stroke and glide work Rest should be followed. Over-work and under work are both bad for the development of an efficient man.

PRINCIPLES OF HEALTH EDUCATION

For a state of well-being a sound mind in a sound body is essential. Health infuses confidence in life. It is an asset by itself. None can afford to neglect or lose it. It helps one to keep oneself fit and maintain one's youth hood. When wealth is lost only something is lost, but when health is lost everything is lost. Therefore, it becomes the duty of everyone to take optimum care of his health. From cradle to grave, the problem of health is one's own. Slight negligence causes great havoc and leads to the end of life itself.

Disciplined way of living, keeping mind calm and composed, nutritious diet, good water, fresh air, sound sleep, useful way of spending, leisure, etc., are the factors that help to maintain health. Ill health and diseases which render negative health, are unavoidable, but a knowledge to overcome them should be acquired at all cost. To the children at school, this knowledge should be imparted. Health Education should be a subject of study and it should find its legitimate place in the curriculum. In case a health education programme is to be planned for a community to protect from the preventable health problems, the community might be suffering and which may be amenable to health education treatment. The following health education principles need to be followed:

1. Pretest Informative Literature: Knowledge is transmitted through various medias. It is always better to involve local talent in preparation of educational material and media for putting up exhibitions or using during educational programme. If these are to be procured from some other sources they may be tested with the community with which it is to be used later on to test whether it conveys the same message for which it is intended. If it does not give the same message it should either be modified or not used.

2. Community Participation: Man is part of the total community system. To generate interest of the community in the educational programme, the community members should be involved in as many organisational tasks as possible, like collecting materials, arranging exhibitions, or making seating arrangement for the programme and even for inviting community people.

3. Knowledge of Locality: Being a part of the whole social system, it is important for a person to have thorough knowledge of his locality and the community. To familiarise with the area, a map should be prepared showing each house with its

number, location of community resources like schools, libraries community halls, entertainment centres, government and non-government health and family welfare facilities. In addition, make note of condition of houses, sanitation status of the community, sewage disposal system, waste disposal arrangements. Any other factors and conditions influencing health positively or adversely should also be noted.

4. Acquaintance with People: Man is a part of total social system and what makes him a social being is his acquaintance and intimacy with other social beings. To have complete and thorough knowledge of and about the people, method should be used are; Survey households to find out occupation of people, their working hours, income, religion, sociocultural practices, educational standard, language spoken, community celebrations and religious festivals organised, religious and opinion leaders, general health needs and interests of people as expressed by their leaders, past experiences of leaders about development programmes in their area, N.G.Os (non-government organisations) working in the field of health and family welfare in the community, health practices, superstitions, health related lifestyles of people like smoking and drinking habits. This information will help while planning health education programme for the community. This information will help in planning an effective health education programme considering their lifestyles if they need to be modified.

5. Identification of Health Problems: Health is the concern of all individuals. If the components of society are healthful and healthy, the society will automatically be a well composed organization. Ask people what problems they and their family members have suffered from during past six months or so. From where they have received or are receiving treatment. Identify health problems of people as recorded in the hospital records.

6. Be Part of the Social System: Man by nature is social. By living in society, he learns various traits and habits. It is the similarity and togetherness, which helps to make social behaviour and society as a unit stronger. People who wear the same dress or speak the same language as people of the community are better accepted by people for discussing their intimate topics and problems. Other ways to build rapport include participation in their cultural programmes, celebrations of festivals. Helping them to solve some of their felt needs which are different from their health needs like getting their ration card made, fixing an appointment with a doctor in the hospital or the like will help in winning peoples confidence and friendship.

IMPORTANCE OF HEALTH EDUCATION

Resistance and immunity are mostly inherited but it can also be acquired through artificial means to keep health unaffected by the enemies of health. Once the health is subjected to unhealthy walk of life, one falls a prey and victim to vicious habits which, in the long run, drains their sources of health and results in irreparable loss. Mind being an inseparable entity, any abnormalities to normal health is bound to upset mental health also. When mind is disturbed it disturb the body. This in turn cast its impact on courage, confidence and determination rendering life to lose its total pleasure. Health education is important for everyone for the following reasons:

1. Every moment new health knowledge, products and services are being generated and advertised to trap the innocent consumer. Health education equips people to analyse and discriminate scientifically about new health knowledge, health products health services and health related advertisements through multimedia before making decisions to use any one of these.
2. Health education also guides students about career opportunities being generated in the field of health and medicine under various systems of medicine which also include public health and teaching fields.
3. Bridges gap between available scientific health knowledge and its usages by common man. Ignorance about such diseases as tuberculosis, leprosy, and AIDS makes even the social life of these patients miserable due to social stigma attached with these diseases. Also that diseases like AIDS, Hepatitis-B, and rabies have no cure but they can be prevented. Health education also reduces deaths from many preventable diseases if correct preventive measures are taken.
4. Reduces burden on health services by helping people to protect themselves from diseases and by helping them to use available health services judiciously. Many a time people with minor diseases or even common ailments rush to the specialists due to their resources whereas people with more serious and chronic conditions are not even able to get an appointment with experts for months together.
5. Helps in understanding technical terminology in layman's language to enable common man to follow healthy lifestyles to protect from serious health problems.
6. Helps people in understanding factors and conditions that affect health favourably or adversely.
7. There are problems like obesity, smoking, drinking, drug addiction illegitimacy, sexual experimentation, insufficient rest, health misconceptions, self medication, lack of exercise, sexually transmitted diseases, AIDS and many more which impair physical, mental and social development. Some reduce the educability of youth. There are some which even lead to disability and death. Health education provides an insight into all such problems and safeguards health and life of people.

CONTEMPORARY HEALTH PROBLEMS

Fast progress in all fields has brought in its wake a number of health problems. Problems arising from pollution of air we breathe in, contamination of water due to the discharge of industrial waste and sewage into our water sources, population explosion, malnutrition, drug addiction and some other problems are growing in gigantic proportions. There is a growing awareness that any slackness on these fronts will have very serious repercussions. Therefore, serious efforts are being made to draw the attention of all concerned towards the solution of these problems. The main areas of concern are the following:

Water Pollution

Of all the types of pollution that affect a child's health, water pollution is by far the most serious. The most harmful pollutants of water come from municipal waste, industrial waste, garbage, human excreta, the drainage of acids from mines, the erosion of soil from farms, roads etc. spillage of oil from tankers and pipelines, the release of sewers, community sewers and acid rains.

Soil Pollution

Most of the activities of children in developing countries like India are on the surface of earth which is contaminated by different polluting agents like industrial waste, fertilizers, pesticides, human and animal excreta and also by contaminated water. Since most of the children play barefoot on the soil and sometimes eat it too, the harmful organisms present in the soil may cause tetanus, enteric fever, diarrhoea, dysentery and other intestinal troubles and worm infestation like hook worm and tape worm.

Noise Pollution

Noise as pollutant contaminate environment which becomes a nuisance and affects the health of a child, his activities and mental abilities. Noise is an unwanted excess sound which disturbs a person. These days there is a lot of noise pollution produce by vehicles, airplanes, factories, loudspeakers, Television, radio, etc. Noise disturbs the sleep of a child and lack of sleep leads to irritation, insomnia and many other behavioral disorders.

Vehicular Pollution

Roads and streets are seen flooded with blind race of different types of automobiles, cars, scooters, tempos and other light and heavy vehicles and, apart from making the city most accident prone,

are the major causes of black smoke that people are forced to breathe. This smoke is full of carbon dioxide, carbon monoxide, sulphur dioxide and lead. These gases cause eye irritation, respiratory disorders and skin diseases.

Nuclear Pollution

In modern times atomic energy is playing an important role for the development and advancement of the world. But at the same time, it has opened its windows to prepare material for the destruction of humanity. Hiroshima and Nagasaki met their ill fate due to atomic explosion. The children are still born disabled with various congenital defect. They suffer from various sorts of cancers. Life is still abnormal in these cities. Natural environment not responding quickly to the new changes.

Food Adulteration

Food and milk which are very essential for the physical growth of a child are also not available in pure forms. The purity of milk is always doubtful. These days synthetic milk containing detergents, urea, refined oil, dirty water of ponds is being produced. Not only milk but the purity of every food stuff is doubtful. In soft drinks and other Foodstuffs, various chemical dyes are used which may cause gastrointestinal disturbances, anemia and various type of cancers. Many poisonous chemicals like calcium carbide are used for ripening fruits. Chemicals used for the preservation of cereals are also harmful to the health of children. Tinned foods may cause food poisoning.

PERSONAL HYGIENE
Meaning of Personal Hygiene

The word '*Hygiene*' has been derived from *Greek* word '*Hygienos*' which means healthful. However, 'Hygiene is also termed as '*Hygia*' in *Greek*, which means the *godess of health*.

In the modern times, it means "*the art of living*". It is true that a healthy mind lives in healthy body. It means that for proper and systematic working of the body it is essential to have proper hygiene, this type of hygiene is called personal hygiene. Hence personal hygiene means the study and application of preventive medicine and physiology for the preservation of the health of the individual. In other words personal hygiene means an individual can maintain his/her health by observing the principles of proper living, paying attention to his cleanliness, exercise, rest, sleep and proper ventilation in the house. Some times when a child in early life neglects the cleanliness, he may develop certain unhygienic habits. Such habits that are generally formed in the early childhood may take a serious turn and become very difficult to break in later life. Therefore, if the proper education is imparted to the children on personal hygiene and bad habits are checked in time, most of the diseases can be kept away, whereas its neglect may cause untold misery.

Importance of Personal Hygiene

Good habits serve as an instrument for the promotion of health and long life. Similarly for proper and systematic functioning of the different organs of the body, it is essential to have proper hygiene. So health and education have relative role for the longivity of life. Both of them go side by side. Education can not go on successfully unless the body is healthy. If good habits are developed among the children by education in the health-instruction class they shall lead to systematic education and successfull living. It has been rightly said that "*healthy body is a source of achieving the highest goal of life*". Therefore, we cannot ignore the importance of personal cleanliness and personal hygiene at home, in the class and institution.

Personal Hygiene helps in :

1. Developing healthy habits and attitudes.
2. Maintaining healthy atmosphere in the home, classroom and institution.
3. Encouraging the individual for reading of health literature.
4. Developing emotional stability.
5. Developing attractive personality.

CLEANLINESS

Personal cleanliness is one of the main ingredients of good health. It is a preventive measure against disease. So one must know how to keep himself clean and healthy. The habit of personal cleanliness must be cultivated in children so that they can keep themselves healthy. *Personal cleanliness includes: cleanliness of teeth, ears, nose, nails, skin, bowels habit, cleanliness / proper clothes etc.*

1. Teeth: Bad teeth result in developing various diseases such as pyorrhoea and also causes a danger to the digestive system whereas healthy teeth contribute to a pleasing appearance and help in chewing and digestion of food. Diseased teeth and gums not only cause pain and discomfort in the oral cavity but also can lead to serious complications like heart dieases, joint pain, abdominal pain and even cancer of mouth. Dental health is a matter of life long concern. Correct dental care can help to keep teeth for a long time. Neglect of teeth care is most likely to reflect on our general well being so we must take care of our teeth and in turn they will take good care of ours. Teeth should be cleaned after every meal so that nothing is left stuck in the denture which can lead to severe pain, abscess, loss of tooth and disfigurement of face. So we must take measure to prevent them as it is well said "*prevention is better than cure.*" We must follow such rules regarding healthy teeth :

(a) Brush teeth daily after every meal especially after dinner.
(b) Brush teeth from up to downward direction and vice-versa.
(c) Don't eat sweet and sticky food in between meals. Children should avoid toffees, candies. Chocolates etc.
(d) Avoid excessive consumption of alcohol, cigarettes, pan chewing to avoid mouth cancer.
(e) Consult dental surgeon regularly.
  With proper personal and professional care one can keep natural denture throughout life.

2. Ears: Hygiene of ears is very essential. Ear is a sense organ because we hear things through ears, good hearing keeps one in active touch with people and events. Whereas poor hearing makes an individual dull and can lead to serious emotional disturbance. The ear is a delicate organ easily prone to injury. Students must learn the precautions to be taken to protect the ear in sports, specifically in swimming and diving. Do not put pins, needles or any sharp thing into the ears. Do not expose ears to loud noise, avoid hitting on ears don't put hydrogen peroxide in child's ear. Don't neglect cough or cold. Learn the early signs of deafness. Treat the illness early. If there is discharge or pain in ear, a doctor must be consulted.

3. Eyes: Eyes are the most important and valuable organs of the body. Every care is essential to retain their sight and keep them healthy. Poor nutrition may cause vision disturbances and inflammatory conditions of eyes and lids, so rich diet is to be taken for better sight. Proper eye hygiene includes good reading habits under lighting conditions and use of glasses when needed. One must practice and learn the following points to protect eyes :

1. Wash eyes with fresh water.
2. Protect the eyes from dust, smoke and bright sunlight and irritating vapours.
3. Avoid rubbing eyes with dirty fingers.
4. Use clean and separate towel or handkerchief.
5. If eyes appear red, swollen or watery, consult doctor immediately.
6. Games with bow and arrow, fire crackers, should be discouraged.
7. Do not neglect eye strain consult doctor immediately.
8. Disease of diabetes should be effectively treated as early as possible because it can lead to complications related with eye sight.
9. Avoid stooping on book or close work.
10. Eye sight should be got tested regularly.

4. Nose and Throat: Nose is another important sense organ responsible for giving the idea of smell, should be kept clean. It is through nose that one breathes and if nose gets stuffed, or disturbed we start breathing through mouth, in such case our respiratory system gets disturbed which can lead to serious lung diseases. Nose should therefore be kept clean, if some problem is experienced in this sense organ, a doctor must be consulted accordingly.

Throat is also a vital organ of the body. It is connected with orther sense organs like ear, nose, tongue etc. if it is not kept clean may cause serious disorders. If there is some complaint, one should take medical advice.

5. Nails and Fingers: The nails are formed by the special horny cells of the epidermis and protect the finger tips of hands and feet. Since hands are used frequently for any work, the nails get dirty very easily and this dirt in the nails becomes a source of infection for food when we touch it with hands. All this dirt may get into our mouth with food and make us sick. It is important to keep the nails of the fingers short, so that no dirt accumulates and chances of infection are reduced. Nails should not be bitten by teeth otherwise dirt of the nails may cause severe ailment of mouth and throat. One must develop the habit of cleaning the hands before cooking, handling and eating food. The nails of the toes be cut straight. The feet should be washed and dried properly before retiring to bed.

6. Skin: In order to avoid the dangerous effects of polluted atmosphere around us, one has to clean or wash the skin daily. If dirt is allowed to remain over the skin for a long time, it may cause skin diseases. By taking bath the body becomes fresh and remain active. During winter sun-bath may also be practised. Exposure of the body in the sun during winter provides vitamin D and K and improves vitality of the human body, which develops resistance against diseases. The best way to clean the skin or face is with soap and water, dry it with a soft towel by simple patting rather than rubbing. It is advisable to use cold creams in winter particularly when the skin is dry, but care should be taken in case of oily skin and skin with acne. One must avoid over exposure of skin or face to hot weather.

7. Clothes: One puts on different types of clothes according to various seasons. Clothes should be fit, clean and tidy, as clean dress adds something to one's personality. Preferably clothes should be washed regularly depending on the weather condition and occupation, and then dried in sun. Under clothes which are in direct contact with the body must be cleaned daily because they constantly come in contact with different body secretions and perspiration of skin. They should be made up of cotton as texture synthetic fiber may cause skin allergy. The clothes should be comfortable to the body and must not obstruct breathing and body development. Avoid wearing tight clothes.

8. Hair: Hair should be brushed or combed with personal brush/comb properly. For healthy hair, these should be washed with a good antiseptic soap or shampoo twice a week and then properly dried up. A gentle massage with oil will improve blood circulation and facilitate proper growth and lustre. The scalp is to be gripped lightly between fingers of both hand and gently moved forward, backward and from side to side over the bony skull. If dandruff is there then use anti dandruff shampoo. In case condition does not improve then consult doctor and follow his instruction carefully. The hair should be free from lice and any other infectious germs.

9. Bowel: The daily habit of emptying the bowel at regular time should be developed and intentional delay should be avoided. The child should be given proper training from the very beginning. A good nutritive diet with sufficient amount of roughage, plenty of water intake, regular exercise will help in cleaning the bowel. Frequent intake of junk and fried food should be avoided.

Therefore, one must develop good habit of keeping personal cleanliness up to the mark. Good habits are formed during childhood which last longer. If bad habits are nipped in the bud, it would be very beneficial in the long run for the individual as well as community. As Dr. Fielden said, "Life is like a house, give it good foundation and it shall give you good service for as long as you want it" So if we develop good habits in child to keep him healthy, he will help the society to give his best.

OBJECTIVE QUESTIONS

1. Which of the following vitamins is concerned with proper bone formation in the young?
(*a*) Vitamin A (*b*) Vitamin B
(*c*) Vitamin D (*d*) Vitamin E

2. The technique of recording and reproducing three dimensional images of objects is known as—
(*a*) Autography (*b*) Lexicography
(*c*) Holography (*d*) Photography

3. Which one of the following contains both vitamins A and D?
(*a*) Codliver oil (*b*) Mutton
(*c*) Orange (*d*) Wheat

4. Which of the following is grown from stem cuttings?
(*a*) Banana (*b*) Maiz
(*c*) Sugarcane (*d*) Turmeric

5. The owl can see most clearly in total darkness because—
(*a*) it has squint eyes
(*b*) it has large eyes with orbs directed forward, giving it binocular sight
(*c*) it has light bulbs in its eyes provided by nature
(*d*) none of these

6. Which of the following vitamins helps in the normal clotting of blood?
(*a*) E (*b*) G
(*c*) H (*d*) K

7. All of the following belong to the vitamin B Group, except
(*a*) folic acid (*b*) nicotinamide
(*c*) riboflavin (*d*) thiamine

8. How many red blood cells does the bone marrow produce every second?
(*a*) 5 million (*b*) 7 million
(*c*) 10 million (*d*) 12 million

9. The portion of the eye as an organ visible from outside is about—
(*a*) 1/5 (*b*) 2/5
(*c*) 3/5 (*d*) 415

10. Morphine is a/an—
(*a*) stimulant (*b*) analgesic
(*c*) tranquilliser (*d*) none of these

11. In the eye, colour vision is affected by the presence of—
(*a*) Choroid coat (*b*) Rods
(*c*) Sclerotic coat (*d*) Cones

12. The disease caused by asbestos is—
(*a*) Emphysema   (*b*) Dysentery
(*c*) Diarrhoea   (*d*) Paralysis

13. Which one of the following substances is used for the preservation of pickles food grains?
(*a*) Vinegar
(*b*) Sodium benzoate
(*c*) Sodium chloride
(*d*) Potassium permanganate

14. Concave mirrors are used as shaving mirrors because they—
(*a*) Do not distort images
(*b*) Always produce real images
(*c*) Produce magnified images
(*d*) never produce inverted images

15. Which of the following is used as a filler in rubber tyres?
(*a*) Graphite   (*b*) Carbon black
(*c*) Coke   (*d*) Chaarcoal

16. The principal organ concerned in the loss of heat from the body is—
(*a*) skin   (*b*) heart
(*c*) liver   (*d*) none of these

17. When light passes from air into glass it experiences change of—
(*a*) frequency and wavelength
(*b*) frequency and speed
(*c*) wavelength and speed
(*d*) frequency, wavelength and speed

18. One of the interesting features of viruses is that they—
(*a*) Multiply only in the host cytoplasm
(*b*) Are made of proteins only
(*c*) Occur only inside bacteria
(*d*) Behave in the same manner as plants

19. To produce sound it is necessary that—
(*a*) the source should execute longitudinal vibrations
(*b*) the source should execute transverse vibrations
(*c*) the source may execute any type of vibration
(*d*) the vibrations of source are not necessary

20. Which one of the following acids is used for etching glass?
(*a*) HIO_4 (*b*) $HBrO_3$
(*c*) H_2F_2 (*d*) $HClO_4$

21. Which of the following vitamins aids night vision?
(*a*) Vitamin A   (*b*) Vitamin B
(*c*) Vitamin C   (*d*) Vitamin D

22. Carbohydrates contain—
(*a*) only Oxygen
(*b*) only hydrogen
(*c*) equal quantities of hydrogen and oxygen
(*d*) hydrogen and oxygen in the same proportion as in water

23. In the human body, urea is produced in the~—
(*a*) Liver   (*b*) Spleen
(*c*) Kidney   (*d*) Pancreas

24. A corked bottle full of water frozen will break because—
(*a*) the bottle contracts on freezing
(*b*) the volume of water decreases on freezing
(*c*) the volume of water increases on freezing
(*d*) glass is a bad conductor of heat

25. Cyclotron is a device which—
(*a*) Detects and analyses the spectrum of light emitted by stars
(*b*) Detects the cyclic variation in the intensity of electromagnetic radiation emitted from stars
(*c*) Accelerates subatomic particles using combined electric and magnetic fields
(*d*) Measures the intensity of X-rays

26. One important product of fermentation is—
(*a*) alcohol   (*b*) water
(*c*) oxygen   (*d*) honey

27. The blood pressure of a young male human being is—
(*a*) 110/70   (*b*) 120/80
(*c*) 135/90   (*d*) 140/100

28. All of the following contain minerals, except—
(*a*) fruits   (*b*) jaggery
(*c*) milk   (*d*) vegetables

29. As the number of animals in pond increases, the number of plants in the same pond—
(*a*) increase   (*b*) decrease
(*c*) remain the same   (*d*) none of these

30. Dialyzer is a/an—
   (*a*) special clock which indicates the day and the date
   (*b*) apparatus used for recharging batteries
   (*c*) apparatus sometimes used in patients with defective renal function
   (*d*) meter used for controlling volume of sound

31. In summer, water is stored in unglazed earthen pots because—
   (*a*) these are cheap
   (*b*) more water can be stored in them
   (*c*) evaporation through pores makes the water cooler
   (*d*) earthen pots do not need as much rinsing and cleaning as metal vessels do

32. Which of the following regulates and controls the entry of light into the human eye?
   (*a*) Anterior chamber (*b*) Cornea
   (*c*) Iris   (*d*) Retina

33. All of the following are caused by viruses except—
   (*a*) jaundice   (*b*) influenza
   (*c*) typhoid   (*d*) mumps

34. Sprain, a condition normally encountered, is related to—
   (*a*) Painful muscular contrition's
   (*b*) Tears or breaks in ligaments or tendons
   (*c*) Tears or breaks in muscles
   (*d*) Inflammation of the connective tissue surrounding a tendon

35. All of the following can be reproduced by the use of respective seeds, except—
   (*a*) Cauliflower   (*b*) Peas
   (*c*) Potato   (*d*) Tomato

36. Which of the following properties of soaps and detergents helps to remove dirt from clothes?
   (*a*) Capillary action (*b*) Interfacial torsion
   (*c*) Osmosis   (*d*) None of these

37. Which of the following statements about diseases is not correct?
   (*a*) Patients suffering from diabetes need to be administered insulin
   (*b*) Diphtheria is not a communicable disease
   (*c*) Chemotherapy is resorted to as a treatment of patients suffering from cancer
   (*d*) Meningitis affects the brain

38. A term that may be applied to all disease producing micro-organisms is—
   (*a*) streptococci   (*b*) viruses
   (*c*) saprophytic   (*d*) pathogenic

39. Toxin is a poisonous substance produced by—
   (*a*) some higher plants
   (*b*) certain animals
   (*c*) pathogenic bacteria
   (*d*) all of these

40. The air we inhale is a mixture of gases. Which of the following gases in this mixture is highest in percentage?
   (*a*) Carbon dioxide (*b*) Nitrogen
   (*c*) Oxygen   (*d*) Ozone

41. A substance used to destroy micro-organisms and render the material sterile is called—
   (*a*) an antigen   (*b*) a disinfectant
   (*c*) an antitoxin (*d*) an antibiotic

42. Absence or inadequacy of proteins in the human diet will produce all of the following results, except—
   (*a*) body's defences against infections will weaken
   (*b*) production of hormones needed by the body will be impaired
   (*c*) conversion of heat by the body cells into energy, which sustains life, will be impaired
   (*d*) body's growth will be impaired

43. Which of the following act as a channel of transmission of blood to the heart in the human body?
   (*a*) Arteries   (*b*) Muscle fibres
   (*c*) Nerves   (*d*) Veins

44. As the number of micro-organisms in a soil increases, the amount of humus in the same soil—
   (*a*) increases
   (*b*) decreases
   (*c*) remains unchanged
   (*d*) micro-organisms do not play any role in the formation of humus

45. To prevent loss of weight, plants reduce transpiration by—
   (*a*) shedding of leaves
   (*b*) reducing the size of leaves
   (*c*) developing hair around stomata
   (*d*) all of these

46. Why is tungsten used in the manufacture of electric bulbs?
(*a*) It has high melting point
(*b*) It is cheaper than other metals
(*c*) It is both durable and economical
(*d*) It makes the bulb-light brighter

47. A labourer doing heavy work requires about—
(*a*) 4,500 calories per day
(*b*) 3,500 calories per day
(*c*) 2,500 calories per day
(*d*) none of these

48. In a normal human being how much time does food take to reach the end of the intestine for complete absorption?
(*a*) about 8 hours   (*b*) about 12 hours
(*c*) about 16 hours   (*d*) about 18 hours

49. A fisherman on the bank of a pond is attempting to spear a fish. He should—
(*a*) aim above where he sees the fish
(*b*) aim directly at the fish
(*c*) aim below the fish
(*d*) none of these

50. Aphasia is an ailment which affects—
(*a*) hearing   (*b*) eyesight
(*c*) memory   (*d*) Speech

51. The catabolism represents—-
(*a*) Series of biochemical reactions leading to release of energy
(*b*) Series of biochemical reactions leading to storage of energy
(*c*) Consumption of energy
(*d*) None of the above

52. Creatine Phosphate releases energy
(*a*) Directly
(*b*) With the help of glucose
(*c*) With the help of ATP
(*d*) All of the above

53. The main postural deformity among young girls is
(*a*) Kyphosis   (*b*) Lordosis
(*c*) Scoliosis   (*d*) Arousal

54. Renal glands produce
(*a*) Adrenalin
(*b*) Renin
(*c*) Pepsin
(*d*) None of the above

55. Which disease is also called 'lockjaw'?

(*a*) Tetanus   (*b*) Rabies
(*c*) Leprosy   (*d*) Measles

56. Which of the following diseases is called hydrophobia?
(*a*) Tetanus   (*b*) Leprosy
(*c*) Rabies   (*d*) Chickenpox

57. Which of the following is a viral disease affecting central nervous system ?
(*a*) Chicken pox   (*b*) Rabies
(*c*) Tetanus   (*d*) Leprosy

58. Which of the following is the measles vaccine
(*a*) DPT   (*b*) Quinine
(*c*) MMR   (*d*) TIG

59. Which disease is transmitted from infected mammals to man?
(*a*) Chickenpox   (*b*) Malaria
(*c*) Rabies   (*d*) AIDS

60. Which of the following is not a source of protein?
(*a*) Eggs   (*b*) Meat
(*c*) Oil   (*d*) Milk

61. How many calories are required per kg of body weight every hour?
(*a*) 1 Kcal   (*b*) 1.3 Kcal
(*c*) 2 Kcal   (*d*) 2.5 Kcal

62. Of the following , the rich source of calcium is
(*a*) Milk   (*b*) Nuts
(*c*) Meat   (*d*) Eggs

63. A rich source of Vitamin A is
(*a*) Citrus fruits   (*b*) Banana
(*c*) Grape-fruit   (*d*) Apricot

64. Citrus fruits are rich in
(*a*) Vitamin A   (*b*) Vitamin B
(*c*) Vitamin C   (*d*) Vitamin D

65. Bread, cereals and rice provide with most of the
(*a*) Carbohydrates   (*b*) Proteins
(*c*) Vitamins   (*d*) Minerals

66. Make correct pairs
A. Milk, Cheese, yogurt 1. Carbohydrates
B. Meat , Poultry, Fish 2. Calcium & nuts
C. Vegetable group   3. Protein
D. Bread, Rice,   4. Vitamins
   Cereal

Codes :
(*a*) A-2, B-4, C-3, D-1
(*b*) A-2, B-3, C-4, D-1
(*c*) A-1, B-3, C-2, D-4
(*d*) A-1, B-4, C-3, D-2

67. Sunlight is a source of
(*a*) Vitamin A　　(*b*) Vitamin B
(*c*) Vitamin C　　(*d*) Vitamin D

68. Nitrogen forms a part of
(*a*) Proteins　　(*b*) Vitamins
(*c*) Fats　　(*d*) Carbohydrates

69. Obesity does not cause
(*a*) Infertility
(*b*) Cancer
(*c*) Diabetes
(*d*) Ischaemic heart diesease

70. The source of acid rain is
(*a*) Nitrous oxide　　(*b*) Nitric oxide
(*c*) CFCS　　(*d*) CO_2

71. Which of the water pollutant is a source of water borne diseases like cholera and gastroenteritis?
(*a*) Animal Waste　　(*b*) Sewage
(*c*) Fertilizers　　(*d*) Mercury

72. Poor illumination in industries is a cause of
(*a*) Physical hazard
(*b*) Chemical hazard
(*c*) Biological hazard
(*d*) Mechanical hazard

73. Exposure to Ultraviolet radiation is a
(*a*) Mechanical hazard
(*b*) Physical hazard
(*c*) Chemical hazard
(*d*) Biological hazard

74. Chilbians , frost , bite are caused due to
(*a*) Physical agents
(*b*) Chemical agents
(*c*) Biological agents
(*d*) Mechanical agents

75. Lung cancer is caused due to
(*a*) Physical agents
(*b*) Chemical agents
(*c*) Biological agents
(*d*) Mechanical agents

76. Diseases like hypertension, industrial neurosis, peptic ulcer are of
(*a*) Physical origin
(*b*) Chemical origin
(*c*) Biological origin
(*d*) Psychological origin

77. Which form of Hepatitis was initially called the serum hepatitis?
(*a*) Hepatitis A　　(*b*) Hepatitis B
(*c*) Hepatitis C　　(*d*) Hepatitis D

78. Which hepatitis virus spreads by direct contact?
(*a*) Hepatitis A　　(*b*) Hepatitis B
(*c*) Hepatitis C　　(*d*) Hepatitis D

79. HIV Virus causes
(*a*) AIDS　　(*b*) Hepatitis C
(*c*) Hepatitis B　　(*d*) TB

80. Match the following
A. Cholera　　1. Mycobacterium
B. Chickenpox 2. Vibrio Cholera
C. Tuberculosis 3. Mycobacterium leprae
D. Leprosy　　4. Varicella virus
Codes :
(*a*) A-2, B-3, C-1, D-4
(*b*) A-2, B-4, C-1, D-3
(*c*) A-1, B-3, C-2, D-4
(*d*) A-3, B-4, C-1, D-2

81. Reye syndrome is associated with
(*a*) Cholera　　(*b*) AIDS
(*c*) Leprosy　　(*d*) Chickenpox

82. Which of the following is a disease caused by virus?
(*a*) Cholera　　(*b*) Tuberculosis
(*c*) Leprosy　　(*d*) Chickenpox

83. Which communicable disease is also known as Hansen's disease?
(*a*) Hepatitis A　　(*b*) Tuberculosis
(*c*) Rabies　　(*d*) Leprosy

84. Which of the following is a bacterial disease of skin and nervous system?
(*a*) Chickenpox　　(*b*) Measles
(*c*) Leprosy　　(*d*) Tetanus

85. Unhealthy eating patterns do not cause
(*a*) Anemia　　(*b*) AIDS
(*c*) Dental Caries　　(*d*) Obesity

86. Which nutrients are essential to growth and repair of muscle and other body tissues?
    (*a*) Proteins   (*b*) Minerals
    (*c*) Roughage   (*d*) Vitamins

87. The inorganic elements occurring in the body and which are critical to its normal functioning are
    (*a*) Vitamins   (*b*) Proteins
    (*c*) Carbohydrates   (*d*) Minerals

89. An athlete weighing 50 kg who trains for two hours required an intake of approximately
    (*a*) 2410 Kcal   (*b*) 2800 Kcal
    (*c*) 3000 Kcal   (*d*) 4500 Kcal

90. Sugar, sweets, bread and cakes are rich sources of :
    (*a*) Carbohydrates   (*b*) Fats
    (*c*) Proteins   (*d*) Roughage

91. Who opened the first Olympics of modern era?
    (*a*) Prince Constantine
    (*b*) Pierre de Coubertin
    (*c*) King George
    (*d*) Georgious Averoff

92. The number of members of IOC on its innception were
    (*a*) 12   (*b*) 13
    (*c*) 14   (*d*) 15

93. Who was the first IOC President?
    (*a*) Pierre de Coubertin
    (*b*) Avery Brundage
    (*c*) Lord Killanin
    (*d*) Demetrius Vikelas

94. Who served as the President of IOC for maximum years?
    (*a*) Demetrius Vikelas
    (*b*) Avery Brundage
    (*c*) Heni de Baillet
    (*d*) Pierre de Coubertin

95. Who is the present President of IOC?
    (*a*) J. sigfrid Edstrom
    (*b*) Lord Killanin
    (*c*) Jvan Antonio Samaranch
    (*d*) Jacques Rogge

96. What is "a state of complete physical, mental and social well being and not merely the absence of disease and deformity"?
    (*a*) Physiology   (*b*) Recreation
    (*c*) Health   (*d*) Growth

97. Physical education as well as sports experienced a 'golden age' in which ancient country?
    (*a*) Greece   (*b*) Italy
    (*c*) Rome   (*d*) Germany

98. The first Olympics were held in honour of which supreme God?
    (*a*) Jupiter   (*b*) Zeus
    (*c*) Venus   (*d*) Helena

99. The first Olympics games were held in
    (*a*) 726 B.C.   (*b*) 776 B.C.
    (*c*) 756 B.C.   (*d*) 784 B.C.

100. The Olympic games are held every
    (*a*) Third year   (*b*) Fifty year
    (*c*) Second year   (*d*) Fourth year

ANSWERS

1. (*c*)	2. (*c*)	3. (*a*)	4. (*c*)	5. (*b*)	6. (*d*)	7. (*a*)	8. (*c*)
9. (*a*)	10. (*b*)	11. (*b*)	12. (*a*)	13. (*b*)	14. (*c*)	15. (*b*)	16. (*a*)
17. (*c*)	18 (*a*)	19. (*c*)	20. (*c*)	21. (*a*)	22. (*d*)	23. (*c*)	24. (*c*)
25. (*c*)	26. (*a*)	27. (*b*)	28. (*c*)	29. (*b*)	30. (*c*)	31. (*c*)	32. (*c*)
33. (*c*)	34. (*b*)	35. (*c*)	36. (*b*)	37. (*b*)	38. (*d*)	39. (*d*)	40. (*b*)
41. (*b*)	42. (*c*)	43. (*d*)	44. (*a*)	45. (*d*)	46. (*a*)	47. (*b*)	48. (*b*)
49. (*c*)	50. (*d*)	51. (*a*)	52. (*c*)	53. (*b*)	54. (*a*)	55. (*a*)	56. (*c*)
57. (*b*)	58. (*c*)	59. (*c*)	60. (*c*)	61. (*d*)	62. (*a*)	63. (*d*)	64. (*c*)
65. (*a*)	66. (*b*)	67. (*d*)	68. (*a*)	69. (*b*)	70. (*b*)	71. (*b*)	72. (*a*)
73. (*b*)	74. (*a*)	75. (*b*)	76. (*d*)	77. (*b*)	78. (*a*)	79. (*a*)	80. (*b*)
81. (*d*)	82. (*d*)	83. (*d*)	84. (*c*)	85. (*b*)	86. (*a*)	87. (*d*)	89. (*a*)
90. (*a*)	91. (*c*)	92. (*c*)	93. (*d*)	94. (*d*)	95. (*d*)	96. (*c*)	97. (*a*)
98. (*b*)	99. (*b*)	100. (*d*)					

7. PHYSICAL FITNESS

INTRODUCTION

Today, there is a growing emphasis on looking good, feeling good and living longer. Increasingly, scientific evidence tells us that one of the keys to achieving these ideals is fitness and exercises. Getting moving is a challenge because today physical activity is less a part of our daily lives. There are fewer jobs that require physical exertion. We have become a mechanically mobile society, relying on machines rather than muscles to get around. In addition, we have become a nation of observers with more people (including children) spending their leisure time pursuing just that - leisure. Consequently, statistics show that obesity and over weight, the problems that come with high blood pressure, diabetes, cardiac arrest, etc. are on the rise. But statistics also show that preventive medicine pays off, so one should not wait until his/her doctor gives an ultimatum. Every one must take the initiative to get active now.

The decision to carry out a physical fitness program cannot be taken lightly. It requires a lifelong commitment of time and effort. Exercise must become one of those things that you do without question, like bathing and brushing your teeth. Unless you are convinced of the benefits of fitness and the risks of unfitness, you will not succeed. It has been realised that fitness adds not only years to one's life, but life to one's years.

Patience is essential. Don't try to do too much too soon and don't quit before you have a chance to experience the rewards of improved fitness. You can't regain physical fitness in a few days or weeks what you have lost in years of sedentary living, but you can get it back if you persevere. And the prize is worth the price.

In the following section you will find the basic information you need to begin and maintain a personal physical fitness program. These guidelines are intended for the average healthy adult. It tells you what your goals should be and how often, how long and how hard you must exercise to achieve them. It also includes information that will make your workouts easier, safer and more satisfying. The rest is up to you.

DEFINITIONS OF PHYSICAL FITNESS

Physical fitness is to the human body what fine-tuning is to an engine. It enables us to perform up to our potential. Fitness can be described as a condition that helps us for better look, pleasant feel and do our best.

More specifically, it is: "The ability to perform daily tasks vigorously and alertly, with energy left over for enjoying leisure-time activities and meeting emergency demands. It is the ability to endure, to hear up, to withstand stress, to carry on in circumstances where an unfit person could not continue, and is a major basis for good health and well-being."

"Physical fitness refers to the organic capacity of the individual to perform the normal task of daily living without undue tiredness or fatigue having reserves of strength and energy available to meet satisfactorily any emergency demands suddenly placed upon him." *– Nixon*

"Fitness is that state which characterizes the degree to which the person is able to function. Fitness is an individual matter. It implies the ability of each person to live most effectively with his potential. Ability to function depends upon physical, mental, emotional and social components of fitness, all of which are related to each other and mutually interdependent." *– Kirchner*

Physical fitness involves the performance of the heart and lungs, and the muscles of the body.

And, since what we do with our bodies also affects what we can do with our minds, fitness influences to some degree qualities such as mental alertness and emotional stability.

As you undertake your fitness program, it's important to remember that fitness is an individual quality that differs from person to person. It is influenced by age, sex, heredity, personal habits, exercise and eating habits, diet, attitude towards life, anxiety, tension and stress, values of physical fitness, institutional curicular and state's policy/ legislation, You can't do anything about the first three factors. However, it is within your power to change and improve the others where needed.

COMPONENTS OF PHYSICAL FITNESS

Exercise scientists have identified nine elements/ components that comprise the definition of fitness. The following lists each of the nine elements and an example of how they are used :

Strength - the extent to which muscles can exert force by contracting against resistance (holding or restraining an object or person)

Power - the ability to exert maximum muscular contraction instantly in an explosive burst of *movements* (*jumping or sprint starting*)

Speed - the quickness of movement of limb, whether this is the leg of a runner or the arm of the shot putter.

Agility - the ability to perform a series of explosive power movements in rapid succession in opposing directions (Zig Zag running or cutting movements)

Balance - the ability to control the body's position, either stationary (e.g. a handstand) or while moving (e.g. a gymnastics stunt)

Flexibility - the ability to achieve an extended range of motion without being impeded by excess tissue, i.e. fat or muscle (Executing a leg split)

***Local Muscle* Endurance -** a single muscle's ability to perform sustained work (Rowing or cycling)

Cardiovascular Endurance - the heart's ability to deliver blood to working muscles and their ability to use it (Running long distances)

Strength Endurance - a muscle's ability to perform a maximum contracture time after time

(Continuous explosive rebounding through an entire basketball game)

Co-ordination - the ability to integrate the above listed components so that effective movements are achieved.

Physical fitness is the most easily understood by examining these components, or elements, or "parts." There is widespread agreement that following four elements are basic.

1. Endurance - the ability to deliver oxygen and nutrients to tissues, and to remove wastes, over sustained periods of time. Long runs and swims are among the methods employed in measuring this component.

2. Strength - the ability of a muscle to exert force for a brief period of time. Upper-body strength, for example, can be measured by various weight-lifting exercises.

3. Speed - the quickness of movement of limb, whether this is the leg of a runner or the arm of the shot putter.

4. Flexibility - the ability to move joints and use muscles through their full range of motion. The sit-and –reach but is a good measure of flexibility of the lower back and backs of the upper legs.

Body Composition is also considered a component of fitness. It refers to the makeup of the body in terms of lean mass (muscle, bone, vital tissue and organs) and fat mass. An optimal ratio of fat to lean mass is an indication of fitness, and the right types of exercise will help you decrease body fat and increase or maintain muscle mass.

BENEFITS OF PHYSICAL FITNESS:

Exercise or fitness is not just for Olympic hopefuls or supermodels. In fact, you are never too unfit, too young or too old to get started. Regardless of your age, gender or role in life, you can benefit from regular physical activity. If you are committed, exercise in combination with a sensible diet can help to provide an overall sense of well-being and can even help to prevent chronic illness, disability and premature death. Some of the benefits of increased physical activity or physical fitness are:

Improved Health
- Increased efficiency of heart and lungs
- Reduced cholesterol levels
- Increased muscle strength
- Reduced blood pressure
- Reduced risk of major illnesses such as diabetes and heart disease
- Weight loss

Improved Sense of Well-Being
- More Energy
- Less stress
- Improved quality of sleep
- Improved ability to cope with stress
- Increased mental sharpness

Improved Appearance
- Weight loss
- Toned muscles
- Improved posture

Enhanced Social Life
- Improved self-image
- Increased opportunities to make new friends.
- Increased opportunities to share an activity with friends or family members

Increased Stamina
- Increased productivity
- Increased physical capabilities
- Less frequent injuries
- Improved immunity to minor illnesses

DEVELOPMENT OF PHYSICAL FITNESS

By improving the basic components physical fitness such as endurance, strength, flexibility, speed and agility (Co-ordinative ability) one can develop physical fitness. These elements can be developed through different means/methods of training. Before hand, one must know about warming and cooling down and its importance.

Endurance : The objective of endurance training is to develop the energy production system(s) to meet the demands of the event. Endurance can be developed using continuous and interval running.

ENERGY PRODUCTION SYSTEMS

In the human body, food energy is used to make adenosine troposphere (ATP) the chemical compound that supplies energy for muscular contraction. Since ATP is in very low concentrations in the muscle, and it decreases only to a minor extent, tightly controlled energy pathways exist for the constant regeneration of ATP as muscular contraction continues. For continuous exercise, ATP must be re-synthesised at the same rate as it is utilised.

Types of endurance: The types of endurance are:
1. Aerobic endurance
2. Anaerobic endurance
3. Speed endurance
4. Strength endurance

A sound basis of aerobic endurance is fundamental for all events.

Aerobic Endurance

Aerobic means 'with oxygen'. During aerobic work the body is working at a level that the demands for oxygen and fuel can be met by the body's intake. The only waste products formed are carbon dioxide and water. These are removed as sweat and by breathing out.

Aerobic endurance can further be sub-divided as follows:
- Short aerobic - 2 minutes to 8 minutes (lactic/aerobic)
- Medium aerobic - 8 minutes to 30 minutes (mainly aerobic)
- Long aerobic - 30 minutes + (aerobic)

Aerobic endurance is developed through the use of
- Duration runs to improve maximum oxygen uptake (VO2max)
- Interval training to improve the heart as a muscular pump.

This can be achieved through different aerobic activities or exercises.

What is Aerobic Exercise?

The American College of Sports Medicine (ACSM) defines aerobic exercise as "any activity that uses large muscle groups, can be maintained continuously, and is rhythmic in nature." It is a type of exercise that overloads the heart and lungs and causes them to work harder than at rest. The important idea behind aerobic exercise today, is to get up and get moving! There are more activities than ever to choose from, whether it is a new activity or an old one. Find something you enjoy doing that keeps your heart rate high for a continuous time period and get moving to a healthier life.

Types of Aerobic Exercise
1. Aerobic Dance
2. Walking for Fitness
3. Rope Skipping
4. Running
5. Stair Climbing
6. Swimming
7. Bicycling
8. Cross Country

Anaerobic Endurance

Anaerobic means 'without oxygen'. During anaerobic work, involving maximum effort, the body is working so hard that the demands for oxygen and fuel go above the rate of supply and the muscles have to rely on the stored reserves of fuel. In this case waste products gather, the main one being lactic acid. The muscles, being hungry of oxygen, take the body into a state known as oxygen debt. The body's stored fuel soon runs out and activity ceases painfully. Activity will not be resumed until the lactic acid is removed and the oxygen debt repaid. Fortunately the body can resume limited activity after even only a small amount of the oxygen debt has been repaid. Since lactic acid is produced the correct term for this pathway is lactic anaerobic energy pathway. The alactic anaerobic pathway is the one in which the body is working anaerobically but without the production of lactic acid. This pathway can exist only so long as the fuel actually stored in the muscle lasts, approximately 4 seconds at maximum effort.

Anaerobic endurance can be sub-divided as follows:

- Short anaerobic - less than 25 seconds (mainly alactic)
- Medium anaerobic - 25 seconds to 60 seconds (mainly lactic)
- Long anaerobic - 60 seconds to 120 seconds (lactic + aerobic)

Using repetition methods of relatively high intensity work with limited recovery can develop anaerobic endurance.

Speed Endurance

Speed endurance is used to develop the co-ordination of muscle contraction in the climate of endurance. Repetition methods are used with a high number of sets, low number of repetitions per set and intensity greater than 85% with distances covered from 60% to 120% of racing distance. Competition and time trials can be used in the development of speed endurance.

Strength Endurance

Strength endurance is used to develop the athlete's capacity to maintain the quality of their muscles' contractile force in a climate of endurance. All athletes need to develop a basic level of strength endurance. Examples of activities to develop strength endurance are weight training, circuit training, Fartlek, hill running etc.

STRENGTH

The common definition is *the ability to exert a force against a resistance.* The strength needed for a sprinter to explode from the blocks is different from the strength needed by a weight lifter to lift a 200 kg barbell. This, therefore, implies that there are different types of strength.

Types of Strength

- Maximum strength -*the greatest force that is possible in a single maximum contraction*
- Explosive strength - *the ability to overcome a resistance with a fast contraction*
- Strength endurance - *the ability to express force many times over*

How do Muscles Get Strong ?

A muscle will only strengthen, when it is worked beyond its normal operation, or it is overloaded. Overload can be progressed by increasing the:

- Number of repetitions of an exercise
- Number of sets of the exercise
- Intensity - reduced recover time

Development of Strength

Maximum strength can be developed with

- Weight training
- Explosive strength can be developed with:
- Conditioning exercises
- Medicine ball exercises
- Polymeric exercises
- Weight training
- Strength endurance can be developed with:
- Circuit training
- Dumbbell exercise
- Weight training
- Hill running

SPEED

Speed is the quickness of movement of limb, whether this is the legs of a runner or the arm of the shot putter. Speed is an integral part of every sport and can be expressed as any one of, or combination of the following

- Maximum speed
- Explosive strength (power)
- Speed endurance

Factors Influencing Speed

Speed is influenced by the athlete's mobility, special strength, strength endurance and technique.

Energy System for Speed

The anaerobic alactic pathway supplies energy for absolute speed. The anaerobic (without Oxygen) alactic (without lactate) energy system is best challenged as an athlete approaches top speed between 30 and 60m while running at 95% to 100% of maximum. This speed component of anaerobic metabolism lasts for approximately six seconds and should be trained when no muscle fatigue is present (usually after 24 to 36 hours of rest).

Development of Speed

The technique of sprinting must be rehearsed at slow speeds and then transferred to run at maximum speed. The stimulation, excitation and correct firing order of the motor units, composed of a motor nerve (Neuron) and the group of muscles that it supplies, makes it possible for high frequency movements to occur. The whole process is not totally clear but the complex coordination and timing of the motor units and muscles most certainly must be rehearsed at high speeds to implant the correct patterns.

Flexibility and a correct warm up will affect stride length and frequency. Stride length can be improved by developing muscular strength, power, strength endurance and running technique. The development of speed is highly specific and to achieve it we should ensure that:

- Flexibility is developed and maintained all year round.
- Strength and speed is developed in parallel
- Skill development (technique) is pre-learned, rehearsed and perfected before it is done at high-speed levels.
- Speed training is developed by using high velocity for brief intervals. This will ultimately bring into play the correct neuromuscular pathways and energy sources used.

FLEXIBILITY

Flexibility is the ability to perform a joint action through a range of movement. In any movement there are two groups of muscles at work:

1. protagonist muscles which cause the movement to take place
2. Opposing the movement and determining the amount of flexibility are the antagonistic muscles.

Flexibility Training

The objective of flexibility training is to improve the range of stretch of the antagonistic muscles.

Benefits of Flexibility

Flexibility plays an important part in the preparation of athletes by developing a range of movement to allow technical development and assisting in the prevention of injury.

Flexibility Exercises

The various techniques of stretching may be grouped as Static, Ballistic and Assisted. In both Static and Ballistic exercises the athlete is in control of the movements. In Assisted the movement is controlled by an external force that is usually a partner.

Static Stretching

Static stretching involves gradually easing into the stretch position and holding the position. The amount of time a static stretch is held may be anything from 6 seconds to 2 minutes. Often in static stretching you are advised to move further into the stretch position as the stretch sensation subsides.

Ballistic Stretching

Ballistic stretching involves some form of rapid movement into the required stretch position. Where the event requires a ballistic movement, it is appropriate and perhaps necessary to conduct ballistic stretching exercises. Start off with the movement at half speed for a couple of repetitions and then gradually work up to full speed. Appropriate preparatory static stretching exercises should be conducted before any ballistic exercises are carried out.

Assisted Stretching

Assisted stretching involves the assistance of a partner who must fully understand what his role is otherwise the risk of injury is high. A partner can be employed to assist with Partner stretches.

Partner Stretches

Your partner assists you to maintain the stretch position or help you ease into the stretch position as the sensation of stretch subsides. You should aim to be full relaxed and breath easily throughout the exercise. Partner assisted stretches are best used as developmental exercises, with each stretch being held for thirty seconds.

Methods

Static methods produce far fewer instances of muscle soreness, injury and damage to connective tissues than ballistic methods. Static methods are simple to carry out and may be conducted virtually anywhere. For maximum gains in flexibility in the shortest possible time ballistic stretches technique is the most appropriate. Where the technique requires ballistic movement, ballistic stretches should be employed.

When conducting flexibility exercises it is recommended to perform them in the following order Static, assisted and then dynamic.

Flexibility exercises could be part of:
- the warm up programme
- a stand alone unit of work.

It is considered beneficial to conduct flexibility exercises as part of the warm down programme but should not include ballistic exercises, as the muscles are fatigued and more prone to injury.

MEASURING YOUR HEART RATE

Heart rate is widely accepted as a good method for measuring intensity during running, swimming, cycling and other aerobic activities. Exercise that doesn't raise your heart rate to a certain level and keep it there for 20 minutes won't contribute significantly to cardiovascular fitness.

The heart rate you should maintain is called your Target Heart Rate. There are several ways of arriving at this figure. One of the simplest is: Maximum Heart Rate (220 - age) × 70%. Thus, the target heart rate for a 40 year-old would be 126.

Some methods for feuding out the target heart rate take individual differences into consideration. Here is one of them

1. Subtract age from 220 to find Maximum Heart Rate.
2. Subtract resting heart rate (see below) from maximum heart rate to determine Heart Rate Reserve.
3. Take 70% of heart rate reserve to determine Heart Rate Raise.
4. Add heart rate raise to resting heart rate to find Target Heart Rate.

Resting heart rate should be determined by taking your pulse after sitting quietly for five minutes. When checking heart rate during a workout, take your pulse within five seconds after interrupting exercise because it starts to go down once you stop moving. Count pulse for 10 seconds and multiply by six to get the per-minute heart rate.

CONTROLLING YOUR WEIGHT

The key to weight control is keeping energy intake (food) and energy output (physical activity) in balance. When you consume only as many calories as your body needs, your weight will usually remain constant. If you take in more calories than your body needs, you will put on excess fat. If you utilise more energy than you take in, you will burn excess fat.

Exercise plays an important role in weight control by increasing energy output, calling on stored calories for extra fuel. Recent studies show that not only does exercise increase metabolism during a workout, but it causes your metabolism to stay increased for a period of time after exercising, allowing you to burn more calories.

How much exercise is needed to make a difference in your weight depends on the amount and type of activity, and on how much you eat. Aerobic exercise burns body fat. A medium-sized adult would have to walk more than 30 miles to burn up 3,500 calories, the equivalent of one pound of fat. Although that may seem like a lot, you don't have to walk the 30 miles all at once. Walking a mile a day for 30 days will achieve the same result, provided you don't increase your food intake to negate the effects of walking

If you consume 100 calories a day more than your body needs, you will gain approximately 10 pounds in year. You could take that weight off, or keep it off, by doing 30 minutes of moderate exercise daily. The combination of exercise and diet offers the most flexible and effective approach to weight control.

Since muscle tissue weighs more than fat tissue, and exercise develops muscle to a certain degree, your bathroom scale won't necessarily tell you whether or not you are "fat." Well-muscled individuals, with relatively little body fat, invariably are "overweight" according to standard weight charts. If you are doing a regular program of strength training, your muscles will increase in weight, and possibly your overall weight will increase. Body composition is a better indicator of your body condition than body weight.

Lack of physical activity causes muscles to get soft, and if food intake is not decreased, added body weight is almost always fat. Once-active people, who continue to eat as they always have after settling into sedentary lifestyles, tend to suffer from "creeping obesity."

FACTORS INFLUENCING PHYSICAL FITNESS
Age

Age is the major factor influencing physical fitness. Usually maturity can be defined by chronological, skeletal and physiological age. The period of life is generally divided into infancy, childhoods, adolescence, adulthood and seniors. So children and adolescence must not be regarded as miniature versions of adults.

They are unique at each stage in their development. Their physiological and physical performance in term of physical fitness mainly depends on the growth and development of their bones, muscles, nerves and other organs. As children size increases, their functional capacities along with physical fitness also increases/ improves.

The child is physiologically distinct from the adult and must be considered differently while planning fitness programme. The training can improve the physical fitness of the child. Generally youngsters, adapt well to the same type of training used by adults. But training programme for children and adolescents should be specifically prepared for each age group, keeping in mind the developmental factors associated with that age

Studies have shown that humans tend to decrease their physical activity as they grow older, which affects the physical fitness. When older people participate in training, most of the changes associated with aging are lessened. It is clear that mode and nature of fitness training is a individual matter, which differs from person to person.

Sex

Prior to adolescence boys and girls do not differ substantially in height, weight, girth, bone width and body composition. But at maturity they differed significantly on various parameters. These Physical, Physiological and anthropometrical differences also affect the physical fitness of male and female. Thus the sex differences affect the type of exercise frequency of participation, duration and intensity of the exercise for developing physical fitness. Due consideration should be given to these factors while preparing a training programme for males and females.

Body Composition

Body composition is the proportion of the lean body mass and depot fat and it is one of the most important morphological features characterising human organisation. Obesity is defined as that percentage of body fat that begins to increase the chances for cardiovascular disease. Ideal body fat levels for men are 12% to 17% and 18% to 22% for women. Body fat is essential for certain bodily functions. Sometimes body type, determined genetically, prevents an individual from achieving unrealistic body shaping goals. There are basically three body types. The Endomorph is characterized by a large block shaped body. The Mesomorph is characterized by a solid muscular structure. The Ectomorph is characterized by a frail, slight build and very little fat.

Body composition assessment has revealed that athletes generally have physique characteristics unique to their specific sports. For example, field event athletes have large quantities of lean tissue and a high percent body fat whereas long distance runners have the least amount of lean body and fat weight. Now a days body composition is considered one of the components of fitness as it plays important role in developing fitness. For athletes, weight gain must be in the form of lean body weight i.e. muscle mass. Strength training seems to increase muscle mass and strength effectively. Actually, individual physiologic variations and training factors affect weight gain. Because of this body weight and body fat should be monitored on a regular basis and training programme should be developed accordingly.

Diet

Diet plays an important role in maintaining physical fitness level. The key to weight control is keeping energy intake (food) and energy output (physical exercises) in balance. When we consume only as many calories as our body needs, our weight will remain constant. If we take in more calories than our body needs, we will put on more fat. If we expand more energy than we take in we will burn excess fat. Diet requirement varies from training to training and form individual to individual. An athlete required good diet while he is undergoing vigorous training schedules. While planning a physical fitness programme diet factor must also be given due consideration.

Diet and Physical Activities

Do you know that you need to burn off 3,500 calories more than you take in to lose just one kg?

If you're overweight, eating your usual amount of calories while increasing activity is good for you, but eating fewer calories and being more active is even better. The following chart gives you an idea of the calories used per hour in common activities. Calories burned differ in proportion to body weight. So these figures are averages.

Activity Calories Burned Per Hour

Calories burned per hour in different activities has been given in the following Table just for reference.

Calories burned per hour in some Activities

    Bicycling 6 mph 240
    Bicycling 12 mph 410
    Jogging 5.5 mph 740
    Jogging 7 mph 920
    Jumping rope 750
    Running in place 650
    Running 10 mph 1,280
    Cross-country 700
    Swimming 25 yds/min 275
    Swimming 50 yds/min 500
    Tennis (singles) 400
    Walking 2 mph 240
    Walking 4 mph 440

Climate

Physical fitness by and large also gets influenced by different climatic conditions such as winter, summer, humid etc.

When it's Hot or Humid:

- Exercise during cooler and/or less humid times of day. Try early morning or late evening.
- Drink plenty of fluids especially water. Avoid alcohol, which encourages dehydration.
- Wear light, loose-fitting clothes.
- Stop at the first sign of muscle cramping or dizziness.

When it's Cold:

- Dress in layers.
- Wear gloves to protect your hands.
- Wear a hat or cap. Up to 40% of body heat is lost through your neck and head.
- Adjust the size of your shoes if you need to wear thicker socks.
- Warm up slowly.
- Drink plenty of fluids. You can get dehydrated in the winter, too.
- Stop if you experience shivering, drowsiness or disorientation.

OBJECTIVE QUESTIONS

1. Ontogeny recapitulates phylogeny is the theory of:
   (*a*) evolution (*b*) reduction
   (*c*) recapitulation (*d*) Darwinism

2. Winter dormancy is:
   (*a*) hibernation (*b*) aestivation
   (*c*) pollination (*d*) none of these

3. Bronchitis is a disease of:
   (*a*) blood (*b*) liver
   (*c*) intestine (*d*) respiratory tract

4. What is meant by 'Organ Culture'?
   (*a*) Maintenance alive of a whole organ, after removal from the organism by partial immersion in a nutrient fluid.
   (*b*) Introduction of a new organ in an animal body with a view to create genetic mutation in the progenies of that animal.
   (*c*) Cultivation of organs in laboratory through the synthesis of tissues.
   (*d*) The aspects of culture in a community which are mainly dedicated by the needs of a specified organ of the human body.

5. BCG is used to prevent:
   (*a*) hydrophobia (*b*) cancer
   (*c*) neuralgia (*d*) tuberculosis

6. The molecules responsible for storing the genetic code are:
   (*a*) DNA (*b*) RNA
   (*c*) protein (*d*) Chromosome

7. Test-tube baby means:
   (*a*) ovum fertilized and developed in test tubes.
   (*b*) ovum fertilized in test tubes and developed in test tubes
   (*c*) ovum fertilized in test tubes and developed in uterus.
   (*d*) ovum developed without fertilization in test tubes.

8. What is the basic characteristic of antigens?
   (*a*) They are capable of stimulating the formation of hemoglobin in the blood.
   (*b*) They destroy hemoglobin.
   (*c*) They are capable of defending themselves against attack by antibodies.
   (*d*) They are capable of stimulating the formation of antibodies.

9. When White-flowered Fl plants were crossed to pure red-flowered plants; the progeny had all plants:
   (*a*) White flowered
   (*b*) Red flowered
   (*c*) Exhibiting 3:1 ratio of red to white-flowered plants.
   (*d*) Exhibiting 1:1 ratio of red to white-flowered plants.

10. A mature living cell without a nucleus is:
    (*a*) sieve cell (*b*) sieve tube
    (*c*) companion cell (*d*) vessel

11. In an adult human being, the number of vertebrae is:
    (*a*) 33 (*b*) 26
    (*c*) 36 (*d*) 56

12. The following bone is not found in man:
    (*a*) hummers (*b*) carpal
    (*c*) astragalus (*d*) atlas

13. Alimentary canal is usually longer in:
    (*a*) carnivores (*b*) herbivores
    (*c*) omnivores (*d*) insectivores

14. Which is the most fast spreading disease?
    (*a*) Malaria (*b*) Plague
    (*c*) Poliomyelitis (*d*) Leprosy

15. Seed dormancy is due to:
    (*a*) Abscisic acid (*b*) Cytokinins
    (*c*) IAA (*d*) Gibberellic acid

16. A bat is:
    (*a*) a mammal (*b*) a reptile
    (*c*) an amphibian (*d*) an avian

17. The Central Building Research Institute is located at:
    (*a*) Roorkee (*b*) Dhanbad
    (*c*) Chennai (*d*) Kolkata

18. A drop of oil is placed on the surface of water. Which of the following statement is correct?
- (*a*) It will remain on in as a sphere
- (*b*) It will spread as a thin layer
- (*c*) It will partly be as spherical droplet and partly as thin film
- (*d*) It will float as a distorted drop on the water surface

19. A drop of water breaks into two droplets of equal size. In this process which of the following statement is correct?
- (*a*) The sum of the temperature of the two droplets together is equal to the original drop
- (*b*) The sum of the masses of the two droplet is equal to the mass of the original drop
- (*c*) The sum of radii of the two droplet is equal to the original drop
- (*d*) The sum of the surface area of the two droplet is equal to the surface area of the original drop

20. If there were smaller gravitational effect which of the following forces do you think would alter in some respect?
- (*a*) Viscous force
- (*b*) Archimedes uplift
- (*c*) Electrostate force
- (*d*) None of the above

21. Which is the correct chronological order?
- A. Mendel's lows of inheritance
- B. Darwin's theory of evolution
- C. Blood circulation by Harvey
- D. De Vireo's theory of mutation
- (*a*) A, B, C, D   (*b*) D, B, C, A
- (*c*) B, D, A, C   (*d*) C, B, A, C

22. Human blood has the highest percentage of:
- (*a*) eosinophils   (*b*) basophils
- (*c*) neutrophils   (*d*) monocytes

23. Most abundant tissues of our body are
- (*a*) muscular   (*b*) connective
- (*c*) epithelial   (*d*) nervous

24. Normal adult human male has:
- (*a*) 10 gm of haemoglobin/1 00 gm of blood.
- (*b*) 14 gm of haemoglobin/100 gm of blood.
- (*c*) 18 gm of haemoglobin/100 gm of blood.
- (*d*) 24 gm of haemoglobin/100 gm of blood.

25. The outer layer of skin is called:
- (*a*) dermis   (*b*) epidermis
- (*c*) endodermis   (*d*) exodermis

26. Blood does not clot in the absence of Vitamin K because it is:
- (*a*) an essential component of the clot.
- (*b*) an essential component of the platelets.
- (*c*) an essential component of the prothrombin.
- (*d*) an esselitial component of the fibrinogen.

27. The nucleus is absent in:
- (*a*) algae   (*b*) fungi
- (*c*) Escherichia coli   (*d*) angiosperm

28. There is no atmosphere on moon because
- (*a*) It is closer to earth
- (*b*) It revolves round the earth
- (*c*) It gets light from the sun
- (*d*) The escape velocity of the gas molecules is less than their root mean square velocity here

29. Treatment of malaria fever by inoculation is out of question because plasmodium produces
- (*a*) a very few antibodies or antitoxins
- (*b*) few antibodies or antitoxins
- (*c*) no antibodies or antitoxins
- (*d*) none of the above

30. Sleeping on left side is useful because:
- (*a*) left side is pressed and given relaxation to the right side.
- (*b*) the heart is found on the left side of our body cavity.
- (*c*) the organs of left side are smaller than those on the right side
- (*d*) it gives maximum relaxation to the muscles of the right side and keeps the liver warm, relaxed and improves bile secretion.

31. The vaccine-preventable diseases associated with children are:
- (*a*) diphtheria, whopping cough, tuberculosis, ringworm, botulism.

(*b*) diphtheria, whopping cough, tuberculosis, botulism, trachoma

(*c*) diphtheria, whopping cough, tuberculosis, poliomyelitis, tetanus.

(*d*) diphtheria, whopping cough, tetanus, ringworm, trachoma.

32. Sugarcane is........plant.
(*a*) C_1 (*b*) C_2
(*c*) C_3 (*d*) C_4

33. The largest flower in the world is:
(*a*) Rafflesia   (*b*) Wolffia
(*c*) Ralffia   (*d*) Kaffia

34. Weightlessness experienced while orbiting the earth in space ships is the result of
(*a*) Inertia   (*b*) Acceleration
(*c*) Zero gravity   (*d*) Centre of gravity

35. What is tissue culture?
(*a*) Preparation of fragments of the cells of organism for biochemical examination.
(*b*) Japanese culture
(*c*) Name given to a special type of surgery
(*d*) None of the above

36. Which of the following glands in the human body is popularly called 'Adam's Apple'?
(*a*) Adernal   (*b*) Liver
(*c*) Thyroid   (*d*) Thymus

37. Which of the following is the richest source of protein?
(*a*) Egg   (*b*) Pulse
(*c*) Fresh milk   (*d*) Ground nut

38. People living in houses far removed from the municipal water tank often find it difficult to get water on the top floor even if is situated lower than the level of the Water tank. This is because
(*a*) There is loss of pressure when water is flowing
(*b*) There is generally some fault with the pipes otherwise water must reach upto the level of tank
(*c*) The pipes are not of uniform diameter
(*d*) People living in the house near the tank consume all the water in the tank

39. What do you mean by biopsy?
(*a*) Examination of tissue cut from living body.
(*b*) A study of organs of dead body
(*c*) A disease of eyes.
(*d*) A study of toxicological effects of plants.

40. 'Amnesia' is related to the loss of:
(*a*) Hearing   (*b*) Memory
(*c*) Sleep   (*d*) Appetite

41. Silver fish is:
(*a*) An insect
(*b*) A fish
(*c*) A fish made of silver
(*d*) A term used in politics

42. A boat with scrap-iron in it is floating in a lake. If the iron is thrown in the lake. What will happen to the water level of the lake?
(*a*) The level will rise
(*b*) The level will go down
(*c*) There will be no change in the water level
(*d*) If the water in the lake is saltish, then the level will go up

43. In a pressure cooker the cooking is fast because
(*a*) The boiling point of water is raised by the increased pressure inside the cooker
(*b*) The boiling point of water is lowered by pressure
(*c*) More steam is available to cook the food at 100°C
(*d*) More pressure is available to cook the food at 100°C

44. Identical twins are born when :
(*a*) two sperms fertilize one ovum
(*b*) two sperms fertilize two ovums simultaneously.
(*c*) one sperm fertilizes the ovum and zygote divides into two separate cells developing independently.
(*d*) one sperm fertilizes two ovums.

45. Which of the following is a physical basis of life ?
(*a*) Nucleus   (*b*) Ribosome
(*c*) Protoplasm   (*d*) Mitochondria

46. "AIDS" affects :
(*a*) blood cells of human body
(*b*) immunity system of humanbody
(*c*) growth of human body
(*d*) all of the above

47. Anatomy is the branch of science which deals with :
(*a*) Study of structure of animals and plants.
(*b*) Study of functioning of body organs.
(*c*) Study of animal behaviour.
(*d*) Study of cells and tissues.

48. Short duration crops are especially suitable for:
(*a*) hilly areas   (*b*) dry farming
(*c*) sandy areas   (*d*) wet farming

49. Fruits infested with larvae of pests, imported from abroad are more dangerous in India than in the country of their origin since :
(*a*) they will cause afforestation.
(*b*) they cannot be eliminated in India.
(*c*) natural predators who prey on them are not available in India.
(*d*) they are likely to transmit exotic diseases to the crops in India.

50. Which of the following factors is most responsible for the damage of stored food-grains ?
(*a*) Moisture content of the grains
(*b*) Aeration of the grains.
(*c*) Environmental humidity
(*d*) Environmental temperature

51. Which of the following phenomena causes removal of blood from the injured area?
(*a*) Muscle contraction
(*b*) Gravity
(*c*) Respiration
(*d*) All of the above

52. Which of the following forms of energy, has the highest velocity
(*a*) Cosmic waves
(*b*) X-rays
(*c*) Short-wave diathermy
(*d*) They are all equal

53. Which of the following forms of energy has the highest frequency?
(*a*) Cosmic waves
(*b*) X-rays
(*c*) FM radio waves
(*d*) Short wave diathermy

54. The method of heat transfer that involves the cooling of one object with the subsequent heating of another object through the circulation of air or water is -
(*a*) Radiation   (*b*) Evaporation
(*c*) Conduction   (*d*) Convection

55. The measure of the number of heat units required to raise a unit of mass by 1°C is termed-
(*a*) Calorie   (*b*) Thermal capacity
(*c*) Specific heat   (*d*) Change of state

56. Which of the following modalities has the greatest likelihood of frostbite?
(*a*) Ice immersion
(*b*) Reusable cold packs
(*c*) Ice massage
(*d*) Ice bag

57. Which of the following is a contradiction for the use of a paraffin bath?
(*a*) No range of motion
(*b*) Chronic condition
(*c*) Pain
(*d*) Skin conditions.

58. In which of the following modalities is, convection used as its method of heat transfer?
(*a*) Ice bag   (*b*) Whirlpool
(*c*) Hot packs   (*d*) Infrared lamp.

59. Which of the following is not a local effect of cold application?
(*a*) Decreased rate of cell metabolism
(*b*) Decreased muscle spindle activity
(*c*) Decreased nerve conduction velocity
(*d*) Decreased viscosity of fluids in the area

60. Which of the following modalities has the greatest dept of penetration?
(*a*) Moist heat pack   (*b*) Hot Whirlpool
(*c*) Infrared lamp   (*d*) Ice bag.

61. Which of the following is not a local effect of heat application?
(*a*) Increased rate of cell metabolism
(*b*) Increased elasticity of soft tissue
(*c*) Increased muscle tone
(*d*) Decreased muscle spasm.

62. Which of the following would be the modality of choice to cause physiochemical changes within the tissues?
(*a*) High voltage pulsed stimulation
(*b*) Interferential stimulation
(*c*) Low-voltage alternating current
(*d*) Low-voltage direct current.

63. Which of the following is contradiction of ultrasound?
(*a*) Scar tissue   (*b*) Infection
(*c*) Warts   (*d*) Trigger points

64. Reflection of ultrasonic energy occurs least between -
(*a*) Water and soft tissue
(*b*) Soft tissue and fat
(*c*) Soft tissue and bone
(*d*) Soft tissue and air.

65. When applying intermittent compression to an extremity, the pressure in the appliance should not exceed -
(*a*) The athlete's diastolic blood pressure
(*b*) The athlete's systolic blood pressure
(*c*) The difference between the athletes diastolic and systolic blood pressure
(*d*) the athlete's resting heart rate.

66. "Petrissage' technique of massage involves—
(*a*) Pounding of the skin
(*b*) Pinching of the skin
(*c*) Kneading of the skin
(*d*) Stroking of the skin

67. "Effleurage" technique of massage involves :
(*a*) Kneading of the skin
(*b*) Pounding of the skin
(*c*) Stroking of the skin
(*d*) None of the above.

68. "Tapoment" of the skin involves -
(*a*) Stroking   (*b*) Kneading
(*c*) Pounding   (*d*) Friction

69. Immediate treatment provided to an athlete upon a sports injury is -
(*a*) Short weve diathermy
(*b*) Cryotherapy
(*c*) Contrast bath
(*d*) Whirlpool

70. Which of the following instruments measures the heart action :
(*a*) Electrocardiogram
(*b*) Sphygmomanometer
(*c*) Electroencephalograph
(*d*) Elctromyograph

71. Green Stick fracture occurs owing to the -
(*a*) Lack of strength
(*b*) Forceful muscular contraction
(*c*) Non-ossification of bone
(*d*) Old age.

72. The degree of chronic fatigue may be assessed through -
(*a*) Observation method
(*b*) Clinical method
(*c*) Introspection method
(*d*) All of the above.

73. The drugs that develop calmness are known as-
(*a*) Diuretics
(*b*) Sedatives
(*c*) Narcotics
(*d*) None above

74. Energy requirements depend upon -
(*a*) Age
(*b*) Sex
(*c*) Physical activity
(*d*) All above

75. Which of the following is not a fat soluable vitamin?
(*a*) Vitamin A   (*b*) Vitamin C
(*c*) Vitamin D   (*d*) Vitamin E

76. Prevention of sudden outbreak of a disease includes-
(*a*) Adequate waste management
(*b*) Health Education
(*c*) Clean water supply
(*d*) All the above.

77. Tendonitis is the -
(*a*) Inflammation of tendon
(*b*) Tearing of tendon
(*c*) Strain
(*d*) Muscle pull

78. Acclimatization is the -
(*a*) Physiological adaptation to environment
(*b*) Constant exposure to climate
(*c*) exposure to high altitude
(*d*) all of the above

79. The drug that stimulates the central nervous system is -
(*a*) Amphetamine   (*b*) anabolic steroid
(*c*) anabolism   (*d*) Adrenalin

80. Increase in the blood lactate is due to -
(*a*) Anaerobic threshold
(*b*) Anaerobic
(*c*) Aerobic potential
(*d*) Absence of oxygen

81. The cardiovascular endurance capacity is
(*a*) Overall body endurance
(*b*) Stamina
(*c*) Aerobic power
(*d*) None of the above

82. What is cardiac hypertrophy?
(*a*) Changes in heart size
(*b*) Due to training the size (volume) of heart increases
(*c*) Normal thickness in the ventricular wall
(*d*) It is an Athletic heart.

83. Name the gadget used for treating chronic sports injuries?
(*a*) Short wave diathermy
(*b*) Infra red rays
(*c*) Ultra-violet rays
(*d*) Ultrasound diathermy

84. The upper two chambers of the heart are known as -
(*a*) Ventricles   (*b*) Arteries
(*c*) Veins   (*d*) Auricles

85. The voluntary muscles are controlled by -
(*a*) Nerves   (*b*) Brain
(*c*) heart   (*d*) muscles

86. Example of slow twitch muscle is —
(*a*) Chest muscles   (*b*) Hip muscles
(*c*) soleus   (*d*) Trapezius

87. Example of fast twitch muscle is -
(*a*) Cluteus maximus
(*b*) Hamstrings
(*c*) Medial gastrocnemius
(*d*) Lateral gastrocnemius

88. What is the percentage of muscles in the body?
(*a*) 40%   (*b*) 60%
(*c*) 80%   (*d*) 100%

89. In case of sprain, the immediate treatment recommended is -
(*a*) Hydrotherapy
(*b*) Cryotherapy
(*c*) heat therapy
(*d*) None of the above.

90. Which of the following is not a local effect of heat application?
(*a*) Increased rate of cell metabolism
(*b*) Increased elasticity of soft tissue
(*c*) Increased muscle tone
(*d*) Decreased muscle spasm.

91. Which artery supplies the blood to posterior and hind limbs?
(*a*) Renal   (*b*) Gastric
(*c*) Iliac   (*d*) Hepatic

92. Which vein drains blood from liver?
(*a*) Renal   (*b*) Iliac
(*c*) Hepatic   (*d*) Gastric

93. One complete heartbeat consisting of one systole and one diastole lasts for
(*a*) 0.72 sec   (*b*) 0.8 sec.
(*c*) 0.85 sec.   (*d*) 1 min.

94. What is known as the pacemaker of heart?
(*a*) Pericardium
(*b*) AV node
(*c*) SA node
(*d*) Both AV and SA node

95. The amount of blood flowing from the heart over a given period of time is known as
(*a*) Stroke volume   (*b*) cardiac output
(*c*) heart rate   (*d*) blood pressure

96. Which of the following properties is not possessed by slow twitch fibres?
(*a*) Red fibres
(*b*) High myoglobin
(*c*) Slow action potential
(*d*) High haemoglobin

97. Number of fibres per neuron in slow twitch muscle is
(*a*) 10-180
(*b*) 300-800
(*c*) 150-300
(*d*) 100-250

98. Number of fibres per neuron in fast twitch muscle is
(*a*) 10-180
(*b*) 300-800
(*c*) 150-300
(*d*) 100-250

99. What is not possessed by fast twitch muscles in comparison to slow twitch muscles?
(*a*) less resistant to fatigue
(*b*) High AT Pase activity
(*c*) less myosin crossbridges
(*d*) Fast contraction speed

100. Elite male and female distance runners posses
(*a*) more of slow twitch fibres
(*b*) more of fast twitch fibres
(*c*) more of intermediate twitch fibres
(*d*) 50% ST and 50% FT fibres

ANSWERS

1. (*c*)	2. (*a*)	3. (*d*)	4. (*a*)	5. (*d*)	6. (*a*)	7. (*c*)	8. (*d*)
9. (*b*)	10. (*b*)	11. (*b*)	12. (*c*)	13. (*b*)	14. (*b*)	15. (*a*)	16. (*a*)
17. (*a*)	18. (*b*)	19. (*b*)	20. (*b*)	21. (*d*)	22. (*c*)	23. (*a*)	24. (*b*)
25. (*b*)	26. (*c*)	27. (*c*)	28. (*d*)	29. (*c*)	30. (*d*)	31. (*c*)	32. (*d*)
33. (*a*)	34. (*b*)	35. (*a*)	36. (*c*)	37. (*a*)	38. (*a*)	39. (*a*)	40. (*b*)
41. (*a*)	42. (*b*)	43. (*a*)	44. (*c*)	45. (*c*)	46. (*b*)	47. (*a*)	48. (*b*)
49. (*c*)	50. (*c*)	51. (*b*)	52. (*d*)	53. (*d*)	54. (*d*)	55. (*b*)	56. (*b*)
57. (*d*)	58. (*b*)	59. (*d*)	60. (*d*)	61. (*c*)	62. (*b*)	63. (*b*)	64. (*b*)
65. (*c*)	66. (*c*)	67. (*c*)	68. (*c*)	69. (*b*)	70. (*a*)	71. (*c*)	72. (*b*)
73. (*b*)	74. (*d*)	75. (*b*)	76. (*d*)	77. (*a*)	78. (*a*)	79. (*a*)	80. (*b*)
81. (*c*)	82. (*c*)	83. (*a*)	84. (*d*)	85. (*b*)	86. (*c*)	87. (*c*)	88. (*a*)
89. (*b*)	90. (*c*)	91. (*c*)	92. (*c*)	93. (*b*)	94. (*c*)	95. (*b*)	96. (*d*)
97. (*a*)	98. (*b*)	99. (*c*)	100. (*a*)				

8. SPORTS TRAINING

MEANING OF SPORTS TRAINING

The training is a process of preparing an individual for any event or an activity or job. Usually in sports we use the term sports training which denote the sense of preparing sportspersons for the highest level of performance. But now a days sports training is not just a term but it is very important subject that affects each and every individual who takes up physical activity or sports either for health and fitness or for competition at different level. Hence, sport training is the physical, technical, intellectual, psychological and moral preparation of an athlete or a player by means of physical exercises.

According to Harre (1982) sports training is a process of athletic improvement, which is conducted on the basis of scientific principles through which systematic development of mental and physical efficiency, capacity and motivation enables athletes to produce outstanding and record breaking athletic performances.

Thus, we can say that sports training is the over all scientific and systematic channel of preparation of sportspersons for the highest level of sports performance. Sports training also consists of all those learning influences and processes that are aimed at enhancing sports performance.

DEFINITION OF SPORTS TRAINING

Some definitions of sports training as given by the experts of this area are as under:

According to **Hardial Singh** (1993), sports training is a pedagogical process, based on scientific principles aiming at preparing sportsmen for higher performances in sports competitions.

Harre (1986) said, "Sports training, based on scientific knowledge, is a pedagogical process of sports perfection which through systematic effect on psycho-physical performance ability and performance readiness aim at leading the sportsman to high and the highest performance. Through active and conscious interaction with the given demands in sports training, the sportsman's personality develops according to the norms and standards of socialist society."

According to **Matveyev** (1981) sports training is the basic form of an athlete's training. It is the preparation systematically organised with the help of exercises, which in fact is a pedagogically organised process of controlling an athlete's development (his sporting perfectioning).

Martin (1979) said, 'sports training is a planned and controlled process in which, for achieving a goal, changes in complex sports motor performance, ability to act and behaviour are made through measures of content, methods and organisation."

In the broad sense sports training is the entire systematic process of preparation of athletes for the highest levels of athletic performance. It comprises all those learning influences and processes, including self tuition by the athlete, which are aimed at improving performance.

AIM OF SPORTS TRAINING

In the light of the meaning and definitions of sports training, the aim of sports training is to improve rapidly the sports performance of a sportsperson particularly in sports competitions, which is mainly based on his physical, psychological, intellectual and technical capacities and capabilities. In other words, the aim of sports training in competitive sports is to prepare the sportspersons for the attainment of highest possible sports performance in competition.

OBJECTIVES OF SPORTS TRAINING

Keeping in view the aim of sports training in competitive sports, the following objectives of sports training may be set to reach the aim.

- Personality Development
- Physical fitness Development
- Skill/Technique Development
- Tactical Development
- Mental Training

Personality Development

One of the main objectives of sports training is the all round development of personality of the sportsperson because a good personality — counts a lot in sports competition and attainment of highest possible performance. Various personality traits such as drive, assertion, drive determination; self-confidence, leadership, emotional maturity, trainability, conscience and mental toughness can be developed through sports training and education. These factors play an essential role in all round development of sportsperson and in achieving higher performance in sports competitions.

Physical Fitness Development

Next important objective of sports training is to develop physical fitness level of the sportsperson. Physical fitness consists of mainly strength, speed, endurance, flexibility and other coordinative abilities. These abilities are essential prerequisites of high sports performance. Sports training should be concentrated mainly on the development of the kind of fitness that is needed for the specific sports event or game concerned. The development of desired level of fitness and its components takes several year of systematic training. This needs the use of different types of physical exercises and various types of training methods in sports training programme for sportspersons/trainees

Skill/Technique Development

Another vital objective of sports training is the development of skills or techniques in a particular sport or event in which sportsperson intend to perform or execute. Good skill or technique helps the sportsperson to make economical and optimum use of his abilities or physical prowess.

The sportspersons learn the skill or techniques and get a mastery over it under condition specific to their sport or event. As the sportsperson develops his/her level of physical fitness he/she must also keep improving the standard of his/her skill or technique. Thus these two aspects of sports training i.e. development of physical fitness and development of skill or technique should also go hand in hand.

Tactical Development

The importance of tactics is gradually increasing due to neck-to-neck competition at national and international levels. Thus, it is very important aspect of any sports training programme particularly at higher level to include tactical training as a part and parcel of all other components of training programme. Because the sportsperson must acquire those skills and abilities that will enable him/her to win the games or event.

Mental Training

Mental training is an integral and important part of sports training. Now a day, in the hi-tech competitive era higher demands are put on the mental faculties of sportspersons. They are under tremendous stress and pressure both internal and external. The sportspersons must be able to act and think for themselves during sports training and also in competition to perform better. This is an important objective of sports training to develop and train the sportsperson's intellectual faculties and improve their knowledge of sports training and learn its application in a unique way in training and competition.

CHARACTERISTICS OF SPORTS TRAINING

Main characteristics of sports training are as follows:
- Sports Training is Performance Oriented
- Sports Training is Individual Matter
- Sports Training is Planned and Systematic
- Sports Training is Scientific Process
- Sports Training is Educational Process
- Coach as a leader/Mentor in Sports Training
- Development and Exploitation of Reserves of sportsperson
- Sports Training is Controlled Process

Sports Training is Performance Oriented

Sports training is always performance oriented as it targeted at achieving high performance in a given sports competition. Each and every aspect or process of sports training leads to improving sports performance whether it is a physical or psychological preparation or skill/technique development or tactical and mental training.

Sports Training is Individual Matter

Sports performance is a result of various factors, may differ from person to person. Thus, sports training is to a great extent an individual matter. But it does not mean that sports training should not be given in group. Rather sports training in groups is essential for mobilising performance potentials by providing necessary emotional basis. Group training is economical and important factor in-group education. It is essential to give due weightage to individual factors while planning load and frequency management in sports training.

Sports Training is Planned and Systematic

Sports training is always a planned and systematic for achieving the highest performance in a given competition. Desired results in any sports/events or game cannot be achieved without proper planning i.e. long tern, intermediate and short term planning and also without systematic process. One cannot have mastery over tactical aspect of any sport/event or game without developing skills or technique first. So sports training is a planned and scientific process to achieve excellent performance.

Sports Training is Scientific Process

Now a days sports training is a highly scientific process, which is based on sound scientific principles. It is also based on advances made in natural and social sciences. Knowledge from these sciences has to be put in use in the process of sports training to attain the highest performance. Thus, sports training itself becomes a science which play a vital role in today's sports.

Sports Training is Educational Process

Actually, sports training is a planned and systematic educational process through which education is imparted to sportspersons regarding various training methods, training process, rules and regulations and regarding his abilities and capabilities. Sports training is a educational process to develop all round personality of an athlete through various means and methods. Without developing sports personality, proper training and high performance are not possible

Coach as a Leader/Mentor in Sports Training

Another important characteristics of sports training is the leadership role of the coach. The coach's role as a mentor covers all aspects and forms of sports training. The coach is responsible to control everything in training i.e. planning, implementation, assessment etc. In sports training, coach assist athletes to follow training programme properly, and he/she communicates effectively with his/her athletes/players on the various aspects of training and performance.

Development and Exploitation Reserves of Sports Persons

One of the main tasks of sports training is to develop the capacities and capabilities of sportsperson besides exploitation of his potentials. Some time sportspersons are unaware about their performance limits. Hidden potentials are tapped through training and sportspersons are educated about these reserves. Through sports training sportsperson scales new heights of his own performance and sets the higher target.

Sports Training is Controlled Process

This is one of the unique characteristics of sports training that each and every element of training is fully controlled. In sports training athlete/player has to be very disciplined, dutiful and committed to all aspects of training to realise the maximum benefit for better performance. His/her training is fully managed through daily training session to micro, meso and macro training.

PRINCIPLES OF SPORTS TRAINING AND CONDITIONING

The following are the basic principles of sports training and conditioning:
- Principle of Overload.
- Principle of individuality.
- Principle of Progressive Development.
- Principle of Specificity.
- Principle of Continuity.
- Principle of Active Participation.
- Principle of Variety.
- Principle of Periodisation.

Principle of Overload

In sports training this is the foremost principle to make any improvement in different abilities of an individual. The overload is that any improvement in fitness needs an increased training load that challenges the trainee's state of fitness. Loading causes fatigue and when loading ends, then recovery starts. If the training load is optimal (just less than maximum which is unknown), the trainee will be more fit after recovery than before the training load was applied.

Principle of Individuality

As no two individuals are identical in this world. Thus each trainee or athlete does not react in the same way to a training method or system rather he or she reacts in a little different way. Age and sex differences also affect the training programme.

According to the principle of individualization the training programme should be prepared and planned as per the trainee's own ability, requirements and his/her potential. So one must not just copy a training programme of any other individual trainee. Trainee's physical, physiological and psychological make-up, his/ her age, experience in sports, skill level, past and present performance, training load capacity and rate of recovery, body build and gender differences must be considered by the coach/trainer while planning a training programme for him/her. The training programme will be most effective and successful only if it is followed by trainee for whom it was planned.

Principle of Progressive Development

This progressive development refers to the general motor skills and fitness development, which are the main goals of the early part of the training year. If there is a more balanced general development at the early stage, then the greater level of performance can be achieved at the latter stage.

In training children and junior athletes/players more emphasis should be given to this principle because it is the first step of the systematic step approach in the sports training.

In sports training there should be increase in the intensity, frequency and/or duration of activity step by step instead of linear increase over periods of time in order to improve.

Principle of Specificity

The principle of specificity is that the nature of the training load determines the training effect The training must be specific to the desired effect. The training programme should be prepared in a specific way that it meets the specific demands of a specific event/activity/game. The training load should also be specific in terms of recovery and intensity. Intensity is the quality or difficulty of the training load.

Principle of Specialization

This principle refers to training programme, which develops the techniques and abilities required for a specific event or activity. A runner needs speed and endurance components. So he/she should develop running technique that uses the most efficient running pattern for the racing distance.

A thrower needs strength in specific parts of the body, just as different specific motor skills are required for each throwing event. All such traits or factors are developed through specialized training programme and specialized specific training exercises.

Principle of Continuity

This principle refers to continuity in training programme. The training effect will reverse itself if there is no continuity and the fitness or conditioning level will fall if the loading does not continue. If the sports training does not, become more challenging, the fitness level will stagnate (plateau). If the sports training ends, the fitness level will slowly come down until it reaches the level needed to maintain normal daily activities

The training load must continue to increase if the trainee's general and specific fitness to continue to improve. If load remains at the same level, the fitness rise for a time, then begin to fall. So there must he a progressive overload for the improvement of performances.

Principle of Active Participation

The principle of active participation means that for good results of sports training programme,

Trainee must be actively involved in this process by his/her own choice. The sports training is a two-way process among the trainee and the coach. The trainee/s should fully understand the aim and objectives of his/her training programme. There must be regular evaluation of every sports training programme. The trainee should not be a passive participant and he/she should follow the coach's directive or dictate. The trainee must provide quality feedback, working with the coach to reach for excellent training effect.

Principle of Variety

In sports training different types of training methods and means should be involved to overcome the problem of boredom or staleness or stagnation.

Principle of Periodisation

Sports training programme are developed through a series of training periods or cycles. Usually there are three training period such as Macrocycle, Mesocycle and Microcycle. Macrocycle is a large or long cycle may be 4 month to 12 months or even longer. Mesocycle is an intermediate or medium length cycle may be weekly cycle. Microcycle is small cycle may consists of 3 to 10 days.

OBJECTIVE QUESTIONS

1. Mark the incorrect statement:
(a) Gall bladder is absent in horse
(b) Iron is stored as ferritin
(c) Fat metabolism takes place in liver
(d) Heart is the largest gland in human body

2. The contraction of muscles is obtained from the:
(a) Stores of chemical compounds in the muscles
(b) Stores of fats in the muscles
(c) Stores of glycogen in the blood
(d) None of these

3. What is oxygen debt?
(a) Excessive inflow of oxygen
(b) The amount of oxygen consumed during recovery from exercise
(c) Transportation of oxygen from one person to another
(d) It is a confusing term in physical education

4. The other name of oxygen debt is;
(a) Oxygen spending
(b) Recovery oxygen
(c) Oxygen regression
(d) None of These

5. Fatigue results from:
(a) Intake of excessive food
(b) Prolonged and excessive exertion
(c) Loosing of weight and health
(d) Failures to hit the target

6. Fatigue can be classified into:
(a) Mental and physical fatigue
(b) Social, cultural and national fatigue
(c) Physical and social fatigue
(d) Mental and psychological fatigue

7. Which among the *following is* not the internal symptoms of the fatigue?
(a) Loss of confidence
(b) Tendency to relax
(c) Loss of coordination
(d) Loss of concentration

8. Which among the following is not the external symptoms of the fatigue:
(a) Increased proneness to injury
(b) Reduction in quality skill
(c) Decreased time sense
(d) Tension in the involved muscles

9. Which is not the method of preventing fatigue?
(a) Limber down after training programme
(b) To continue vigorous exercise non stop
(a) Consume adequate calories
(d) Perform warming up

10. What is the main cause of fatigue?
(a) Toxic action of waste products together with the lose of energy in the functioning of cells
(b) Excessive eating and drinking
(c) Preparation for world level competition
(d) None of the above

11. Mind is—
    (*a*) An organ of the body
    (*b*) Super organ of the body
    (*a*) Only a process of the nervous system
    (*d*) It is only a mythical conception

12. In the 18th century psychology was defined as:
    (*a*) Science of mind
    (*b*) Science of human behaviour
    (*c*) Supernatural phenomenon dealing with social behaviour
    (*d*) Only a general behaviour science

13. Who said "first psychology lost its soul then it lost its mind, then it lost consciousness. It still has behaviour of sort'—
    (*a*) Segment Freud   (*b*) John D. Lawther
    (*c*) Wordsworth   (*d*) Akanksha Jha

14. The basic process involved in physical education learning is;
    (*a*) Hele-learning   (*b*) Motor learning
    (*c*) Plane learning   (*d*) Auto learning

15. Achievements may be referred as—
    (*a*) A partial success
    (*b*) Successful completion of some task or goal
    (*c*) When one feels psychologically satisfied
    (*d*) When some one wins gold medal in an event

16. Who said that "motivation is the process by which a man is inspired to seek some goal"?
    (*a*) Wordsworth   (*b*) Lincoln
    (*c*) Frost   (*d*) John D. Lawther

17. Mark the incorrect statement—
    (*a*) The teacher who is interested to promote learning can't afford to ignore motivation
    (*b*) Motivation helps to achieve desired result
    (*c*) Motivation is not as necessary as the quality food
    (*d*) Awards and honours assist potential sports persons to achieve higher goals

18. Which is not the motivating factor:
    (*a*) Appreciation and praise
    (*b*) Awards and rewards
    (*c*) threatening with due consequences if not achieved the goal
    (*d*) Personality of the teacher

19. Mark the incorrect statement—
    (*a*) learning by doing itself is a great motivational factor
    (*b*) physical and mental health also contributes to motivation
    (*c*) sport and games serve as strong outlet for pent up feelings
    (*d*) material rewards are promotion, praise and honours

20. Motivation is not an effective device to bring change in:
    (*a*) Behaviour   (*b*) Attitude
    (*c*) Performance   (*d*) Physical outlook

21. The word emotion originated from 'emover' belonging to the:
    (*a*) Latin language   (*b*) Greek language
    (*c*) English language (*d*) Chinese language

22. What is the etymological meaning of the world 'emovere' ?
    (*a*) Emotions   (*b*) Movements
    (*c*) Spirit   (*d*) Desire

23. Which among the following is a unpleasant feeling?
    (*a*) Love   (*c*) Anger
    (*b*) Affection   (*d*) Sympathy

24. What is responsible for the persistent and constant behaviour of an individual?
    (*a*) Attitude   (*b*) Interest
    (*c*) Emotions   (*d*) Tension

25. Do we need ethics in sport?
    (*a*) Yes, ethics have greater value in sports
    (*b*) No, it is not mandatory
    (*c*) Ethics may have some place somewhere
    (*d*) Ethics are most unwanted things

26. Shubhangi Kulkarni was associated with:
    (*a*) Chess   (*b*) Badminton
    (*c*) Cricket   (*d*) Billiards

27. Monica Nath was a famous player of:
    (*a*) Football   (*b*) Basketball
    (*c*) Kabaddi   (*d*) Kho-Kho

28. Who among the following have received the Padam Bhushan Award?
    (*a*) Ajit Wadekar
    (*b*) Kanwaljeet Sandhu
    (*c*) Balbir Singh
    (*d*) Dilip Vengsarkar

29. Sh. Om Prakash the receipient of Chan Award was associated with:
 (*a*) Hockey   (*b*) Boxing
 (*c*) Basketball   (*d*) Volleyball

30. Sayyed Naimuddin the receipient of Dronacharya Award was associated with which game?
 (*a*) Football   (*b*) Hockey
 (*c*) Athletics   (*d*) Vollyball

31. In which year Arjuna Award were instituted?
 (*a*) 1961 A.D.   (*b*) 1963A.D.
 (*c*) 1965 A.D.   (*d*) 1970 A.D.

32. Which University has won the Maulana Abul Kalam Azad trophy for the highest number of times so far:
 (*a*) University of Delhi
 (*b*) Mumbai University
 (*c*) Guru Nanak Dev University
 (*d*) Punjab University

33. Abhinav Bindra and Anjali Bhagwat are associated with:
 (*a*) Chess   (*b*) Snooker
 (*c*) Billiards   (*d*) Shooting

34. Ghos Mohammed Khan was a famous player of:
 (*a*) Hockey   (*b*) Lawn tennis
 (*c*) Kabaddi   (*d*) Football

35. Name the first cricketer who received Padam Shri Award in the year 1960?
 (*a*) Lala Amarnath   (*b*) Vijay Hazare
 (*c*) C.G. Borde   (*d*) D.V. Deodhar

36. Sukhchain Singh Cheema was associated with:
 (*a*) Boxing   (*b*) Athletics
 (*c*) Wrestling   (*d*) Kabaddi

37. Who among the following won "Dhyan Chand Award"
 (*a*) Ashok Diwan   (*b*) Aparna Ghosh
 (*c*) Charles Kamolias (*d*) All the above

38. Chand Ram was a famous:
 (*a*) Cricketer   (*b*) Footballer
 (*c*) Athlete   (*d*) Boxer

39. Mark incorrect about Anabolic Steroid is:
 (*a*) A drug that produces nitrogen potassium and phosphate

 (*b*) A drug that helps body to perform rythmic exercises with greater speed
 (*c*) Increases protein synthesis
 (*d*) Decreases amino acid breakdown

40. What is wrong about Bacteria?
 (*a*) Also called as Germs
 (*b*) These are single cell organism
 (*c*) They are visible to naked eyes
 (*d*) They are treated with antibiotics

41. What is heterosexual?
 (*a*) A person having extra sexual relations
 (*b*) A person having sex relations with opposite sex
 (*c*) A person having sex with similar sex
 (*d*) None of these

42. Who was the first President of International Football Association from 1904-1906?
 (*a*) Daniel Barley   (*b*) Sir Stanley Bose
 (*c*) Robert   (*d*) Juleus Rime

43. Which country host first World Cup football championship
 (*a*) France   (*b*) Russi
 (*c*) Brazil   (*d*) Uruguay

44. In which year Winter Olympic Games were started?
 (*a*) 1900A.D.   (*b*) 1908A.D.
 (*c*) 1916A.D.   (*d*) 1924A.D.

45. In which country first Commonwealth Games were held in the year 1930 A.D.?
 (*a*) Great Britain   (*b*) Canada
 (*c*) Australia   (*d*) Malayasia

46. Yuva Bharti Stadium is located at:
 (*a*) Mumbai   (*b*) Chennai
 (*c*) Kolkata   (*d*) Patiala

47. Sheesh Mahal trophy is associated with which game?
 (*a*) Football   (*b*) Cricket
 (*c*) Kabaddi   (*d*) Chess

48. "Ping Pong" is popularly known as:
 (*a*) Lawn Tennis   (*b*) TableTennis
 (*c*) Chess   (*d*) Baseball

49. What is the National Game of Malayasia?
 (*a*) Judo   (*b*) Badminton
 (*c*) Bull fighting   (*d*) Lacrosse

50. The National Game of America is
 (*a*) Hockey   (*b*) Lawn Tennis
 (*c*) Baseball   (*d*) Rugby

51. The first metamorphosis falls between the age of—
- (*a*) 7-10 years
- (*b*) 3-5 years
- (*c*) 11-14 years
- (*d*) 2-4 years

52. In selecting talent, the most important factor to be considered is—-
- (*a*) Training State
- (*b*) Health
- (*c*) Interest and attitude
- (*d*) All of the above.

53. An efficient coach is he who—-
- (*a*) Tells
- (*b*) Tells and demonstrates
- (*c*) Tells, demonstrates and explain
- (*d*) Tells, demonstrates, explains and inspires.

54. While exercising on a Multigym the type of muscular contraction that occurs is—-
- (*a*) Isotonic
- (*b*) Isometric
- (*c*) Isokinetic
- (*d*) Kinetic

55. What is the weight of a Football?
- (*a*) 14-16 oz
- (*b*) 16-18 oz
- (*c*) 18-20 oz
- (*d*) 20-22 oz

56. What is the duration of a Football game?
- (*a*) 45-10-45 (min.)
- (*b*) 40-10-40 (min.)
- (*c*) 35-10-35 (min.)
- (*d*) 45-2-45 (min.)

57. How many referees are required for a Football match?
- (*a*) 4
- (*b*) 3
- (*c*) 2
- (*d*) 1

58. The number of umpires required to conduct a Hockey match is:
- (*a*) One
- (*b*) Three
- (*c*) Four
- (*d*) Two

59. In Hockey, the ball gets trapped in a goal keeper's pads, how does the game restart?
- (*a*) With bully
- (*b*) Center hit
- (*c*) Hit from the goal
- (*d*) Toss.

60. How does the game of Hockey start?
- (*a*) With a bully
- (*b*) With forward pass
- (*c*) With back pass
- (*d*) None of the above

61. From what distance is the penalty stroke taken in Hockey?
- (*a*) 6 yards
- (*b*) 8 yards
- (*c*) 9 yards
- (*d*) 7 yards

62. What is the duration of one half in the game of Hockey?
- (*a*) 34 minutes
- (*b*) 40 minutes
- (*c*) 35 minutes
- (*d*) 30 minutes

63. Width of lanes in a standard track is:
- (*a*) 1.22-1.25 m
- (*b*) 1.22 m
- (*c*) 1.25 m
- (*d*) 1.21 m

64. What is the angle at which the throwing sector is marked?
- (*a*) 40°
- (*b*) 45°
- (*c*) 50°
- (*d*) 35°

65. Decathlon consists of:
- (*a*) 6 track and 4 filed events
- (*b*) 4 track and 4 filed events
- (*c*) 3 track and 7 filed events
- (*d*) 7 track and 3 filed events

66. The range of points awarded in 'Decathlon' is:
- (*a*) 1-1200
- (*b*) 1-1000
- (*c*) 5-1000
- (*d*) 12000.

67. To break tie in the triple jumps competition:
- (*a*) Consider the next best performance
- (*b*) Provide an additional trial
- (*c*) Consider all the attempts
- (*d*) Adopt any one of the above.

68. Number of flights in 110m (Hurdle) race is
- (*a*) 8
- (*b*) 9
- (*c*) 10
- (*d*) 11

69. To break tie in Long Jump :
- (*a*) Consider the performance of the first attempt
- (*b*) Consider the performance of the last attempt
- (*c*) Consider the next best performance
- (*d*) Change the venue of competition.

70. In 110 m Hurdles, the number of strides performed between two Hurdles is :
(*a*) 5   (*b*) 8
(*c*) 3   (*d*) 4

71. In 300 m Steeple Chase, the number of Water jumps is -
(*a*) 6   (*b*) 7
(*c*) 8   (*d*) 9

72. The length of exchange zone in 4 × 100 m relay is :
(*a*) 10 meters   (*b*) 15 meters
(*c*) 20 meters   (*d*) 30 meters

73. The weight of men's Javelin is :
(*a*) 600 gms   (*b*) 800 gms
(*c*) 900 gms   (*d*) 1000 gms

74. Distance of Marathon race is :
(*a*) 43.195 km   (*b*) 42.195 km
(*c*) 41.185 km   (*d*) 40.165 km

75. How many total jumps are there in 3000 m steeple chase race?
(*a*) 34   (*b*) 36
(*c*) 35   (*d*) 33

76. How many time keepers should check the performance before a world record can be considered in the track events :
(*a*) 3 including one chief time keeper
(*b*) 2 including one chief time keeper
(*c*) 4 including one chief time keeper
(*d*) 5 including one chief time keeper.

77. Events of the modern pentathlon are :
(*a*) Riding, Shooting, Fencing, Swimming and Cross Country Running
(*b*) Riding, Shooting, Fencing, Swimming and Kayaking
(*c*) Riding, Shooting, Fencing, Swimming and Canoeing
(*d*) 800 m, Shot Put, Long Jump, 100 m and Discuss

78. What is the width of lines in Athletics track events?
(*a*) 4 cm   (*b*) 5 cm
(*c*) 6 cm   (*d*) 7 cm

79. Dimensions of the Volleyball Court are :
(*a*) 9 m × 18 m (B × L)
(*b*) 10 m × 20 m (B × L)
(*c*) 11 m × 21m (B × L)
(*d*) 8 m × 16 m (B × L)

80. Width of the Volleyball Net is :
(*a*) 1.80 m   (*b*) 1.20 m
(*c*) 1.10 m   (*d*) 1 m.

81. Height of Antena in Volleyball is :
(*a*) 1.80 m   (*b*) 1.60 m
(*c*) 1.40 m   (*d*) 1.20 m

82. Height of the Volleyball net for men is :
(*a*) 2.40 m   (*b*) 2.41 m
(*c*) 2.42 m   (*d*) 2.43 m

83. Height of the volleyball net for women is :
(*a*) 2.21 m   (*b*) 2.22 m
(*c*) 2.23 m   (*d*) 2.24 m

84. Height of the antenna above the net in Volleyball is :
(*a*) 50 cm   (*b*) 60 cm
(*c*) 70 cm   (*d*) 80 cm

85. In Volleyball, the distance of the attack line from centre line is :
(*a*) One metre   (*b*) Two metres
(*c*) Three metres   (*d*) Five metres

86. According to the new rules, maximum points in the first 4 sets of a game in volleyball is :
(*a*) 15   (*b*) 14
(*c*) 25   (*d*) 24

87. Weight of a Volleyball is :
(*a*) 260-280 gms.   (*b*) 260-280 oz
(*c*) 280-300 gms.   d) 300-320 gms.

88. How many field players are there in one team in Volleyball?
(*a*) 12   (*b*) 10
(*c*) 9   (*d*) 6

89. What is the width of boundary lines in Volleyball?
(*a*) 6 cm   (*b*) 5 cm
(*c*) 3 cm   (*d*) 2 cm

90. Rotation in Volleyball takes place in the :
(*a*) Clockwise direction
(*b*) Anticlockwise direction
(*c*) Both (*a*) and (*b*)
(*d*) Zig-zag direction

ANSWERS

1. (c)	2. (c)	3. (c)	4. (d)	5. (a)	6. (c)	7. (c)	8. (d)
9. (b)	10. (b)	11. (c)	12. (d)	13. (c)	14. (b)	15. (c)	16. (b)
17. (c)	18. (d)	19. (d)	20. (b)	21. (c)	22. (b)	23. (b)	24. (b)
25. (c)	26. (c)	27. (c)	28. (d)	29. (b)	30. (b)	31. (d)	32. (b)
33. (b)	34. (d)	35. (a)	36. (b)	37. (c)	38. (c)	39. (c)	40. (b)
41. (a)	42. (b)	43. (a)	44. (b)	45. (b)	46. (a)	47. (b)	48. (b)
49. (b)	50. (c)	51. (a)	52. (d)	53. (d)	54. (c)	55. (a)	56. (a)
57. (d)	58. (d)	59. (a)	60. (c)	61. (b)	62. (c)	63. (a)	64. (a)
65. (b)	66. (a)	67. (d)	68. (c)	69. (c)	70. (c)	71. (b)	72. (c)
73. (b)	74. (b)	75. (c)	76. (a)	77. (a)	78. (b)	79. (a)	80. (d)
81. (a)	82. (d)	83. (d)	84. (d)	85. (c)	86. (c)	87. (a)	88. (d)
89. (b)	90. (a)						

9. SCHOOL SPORTS

Can you imagine an American junior or senior high school without an interschool sports program for students? Probably not, because virtually every school has such a program. The universality of sports in educational settings implies that sport must accomplish educational objectives. That, however, is the ideal. Rather, the pressure to win is foremost and when taken to its extreme, runs counter to the stated goal of athletics - to foster the optimum physical, mental, emotional, social, and moral growth of the participants. Schools demand that their athletic teams win but there is something fundamentally wrong with such a demand. It means, for example, that the livelihood of coaches and their families depends exclusively on whether their teams win. Thus, many coaches drive their players too hard, bend the rules, teach unfair tactics, and demand the total control of their players. These reactions to the win ethic are understandable but they are wrong because they are antithetical to the stated purposes of educational institutions.

The assumption is often made that "sports build character." But do they? Those responsible for educational programs must continually monitor the athletic program to assess whether educational objectives are being met. Some questions these monitors might ask are

- Are educational goals being met when coaches are selected primarily for their win-loss record?
- Are educational goals being met when practice sessions are run like a marine boot camp?
- Are educational goals being met when coaches physically or verbally assault their athletes?
- Are educational goals being met when players are denied the rights and freedoms guaranteed by the Constitution (e.g., freedom of speech)?
- Are educational goals being met when athletes, coaches, and fans taunt and intimidate their opponents?
- Are educational goals being met when all decisions are made for the young athletes by adults?
- Are educational goals being met when players are treated as interchangeable parts?
- Are educational goals being met when athletes are encouraged to use certain drugs to enhance their performance artificially?
- Are educational goals being met when athletes are taught to cheat (how to hold in football without getting caught or how to feign a foul to receive an undeserved free throw in basketball)?
- Are educational goals being met when the athletic program is reserved for the elite few?
- Are educational goals being met when administrators and coaches resist giving equal importance to women's athletics?

These queries call into question many existing practices allowed in educational settings from junior high school to our most prestigious universities. They suggest that sports programs tend to be win-oriented rather than player-oriented. Educators must ask is this the way it should be, or is there a better way?

The pressures on school personnel to win in sports are enormous and unrelenting. But to give in to these pressures is the easy way out. The leaders of schools (school board members, administrators, coaches) must have integrity and be sincerely interested principal in the development of youth. This means that educational goals must always remain paramount and not be sacrificed for a "win-at-any-costs" philosophy. Neither individual coaches nor administrators can accomplish this, however, without the support of their counterparts in other schools. Otherwise the demand to win will result in their dismissal. This problem can be countered by State High School Athletic Associations or leagues adopting rules that maximize the probability that educational goals remain central for all member schools. Here are some possible rule chances that would help bring this about:

- Eliminate all play-offs and championships to reduce pressure and to allow more individuals and teams to experience success. Tom Meschery, former professional basketball player, has said that school sports "should be directed toward lessening tension, not creating it. There is no need for high school state basketball tournaments. This may seem drastic, but at that age it seems counterproductive to arrive at an ultimate winner when we could have half a dozen winners. It is good for the young to argue the never-to-be-settled championship."

- Establish rules and demand proper equipment to insure the maximum safety of the athletes. There is strong evidence that playing football on artificial turf, for example, is much more dangerous than natural turf. How can school administrators allow their teams to play in situations where the probability of injury is higher than is absolutely necessary?

- Establish leagues for all levels of playing ability and size. This would allow maximum participation for students.

- Make it mandatory that all players participate in every game. For example, in baseball players could be required to play at least one full inning, once substituted for a player could return to the game, and all players (starters and substitutes) could constitute the batting rotation. In

basketball starters could play the first and fourth quarters but not be allowed to play in the middle two quarters.

Allow teams to practice and/or play games but only three times a week, leaving the remaining two days for participation in other extracurricular activities. This would open the facilities for use by others and allow athletes to broaden their interests and skills.

These suggestions, if implemented, would work to accomplish educational goals within the leagues organized to achieve them. Competition would remain keen but coaches, players, and teams would be organized to be player-oriented rather than exclusively win-oriented. Within each school, the goal of promoting educational objectives would be enhanced further

By hiring coaches who are absolutely honest. Second schools should insist that these coaches emphasize sport as an enjoyable activity. Third, coaches should be encouraged to promote democracy by allowing athletes to make their own training rules, make decisions during the game, select their own captains, and have a voice in starting lineups. As it is, the norm is for an athletic team to be a dictatorship. Is that organizational form an appropriate setting to learn how to participate effectively in a democracy ?

Moreover, coaches should allow their charges to express grievances without reprisal and to express their individuality in clothing and hair styles. Coaches have no business requiring conformity to their or the community's standards if they are unrelated to athlete training or performance. What is the educational value of controlling athletes on and off the field? It would appear that a system which denies personal autonomy fosters dependence and immaturity, rather than the presumed virtues of participation - leadership, independence, and self-motivation.

Finally, the aim of every athletic program should be maximum participation. If being on a team promotes physical health as well as teamwork and discipline, then that privilege should be open to all students not just the gifted. This has at least three implications for school policy. First, the programs for boys and girls should be given equal priority. Second, if there are too few teams to 'accommodate the persons who want to take part, then more coaches should be hired and teams added. The typical response, however, is to cut players from the teams, which most likely means removing those persons who could most benefit from the experience. Last, each participant should be considered a vital part of his or her team and be given equal coaching during practice sessions and approximately equal playing time for games.

This essay has raised some serious doubts about the educational value of sports as they are presently organized in America's schools. The "win-at-any-costs" philosophy, taken to its extreme led to such events as Watergate and the bombing of neutral Cambodia. And it is this very philosophy, so common in our schools, that has been tolerated, even encouraged, by those in authority. While winning is a worthy goal, is a natural high, and promotes unity, we should not lose sight of its negative effects. An over-zealous drive to win may promote dishonest practices, make fun work, and lead to failure for so many. If, on the other hand, participation for fun were stressed, if democracy superseded autocracy, and if the personal growth of persons were more important than winning, then school sports would deserve the disproportionate amounts of time and money that are now spent on them.

PARTICIPATION IN SPORTS

There is a persistent belief held by most persons that sports participation has positive benefits for those involved. The following quotation from *Time* summarizes this assumption:

"Sport has always been one of the primary means of civilizing the human animal, of inculcating the character traits a society desires. Wellington in his famous aphorism insisted that the Battle of Waterloo had been won on the playing fields of Eton. The lessons learned on the playing field are among the most basic : the setting of goals and joining with others to achieve them; an understanding of and respect for rules; the persistence to hone ability into skill, prowess into

perfection. In games, children learn that success is possible and that failure can be overcome. Championships may be won; when lost, wait until next year. In practicing such skills as fielding a grounder and hitting a tennis ball, young athletes develop work patterns and attitudes that carry over into college, the marketplace and all of life."

It is no wonder, given the universality of this belief, that parents, schools, and communities push sports programs for youth so vigorously. Mostly forgotten or ignored, however, is the negative side of sports participation, a position that is summarized by Charles Banham:

"If (the conventional argument that sport builds character) is not sound because it assumes that everyone will benefit from sport in the complacently prescribed manner. A minority do so benefit. A few have the temperament that responds healthily to all the demands. These are the only ones able to develop an attractively active character. Sport can put fresh air in the mind, if it's the right mind; it can give muscle to the personality, if it's the right personality. But for the rest, it encourages selfishness, envy, conceit, hostility, and bad temper. Far from ventilating the mind, it stifles it. Good sportsmanship may be a product of sport, but so is bad sportsmanship."

The problem is that sports produce positive and negative outcomes. This dualistic quality of sport is summarized by Terry Orlick:

"For every positive psychological or social outcome in sports, there are possible negative outcomes. For example, sports can offer a child group membership or group exclusion, acceptance or rejection, positive feedback or negative feedback, a sense of accomplishment or a sense of failure, evidence of self-worth or a lack of evidence of self-worth. Likewise, sports can develop cooperation and a concern for others, but they can also develop intense rivalry and a complete lack of concern for others."

The selections in this section summarize what we know about the ability of sports participation to build character. The first essay, by Charles Kniker, a professor of education, reviews the research and concludes that neither the proponents nor the critics of athletics can offer substantial evidence to prove that sports are either beneficial or harmful.

Tutko and Bruns also look carefully at this issue, but they conclude that sport does not build positive character for all participants. This conclusion should not be taken lightly because Tutko, along with his colleague in sport psychology, Bruce Ogilvie, have studied the effects of competition on personality more comprehensively than any other research team. In over twenty years of research, for example, they have studied approximately 60,000 athletes, including more than 15,000 who have taken a test that measures eleven traits common to athletes. Tutko's conclusions, then, are not based on his particular ideological bent but on hard data.

The final selection, by Glenn Dickey, examines the effects of sports participation on one character trait - self-discipline. He argues that, contrary to the commonly accepted belief sport produces followers, not leaders.

OBJECTIVE QUESTIONS

1. Who raised the slogan Back to Nature?
(*a*) Realism   (*b*) Pragmatism
(*c*) Naturalism   (*d*) Existentialism

2. Which statement is *Not* correct about Naturalism?
(*a*) A reaction against the degenerated humanism of the Renaissance period
(*b*) A reaction against the degenerated humanism of the Renaissance period.
(*c*) A reaction against sophistication, artificially and paraphernalia in education.
(*d*) A reaction against a mere study of books and linguistic forms.

3. Which is *Not* a form Naturalism?
(*a*) Scientific Naturalism
(*b*) Mechanical Naturalism
(*c*) Naturalism of physical science
(*d*) Biological Naturalism

4. Who said, "Reverse the usual practice and you will almost always do right"?
(*a*) Mahatma Gandhi   (*b*) J.J. Rousseau
(*c*) John Dewey   (*d*) Plato

5. "Human institutions are one mass of folly and contradiction "Whose statement is this?
(*a*) Bernard Shaw   (*b*) J.J. Rousseau
(*c*) John Dewey   (*d*) R.N.Tagore

6. Which school of philosophy of education maintained "The universe is governed by the laws of nature"?
(*a*) Mechanical Naturalism
(*b*) Biological Naturalism
(*c*) Naturalism of physical science
(*d*) Scientific Naturalism

7. Which school of philosophy of education maintained *"Values are inherent in the individual"*.
(*a*) Pragmatism   (*b*) Realis
(*c*) Idealism   (*d*) Existentialism

8. According to which school of philosophy of education exaltation of individual's personality is a function of education?
(*a*) Pragmatism   (*b*) Idealis
(*c*) Marxism   (*d*) both (b) & (c)

9. Which is *Not* about Naturalism's aim of Education?
(*a*) Founded on the notion of man's evolution from lower forms of life
(*b*) To equip the individual or the nation for the struggle for existence so as to ensure survival
(*c*) To help the pupils to learn to be in harmony with and well-adapted to their surroundings
(*d*) To inculcate ethical and moral values in the pupils

10. What do the Naturalists *Not* accept?
(*a*) The view that the "Child comes from heaven trailing clouds of glory".
(*b*) The view that the heart is deceitful above all things and desperately wicked."
(*c*) Interested in the child as he is, rather than as he will be
(*d*) Education not so much as preparation for living as living itself

11. According to which philosophy of education *"childhood is some thing desirable for its own sake and children should be children "*:
    (*a*) Idealism
    (*b*) Pragmatism
    (*c*) Naturalism
    (*d*) Realism

12. What is *Not* applicable to Naturalism:
    (*a*) It condemns sacrificing the present of the child to an uncertain future
    (*b*) It discards the idea of burdening a child with so many restrictions
    (*c*) It recommends discipline and control in education in order to prepare the child for some far off happiness of education.
    (*d*) It favours finding the purpose, process and means wholly with in the child

13. Who emphasized that education is a man-making process:
    (*a*) Swami Vivekanand
    (*b*) J.J. Rousseau
    (*c*) John Dewey
    (*d*) Pestalozzi

14. *"Education is the process of natural development of the child into an enjoyable, rational, harmoniously balanced, useful and hence, natural life"*. Which school of philosophy of education believes that?
    (*a*) Realism
    (*b*) Existentialism
    (*c*) Naturalism
    (*d*) Idealism

15. According to which school of philosophy of education anything that impedes child's free choice of activities stands condemned according to the:
    (*a*) Naturalism
    (*b*) Pragmatism
    (*c*) Idealism
    (*d*) Marxism

16. Which school calls the classroom unnecessary:
    (*a*) Idealism
    (*b*) Marxism
    (*c*) Naturalism
    (*d*) Pragmatism

17. To which school is it unacceptable that all children are going at one place and learning by one method?
    (*a*) Pragmatism
    (*b*) Realism
    (*c*) Naturalism
    (*d*) Idealism

18. According to which school teacher's place in teaching-learning is behind the scene; he is an observer of the child's development rather than a moulder of child's character.
    (*a*) Idealism
    (*b*) Pragmatism
    (*c*) Naturalism
    (*d*) Realism

19. Evaluate the viewpoint *"The child knows better than any educator what he should learn, when and now he should learn it"* is-
    (*a*) Hundred percent correct
    (*b*) Correct, but not practical
    (*c*) Correct and practical both
    (*d*) Practical, but not correct.

20. Which school asserted, *"Child's nature is the chief claim in the educative process "*-
    (*a*) Pragmatism
    (*b*) Realism
    (*c*) Naturalism
    (*d*) Idealism

21. All of the following are true about phobias, except that:
    (*a*) They are generated by an early emotional experience
    (*b*) The sufferer cannot control the impulse to avoid them
    (*c*) The sufferer will resort to reckless activities to conceal them
    (*d*) They can be overcome
    (*e*) Acrophobia is a fear of open places; agoraphobia is a fear of high places

22. The current movement of behaviour modification, where in tokens are awarded for correct responses, is a reflection of:
    (*a*) Herbert's Five Steps
    (*b*) Locke's Tabularasa
    (*c*) Thorndike's Law of Effect
    (*d*) Thorndike's Law of Exercise
    (*e*) Pavlov's stimulus-response

23. The evaluation of personality is best made through the use of a/an:
    (*a*) Inventory test
    (*b*) Preference test
    (*c*) Survey test
    (*d*) Projective
    (*e*) Power test

24. During the first year of life a child's height increases by about:
    (*a*) 10 percent
    (*b*) 30 percent
    (*c*) 50 percent
    (*d*) 80 percent
    (*e*) 100 percent

25. The term *identical elements* is closely associated with:
    (*a*) Group instruction
    (*b*) Transfer of learning

(*c*)   Jealousy between twins

(*d*)   Similar test questions

(*e*)   The scientific method

26. The normal twelve-year-old child is most likely to:

(*a*)   Have difficulty with gross motor co-ordination

(*b*)   Have anxiety feelings about pleasing adults

(*c*)   Confine his/her interests to the here and how

(*d*)   Be eager for peer approval

(*e*)   Be concerned with boy-girl relationships

27. The statement least characteristic of first grade children is that they are:

(*a*)   Too young to be taught classroom routines

(*b*)   Not yet concerned with group approval

(*c*)   Very concerned with adult approval

(*d*)   Not concerned with neatness

(*e*)   Curious and exploratory

28. When an individual repeats those learning that, in the past, proved to be highly satisfying, such behaviour can best be explained by the law of:

(*a*)   Recency   (*b*)   Frequency

(*c*)   Readiness   (*d*)   Effect

(*e*)   Exercise

29. Children's attitudes toward persons of different ethnic groups are generally based upon:

(*a*)   Their parent's attitudes

(*b*)   The attitudes of their peers

(*c*)   The influence of television

(*d*)   Their siblings attitudes

(*e*)   Their religious affiliation

30. All of the following are sound mental hygiene practices, except:

(*a*)   Asking pupils to correct their answers after their tests have been marked

(*b*)   Discussing an individual pupil's test marks with in class

(*c*)   Asking parents to sign test papers so that they are aware of their child's marks

(*d*)   Having pupils keep a record of their own test marks

(*e*)   conferring with pupils about the results of a group of tests

31. All of the following advocated principles of child development are closely allied to the stimulus response learning theory, except:

(*a*)   Pavlov   (*b*)   J.B. Watson

(*c*)   Hull   (*d*)   Gesell

(*e*)   Skinner

32. Abhinav and Akanksha have the same mental age, 8-0.We can conclude that:

(*a*)   They have the same potential for success in school

(*b*)   They have the same 19

(*c*)   Their interest are similar

(*d*)   Their ability to learn may be quite different

(*e*)   They copied from each other on the test

33. A child whose class is in a windowless room may have to be assigned to another class if he/she suffers from:

(*a*)   Acrophobia   (*b*)   Agoraphobia

(*c*)   Claustrophobia   (*d*)   Hydrophobia

(*e*)   Toxophobia

34. The self -adjustive mechanism that teachers often unwittingly encourage is:

(*a*)   An attention-getting device

(*b*)   Daydreaming

(*c*)   regression

(*d*)   Fantasy

(*e*)   withdrawal

35. The incorrectly associated pair is:

(*a*)   Joseph Lancaster—contract plan

(*b*)   Benjamin Franklin—academy

(*c*)   James B. Contant—high school

(*d*)   Horace Mann—elementary education

(*e*)   Elizabeth Peabody—Kindergarten

36. The regular teacher should be aware of the disability because:

(*a*)   It interfere with the child's learning

(*b*)   He can serve society better

(*c*)   It will improve his teaching

(*d*)   It improves understanding of the self

37. The teacher can help the child with lower mental ability by:
(*a*) Diagnosis of his problems
(*b*) Referring to special schools
(*c*) Sending him to a special remedial class
(*d*) Providing concrete learning experiences

38. To meet the educational needs of the hearing Impaired child in the regular classroom, the teacher has to face student while speaking so that:
(*a*) The social distance between teacher and student is reduced
(*b*) The students remain under control
(*c*) The students can listen better
(*d*) The students can lip-read

39. Learning disability is because of:
(*a*) Low intelligence
(*b*) Poor socio-economic background
(*c*) Damage to psychological processes
(*d*) Physical injury

40. Learning disability refers to specific problem in:
(*a*) All academic areas
(*b*) Reading and writing
(*c*) Reading, writing and spelling
(*d*) Reading, writing and arithmetic

41. How many members are there in one team in the game of Rugby?
(*a*) 14   (*b*) 15
(*c*) 16   (*d*) 17

42. Total number of substitutes in a team of Rugby are
(*a*) 7   (*b*) 8
(*c*) 9   (*d*) 10

43. The apparatus used in women Gymnastics is-
(*a*) Parallel Bars, Balancing Beam, Vaulting Horse and Uneven Bar.
(*b*) Balancing Beam, Horizontal Bar and Uneven Bars
(*c*) Balancing Beam, Vaulting Horse, Uneven Bars and Floor
(*d*) All of the above.

44. What is the duration of a round in Boxing?
(*a*) 1 minute   (*b*) 2 minutes
(*c*) 3 minutes   (*d*) 4 minutes

45. What is the duration of Rest period in between the two rounds of a professional bout in Boxing?
(*a*) 20 seconds (*b*) 30 seconds
(*c*) 1 minute   (*d*) 1.30 minutes

46. 'Going into the tank' in Boxing means-
(*a*) Abusing the referee
(*b*) A Boxer losing the fight deliberately
(*c*) Throwing towel in the rink
(*d*) None of the above.

47. How many cross lanes are there in Kho-Kho
(*a*) 6   (*b*) 7
(*c*) 8   (*d*) 9

48. How may weight categories are in the game of Judo (Senio men)?
(*a*) 7   (*b*) 8
(*c*) 9   (*d*) 10.

49. Opening command to start the Judo bouts is
(*a*) Hajime   (*b*) Koka
(*c*) Ippon   (*d*) Wazari

50. Highest penalty in Judo is
(*a*) Hanso ko-make (*b*) kei koku
(*c*) Chui   (*d*) Shido

51. Highest point in Judo is-
(*a*) Koka   (*b*) Ippon
(*c*) Waza-ari   (*d*) Yuko

52. How many feathers are there in a shuttle cock?
(*a*) 14 to 16   (*b*) 15 to 17
(*c*) 17 to 19   (*d*) 21 to 24

53. What is the length of a standard swimming pool?
(*a*) 50 meters   (*b*) 60 meters
(*c*) 70 meters   (*d*) 80 meters

54. What is the depth of the water, in a standard size swimming pool?
(*a*) More than 1.8 metres
(*b*) Less than1.8 metres
(*c*) More than 2.0 meters
(*d*) More than 3 metres

55. Which of the following can not be the shape of a swimming pool?
(*a*) A type   (*b*) L type
(*c*) U type   (*d*) V type

56. What is the height of the net in tennis?
(*a*) 2 ft.　　(*b*) 3 ft.
(*c*) 4 ft.　　(*d*) 5 ft.

57. In cricket terminology 'trimmer' is referred to as-
(*a*) A delivery that knocks off the bails only
(*b*) A delivery that does not knocks off the bails
(*c*) A delivery that knocks off the bails but the bails fall back of the stumps
(*d*) A delivery when the ball just touches the batsman and goes for a boundary.

58. How many bouncers can be bowled in one over in a test match in cricket?
(*a*) 1　　(*b*) 2
(*c*) 3　　(*d*) 4

59. What is the length of pitch in cricket?
(*a*) 21 yds　　(*b*) 22 yds
(*c*) 23 yds　　(*d*) 24 yds

60. How many legs does a Billiards Table has?
(*a*) 7　　(*b*) 8
(*c*) 9　　(*d*) 10

61. What is "hiki-wake' in Judo?
(*a*) A draw　　(*b*) A penalty
(*c*) A point　　(*d*) A player

62. Three second rule is applied in the game of-
(*a*) Basketball　　(*b*) Kabaddi
(*c*) Kho-Kho　　(*d*) Table Tennis

63. In weight lifting competition the increase is weight between two attempts must not be less than-
(*a*) 2.5 kg.　　(*b*) 5 kg.
(*c*) 10 kg.　　(*d*) 2 kg.

64. During the conduct of a Penalty stroke in hockey, the umpire takes position over-
(*a*) Cetnre line　　(*b*) 25 yrds
(*c*) Striking circle　　(*d*) Goal line.

65. The height of the backboard of hockey goal is
(*a*) 12 inches　　(*b*) 10 inches
(*c*) 18 inches　　(*d*) 24 inches

66. To take penalty stroke in hockey, any skill can be used except-
(*a*) Push　　(*b*) Flick
(*c*) Scoop　　(*d*) Hit.

67. In soccer the penalty kick spot is marked at a distance of -
(*a*) 12 yards　　(*b*) 8 yards
(*c*) 10 yards　　(*d*) 16 yards

68. In hockey the corner hit is taken from the -
(*a*) back line　　(*b*) Centre line
(*c*) Side linc　　(*d*) Goal line

69. 'Round Robin" is a name given to-
(*a*) Knock out tournament
(*b*) Ladder tournament
(*c*) League type composition
(*d*) None of the above

70. The final event in "Decathlon' is always
(*a*) Javelin throw
(*b*) 1500 meter race
(*c*) 110 meter Hurdles
(*d*) 800 meter race

71. The ability to release maximum muscular force in the shortest possible time is called-
(*a*) Muscular endurance
(*b*) Muscular strength
(*c*) Muscular power
(*d*) Agility

72. Shortening of the muscle occurs during which type of contraction?
(*a*) Concentric contraction
(*b*) Eccentric contraction
(*c*) Isokinetic
(*d*) None of the above

73. Name the device used for recording muscular work-
(*a*) Ergometer　　(*b*) Electromyogram
(*c*) Eergograph　　(*d*) All the above

74. Aerobic exercises contribute to the development of -
(*a*) Speed　　(*b*) Strength
(*c*) Agility　　(*d*) Endurance

75. Which of the following is test trainable-
(*a*) Flexibility　　(*b*) Endurance
(*c*) Speed　　(*d*) Strength

76. Which of the following is the longest cycle of training?
(*a*) Macrocycle　　(*b*) Microcycle
(*c*) Mesocycle　　(*d*) Weekly cycle

77. Duration of a macro-cycle is usually
(*a*) 3-4 months to even 12 months
(*b*) 3-6 weeks
(*c*) One week
(*d*) 3-10 days

78. Mesocycle can be logically achieved in
(*a*) One week   (*b*) 2-5 weeks
(*c*) 3-6 weeks   (*d*) 10 days

79. The first person to give a theoretical base to periodization was
(*a*) Hardayal Singh   (*b*) L. P. Matweyew
(*c*) Minow   (*d*) Bastion

80. The Shortest training cycle is the
(*a*) Mesocycle   (*b*) Microcycle
(*c*) Macro cycle   (*d*) None

81. Continuous training method was introduced by
(*a*) Dr. Ernst Van Aaken
(*b*) Woldemar Gerschler
(*c*) Reindell
(*d*) Morgan

82. LSD (low slow distance) training and – can provide an athlete some relief from high intensity training
(*a*) Interval training (*b*) Fartlek training
(*c*) Speed training   (*d*) Weight training

83. Interval training methods was introduced by
(*a*) Morgan   (*b*) Reindall
(*c*) Gerschler   (*d*) Van Aaken

84. Circuit training was developed by
(*a*) Morgan and Adamson

(*b*) Reindall
(*c*) Van Aaken
(*d*) Marlow

85. Dumb bells, Bar bells and Pulley machines are used in
(*a*) Weight training   (*b*) Speed training
(*c*) Circuit training   (*d*) Strength training

86. Method of training for power or explosiveness is called
(*a*) Fartlek   (*b*) Circuit training
(*c*) Plyometrics   (*d*) Strength training

87. Which of the following is not the technique of flexibility training?
(*a*) Static   (*b*) Ballistic
(*c*) Assisted   (*d*) Circuit

88. Speed endurance can be developed by the use of
(*a*) Circuit training
(*b*) Running
(*c*) Fartlek
(*d*) Competition and time trial

89. Speed endurance cannot be developed with the help of
(*a*) Fartlek   (*b*) Interval training
(*c*) Weight training   (*d*) Circuit training

90. The training method which increases the heart's stroke volume and hence its ability to deliver blood and oxygen to legs is
(*a*) Continuous Training method
(*b*) Fartlek
(*c*) Interval training method
(*d*) Weight training method

ANSWERS

1. (*c*)	2. (*d*)	3. (*a*)	4. (*b*)	5. (*b*)	6. (*c*)	7. (*c*)	8. (*d*)
9. (*d*)	10. (*b*)	11. (*c*)	12. (*c*)	13. (*a*)	14. (*c*)	15. (*a*)	16. (*c*)
17. (*c*)	18. (*c*)	19. (*b*)	20. (*c*)	21. (*e*)	22. (*c*)	23. (*d*)	24. (*c*)
25. (*b*)	26. (*d*)	27. (*a*)	28. (*d*)	29. (*a*)	30. (*b*)	31. (*d*)	32. (*d*)
33. (*c*)	34. (*a*)	35. (*a*)	36. (*a*)	37. (*d*)	38. (*d*)	39. (*c*)	40. (*d*)
41. (*b*)	42. (*a*)	43. (*c*)	44. (*c*)	45. (*c*)	46. (*b*)	47. (*c*)	48. (*b*)
49. (*a*)	50. (*d*)	51. (*b*)	52. (*a*)	53. (*a*)	54. (*c*)	55. (*c*)	56. (*b*)
57. (*a*)	58. (*b*)	59. (*b*)	60. (*b*)	61. (*a*)	62. (*a*)	63. (*b*)	64. (*d*)
65. (*c*)	66. (*d*)	67. (*a*)	68. (*c*)	69. (*c*)	70. (*b*)	71. (*c*)	72. (*a*)
73. (*c*)	74. (*d*)	75. (*c*)	76. (*a*)	77. (*a*)	78. (*c*)	79. (*b*)	80. (*b*)
81. (*a*)	82. (*b*)	83. (*c*)	84. (*a*)	85. (*a*)	86. (*c*)	87. (*d*)	88. (*d*)
89. (*b*)	90. (*c*)						

10. PLAY AND ITS THEORIES

MEANING AND DEFINITION OF PLAY

Play is a recreational activity, with which joy is associated.

Various psychologists have given different definitions of play. They are as follows:

1. According to Ross, *"Play is joyful, spontaneous, creative activity, in which man finds fullest expression."*
2. According to Valentine, *"Play is joyful activity, carried on for its own sake."*
3. According to Ruskin, *'Play is the exerting of body and mind made to please ourselves without a determined end."*
4. In the view of Gollick, *"Play is what we do when we are fit to do what we like."*
5. According to Lazarus, *"Play is an activity which is in itself free, aimless, amusing and diverting."*
6. In the view of T.P. Nunn, *"Play is powerful manifestation of creative activities."*
7. According to Stern, *"Play is a kind of self-constrained activity."*
8. In the opinion of Hurlock, *"Play relates to any activity. engaged in for the engaged in for the enjoyment it gives, without consideration of the end result."*
9. According Co Crow and Crow, *"Play can be defined as the activity which a person engages when he is free to do which he wants to do."*

These definitions reveal one aspect or more of play. However, each of these definitions regards play essentially a motor activity and points out the type of its motor activity. We can summarize the results these definitions in the following way:

1. Play is an activity which is undertaken for its own sake.
2. It gives enjoyment or amusement. The enjoyment or amusement lies in the activity itself.
3. It provides opportunity for self-expression.
4. It is purely a voluntary activity. There is no compulsion of any kind in it.
5. It is performed completely in a spirit of freedom and liberty.
6. It brings us into free and easy company with our fellows with whom we play.

DIFFERENCE BETWEEN WORK AND PLAY

Valentine has said, *"Play is an activity carried out for its own sake"*. If we accept his views on play, then what is the difference between work which is enjoyed and play.

It is very difficult to differentiate between enjoyed work and play. They may differ in relation to the individual's attitudes towards any activity and not in the forms of activities. The same activity can be play as well as work according to the attitude of a person towards it. For example, gardening can be play for a person interested in it, but it will become work if it is the part of a person's instruction duty.

We should remember here that work is something which we have to do. It has some motive behind it. Work is always carried out for some end or purpose. But play has no specific end or purpose behind it. In fact, play is something which we can do if we like. When a player plays a game, there is no specific purpose in his mind. But if a professional player plays the same merely for getting money or earning his livelihood, it becomes work for him.

Ross has differentiated work and play in the following way

"If we perform any activity joyfully and on our owe accord, with a minimum of external

compulsion and restraint and if in much activity our instincts, either in a crude or sublimated form are finding their satisfactions, then that activity is play to us. If on the other hand, there Is neither joy nor spontaneity, if our whole heart and soul are not in what we are doing, then the spirit of play is absent and the activity must be called work."

Another difference between work and play is that work is undertaken for necessity and play for its own sake.

According to Drever, *"In play, the value and significance of the activity are found in the activity itself, whereas in work they lie outside. It is true for every play and every work."*

Play is a recreational activity and joy is associated with it. In work joy is associated with the successful completion of that work. There is no undue strain or pressure on the mind in play, but work is strenuous.

In play all the players are very serious in playing but that seriousness is self-imposed while in work the worker has to be serious by external control.

In work the ends or purposes are of real world, but in play the ends or purposes are of make-believe shape. Play can be changed according to one's desire, but work is such a duty, which cannot be changed so easily as desired.

THEORIES OF PLAY

There is tendency to play in all children and grown-up people. This leads us to a burning question as to what is the purpose of play or why do we play. Mc Dougall has called play a 'non-specific' or general tendency. So it must have some purpose behind it. Our question 'why do we play' can be expressed by the theory of play. Many psychologists have given various theories of play. Some of them are given below :–

1. Surplus Energy Theory: It is one of the oldest and widely accepted theories of play. It defines play as an excess of energy in children because they are free from all kinds of pressures like economic, social and domestic pressures. Hence they express their surplus energy in play. This theory was first propounded by Schiller and later on developed by Herbert Spencer. According to their views the child has not to worry about earning his livelihood. He does not have to search for food. Hence the surplus. energy that overflows his nervous channel is expressed in purposeless movements. Therefore play is just like a safety valve of an engine. It is a healthy outlet for super abundant energy.

Criticism: No doubt, there is some element of truth in this theory but it is inadequate to account for all kinds of play.

Secondly, sometimes play is undertaken when there is no abundant energy. When the child is tired and asked to go to bed by the mother, he requests for more game to play.

Thirdly, play is wrongly compared with safety valve of an engine. The safety valve has no productive effect upon engine, though it may save it from bursting. But play has productive value for human body. It builds the tissues and develops the muscles of human body.

2. Recreational Theory: Lazarus has, propounded recreational theory of play. He has regarded play as recreative. According to his view play builds up and restores energy lost through work. It removes fatigue and boredom.

Lovell has seconded this theory of play. According to his view, "while sleep and rest are necessary for rest, a change to an interesting and active play is more restful."

Criticism: This theory is also partly correct as it explains one aspect of play *i.e.* recreation. The games of competition are not played for the sake of recreation.

Secondly, body and mind are interrelated. The fatigue of one brings fatigue to the other also. So there is little scope of recreation through play.

3. Anticipatory Theory: Karl Groose has propounded the anticipatory theory of play. He claimed that the key to play lies in preparation for future life. He has explained this theory with reference to the plays of animals and human children. He has given a number of examples to prove this theory. Building of clay or sand houses, Mechano toys, group games and playing with dolls are for the preparation of future life. The 'make-believe' world of the child is to be restored in future by the real world of adulthood.

According to Ross, *"Play is perfecting by experience of the more specialized and difficult kinds of activity on the successful exercise of which their survival in the struggle for existence must depend."*

This theory is called "Practice Theory." A kitten pounces on a ball on the floor, thus practicing to catch its prey or mouse in the future life. Puppies wrestling with each other prepare themselves to become good fighters. Hence T. P Nunn has said, *"Nature has invented play not merely as a mean of disposing off the young animal's superfluous energy, but as a device for using that energy to prepare him for serious business of life."*

In fact play serves biological utility to the race. It is the nature's most important mode of education for future life. That is why Karl Croose has said, *"We do not play because we are young, but we are young in order to play and prepare for future life."*

Criticism: The theory is quite convincing as regards the plays of children are concerned. But it does not explain as to why the adults play even when they have other serious business of life.

Moreover, it is hardly believable that all plays of children, animals and human beings are anticipatory in nature. In case of human children Interests vary at various age levels. Therefore all the players cannot be predictors of the future career of a person.

4. Recapitulatory Theory: This theory has been propounded by Stanely Hall. He maintained that child relives the life of his ancestors. He also maintained that various games of children are simply revival of the various stages of human history. In the past, primitive man adopted various rudimentary techniques of house building. Hence the child in his play builds a house of sand. He thus repeats the old history of building of houses by human beings in the simplest forms.

Criticism: This theory is too far fetched and can hardly be accepted. The child in fact uses in his play old and new techniques used by human race. If the child builds houses of sand while playing, he also plays with Mechano which is a toy resembling a modern machine.

5. Cathartic Theory: According to this theory play is cathartic in its action. It provides an outlet for certain part of energies, instincts and emotions, which cannot find expression in the childhood or adult life.

In fact, play activities provide opportunities for the expression of the feelings that would otherwise remain bottled up in the mind. For example, children while taking part in a dramatic play, can ridicule their teacher or parents. But they cannot do so actually in life. Similarly there is catharis of instructive and emotional energy when children engage themselves in in-door as well as out-door games.

Criticism: This theory of play has certain defects. All the children do not 'have repressed and unbalanced emotions to be purged out through play, but still they play with great interest.

Moreover, all the play activities are not related with emotions. This theory takes into account only the release of psychric energy and neglects the physical aspect of play activities.

CONCLUSION

The various theories of play try to explain the purpose of particular types of play activities. But none of them gives valid reasons for explaining all the forms of play activities.

Moreover, all human beings differ in their interests, needs, abilities and capacities. So the purpose for playing cannot be the same for all persons, whether they are children or adults.

Hence we should try to synthesize the different view-points expressed by these theories. By combining all the view points and explanations put forth by these theories, we can get proper answer to our question. "Why do we adults or children play?' Hence there is no single theory of play to depend upon.

IMPORTANCE OF PLAY IN EDUCATION

The importance of play in the educative percess can scarcely he exaggerated. Begehot has remarked, *"Before letters were invented, the outdoor life, the fights and wrestling sinew, the old games, foot ball and cricket, the hard blows given and the hard blows received, all these were education."*

There are many educational aspects of play. Out of them two educational aspects are very important. One aspect is of physical development and the second is relation of play with school subjects.

The physical games provide complete enjoyment and recreation. They make the minds and brains of children quite fresh after they have put in hard mental labour over their studies. Moreover, they furnish opportunities for the development of good personality through the maxim of 'sound mind in sound body,' They also develop desirable social qualities in children.

Moreover the play spirit in the class room makes education very easy. The play spirit educates without letting the students know that they are being educated. It provides free activities in the school programme in which the students play and get educated by themselves.

PLAY AND ITS THEORIES

The physical games give the body practice in co-ordination its movements. Through these games children acquire various forms of bodily skills, habits of frankness, punctuality, co-operation and unselfishness.

Moreover play provides opportunities for gratifying needs and desires in a socially acceptable manner, thus helping in maintaining good mental health besides good physical health. Even in their crudest forms, games, competitions and athletic contests not only mould the behaviour of children, but also prepare them for social life, leadership, sacrifice and discipline. They train them to sacrifice personal ends for collective ends.

Play impulse is also regarded as one of the principal sources of artistic creacion. Plays provides ample opportunities for information regarding new colours and new textures. Even mentally upset and mal-adjusted children get freedom for self expression in socially approved manner by various forms of play.

VARIOUS TYPES OF PLAY

There are many types of play. Some of the important types are as follows :

1. Experimental plays: These plays include random handling of objects, through which children get sensory experience. Children also get acquaintance with the environment through the experimental games.

2. Movement plays: These types of plays refer to random movements of children. In fact, children get muscular control by these plays.

Little children make meaningless sound, run aimlessly and show complete restlessness. In bigger children such movements take the form of hide and seek and other such movement plays.

3. Constructive plays: In constructive plays children make the different objects with blocks and sticks. Girls generally play with Mechano etc.

4. Fighting plays: Fighting plays are meant for grown-up children. These plays include wresting, boxing and kabaddi.

5. Group or team plays: Group or team plays include games of group competition and team work games, such as football, hockey, cricket, basket ball, volley ball etc.

6. Athletics and Elastic Games: These plays include athletics and gymnastics involving single competition, instead of team competition.

7. Intellectual and emotional play: These plays include games, which employ mental power of children. Some of these games are word-building, crossword puzzles, story telling and dramatization etc.

All the above games are very beneficial for the physical, mental and intellectual development of children.

PLAYWAY METHODS

Meaning

According to Levell *"Such method is as try to harness the natural and acquired tendencies of the child to provide motivation for learning in an easy and quick way are called playway methods."*

In the words of B.M. Jha, *"When the element of enjoyment is introduced in a serious activity, it is carried out in a play way method."*

Benefits of Playway Methods

An activity in which the doer is allowed complete freedom of self expression and enjoyment always gives pleasure to the individual. The advocates of playway methods believe that children learn most rapidly when their interests and attitudes are catered for and when they work freely in a group.

Social psychologists believe that if in a classroom situation the teacher is dominating, child's social and natural impulses are likely to be frustrated. But if children work in a team spirit, they work with full enjoyment jointly and easily.

Playway Method of Education

In recent times many modern playway methods have been introduced in education. They are as follows

1. Montessorie Method: This method was devised by Madam Montessorie. It includes a number of play activities. It eliminates drudgery and provides joyful spirit to children for learning easily. The children play with a special pidactic apparatus in this method. The Intellectual training proceeds side by side with the physical development. The apparatus is designed in such a manner that it can provide proper education of the senses through playway methods.

2. Kindergarten Method: Play occupies a very important place in Kindergarten Method. This method was devised by Froebel, who tried to bring play and work together. 'Kindergarten' means garden of children. In it the teacher is the gardener who cultivates the plants of children and helps them to grow on healthy lines.

The children are given full freedom to work and play as they desire. The teacher is there only to guide them with tender love and fondness.

3. School Journey Method: It is very interesting and successful method for teaching children. They are taken out of doors. They study Geography from rivers, mountains, valleys, seas, sea shores and oceans. They study history from ancient castles, cathedrals and relics of ancient ages.

4. Boy Scout and Girl Guide Movement: These movements are purely the outcome of playway method. These activities emphasize the importance of utilising leisure in a useful and playful way. They provide opportunities for self expression through various joyful activities like games, sports and camp fires. They lay emphasis on doing everything through self-effort.

5. Self Government Method: All good schools have arrangement for Perfect System, 'House System', Monitor System, Student Unions and Student Associations. In these systems the students are given a chance for self-government. The emphasis is on playway spirit in school government, so that the students may recognise school as a joyful society in miniature, which is organised on the lines of democracy. The natural instincts of students like self-assertion, self-abasement, pugnacity etc. get free expression through it. The children also get best training for citizenship of a broad society through this method.

6. Intellectual Games Method: Many intellectual games are included in this method. The games sharpen the intellect of children and give them chance to learn things by their own efforts. Some of such intellectual games are word-building, Mechano, trade game. They are also based on the principle of play.

7. Dramatisation Method: This method gives a free chance to the students to express their view points through the stage and learn easily through dramatic performance. Imaginative activity of the children finds its firm basis in this method.

8. Method of Hobbies: This method utilizes hobbies for educative purposes. Many hobbies can be pursued by children according to their interest. Some of the hobbies are stamp collecting, feather collecting, coin collecting, drawing, painting, collection of plants, weeds, samples of soil and stones, leaves and fossils. These hobbies can help the children in learning Natural Science, History and Geography through self effort. They enjoy the activities connected with hobbies of their own interest and learn many things very easily.

9. Method of Audio-Visual Aids: Children play with as well learn from Audio Visual Aids. They enjoy them also. These aids are very useful for educational purposes as well for the physical health of children. There are many Audio-Visual Aids, such as cinema strips, slides, tape records, television, radio, charts, models, phonogramme etc. They attract the attention of children and provide them great pleasure.

10. Conclusion: We can conclude that playway methods perform very important role in the education of young children. If we thrust and force a prescribed syllabus or fixed time table upon the children, we cannot get the desired results of teaching them easily.

No doubt, there are some people who criticize playway methods and call them non-serious, but even in the face of certain limitations playway methods have shown wonderful results in the field of education. Hence full use should be made of them to help children in self-education process.

DIMENSIONS OF PERSONALITY

1. Physical Dimension: The physical body structure or the physique is the primary aspect or dimension of human personality and all other dimensions are subservient to it. No doubt that heredity has a very important role in the development of this aspect of personality, but heredity alone would be helpless if appropriate environment is not available, and vice–versa environment alone is not sufficient enough for development of physical aspect of personality as without genetic support, it would be without any base. It will be appropriate to suggest that genetics provide the plinth or base of personality and environment helps in raising a beautiful structure thereon.

The comments such as "he has got a wonderful personality" or "he is not having a good personality" are quite common. This common conception of personality reflects the importance attached to the physical dimension of personality by the society . We everyday hear that first impression is the last impression. This first impression, obviously, refers to one's physical appearance i.e. the outward mask, and how one carries himself. Physique i.e., the height structure and muscular framework, has profound effect on the onlookers. An individual possessing a well built physique tends to be more confident of himself . The manner or the way he carries himself, not only has aesthetic appeal, but is also a source of admiration from others. It has been generally

observed that persons having weak, sick and deformed physique are not sure of themselves whereas persons having tall, robust and athletic built have commanding and effective appearance. Good physique and health do have positive relationship. A person having good healthy physique is able to mobilize all his resources to lead zestful and harmonious life. A healthy individual not only contributes to the welfare of the society but is an asset to it.

Physical dimension has attracted the attention of psychologists as well as physiologists from the time immemorial, almost since the start of our civilization. Classification of human beings on the basis of their physical built-up and structure is probably, the oldest type of classification in the history of our evolution.

Since early times there have been serious efforts to discover types of physique and to relate the same to various aspects of personality. *Naccarati* (1921) adopted a morphological index the ratio of height to weight, as the most satisfactory indicator of physical type, and gave threefold classification:

1. miscroplanchnics, characterized by small trunks and development of the limbs in excess of the trunk (the thin, slender body build);

2. macrosplanchnics (or megalos-planchnics), denoted by large trunks, excessively developed (the short and fat body build); and

3. n*ormosplanchnics,* who show a harmonious development of physical constitution. Hall lateron, classified persons into four types : *Muscular, thoracic abdominal, and nervous.*

In the early twentienth century, *Kretchmer* in his book "physique and Character" based his classification on three biological types according to physical structure, and using Greek terminology, described the same as :

1. Picknik (having round and fat bodies) who were good natured, happy sociable and easy going,

2. Athletic (having robust, well built, and balanced body) who were energetic,

adjustable and social by temperament; and

3. Asthenic (having lean, thin long limbed, slender body structure) who were sensitive, imaginary, emotional and idealistic.

Berman suggested six body types on the assumption that one or two glands may have an ascendant function in a given individual :

1. *Thymocentric personality* marked by lack of inhibitory capacity, moral irresponsibi-lity, criminality, and general incapacity to meet the demands of a taxing environment;

2. *Thyroid personality*, having excessive activity, quick mentality, impulsiveness restlessness , and great energy;

3. *Adrenal personality*, having intense energy, vigour, and persistence in case of hyper adrenals, and in case of adrenal insufficiency revealing lack of energy, irritability, dullness, fatigability, and loss of appetite;

4. *Pituitary personality* which is of two types, one which tends to be masculine, and the other which tends to be feminine;

5. *Eidetic type personality*, who are perpetually restless, eternally unsatisfied, and who hold themselves aloof from others,

6. *Gonadocentric personality*, those lacking proper and normal development of masculinity.

In his book "The Varieties of Temperament" Sheldon based his classification on the temperamental and physical characteristics to provide three types of personalities :

1. *Endomorphic* (having round, fat, and soft bodies), who were fond of food, easy going, slow in reactions, and sociable.

2. *Mesomorphic* (having well developed, rugged and athletic body) who were adventurous, assertive, courageous, and having a liking for physical activity; and

3. *Ectomorphic* (having weak, fragile, and delicate body build) who were reserved, anxious pessimistic, and having inhibition towards physical activity.

2. Mental and Intellectual Dimension: A well built physical stature of an individual, devoid of mental and intellectual abilities, is just like a statue without life. The fact that human beings have been bestowed with higher mental and intellectual abilities, is an important distinguishing feature between them and other living organisms. Human personality loses its meaning if conceived without mind and intellect. Man is a psychophysical organism i.e. a mind and body unit and one part is incapable of effective survival without the other. It is the marvel of human intellect that has made it possible for us to explore the universe. Renowned psychologists, physiologists, scientists, philosophers, and leaders are known for their mental and intellectual abilities. Those of us who are more intelligent and mentally alert, react and respond quickly to any sort of stimulation, and understand the things in a better way, are always in an advantageous position in the society. Mental and intellectual capabilities of an individual help him in adjusting to new requirements, circumstances, and overchanging conditions of present day life in a most appropriate way. Importance of mental and intellectual dimension can never be over emphasized.

As with many other modern ideas it was the Greeks, especially *Hippocrates* who first introduced the concept of type on the basis of emotional or temperamental features of personality. He divided people into four types of temperamental personalities, on the basis of four fluids or "humors" i.e. black bile, yellow bile, blood and phlegm. As per his classification, predominance of any of these fluids gave an individual a unique and different type of temperament :

1. those who had predominance of black bile (melancholic) were considered bad tempered, depressed, dejected, and pessimistic;

2. those with yellow bile (choleric) were irritable, short tempered, strong and imaginative:

3.   those having predominance of blood (sanguine) were light hearted, cheerful, and happy; and

4.   those having predominance of phlegm (phlegmatic) were considered slow, cold indifferent, and unresolved.

Perhaps the best known and the most important classification of personality is give by *Jung*. He begins with the assumption of a fundamental life force or energy in human beings which tend to take one or the other of the two directions; either outward i.e. towards the external environment, or inward i.e. towards one's subjective life patterns. On this basis, he divided the personality into two divisions extrovert and introvert. Each type, extrovert or introvert, is organized around one of the four fold features : thinking, feeling, sensation or intuition. The extroverts have more self confidence, take more interest in others, are outgoing lively and realistic. They are very social and form friends quite easily. Actors, social and political leaders, etc. belong to this group. On the other hand, introverts are too self conscious, they are more interested in their own thoughts and ideas, are self centerd, shy, reserved, and lovers of solitude. They do not make friends easily and keep in background on social occasions. Philosophers, poets, artists, scientists etc. belong to this class. Doubting whether people can be divided into these two distinctive classes, it has been suggested that between these two extremes lie most of the people, who have been labelled as *Ambiverts*. The ambiverts are a mixture of both the extremes in a balanced manner. Ambiverts are neither out-going nor reserved to themselves, they are able to adjust themselves with any situation.

Sheldon, apart from providing classification on the basis of physique, also gave three types of personalities on the basis of temperament:

1.   Vicerotonic (happy outgoing and lovers of food);

2.   Somatotonic (assertive, bold and risk taking) and

3.   Cerebrotonic (studious, tense, and introverted).

3. Social Dimension: Inherently, by nature man is a social being. He has learnt speaking reading, writing and behaving with others from the society in which he lives. If he is isolated completely from the society, he will not be able to survive for long. Human beings are not only gregarious, liking to be in sight of his fellows, but also have an innate propensity to get themselves noticed, and noticed favourably. Man besides gratification of his biological needs and values, must fulfill such emergent social values as status, power, affection and good will. This is necessary in order that he may have a feeling of being at home in the social world. Sociological and psychological tendencies are intimately related to each other. Psychologically each individual is born with specific inherent attitudes, interest, tendencies, and capacities. In order to be an acceptable member of the society, he has to mould and modify his behaviour, learn and acquire various manners qualities and etiquettes, and has to follow the rules, customs and traditions of the society. The social interaction enables an individual to develop social attributes like tolerance, cooperation and fair play. It inculcates the spirit of service and sacrifice, and cultivates a sense of responsibility and duty besides providing social efficiency. It can thus be said that the essence of an individual's development is the development of the society.

An individual has to discipline all his wishes and desires and be prepared for sacrifices in order to live smoothly in the society. The real recognition of one's personality comes from the society in which he lives. The truth is that both, the individual and the society, are mutually interdependent and inseparable. One cannot exist without the other. Both develop each other integrally and har-moniously, with full sense of responsibility.

Undoubtedly sociability is a very important quality of human beings. The manner in which he interacts with other members of the society, how he influences their work and conduct, and how he himself is influenced by others is an important aspect of personality. Sociality or social dimension of personality has much wider implications than the other dimensions of personality. Social dimension is the sum of integration of those traits which categorize the typical reactions of one person towards other persons. Social dimension is, essentially, a matter of how one responds to himself and others.

The possibility of classifying people in terms of their principal social roles has been recognized since long. Theophrastus, a disciple of Aristotle, in the third century before Christian era, attempted to classify the role and status of individuals in society. In his book "Ethical Character" he has described three types. "the flatterer". "The boor", and "the coward". *Lateron, Thomas* and *Znnaiaecki* predicted three types of personality development:

1. The philistine, or a practical man, who over emphasizes the wish for security and safety,
2. The Bohemian, who inclines toward new experiences, is flighty, and has consistent interests which determine much of his behaviour; and
3. The creative man, who though relatively stable, possesses the capacity for modification of attitudes and wishes in terms of some goal or aim of a creative sort in the fields of art, religion, politics, economics etc.

Burgess, while attempting a sociological interpretation of personality, offered a classification of three types of personality :
1. The objective or direct, with such features as equability, enthusiasm, franknes, and aggressiveness,
2. Introspective or indirect, marked by imaginative, sensitive, and inhibited forms of thinking, and
3. The psychopathic or perverse, categorized by eccentricity, egocentrism, emotional instability, and strong sense of inferiority.

Basing his analysis of personality on one's reactions towards society, **Spranger** suggested six categories :
1. *Theoretical* – metaphysician and pure scientists,
2. *Economic* – Typical business man.
3. *Esthetic* – sensuous gratification unreliable,
4. *Social* – interested in fellow beings and social movements,
5. *Political* – desires power over others, and
6. *Religious* – either mystic or missionary type.

4. Emotional Dimension: Emotion is an all important factor in life and occupies a very prominent position in our daily life. A life devoid of emotions is insipid and unattractive. Love, affection, etc are not the only emotions by which our life is made worth living. Emotions make our life interesting as well as dull, happy as well as unhappy. These are present in each and every living organism at all the stages of development. Emotions are personal in nature, and differ from an individual to individual. A child is not born with innate emotional experiences but he learns to show different emotions by experience. Every person responds to the situations as a result of emotions differently. Every emotional experience involves many physical and physiological changes in our body. Emotions increase energy mobilization in our body. The effect of emotions on our body may be beneficial or harmful, According to *Ruch*, " Emotions play a vital part in our motivational pattern. Life without emotions would be, virtually a life without motion." They determine as to what kind of personal and social adjustments an individual will make, not only as a child but also as an adult. They are responsible for finest human characteristics as well as for the most horrible and mean things of life. Dominance of unpleasant emotions is harmful to good personal and social adjustments and any interference with good emotional development will play havoc with an individual's adjustment in life. Since control over the life environment becomes increasingly difficult as we grow up, we should learn to control emotions and develop emotional tolerance – the ability to accept and adjust to unpleasant emotional experiences. A well controlled person has the ability to quickly control shift on emotional reaction. On the basis of emotions, **Morgan and Gilliland** classified personality into four types :

1. Elated (happy and optimistic),
2. Depressed (pessimistic and emotional)
3. Irritable (short tempered), and
4. Unstable (Unbalanced and emotional).

PERSONALITY TRAITS

In every day life, no one, not even psychologists, doubt that underlying the conduct of a mature person there are characteristic dispositions or traits. We usually think of personality as being made up of traits. Psychologists have defined a trait as a mode of behaviour. Traits are not creations in the mind of the observer, nor are they verbal fictions; they are accepted biophysical facts, actual psychological dispositions . These are specific qualities of bahaviour or adjustive patterns, such as reactions to frustrations, ways of meeting problems, specific patterns, aggressive or defensive behaviour, and outgoing or withdrawing behaviour in the presence of others. The traits are outward signs of dynamic forces that act and interact in an infinite number of ways. That is why the integration of these traits or personality – is never the same in any two individuals. In the opinion of *Gordon Allport*, the personality traits are dynamic and flexible dispositions, resulting, at least in part, from the integration of specific habits, expressing characteristic modes of adaptation to one's surroundings." *M. A. May*, in his article "Problems of Measuring Character and Personality:" has concluded that "traits are only convenient names given to types or qualities of behaviour which have elements in common. They are not psychological entities, but rather categories for the classification of habits". An individual's patterns of behaviour are influenced by the sanctions and restrictions imposed by the social environment wherein he grows up. As he develops towards maturity, many characteristic traits tend to become a permanent habit, and his behaviour reflects inner adjustments towards life situations attained through varied experiences at home, in school, and in social set ups. These adjustments

have direct influence on the kind of behaviour expected from him to the normal life situation.

Traits are a product of learning, though they are based on hereditary foundations. They are moulded mainly by child's training in the home and school, and by imitating a person with whom the child identifies himself. Later the child will emulate the traits of members of the peer group, developing characteristic methods of adjustment accepted and approved by that group. Traits continue in a relatively unchanged form over a period of time and can, however be modified with experience. Traits are not directly observable; they are inferred. We do not directly observe a trait in another person. We observe specific indictions, acts, and verbalizations, and from these we generalize and draw conclusions. If we see an individual lose his temper with slight provocation in several situations, we say that he has a trait of irritability. What we have observed, is in essence, a correlation, a functional consistency across situations. Traits are not at all times active, but they are persistent even when latent.

Each person is unique, not only by virtue of an inherited physiological organism which will not be exactly like that of anyone else, but more importantly, by virtue of his unique pattern of experiences which induce perceptions distinctively his own. Strictly speaking, no two persons have precisely the same trait. Though each of two men may be aggressive, the style and range of the aggression in each case will be noticeably different. In contrast to this position, it must be noted that all of us have certain experiences in common. This fact enables us to quite safely assume that certain common traits can also be identified in a population having a fairly uniform cultural milieu. However, in the strict sense of the definition of traits, only the individual trait is a true trait : (a) because traits are always in individuals and not in the community at large, and (*b*) because they develop and generalize into dynamic dispositions in unique ways according to the experiences of each individual . The common trait is not a true trait at all, but is merely a measurable aspect of complex individual traits.

Classification of Personality Traits

In every personality there are traits of major significance and traits of minor significance. **Allport** was of the view that traits may exist at several levels, and classified the same as cardinal traits, central traits, and secondary traits :

1. ***Cardinal Traits :*** occasionally, some traits are so pervasive and so outstanding in life that they deserve to be called the *cardinal traits.* These are so dominant that there are few activities that cannot be traced. Directly or indirectly to their influence, these are so powerful that they permeate every aspect of an individual's life. No such trait can remain hidden for long; an individual is known by it, and may even become famous for it. Though pervasive and pivotal, a cardinal trait still remains within the personality; it never coincides with it.

2. ***Central Traits :*** Next in the hierarchy are a handful of distinguishable central traits. *Central traits* are those which are usually mentioned in careful letters of recommendations, in rating scale where the rater starts the outstanding characteristics of the individual, or in brief verbal descriptions of a person. These traits are the characteristics that are, although important, but not as all pervasive as cardinal traits, eg. aggressiveness, kindness, etc.

3. ***Secondary Traits :*** On still lower pedestal, and less important level, are *secondary traits*, which are less conspicuous, less generalized, less consistent and less often called into play than central traits. They may escape the notice of all but close acquaintances. These traits are characteristics that emerge as situational preferences and behaviours.

Certain traits are readily observable; they appear in interpersonal contacts, in one's way of doing of a job, in responses to questionnaires.

Cattell has designated them as Surface traits. Cheerfulness, liveliness and quarrelsomeness are such traits. On the other hand are Source traits, which may be thought as underlying structures, expressed not directly but through the medium of surface traits. Source traits and surface traits are interchangeable means of personality description. A single surface trait may be a result of the action of one, two, or more underlying source traits. Source traits are thus, in part explanatory whereas surface traits are merely descriptive. Source traits have wider utility, stability, and meaning than surface traits. Source traits spring from influences that may be either in environmental objects and institutions – in which case they are called *"environmental mould traits"* or from sources within the constitution of an individual, in which case they are called "constitutional traits". Surface traits may be a combination of both these two. Both the source and surface traits are likely to vary with the cultural pattern and with the range of genetics and racial constitutions in the population. After examining 4500 traits, Cattell stated that there were 46 surface traits and 16 source traits,   Lateron, he added three more source traits (zestfulness , excitability, and boorishness) in this list.

Cattell postulated that human behaviour is a result of interaction between external situations and an individual's traits. He has further divided personality traits into three categories on the basis of qualities of personality; temperamental traits (being persistently irritable, easy going, or bold), ability traits (such as intelligence and skill, while dealing complex situations) and dynamic traits (such as motivation, interest and attitude). He further sub-divided dynamic traits into attitudes, sentiments, and urges.

Functioning of the Traits

Two views have been put forward with regard to the functioning of the traits. According to one of them it can be said that behaviour of an individual is regulated from within and is independent of external environment i.e. a sincere person will be sincere in all the situations while dealing with other people. This approach may be referred as the *theory of "unitary" or general traits*. On the other hand, some psychologists while explaining the functioning of the traits lay emphasis on behaviour response while facing the demands of situation rather than upon any integration of traits within the Individual. This view has been labelled as *the theory of "specificity" of traits*. On the basis of extensive investigations, *Cattell* has developed 16 Personality Factor Questionnaire to assess the dimensions of personality.

FACTORS AFFECTING DEVELOPMENT OF PERSONALITY (HEREDITY AND ENVIRONMENT)

Our planet is inhabited by countless species, and all the species have some features unique to themselves which distinguish them not only from other species but within themselves also. Each living organism is born with a unique genetic code, a genetic blueprint , which is passed on to it from its parents. Many authors have termed this as Nature. Once born, every living organism is subjected to diverse environmental conditions, some favourable and some hostile, which influence its growth and development . This environment has been termed as Nurture.

Heredity

Human life starts from a single cell, the zygot, produced by the union of two germ cells, one each from the parents, It is this tiny cell which contains all that a child is to biologically inherit form his parents .Genes are very small units present on the chromosomes carried by this cell, it has 23 pairs of chromosomes. These genes are the most powerful indicators of what is being passed on to the child. Genes do not just orchestrate our growth before birth and then leave us alone. Instead, they are "turning on" and "turning off" in patterned ways throughout our life span and they are partly responsible for attributes and behaviour patterns that we carry with us through out our lives. Unique individual genetic make-ups cause us to develop and age in our own ways. The genetic make up or genotype determines our physiological and even some psychological peculiarities. These genotypes or the cluster of genes, transmit the sum total of the traits which we are to inherit from our parents. Heredity is the nature's process of passing on certain physical and mental characteristics from one generation to another. Heredity is the development potential one receives from its parents, which may be similar or dissimilar to the parents.

Environment

Environment, plays a very significant role in shaping one's personality. According to **Woodworth** "Environment covers all the outside factors that have acted on the individual since he began life." Soon after his birth, a Child is exposed to complex external environment physical as well as social, or cultural.

Heredity Versus Environment

The natural question, that then, arises is whether it is the heredity (the nature) or the environment (the nurture) that plays the 'title' role in one's development. Psychologists like *Galton, Karl Pearson* and others hold the view that heredity is more important than the environment. On the other hand, *Locke, Watson* and others have completely divergent opinion and believe that environment alone is responsible for moulding and shaping human personality. To understand the implication of this controversy, let us examine the example of a plant's life cycle. The seed, on whose germination depends the emergence of the plant, has within it all the characteristics that the plant is to have : its type — whether it will be a bush or a tall tree, its shape and size, shape and structure of its leaves, shape, colour and even fragrance of its flowers the type and taste of its fruit and even the mode of dispersal of seeds for further propagation, are all encoded there in. In short, the seed contains the whole life story of the plant. But the climatic conditions of the place where it is sown, availability of water and sunlight, the composition of the soil, mineral and nutritional elements available in the soil, all influence (positively or negatively) to give shape to the final product, the plant, i.e., the expression of the traits within the seed is to some extent dependent upon the environment. Similarly, in case of human beings also, the environment, physical and social, in which a child is brought up, do influence and mould his personality characteristics.

In reality, it is to the Nature OR Nurture which influence the human development but it is the Nature AND Nurture combination which produce the end result – the human personality. Human characteristics do not fall into two mutually exclusive classes, one hereditary and other the environmental. The genetic constitution sets the limits and the general direction of development, and the environment works on it. The development of personality is a result of constant interaction of the organism and its environment. *Lefton* has very appropriately stated that "A person's genetic make-up is the foundation on which all his or her behaviours are built. Experiences in the environment act in collaboration with inheritance to shape day today behaviour." Environment is incapable of changing the basic hereditary characteristics, what it does is to provide opportunities for full expression of these characteristics. We change in response to the environment. All the external physical and social conditions and events can affect us. From crowded living accommodations to stimulating social interactions, all do affect us. Developmental changes are generally the product of a complex interplay between "Nature"- the genetic endowment and the "Nurture" the environmental influences. *Ann Anastasi* had asserted many years ago that "instead of asking how much is due to genes and how much is due to environment, we should be asking how heredity and environment work together to make us what we are."

It is quite clear that genes do not determine anything; instead, they provide us the potentials that are realized or not, depending on the quality of our experiences. The development of personality characteristics is result of not only the genetic and environmental interaction but those are also inter-related. It will not be incorrect to say that they are intimately intertwined. How our genotypes are expressed depends on what kind of environment we experience, and how we respond to the environment depends on what kinds of genes we have. Growing up in a deprived environment can make a child with the genetic potential to be genius to perform as a poorly child with far les genetic potential.

The concept of gene environment interaction tells us that people with different genes react differently to the environments they encounter. The concept of gene–environment correlation also tells us that people with different genes, encounter different environments.

The gene–environment correlation can be of three types : passive, evocative and active.

1. ***Passive correlations :*** The kind of home environment that parents provide for their children is influenced in party by the parents own genotypes. For example sociable parents not only transmit their "social" genes, they create a very social home environment. Such children not only inherit genes, for sociability, but also receive environment that matches their genes and that makes them even more sociable. Such correlation between gene and environment is called passive correlation.

2. ***Evocative correlations :*** An individual's genotype also evokes certain kinds of reactions from other people. The smiling, sociable baby is likely to get more smiles and social stimulation than the withdrawn, shy baby does. The genetic make-up of an individual may affect the relations of other people, and hence affect the kind of social environment that one will experience.

3. ***Active correlation :*** an individual's genotype influence what kind of environment he will actively seek. The individual with a genetic predisposition to be extrovert is likely to seek out parties whereas those with genes for shyness may actively avoid large group activities and remain confined to themselves. *Scarr and McCartney* have found that the balance among these three types of correlations keep on shifting alongwith an individuals' development.

To sum up, both heredity and environment are at work over the entire life span of an individual, although the relative contribution of these two forces change with age.

Environmental forces determine whether we achieve our genetic potential, and heredity determines how we respond to environmental experiences. We are shaped by an incredibly complex interplay of hereditary and environmental influences from conception to death.

ROLE OF PHYSICAL ACTIVITIES IN THE DEVELOPMENT OF PERSONALITY

Physical activities and sports play an important role in the development of personality of an individual. The aim of physical education is to strive for optimum development of an individual in all spheres of life and thus, *physical activities play pivotal role in development of one's personality. Book Walters* clearly illustrates the role of physical education and physical activities in shaping up the personality of an individual. In his own words "The aim of physical education is the optimum development of the physically, socially, and mentally integrated and adjusted individual through guided instructions and participation in selected total – body sports rhythmic and gymnastic activities conducted according to social and hygienic standards".

As one participates in physical activities of his own volition, it provides a free, pleasurable, immediate natural expression of his Innate desires. Such exercise unfolds the hidden talents and desire, and helps in shaping up the personality. Physical activities meet the basic needs of human beings, such as the sense of security, the sence of belonging, happiness, experience etc. Physical activities also provide recreation which go a long way in producing perfectly happy, satisfied and balanced individual, having pleasing and energetic personality, having zest for life experiences.

One of the primary and apparent aspect of one's personality is his physical appearance. Children as well as adults, boys as well as girls, all are very much concerned as to how they look. Adolescents spend quite some time before the mirror to put on their best appearance. Physical activities are conducive to the growth and development of the physique. Robust and athletic physique does enhance one's personality. Poise, grace, agility, and the manner one carries himself, have great impact on one's personality. An individual is able to develop appropriate neuro – muscular coordination for such movements through physical activities and rigorous training only. Workouts in gym are becoming a must for all the youngsters of today, who are becoming more and more conscious about their bulging biceps, broad shoulders, expanded chest, and trim waistline. Actors like Arnold Sch-warzenegger and Sylvestor Stallone are their ideals, blowups are pinned up in each youngsters wardrobe quite prominently.

All physical activities must be learned and that involves analytic thinking, analyzing and interpreting new situations. This, mental exercise enhances the intellectual abilities of the participants and broadens their mental horizon. One also learns to control and regulate one's emotions while participating in competitions as well as during practice sessions. Sports persons are not unduly disturbed by their emotions. They learn to take the successes and failures, achievements and disappointments as part of the game and accept the same in their stride. Unutilized energy, undoubtedly has harmful effect on one's personality makeup. Physical activities and sports provide an interesting and challenging outlet for such energy as well as for blowing out other emotional storms building within.

Participation in sports and other physical activities provides avenues for social interactions, and lays foundations for amicable relationships. Success in such activities also provides social recognition, status, social acceptance and respect. Sports team comprise athletes coming from different , and many times, diverse social, economical and cultural matrix. Physical activities and sports provide opportunities of interaction between athletes coming from different regions speaking different language, belonging to different caste and religions, and thus help an individual to develop multi-dimensional personality. The inculcation of qualities like honesty, sincerity, fair play, punctuality, dedication, obedience of rules, respect for elders, and moral values through sports is responsible for development of sound and ideal character, a very essential attribute of personality. One cannot succeed or achieve any goal unless one sincerely strives to achieve the same. In sports, one learns to make sincere efforts, which reflect positively in the development of an individual's personality. Group effort, loyalty to the team and strong ties are much in evidence in sports and physical activities. The varied experiences and opportunities provided by sport situations make valuable contribution in development of one's personality. Participation in physical activities and sports enables us to develop tolerant attitude toward other players as well as spectators. Participation in sports and physical activities provides many such situations where tolerance pays. Adherence to the code of descipline is fundamental not only to the learning of any physical activity, but also for effective participation in sports. Team spirit or joint efforts are the primary characteristics of any athletic endeavour. Cohesiveness is one of the pre-requisites for team's success. As a member of the team one learns the habit of adjustment in order to achieve the goal. Members of a sport team may be many , their role in the play field may be different, but it is their joint effort, cooperation and helping each other that produces the results. In the play fields as well as off the play fields, a member of the team learns to adjust socially and emotionally with other team members. All these are attributes of a well developed personality.

Competitive situations are inherent in sports and physical activities. One learns to excel and out-beat the others while following the rules of the game. Unless the aim or the goal to be achieved is clear, the physical effort or the athletic endeavour would be directionless. To set realistic goals is one of the fundamental principles of sports. Setting realistic goal enables an individual to organise his way of living in different life situations in a better way. Aggression and hostility, to some extent, is necessary for any successful athletic endeavour. At the same time, too much or too less of the same, would hamper the performance and jeopardize the results. Similarly, fickle and temperamental behaviour is beyond comprehension of any sincere athlete. *Participation in physical activities and sports trains an athlete to manage and control his aggression and temper, which help in the development of a balanced personality.*

While making efforts to win, an athlete also learns to face failure. He learns to overcome and correct his mistakes and try again for success. Pessimistic and negative approach is alien to sport environment and an individual develops a positive outlook towards life, which leaves a permanent impression on his personality. Successful sport performance also contributes to self confidence of the athlete. He has to face many problems some on the play field and some off the play field. Sport settings quite often pose many challenging situations. Through dedicated effort and foresight, an individual learns to solve the problems and to face the challenges of the life with full confidence. *Perseverance and persistence are two important attributes of an athletic performance. These traits provide stability to an individual and are helpful in developing his personality.*

INTEREST

Life will be colourless and barron unless one has something to work for. Boredom and depression are frequent companions of one who lacks personal goals and interests. A sense of direction and enthusiastic concern stabilizes one's life. It gives impetus and interest to daily activities and keeps one going when difficulties are encountered. Interest is not an activity. It is a permanent tendency or a mental structure which supplies sufficient motivating power to maintain the motor activity. Interest can be the cause of an activity and the result participation in the activity. Interest many refer to the motivating force. It compels us to attend to a person, a thing or an activity, or it may be the effective experience that has been stimulated by the activity itself. *Drever has defined interest by stating that "An interest is a disposition in its dynamic aspects".*

Interest builds up either by past satisfaction or by an anticipated future   satisfaction. It is important to note that even failure win hope leads to continued interest. Individuals develop different interests according to their disposition, attention, economic, social or political status etc. Acquired interest depends to a large extent on one's experience. A child's interest reflects the structure of his personality, particularly of the way previous experiences influence his perceptions of himself. While children pursue their interest in group activities, they simultaneously develop their social and technical skills. They find opportunities for outlets in creative expressions and social interaction while exploring their own interests. Interests lead to exploratory activities in many new fields. Such an understanding is quite helpful when interests are used in vocational guidance and classroom planning

Likes and dislikes are often reflected through the interests one develops, The scope of likes and dislikes of an individual is modified by his abilities and the environmental opportunities. A high level of aptitude permits him to engage successfully in a number of activities. Similarly, the richer an individual's environment, the more opportunities he will have for a wide range of experiences. The needs and value system of an individual provides direction to his selection of takes. Only those activities that satisfy relevant needs will continue to be attractive. If the needs can be satisfied in only a small range of possibilities, interests become limited accordingly. Variation in interests reflects the influence of the individual's experience. Now where do differences in interests appear to strikingly as between the two sexes. Such differences begin to appear quite early in the children. Helping around the home, for example, appears as a definitely feminine preferences in the early childhood years, whereas boys prefer outdoor activities. At the age of about ten extremely feminine or masculine activities are almost unanimously disliked by the opposite sex. At this age the preferences and interests of the boys are characterized by anti-sissy, anti-work in home and anti-intellectual factors, more interested in aggressive outdoor plays, riding bicycles etc. On the other hand, interests of girls at this age are typically anti-physical activity and anti-

aggressive. Sex differences indicate the part played by cultural influence in the development of interest. Most boys are expected (and taught) to identify with the masculine and the girls with the feminine roles. The distinctiveness of the experiences imposed by each of theses paths is highly influential in determining the basic interest patterns of each sex.

Interests need not be permanent at all the times. Any action or object which is not associated with fulfillment of any permanent need evokes only temporary interests. The moment the purpose is served or the need fulfilled, one loses interest in that thing or the work. On the other hand when the action or object is associated with fulfillment of permanent needs, it develops permanent interest which subsists to evoke constant response towards fulfilling the need. Interests are more than static qualities of the personality, more than favoured clusters of activities. Interest has important dynamic qualities, Interest is sometimes innate but mostly acquired. It is through the development of interest and the activities pursued in interest satisfaction that one explores and tests his skills and abilities. By this process one eventually acquires a realistic concept of his personal characteristics, capacities and abilities, and his strengths and weaknesses. Through this medium he learns about the characteristics of his social environment, resources available in his physical environment, and the means and skills through which his personally can reach a maximum of his life's need fulfillments.

ATTITUDE

Early psychologists had defined attitude simply as a tendency to seek or avoid something. Merely liking or disliking, approval and disapproval do not convey the real meaning of attitudes. *Stagner* has defined attitude in much broader sense. According to him, ''An attitude can be defined as the meanings that one associates with a certain object (or idea) and which influence his acceptance of it. An element of acceptance or avoidance is present in any attitude, but additional association are also involved.''

Lahey has defined, "Attitudes as beliefs that predispose one to act and feel in certain ways." This definition suggests three basic components of attitude : beliefs, feelings and, dispositions to behave, Most of the attitudes are learnt directly from our experiences and we learn them from others. Many of the specific attitudes closely reflect the prevailing attitudes in our homes and communities. When members of a community have almost same attitude on a topic, anyone growing up in that community is almost sure to adopt it too. The religious and communal hatreds are such examples. Attitudes are learned by a process of interpretation, response and confirmation. The attitude retained is the one that is confirmed by experiences. Like any other response, attitudes are confirmed or modified through repeated trials. We may take the example of a child learning about dogs. Any child almost instantly reaches out and tries to touch almost any object, just to explore it. When he comes near a dog, he tries to touch it, treating it like any other toy he likes to play with. Here an attitude or belief is being tested and the same will be confirmed if it is followed by pleasant results i.e. if the dog licks the child or plays with him and this conveys pleasant feelings to the child. But if the dog reacts and pounces at the child's fingers or barks loudly in protest, child may cry and move away. This will give unpleasant result and next time the child may not try to come near the dog and will try to avoid it. Behaviour of the child in both the situation shows a learned attitude. An attitude can be confirmed or contradicted by further experience. We can say that attitudes are a realistic summary of experience that one likes what works out well and avoids what works out badly. An attitude is generally build on previous attitude. A child growing up in a family, a neighbourhood, and a town tries on their outlooks and behaviours and finds that they work. He continuously responds in these ways and so on he has learned an attitude. Does this mean that attitudes can not be altered or changed? The answer to such a question is that the attitudes can be changed although the process is slow and change is generally partial. Among the attitudes hardest to alter are those rooted in emotional needs.

People conform to and up hold the systems of attitudes they have developed for themselves. Ordinarily any contradiction to their views will not immediately bring any change rather they will try to give meaning to such situations so that the same can be viewed according to their beliefs. We everyday see that we accept views and opinions of persons we respect more quickly than if the same view or opinion is expressed by adversary. This reflects our acceptance on one hand and rejection on the other hand.

OBJECTIVE QUESTIONS

1. In Indian philosophy the validity of scriptures has been challenged by:
    (*a*) The Charvakas   (*b*) Nyaya
    (*c*) Samkhya   (*d*) The Vedanta

2. The only valid Pramana according to Charvaka is:
    (*a*) Perception   (*b*) Scriptures
    (*c*) Inference   (*d*) None of the above

3. According to materialism the only valid Pramana is:
    (*a*) Perception   (*b*) Scriptures
    (*c*) Inference   (*d*) None of the above

4. Perception coming through the contact of external senses with objects according to Charvaka is known as:
    (*a*) External   (*b*) Internal
    (*c*) Both   (*d*) Neither

5. The nature of perception according to Charvaka can be said to be:
    (*a*) Authentic   (*b*) Unauthentic
    (*c*) Both   (*d*) Neither

6. The validity of inference according to Charvaka is:
    (*a*) Authentic   (*b*) Unauthentic
    (*c*) Both   (*d*) Neither

7. Charvaka arguments against inference include:
    (*a*) Rejection of Vyapti
    (*b*) Rejection of testimony

    (*c*) Rejection of comparison
    (*d*) All the above

8. Pramana in Indian philosophy means:
    (*a*) Means of knowledge
    (*b*) Means of valid knowledge
    (*c*) Means of invalid knowledge
    (*d*) All the above

9. The Charvakas have challenged the validity of:
    (*a*) Inference   (*b*) Scriptures
    (*c*) Both   (*d*) Neither

10. The validity of scriptures has been challenged by Charvakas in the field of:
    (*a*) Perceptible things
    (*b*) Imperceptible things
    (*c*) Both
    (*d*) Neither

11. Charvaka have rejected the authenticity of the Vedic statement concerning:
    (*a*) Imperceptible thing
    (*b*) Heaven and Hell
    (*c*) Rebirth
    (*d*) All the above

12. Charvakas have rejected the validity of scriptures on the basis of:
    (*a*) Absence of physical proof
    (*b*) Criticism of inference
    (*c*) Contradictions and tautologies
    (*d*) All the above

13. Charvaka criticism of scriptures has been challenged by:
    (*a*) Nyaya   (*b*) Advaita Vedanta
    (*c*) Samkhya   (*d*) All the above

14. The philosophers who have condemned Charvaka challenge to Vedas include:
    (*a*) Udayana   (*b*) Vainkathnath
    (*c*) Samkara   (*d*) All the above

15. The arguments presented in favour of the Vedas include:
    (*a*) Authenticity of the authors
    (*b*) Character of the authors
    (*c*) Purpose of the authors
    (*d*) All the above

16. The most important element in the Jain *'theory of Pramanas'* is:
    (*a*) Perception   (*b*) Nyaya
    (*c*) Scriptures   (*d*) Inference

17. Knowledge according to Jain philosophers can be called:
    (*a*) Pramana   (*b*) Nyaya
    (*c*) Both   (*d*) Neither

18. The knowledge of a thing as it is, according to Jain philosophers, is known as:
    (*a*) Pramana   (*b*) Nyaya
    (*c*) Both   (*d*) Neither

19. The knowledge of a thing in a particular context or relationship of the knower is known as:
    (*a*) Pramana   (*b*) Nyaya
    (*c*) Both   (*d*) Neither

20. The *theory of Nyaya* is based upon:
    (*a*) Anekantvada   (*b*) Ekantvada
    (*c*) Both   (*d*) Neither

21. Of the following, the educator associated with radical educational reform is:
    (*a*) Hutchins   (*b*) Adler
    (*c*) Bestor   (*d*) Illich
    (*e*) Butler

22. When parents ask teachers about their children's television habits, it is best to suggest that they:
    (*a*) Prohibit television viewing.
    (*b*) Use television for rewards and punishments
    (*c*) Allow children to watch only those programmes selected by the parents.
    (*d*) Encourage family viewing and discussion of jointly selected programmes.
    (*e*) Give freedom to children to select whatever they want to see.

23. Curriculum makers face the greates difficulty when:
    (*a*) There is an inflationary cycle.
    (*b*) The nature of the student population is changing
    (*c*) Parents are participants
    (*d*) Teachers unions insist on input

(*e*) School boards must give their final approval

24. That the mind of an infant is tabularasa the contribution of:
(*a*) Plato   (*b*) Horace Mann
(*c*) John Locke   (*d*) J.J. Rousseau
(*e*) Johann Herbart

25. The educator who advanced the idea of the five formal steps in learning was:
(*a*) Rousseau   (*b*) Comenius
(*c*) Pestalozzi   (*d*) Herbart
(*e*) Froebel

26. De facto school segregation is segregation that Is primarily a result of:
(*a*) guidelines issued by the State Commissioner of Education.
(*b*) Discriminatory zoning of a local school board
(*c*) Residence patterns of the community
(*d*) Federal education laws
(*e*) Rulings of the courts

27. A major contribution of the Jesuits to education includes all of the following except:
(*a*) insistence on well-trained teachers
(*b*) repetition arid memorization as teaching methods.
(*c*) self-discipline
(*d*) concentration on the early education of children.
(*e*) emphasis on the classics as the basis of curriculum.

28. A school district has adopted a policy that prevents teachers from marking the examinations of their own students. The most valid Justification for this policy is that:
(*a*) Teachers favour their pet students.
(*b*) Some parents pressure teachers to give their children high marks.
(*c*) Teachers should not be in a position to evaluate the results of their own teaching
(*d*) This is the best way for principals to evaluate how well pupils are learning.
(*e*) Pupils will have no reason to bring presents to their teachers.

29. All of the following can be sins that a child is gifted, except:
(*a*) Early development of a sense of time
(*b*) Interest in encyclopedias and dictionaries
(*c*) Uneasy relationships with peers
(*d*) Easy retention of facts
(*e*) High intellectual curiosity.

30. Froebel's most Important contribution to education was his development of the:
(*a*) Vocational school
(*b*) Public high school
(*c*) Kindergarten
(*d*) Latin School
(e) Play school

31. Teacher tenure laws can best be justified because they:
(*a*) Protect teachers whose political views differ sharply from those of the community
(*b*) Provide for stability staffing
(*c*) Allow an experienced teacher to plan creatively
(*d*) Protect teachers from excessive requirements of principals
(*e*) Prevent teachers from leaving to accept positions in higher paying school districts.

32. All of the following are contributing to the crisis in urban schools except:
(*a*) The rapid increase in school population
(*b*) The disappearance of taxable property
(*c*) The deterioration and decline of real property
(*d*) The displacement of people
(*e*) High mobility

33. Of the following, the main purpose of state certification of teachers is to:
(*a*) Monitor the quality of teacher training institutions
(*b*) Provide for a uniform standard of entry-level teacher competency throughout the state.
(*c*) Exclude from the profession those not trained in pedagogy

(*d*) Exclude from the profession those who are mentally unhealthy

(*e*) Provide a basis for acceptable performance based on teacher evaluation.

34. A fourth-grade child takes the possessions of pupil who sit near her. The teacher's beat initial step is to:

(*a*) Isolate the child in a corner of the room

(*b*) Make a note of this behaviour in the child's permanent record

(*c*) Ignore the behaviour, as it will eventually disappear.

(*d*) Arrange a parent conference to try to determine causation.

(*e*) Assign the pupil to detention.

35. In dealing with a class that is misbehaving, the teacher's least effective course of action is to:

(*a*) Ask the principal to observe him/her and make recommendations.

(*b*) Lower the grades of pupils who create the most serious infractions

(*c*) Isolate those most responsible for the mis-behaviour.

(*d*) Ascertain the extent to which his/her methods and/or curriculum are responsible.

(*e*) Ask the advice of his/her grade leader.

36. Why would you like to ask question from your students in the classroom of and on?

(*a*) To know if they were listening carefully

(*b*) To know, which student is most attentive and intelligent

(*c*) To Know if they were following the lesson properly or not

(*d*) For the help of the students

37. What type of children would you like to teach?

(*a*) Intelligent   (*b*) Hard-working

(*c*) Disciplined   (*d*) All of the above

38. If a student comes to seek your help, when you are relaxing, what would you do?

(*a*) Reprimand him and ask to go

(*b*) Listen to his problem and ask to go

(*c*) Ask him to raise this issue in the class room on next day

(*d*) Will solve his problem to his satisfaction

39. Home work should be given:

(*a*) According to the interest of the student

(*b*) Keeping in view their age

(*c*) Keeping in view the mental calibre of students

(*d*) Keeping in view the final annual examination

40. What type of questions a teacher should ask in the class room?

(*a*) Which should be answered easily by the students

(*b*) Should be difficult and could not be answered easily

(*c*) Which should be helpful to assess the learning and memory of the pupils

(*d*) Which should be targeted impression about teaching

41. Emotion is defined as -

(*a*) Feeling   (*b*) Disturbed

(*c*) Fear of future   (*d*) State of Organism

42. A reliable psychological test means-

(*a*) Accuracy of measurement

(*b*) Forecasting behaviour

(*c*) Consistency of measurement

(*d*) None of the above

43. The first test intelligence was developed by

(*a*) Binet and Simon

(*b*) Pavlov and Watson

(*c*) Terman and Merril

(*d*) Maslow and McDougall

44. In developmental process the terms "gang-age" occurs during -

(*a*) Early childhood

(*b*) Puberty

(*c*) Infancy

(*d*) Later Childhood

45. Cognition deals with -

(*a*) Learning   (*b*) Memory

(*c*) Creativity   (*d*) All of the above

46. Which is not a primary motive -

(*a*) Affection   (*b*) Hunger

(*c*) Sex   (*d*) Thirst

47. What processes are part of classical conditioning?
(*a*) Generalization (*b*) Discrimination
(*c*) Extinction (*d*) All the above.

48. Psychology is taught to the student of physical education because -
(*a*) It enhances performance
(*b*) It is related to behaviour
(*c*) It helps in learning
(*d*) It motivates athletes

49. In psychological testing, norm is defined as -
(*a*) Record of performance
(*b*) Unique performance of a team
(*c*) Average performance of the team
(*d*) Highest performance of athlete

50. What level of stress may enhance performance of athletes?
(*a*) Heightened (*b*) Moderate
(*c*) Optimal (*d*) None of the above

51. Outstanding athletes usually posses certain personality characteristics, such as -
(*a*) Aggressiveness (*b*) Neurotic
(*c*) Ambivalence (*d*) Submissiveness

52. Psycho-Sexual development takes place during-
(*a*) Later childhood (*b*) Adolescence
(*c*) Young Age (*d*) Adulthood

53. The psychologist who has been most closely related with the study of achievement motivation is-
(*a*) Eclelland (*b*) Maslow
(*c*) Croom (*d*) Mc Gregor

54. The concept of mental age was given by -
(*a*) Stern (*b*) Galton
(*c*) Binet (*d*) Watson

55. The impulses that travel from CNS to muscle are called-
(*a*) Efferent (*b*) Afferent
(*c*) Sensation (*d*) All the above

56. Which one is the simplest form of Cognition-
(*a*) Conception (*b*) Perception
(*c*) Sensation (*d*) Affection

57. The functional division of spinal cord are
(*a*) Somatic motor (*b*) Somatic Sensory
(*c*) Visceral motor (*d*) None of the above

58. The response defined as a result of training is called -
(*a*) Conditioned stimulus
(*b*) Unconditioned reflex
(*c*) Conditioned reflex
(*d*) Conation

59. Sports performance is the bi-product of -
(*a*) Skill
(*b*) Conditional ability
(*c*) Total personality
(*d*) Tactical ability

60. The first metamorphosis falls between the age of
(*a*) 7-10 years (*b*) 3-5 years
(*c*) 11-14 years (*d*) 2-4 years

61. Which is the most effective method for encouraging self learning -
(*a*) Demonstration method
(*b*) Lecture method
(*c*) Observation method
(*d*) Task method

62. Body mind relationship was first promulgated by?
(*a*) Socrates (*b*) Plato
(*c*) Hitler (*d*) Homer.

63. Who said, 'I think therefore I am?'
(*a*) Discartes (*b*) Plato
(*c*) Aristotle (*d*) Rousseau

64. Who said, 'sound mind in a sound body?'
(*a*) Discartes (*b*) Rousseau
(*c*) Aristotle (*d*) Plato.

65. The hereditary factors of learning are -
(*a*) Height and weight
(*b*) Physical structure
(*c*) Body composition
(*d*) All of the above.

66. Autogenic training is a technique
(*a*) To bring about relaxation in body
(*b*) To increase anxiety level
(*c*) To counter avoidance syndrome
(*d*) None of the above.

67. The stress condition is -
   (*a*) Advantageous to the performer
   (*b*) Detrimental to the performer
   (*c*) Neither (*a*) nor (*b*)
   (*d*) Helpful in the development of strength

68. The leader who allows complete freedom in decision making and does not participate in the group activities
   (*a*) Autocratic
   (*b*) Democratic
   (*c*) Lassez fair
   (*d*) None of the above

69. The personal factors in learning are -
   (*a*) Heredity factors
   (*b*) Fitness factors
   (*c*) Psychological factors
   (*d*) All of the above

70. Gestalt has propounded -
   (*a*) Theory of trial and error
   (*b*) Theory of conditioning
   (*c*) Theory of learning
   (*d*) None of the above.

71. Feedback method -
   (*a*) is helpful to the learner
   (*b*) is detrimental to the learner
   (*c*) is neither helpful nor detrimental
   (*d*) none of the above

72. Learning of physical skills is concerned with-
   (*a*) Cognitive learning
   (*b*) Affective learning
   (*c*) Motor learning
   (*d*) All of the above

73. Natural motivation is also known as -
   (*a*) Intrinsic
   (*b*) Self assertion
   (*c*) Self actualization
   (*d*) Extrinsic.

74. Human psychology is confined to the study of-
   (*a*) Behaviour   (*b*) Mind
   (*c*) Soul   (*d*) Relationship

75. Which of the following is a law of learning?
   (*a*) Law of readiness
   (*b*) Law of exercise
   (*c*) Law of effect
   (*d*) All of the above

76. Mental development includes -
   (*a*) External and internal organs
   (*b*) Reasoning and thinking
   (*c*) Ethical and moral
   (*d*) Emotional maturity

77. Through which of the following methods, desirable channels are provided for the release of emotional energy
   (*a*) Inhibition   (*b*) Sublimation
   (*c*) Catharsis   (*d*) Repression

78. The rate of progress in learning slows down and reaches a limit beyond which further improvement seems impossible. It is known as-
   (*a*) Plateau   (*b*) Loss of interest
   (*c*) Boredom   (*d*) Difficult stage

79. The therapy of psychoanalysis was developed by -
   (*a*) Skinner   (*b*) Sigmund Freud
   (*c*) Plato   (*d*) Darwin

80. Which is the description of the methods of personality measurements?
   (*a*) Rating scale.
   (*b*) Interviews &observations
   (*c*) Paper & pencil test
   (*d*) All of the above

81. Eros refers to
   (*a*) Life instincts
   (*b*) Energy
   (*c*) Aggressive and destructive urges
   (*d*) Judge for thought of ego

82. According to Frieud's psychoanalytic theory, internalized parent is
   (*a*) Ego   (*b*) Superego
   (*c*) Conscience   (*d*) Ego ideal

83. Which level of consciousness contains material that can be easily brought to awareness?
   (*a*) Unconscious
   (*b*) Conscious
   (*c*) Preconscious
   (*d*) Conscious and preconscious

84. The conflict where the boy feels rivalry with his father for the affection of the mother is
(*a*) Oedipus conflict (*b*) Electra conflict
(*c*) Both (*d*) None

85. Which leadership style takes full charge of his team?
(*a*) Permissive (*b*) Autocratic
(*c*) Directive (*d*) Democratic

86. Encouragement by spectators is a
(*a*) Social incentive
(*b*) Monetary incentive
(*c*) Reward incentive
(*d*) Social competitive incentive

87. Cognitive evaluation theory of motivation was propounded by
(*a*) Thorndike (*b*) Kohler
(*c*) Pavlov (*d*) Deci

88. Behaviour carried out with the intention of harming another person is called
(*a*) Stress (*b*) Tension
(*c*) Aggression (*d*) Anxiety

89. According to Frieud, the typical moral arm of the personality is
(*a*) ID
(*b*) Ego
(*c*) Super Ego
(*d*) Both ego and superego

90. On the basis of nature of the activity the endurance can be classified into:
(*a*) Two types (*b*) Three types
(*c*) Five types (*d*) Four types

ANSWERS

1. (*a*)	2. (*a*)	3. (*a*)	4. (*c*)	5. (*c*)	6. (*b*)	7. (*c*)	8. (*b*)
9. (*c*)	10. (*b*)	11. (*d*)	12. (*d*)	13. (*d*)	14. (*d*)	15. (*d*)	16. (*b*)
17. (*c*)	18. (*b*)	19. (*a*)	20. (*c*)	21. (*d*)	22. (*d*)	23. (*b*)	24. (*c*)
25. (*d*)	26. (*c*)	27. (*d*)	28. (*c*)	29. (*c*)	30. (*c*)	31. (*a*)	32. (*a*)
33. (*b*)	34. (*d*)	35. (*b*)	36. (*c*)	37. (*d*)	38. (*d*)	39. (*c*)	40. (*c*)
41. (*b*)	42. (*c*)	43. (*a*)	44. (*b*)	45. (*d*)	46. (*a*)	47. (*d*)	48. (*b*)
49. (*c*)	50. (*c*)	51. (*a*)	52. (*b*)	53. (*a*)	54. (*c*)	55. (*a*)	56. (*c*)
57. (*b*)	58. (*c*)	59. (*c*)	60. (*a*)	61. (*c*)	62. (*b*)	63. (*a*)	64. (*d*)
65. (*d*)	66. (*a*)	67. (*b*)	68. (*c*)	69. (*d*)	70. (*c*)	71. (*a*)	72. (*c*)
73. (*a*)	74. (*a*)	75. (*d*)	76. (*b*)	77. (*c*)	78. (*a*)	79. (*b*)	80. (*d*)
81. (*a*)	82. (*b*)	83. (*c*)	84. (*a*)	85. (*c*)	86. (*a*)	87. (*d*)	88. (*c*)
89. (*c*)	90. (*d*)						

11. PLAYGROUND AND MAINTENANCE

INTRODUCTION

Just as we need good coaches and physical training teachers to teach games, so also we need good playgrounds. It is often seen that school sometime do not have playground at all. Again, those who are lucky to have playground cannot maintain these properly. Animals are seen roaming about on the playgrounds. The authorities and those in charge of the playfield should keep in mind that there must be no football, hockey or handball playground in between 400 m athletic track. It is necessary to use the playground available to the maximum. Ordinarily the tracks are grassy grounds though not synthetic and astro-turf is fast becoming popular. The following points should be borne in mind:

1. There should be passage for the proper outlet of water around the playground.
2. There should be one entry, form other points should be barred.
3. The playground should be watered at interval of 8 or 15 days.
4. The playground should be kept clean.
5. The playground should be level with a 1 : 1000 incline, North to South.
6. A barbed wire or high wall should bar unauthorised entry.
7. Playground should be manured.
8. There should be permanent lines drawn on the ground
9. It should be shaded from all sides.
10. Timely repairs should be carried out.
11. No heavy vehicle should be allowed to go within.
12. It should be inspected daily.
13. No unauthorised function should be allowed within.
14. The equipments should be properly looked often.

GYMNASIUM

A gymnasium is an enclosure for taking physical exercises. In the olden days a gymnasium could be at any place, open or enclosed, where players would assemble and take exercises. With the passage of time, heir shape is changed though function remains mostly the same. Today, open spaces have given place to enclosures. In morden condition the gymnasiums are temperature-controlled. The following point should be kept in mind regarding the gymnasiums:

1. Gymnasiums too, like playground, should be in clean environment.
2. Gymnasiums should be built according to national and international standards.
3. There should be arrangement for all essential equipment.
4. There may be made of concrete or wood.
5. The floor should be either of wood or of synthetic matter.
6. There should be provision for toilet and bathroom.
7. No one not connected with training of any kind should not be allowed to enter.

General Equipment Of Gymnasium

Wall-bar; Rope-climbing; Balance- beam; Loy-house; Pommell-horse; Parellel-bar; Horizontal-bar; Weightlifting rod and weights, pull-ups beam; Weighting machine etc.

SWIMMING POOL

The Swimming pools are built in various sizes, as 25 m length × 25 m breath, or 40 m length × 20 m breadth. The National and International competitions are organised on ideal Swimming pools, which are 50 m length × 21 m breath × 10 m depth. For Swimming the pool is divided into eight artificial lanes each 2.40 m broad, with the help of plastic balls linked by ropes. At the start of each lane there is a box 2 ft length × 2 ft breadth × 2 ft height. The lane number is written on each box.

It should be remember that any person suffering from a communicable diseases is not allowed to enter. A good Swimming pool must have its water changed every one week. The walls and floor should be scrubbed clean. The swimming pool is either L- shaped, or T-shaped.

Details of Swimming Competitions

For women					
Free Style	100	200	400	800	4 x 100m
Backstroke	100	200	x	x	x
Breast Stroke	100	200	x	x	x
Butterfly	100	200	x	x	x
Medley Relay	x	200	400	x	4 x 200m
Individual Medley	x	200	400	x	x
For Men					
Free Style	100	200	400	2400	4 x 200m
Free Style	x	x		x	4 x 400m
Backstroke	100	200	x	x	x
Breast stroke	100	200	x	x	x
Butterfly	100	200	x	x	x
Medley Relay	x	200	400	x	4 x 200m
Individual Medley	x		200	400	x

National Fitness Core-N.F.C.

The central government set up a programme which, as per the recommendations of a committee on physical Education formed under the Presidentship of Pandit Hridyanath Kunzru in 1959, was aimed at checking the increasing indiscipline among students. The idea was to channelise their energies towards becoming ideal citizens.

In 1963, Dr. Kunzru presented his Report based on his deliberations with experts, principals, vice chancellors and Physical Education experts. The issues before the committee were—

1. To examine various schemes of Physical Education. Entertainments, character-building and of discipline current in education institution.
2. To suggest ways and means to avoid duplicating of programmes and then saving expenditure.
3. To suggest schemes to augment and develop discipline, physical education, Entertainment, character-building etc.

The programme developed based on the above three issues is known as the National fitness core" programme.

National Cadet Corps (N.C.C.)

National Cadet corps, or NCC, came into being upon suggestions given by Dr. Kunzru's committee. A directorate was set up on an All-India basis and NCC units were set up in schools and colleges. There are separate divisions for boys and girls. These are controlled by Central Advisory Committee of which the Defence Minister is the head. The objectives of NCC are—

1. To develop high character, service and leadership.
2. To cultivate spirit of Nationalism among boys/girls.
3. To co-operate in country's defence in emergencies.

During Chinese aggression in 1962 the scheme was made compulsory. Later, ACC replaced Junior NCC units in same schools. When NFC was introduced in 1965. ACC was abolished.

Indian School Sports Federation

In 1964 a meeting of the All-India Physical Education was held in Calcutta. It was then decided that inter-state or national level competitions should be held annually for the secondary schools students. In 1955 such a National Games competition was held at Pachmari in Madhya Pradesh. Only seven States took part. Now this competition is held every year during winters.

Netaji Subhash National Sports Institute, Moti Bagh, Patiala, Punjab

In 1958, upon recommendations, a national Institute of sports was set up in Patiala, Punjab. Dr. F.S. Shrimali, the then Education Minister, inaugurated it. The following were to be its objectives—

1. To impart higher training in various games.
2. To train coaches/Physical teachers.
3. To assist various sports organisations to spot new players.
4. To coach teams on national and international Levels.
5. To give short-term training to physical education teachers.

6. To hold discussion-groups, seminars on matters related to sports.
7. To train coaches from other countries.
8. To award scholarships to students studying in colleges and universities.
9. To give technical advice to firms manufacturing sports goods.
10. To extend activities of yuvakundras
11. To hold office for Indian Association Track & field.
12. To hold village-level games competition.

A committee was formed for running the Institute. It is known as society of National Physical Education and sports. In 1974 a branch was established in Bangalore. Now there are various branches working in Calcutta, Gandhinagar, Aurangabad, Bangalore. They are serving the nation by giving intensive training.

Y.M.C.A

YM.C.A must be given credit for popularising physical education in the world. Its members got training themselves from Springfield University in America and then went to different countries to spread the idea. In India, YMCA set up its first branch in 1908 in Calcutta. It was under the supervision of Dr. Henry Gire. He attracted people through his speeches and demonstrations. It was here that Dr. A.G. Norherow met Dr. Gire and then took the message to Madras City where he set up its branch.

Dr. H.C. Buck came over to Madras in 1919. He along with Dr. Noeheron set up the branch here in 1920, and also the first YMCA Physical Training Institute. Dr. Buck was its principal and occupied the post till 1943. He contributed to physical Education in the following ways:

1. He included Indian exercises along with western exercises.
2. Dr. Buck was one of the advisors to Madras govt. He got the govt. declare sports as a compulsory subject in schools in 1928.
3. Upon a request from Madras University, Physical Education was made compulsory in class 11 & 12.
4. He wrote several books on various games.
5. Along with Dr. Noeheron, Dr. Buck went all over India and started Olympic movement.
6. Dr. Buck was the official coach of Indian teams which participated in 1920 & 1924 International Olympics.

BADMINTON

1. The total length of a Badminton court is 13.40 metres and breath 6.10 metres (i.e. 20 ft. × 44 ft.).
2. The court is rectangular and is divided into many Darts.
3. There is a lane, 40 cms broad, on both sides of the court which is used for Doubles game only.
4. Along the back boundary line there are lanes 76 cms broad.
5. There is a short-service line on both sides of the centre line, at a distance of 1.98 metres.

Badminton

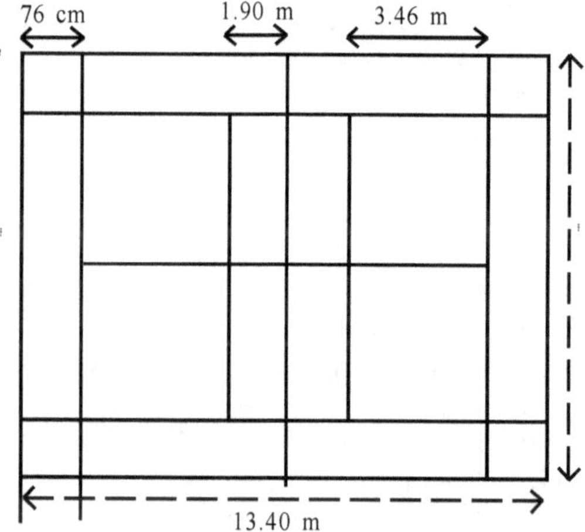

6. Back part of short-service line is divided into two parts. These are called the Right service court and left service court.
7. The pole for net is 1.55 metres high (on both sides).
8. The lower part of the net is 76 cms above ground.
9. Net is 1.55 metres high. It is kept taut always.

10. Shuttle cock is 4.50 to 4.73 gms in weight. It must bear 14 to 16 wings.
11. The squares within the net are 5 cms square
12. Badmintion racket is 66 cms in length, 20-22 cms in breadth, total weight of a racket for man is 1.55 gms, and for women it is 1.42 gms.
13. Game is played single as well as double.
14. The male game is of 21 points, while for women single of 11 points.
15. In each game there are one service Examiner two line Examiners, two umpires and one scorer.

BASKET BALL

1. A team consists of 10 players. Only five at a time occupy the field.
2. Basketball court is 28 metres long, 14 metres wide.
3. Circles are of 3.60 metres radius.
4. Ring is 3.05 metres above the ground.
5. Board is 1.80 metres in length, 1.20 metres wide, 3 cms thick.
6. Ring is 20 mm in thickness and 45 cms radius.

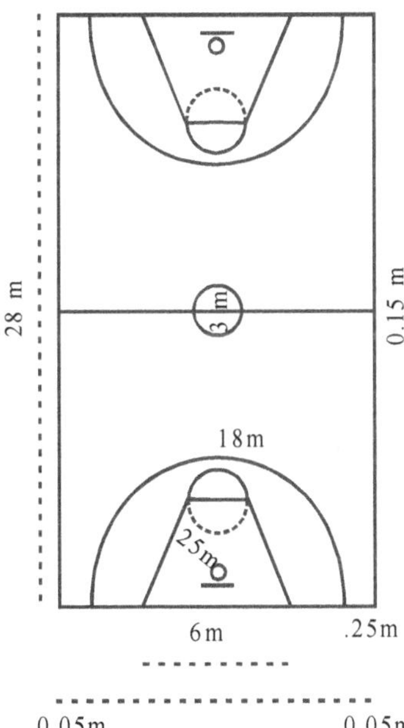

Basket Ball Court

BASKET BALL COURT

7. Basketball is 600-625 gm in weight, 75 cms in thickness.
8. Ball when struck on a wooden surface from 1.80 metres height must bounce 1.30 metres. That is test of air contained within.
9. Each game lasts 20 minutes with a rest period of 20 minutes. For women, it is of 15 minutes duration, with a rest period of 15 minutes.
10. Above the ring there is a rectangle drawn (on the board) which is 0.59 m long, 0.45 metres wide in black colour lines are 5 cms thick.
11. Ring net is made of cotton or nyloan fibre and is hanging loose 40 cms low.
12. Each match is supervised by one Referee, one Umpire, one Time Keeper one scorer and one 30-seconds operator.
13. In case of a tie in a match, each team is given 5 minutes. In case there is a tie again, then match continues with 5 minutes extra time allotted each time.

CRICKET

1. Eleven players play the game as a team.
2. Batting or Bowling is chosen by toss.
3. The Bat is 96.5 cm in length and is 10.8 cm wide.
4. The playing field or pitch is 20.12 m long and 3.05 m wide.
5. Stumps are 71.12 cms in height, 22.86 cms (9 inches) wide.
6. There are 3 stumps and bales upon them are two, 11.11 cms. weight of $5^{1}/2$ ounces (150 gms) and
7. Cricket ball has a circumference 9 inches
8. Stumps are 1.50 inches thick. With a radius of 50 m from the middle stump.
9. The ground is oval in shape.
10. Six balls are thrown in each over.
11. 1.22 metres from stumps is the pop-in crease and a bowling crease again 1.22 m

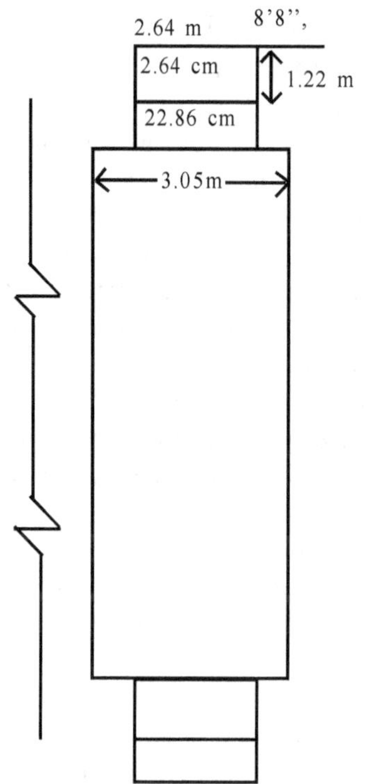

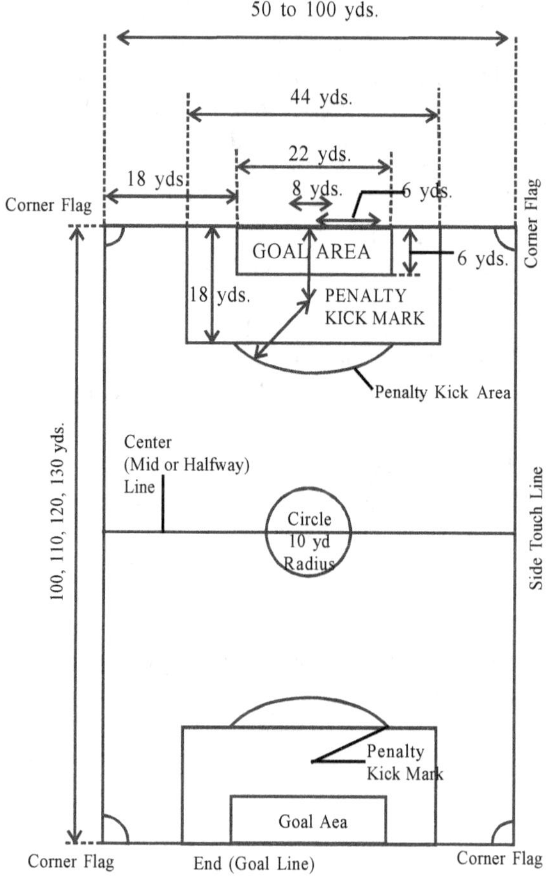

outwards. Width is then 2.64 in between the two lines.

12. Victory is on the runs scored.

13. When injured, a substituted player may do fielding, or running between wickets, not batting or bowling.

14. There are two umpires and one scorer to supervise a match.

FOOTBALL

1. The playing field for football is 120×73.22 metre length and in breadth.

2. Eleven player comprise a team. Five are substitute players.

3. Ball weights 396 to 450 gm and has a circumference of 72 cm.

4. There is a penalty spot 11 m distant from the middle of goal line.

5. Goal area is 5.5 m between two goal posts.

6. Penalty area is 16.5 m on either side of goal posts.

7. Goal posts are 7.32 m (or 8 yards) from another.

8. Goal posts are 2.44 m (8 ft) high.

9. Penalty half- circle is 9.15 m from goal-line.

10. Central kick- circle is a Circle with 9.15 m (10 yds) radius.

11. Corners are 91 cm.

12. Playing time is 45 in with a rest of 5 minutes.

13. One referee, two linesmen one time-keeper supervise the match

14. In case of a tie two extra, timing of 15 minutes are allowed with a change of field. In case of another tie each team is allowed 5 penalty kicks. That will decide the winner.

Football/Hockey score sheet

Name of tournament ....

Team's name..v/s. ....

Date..Time ....

Who won toss...Toss winner's choice ....

S. No.	Name of players	Chest No	S.No.	Names of Players	Chest No.
1.					
2.					
3.					
4.					
5.					
6.					
7.					
8.					
9.					
10.					
11.					

Name of substitute players		Name of substitute player.	
1.	Chest No.	1.	Chest No.
2.		2.	
3.		3.	
4.		4.	
5.		5.	

Goal scored 1,2,3,4,5,6,7,8,9,10,11,12,13,14,15
Goal scored 1.2.3.4,5,6,7,8,9,10,11,12,13,14,15,
...................Team...............won/equalised by goal
Signature.. .scores   signature- Referee
Signature-Team Manager   1 line Man
Signature-team Manager 2 2 Lines Man

HOCKEY

1. Hockey team consists of 11 players and 5 substitutes.
2. Field is 92 metre long, 55 metre wide.
3. Hockey ball weight's 150 gm, has circumference of 23 cm and is always white in colour.
4. Hockey stick weight's 600 gm (12-18 ounces). Ring should be able to pass through a ring of 5 cm.
5. Playing time is 35 minutes with 5 mintues rest and another round of 35 minutes. (Total 70 minutes)
6. Goal-posts are 2.10 metres high with a bar above in between.
7. Goal posts are 3.60 metres (or 4 yard) from one another
8. Goal posts are 5×5 cm in thickness.
9. D-area is 3.60 metres (or 4 yards) semi-circular in shape. Penalty-spot is 7 metres from the middle of Goal line.
10. Banners are 1.22 metres (4 ft) high.
11. Win is decided on the strength of goal scored. In case of a tie, each side is given 15 minutes extra time. In case of another tie, penalty strokes are awarded till a decision is reached.
12. Two umpires, one time-keeper, one scorer supervise the match.
13. Goal Board is 45 cms wide & is placed 2 yards behind. Net is bound to both sides of the Board.

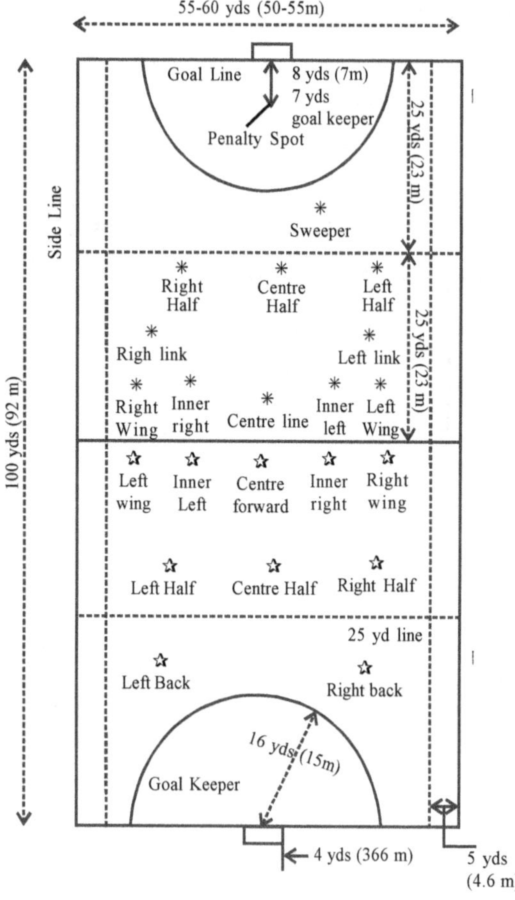

14. Game starts with a toss. Winner has the choice of which side he wishes to play.
15. Game starts with a bully.

KABADDI

1. Kabaddi field for men is 12.50 metres long and 10 m wide
2. For women, play field is 11 m long, 8 m wide.
3. In men, cross line is 3.25 m away from the centre; for women it is 2.25 metres.
4. Lobby is used only for confrontation. It is one metre wide.
5. For men, there is waiting Block 8 m × 1 m for women 6 m × 1 m
6. At a time seven players play. Five are waiting.

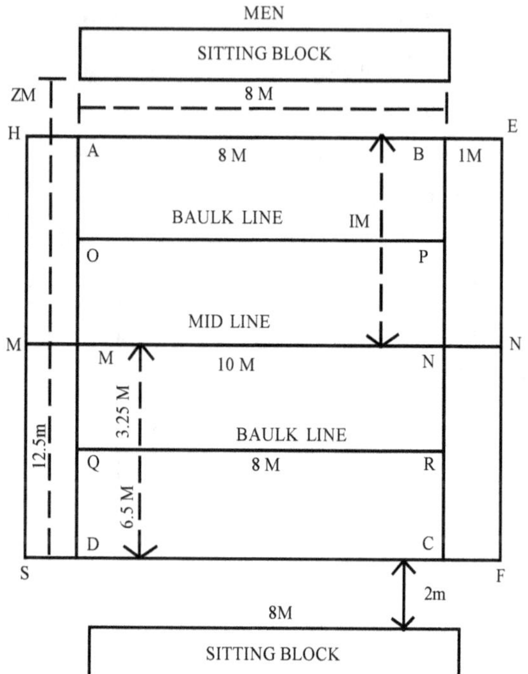

7. Game is of 20 minutes duration, rest of 5 min and then 20 mintues playing time. For juniors, and for women, playing time is 15 minutes +5 min rest + 15 minutes.
8. If all players (of a team) are declared out, the opposite team scores 2 points called Lona.
9. According to new Rules, if any player (from any team) does not score by declaring the opponent player out for 3 consecutive turns, their he is himself declared out and the other team scores one point.
10. Three players can be replaced during one game.
11. In case of a Tie, each team is given 5 minutes extra time. In case of another tie, winner is the team who scores first.
12. Toss will decide Raid as well as choice of playing side.
13. One Referee, two Judges, one scorer, one time-keeper supervise the match.
14. Sitting Blocks are made on both sides.

Kabaddi Score Sheet

Name of Tournament .... (For men/women)

Team's Name ....v/s ....

Date................................Time..Place..

Winner of Toss...Name ....

Time out.........................(no) change of place ....Change of place...................Tme out

S.No.	Names of Players	Chest No.	S.No.	Names of Players	Chest No.
1.			1.		
2.			2.		
3.			3.		
4.			4.		
5.			5.		
6.			6.		
7.			7.		
8.			8.		
9.			9.		
10.			10.		
11.		Head	11.		Head
12.		Captain	12.		Captain

Running Score
    1, 2, 3, 4, 5, 6, 7, 8, 9, 10, 11, 12, 13, 14, 15, 16, 17, 18
Running Score
    1, 2, 3, 4, 5, 6, 7, 8, 9, 10, 11, 12, 13, 14, 15, 16, 17, 18
    First Turn.............Second Turn.................First Turn................Second Turn
    Total Score..............   Total Score.........
    Result...................   Result...............
    Signature
    Head Scorer...........Umpire...........Referee.........
    1
    2
Note : Running score can be more.

KHO-KHO

1. Kho-Kho field is 27 metres long and 15 metres wide
2. Two rectangular areas within the playing field are 2.70 m wide and are called free Areas. For juniors these are 22 × 15 metres.
3. Each team has 9 players, along with three replacement substitutes.
4. The runner is one who runs, chaser is the one who tries to catch him
5. The team scoring higher marks is declared the winner.
6. Playing time is 7—2—7 = 5 = 7—2—7 minutes.
7. Eight players sit is squares. One is standing as a chaser
8. Runners enter in groups of 3 on receiving signal from the referee
9. Kho-Kho pole is 100 m long. It must be clean and thickness should be 10 cm diameter.
10. All lanes are 30 cm (1 ft.) wide.
11. Area near free-area is 2.25 metres wide.
12. All other lanes are 2.10 metres distant in between.
13. There is a lobby 3 metres wide running all round the field
14. In case of a Tie, decistion is reached giving 7-7 minites extra time in case of a Tie further, three players of each team are invited to come and play. Time (upto %

second) is noted when the first player of any team is declared out. The team which takes lesser time is declaring players out, in declared the winner.

15. One referee, two umpires, one scorer, one Time-keeper will supervise

SOFT BALL

1. The Soft Ball playfield is rectangular.
2. The playfield is called softball Diamond.
3. The playing bat is made of solid wood and is circular. The length is 34 inches and the climates of the thicker portion is $2^{1/4}$ inches.
4. The weight of Soft Ball is 6 ozs to 6.25 ozs.
5. Each team has 9 players.
6. One team does batting, as in Cricket, while the other team fields.
7. Each game has five innings. Runs are counted.
8. If the player strikes the Soft Ball and then touches third base and returns to the crease, one run is accord.
9. The full field is divided into two parts, internal and external fields.
10. The catchers are at, the appointed positions.

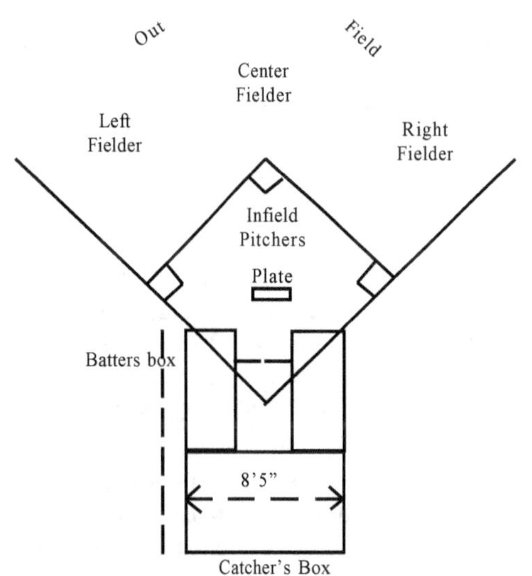

11. The catcher box is loft long and 8.5 ft broad.
12. Each base is made 15 × 15 inches square.
13. Each baseline is 60 ft. long. Between the first and third bases, there is a pitcher-plate. It is 2 ft. long, 6 inches broad.
14. Play begins after a toss.
15. In case of a tie, more innings are played till one team wins.
16. There is a referee, a scorer and two umpires.

TABLE TENNIS

1. Table Tennis is divided centrally by a net.
2. The height of the table from surface below is 76 metres.
3. All around the table, a white band 2 cm wide is drawn or painted.
4. For doubles each part of the table is sub-divided by a 3 mm wide band painted on the table.
5. Length of net is 183 cm.
6. Breadth of table is 15.25 cm.
7. Ball is white and round with a dia of 37.2 mm and weight 2.4 to 2.52 gm.
8. Match is played with 21 points. For a win, the winner must secure two points more than his adversary.
9. A standard match has 5 sets.
10. After every 5 points, service is changed.
11. Match begins after a toss.
12. In case a match is being played at night, the room and the table, must be lighted with a 1500 lumex bulb or tube.
13. The table is made of wood, or a synthetic of.
14. Play is either single or in doubles.

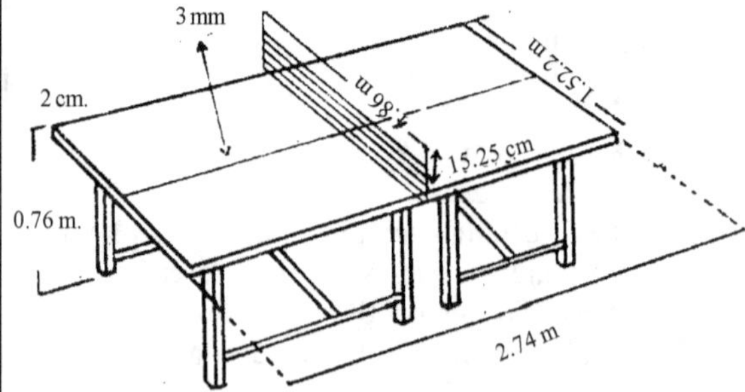

15. The racquet is fitted with a rubber surface.
16. Officials for a game are—scorer, referee and line keeper.

VOLLEYBALL

1. Play ground for Volleyball is 18 metres long and divided into two equal parts.
2. Width is 9 metres.
3. Three metres from the central line is the attacking line.
4. Height between poles is 2.43 metres.
5. Poles are equal to the side line.
6. Net is 9.50 metres is length. Each space in the net is 10 cm long and 10 cm broad.
7. An antenna is fitted above the side line 1.80 metres above and a side-mark is made above the side line. It is .55 mm thick.
8. Volleyball has a circumference of 66 cm.
9. Weight of Volleyball is 260-280 grams.
10. Air pressure is between 0.4 to 0.45 kg/cms.
11. Net is 1 metre in width.
12. Players are in a clock-wise serial.
13. Pole is 2.45 metres high.
14. For females, height of net is 2.24 m.
15. An interval of 3 minutes is observed between two matches.
16. A team has 6 players and they are all playing members.
17. In a standard match there are 5 sets.
18. In the decisive match, there is a change of sides after 8 points.
19. If both players happen to score 14 each, then any one player who makes two connective points is the winner. If the tie is at 16-16, then the player who is able to score 17 first is the winner.
20. A match has a scorer, a referee and two line men.

TEST AND MEASUREMENT

It is a known fact that Education and assessments or tests go hand in hand. Education can have no meaning if it is not timely evaluated. The early educationists wisely built the scheme of examinations into the entire system of education. The same system prevails almost everywhere; examinations are part and parcel of all schools, colleges and universities everywhere. Physical Education is no exception and it cannot be. Rather it needs and so there are, tests and measurements at every step. Its sphere is extensive and vast. The boys and girls are tested, examined and approved in different games for a proper and timely evaluation

Difference between Test and Measurement

Tests are held after every physical activity, that is a universal way. Tests may be individual, or in team. All tests have to be assessed against accepted or standard norms. In normal education, tests are conducted to assess the mental abilities of the performer. In testing certains norms have to be observed. In measurements, such things as length, width, height, weight have to be taken into account. Tests are for everyone. Measurements are based on individual abilities

Aims of Test and Measurement

The following are the main aims of tests and measurements in physical Education:

1. To assess rightly the attainments in different subjects/games.
2. To know about the different handicaps, difficulties and problems in a subject and to find solutions.
3. For the development of a student, tests are necessary.
4. Tests are useful in framing further plans.
5. Tests help in finding better ways of education.
6. Tests help in eradicating weaknesses of an individual.
7. They help in the overall development.
8. Tests show individual's interest in games.
9. Tests help in individual assessments.
10. It helps in the classification.
11. It helps to encourage those who are normally lagging behind.
12. To assist boys and girls in their effort to collect research material.

Besides, Tests and measurements are most helpful to the players and participants to learn about their drawbacks and weaknesses and also helps authorities in informing them about any possible episodemic or disease breaking out.

Qualities or characteristics of Good Test and Measurement

It is difficult to say what test is hundred percent appropriate and without drawbacks. Each one has certain good points, and some bad points too. The fundamental point is that a test should really help a student. Some of its characteristics are :

1. Any kind of test must have received wide recognition, not only by one department or organisation but by others as well. It should have been duly approved by the concerned departments.

2. The people must have full faith in the method or system of tests adopted. The equipment used must be approved.

3. The system of Test should have the approval of the concerned students. Answers to questions should be short and apt, timesaving and to such that assessment should be easy.

4. While testing, a student should feel at ease. If a child is tense, he is not likely to put up his (or her) best performance. If a child is tense, his mental balance and muscular equilibrium is never in order.

5. The method of tests should not he very expensive and should be within reach.

6. The tests should be such that the examinee is able to answer almost all questions. Sometimes too many questions are set and a child has no time to answer them. The number of questions and time allotted to answer them should be in balance.

7. The questions should be set from the entire courses of study or syllabus.
   The teachers should see that they are able to teach the entire syllabus before the examination. Sometimes questions are set out of syllabus. The examiner must see what is in the syllabus and keep his questions within its purview.

8. The questions set should be such that they are able to test all aspects. The students otherwise have a feeling that justice has not been done to them. Sometimes those who are ill-prepared are able to excel those who are far better prepared. This should not be allowed to happen.

Kinds of Tests

The following are some of the tests which the students often have to face:

1. Medical Test: In a medical test, the students are examined regarding health. Here tests are conducted to see if the student may not be suffering from any inherited or communicable discease, as also any defect in eyes, nose, throat, lungs chest, spine etc. The heart-beat is tested under different conditions. All these tests must be carried out by qualified medical doctors.

2. Physical Capacity and Ability Test: Such tests are meant to indicate a boy (or girl's) physical capacity. We can know what is the maximum capacity of strain. Some of the tests in this category are jumps with both feet together, straining hands backward, taking a round in air during jump etc. These tests are necessary for success in physical activities.

3. Physical Fitness Test: In physical education, a healthy body is the first fundamental. The body must be free from all diseases and its hearing and sight must be absolutely normal. Indeed all physical activites should be normal.

To test the strength, speed, stamina and physical agility there are certain tests. The govt of India has formulated certain measurements for men and women under its national physical health programme.

4. Achievement Test: The students achieve certain achievements through practice. These may be individual or in a team. It is necessary to know what has been achieved by which player and in what game, or event. Here achievements in team games, athletics, gymnastics, swimming etc. are examined.

5. Laws, Technique and Skill Testing: It is necessary to know if students understand different rules and laws in the sphere of physical education. What techniques and skills have they adopted and how much do they know about them. What strategies do they know should be adopted in different team-games.

6. Personality Testing: Personality testing is the most important of all tests. Personality tests are necessary to know how does a student discharge his duties and responsibilities, how disciplined is he, whether he has inner capability of becoming and acting as a good leader or not. The character of a player is of great importance. Personality tests are necessary to find out weaknesses, and strength, of his or her character. It is also essential to find about his individual virtues, like humility, discipline, steadfastness etc.

Tests therefore are essential both for finding out his or her weaknesses and also showing the possible goals which he or she can achieve. Thus, tests are both backward-looking and forward looking.

Tests should be normally conducted regularly and month after practice. It should be recorded regularly. If possible the outstanding students should be applauded and encouraged before the entire class. The students not showing good results should not be discouraged. They should be told how they can improve themselves through better techniques and skills.

OBJECTIVE QUESTIONS

1. Forward inclination of the shoulder girdle is known as
   (*a*) Kyphosis   (*b*) Scoliosis
   (*c*) Lordosis   (*d*) Round shoulders

2. Tennis skill is measures by
   (*a*) Miller wall volley test
   (*b*) Mc Donald's Test
   (*c*) Dyers test
   (*d*) All of the above.

3. The ability to carry out daily task is
   (*a*) Physical fitness
   (*b*) Fitness
   (*c*) Minimum muscular fitness
   (*d*) Cardio vascular fitness

4. "Miller wall volley test" is a test of
   (*a*) Badminton   (*b*) Squash
   (*c*) Volley ball   (*d*) Foot ball.

5. The instrument used for estimation of body fat is
   (*a*) Flexometer   (*b*) Goniometer
   (*c*) Dynamometer   (*d*) Skinfold caliper

6. Tournament standing serves as adequate standard for establishing
   (*a*) Validity   (*b*) Reliability
   (*c*) Subjectivity   (*d*) Norms

7. Sargent jump measures
   (*a*) Horizontal jumping ability
   (*b*) Vertical jumping ability
   (*c*) Both (a) and (b)
   (*d*) Neither (a) nor (b)

8. Which of the following terms has nothing to do with a test?
   (*a*) Creativity   (*b*) Validity
   (*c*) Reliability   (*d*) Objectivity

9. Ergometry is a process by which we measure
   (*a*) Brain activity   (*b*) Muscle potential
   (*c*) Lung capacity   (*d*) Cardiac output

10. The major cause of bad posture in school children is
    (*a*) Carrying a load of books
    (*b*) Bad habits of reading, sitting, standing, walking etc.
    (*c*) Muscle weakness
    (*d*) Tight dress

11. Pedograph is used for measuring a
    (*a*) Kyphosis   (*b*) Flat foot
    (*c*) Scoliosis   (*d*) Lordosis

12. Kraus weber test is used for measuring
    (*a*) Physical fitness
    (*b*) Motor educability
    (*c*) Minimum muscular strength
    (*d*) Skill ability in a sport

13. 'Copper's 12 minute run/walk test measures
    (*a*) Speed
    (*b*) Cardio-respiratory endurance
    (*c*) Agility
    (*d*) Strength

14. Test-retest method is used for determining
    (*a*) Validity   (*b*) Reliability
    (*c*) Objectivity   (*d*) Norms

15. Which of the following test measures cardio-respiratory function?
   (*a*) Harvard step test
   (*b*) J.C.R
   (*c*) Oregen motor fitness test
   (*d*) Kraus weber test

16. Which of the following is not a criteria of test selection?
   (*a*) Classification of test
   (*b*) Scientific authenticity
   (*c*) Educational application
   (*d*) Administrative feasibility

17. A test measures what is the purpose to measure is assessed by
   (*a*) Validity   (*b*) Reliability
   (*c*) Objectivity   (*d*) Norms

18. Soccer skill is measured by
   (*a*) Miller wall volley test
   (*b*) MC Donald's test
   (*c*) Sports knowledge test
   (*d*) All the above

19. Dyer test is associated with
   (*a*) Tennis   (*b*) Badminton
   (*c*) Athletics   (*d*) Football

20. Physical fitness is the ability to
   (*a*) Carry out daily task
   (*b*) Measure fundamental skills
   (*c*) Classify the groups
   (*d*) None of the above

21. Tests are
   (*a*) Designed to ascertain the quantity
   (*b*) Rendering service to the society
   (*c*) Appraisal of pupils programme
   (*d*) Instructional methodology

22. Wet spirometer is used for assessing
   (*a*) Vital capacity   (*b*) Blood pressure
   (*c*) Pulse rate   (*d*) Flexibility

23. Twelve minutes run and walk test is used to assess
   (*a*) Strength
   (*b*) Speed
   (*c*) Cardio-respiratory endurance
   (*d*) None of the above

24. Types of muscle fibres are determined by
   (*a*) Calorimeter
   (*b*) Biopsy
   (*c*) Spectrophotometer
   (*d*) All of the above

25. Criteria of tests depends on
   (*a*) Validity   (*b*) Reliability
   (*c*) Objectivity   (*d*) All of these

26. Validity means
   (*a*) The test measures the quality for which it is to be used
   (*b*) The test can be administered accurately
   (*c*) Both
   (*d*) None of these

27. Reliability means
   (*a*) The test measure the quality for which it is to be used
   (*b*) The test can be administered accurately
   (*c*) Both
   (*d*) None of these

28. If test yields the same or approximately the same scores when administered twice to the same individual in same conditions it is called as
   (*a*) Valid test   (*b*) Reliable test
   (*c*) Objective test   (*d*) None of these

29. The sum of all the scores made by each individual on all the tests included in the experimental situation is known as
   (*a*) Composite score (*b*) Standard score
   (*c*) Both   (*d*) None of these

30. The reliability of objective written test is determined by
   (*a*) Correlation between equivalent form of the test
   (*b*) Correlation between split halves test
   (*c*) Correlation between repeated test
   (*d*) All the above

31. The direct measurement of fat deposits sub cutaneously is done by
   (*a*) Skin fold caliper
   (*b*) Harvard instrument
   (*c*) Both
   (*d*) None

32. How many skin fold are taken for measurement of fat in human body
(*a*) Two   (*b*) Three
(*c*) Four   (*d*) None of these

33. The measurement of the size and proportion of the human body is called
(*a*) Anthropometry   (*b*) Plyometry
(*c*) Corrective   (*d*) None of these

34. When the digestive Viscera dominates the body economy the body composition is
(*a*) Mesomorphy   (*b*) Endomorphy
(*c*) Ectomorphy   (*d*) None of these

35. When the cervical spine is curved forward but the head and chin are not dropped
(*a*) Cervical Lordosis (*b*) Poke neck
(*c*) Both   (*d*) None of these

36. When muscle, bone and connective tissue are dominating the body composition is
(*a*) Mesomorphy   (*b*) Endomorphy
(*c*) Ectomorphy   (*d*) None

37. When the normal curve in the thoracic region is increased it is known as
(*a*) Thoracic kyphosis(*b*) Forward head
(*c*) Round shoulder   (*d*) None

38. The Lumber Lordosis is also known as
(*a*) Hollow back   (*b*) Flat back
(*c*) Both   (*d*) None

39. The flat back is also known as
(*a*) Lumbar lordosis   (*b*) Lumber kyphosis
(*c*) Lordosis   (*d*) None of these

40. A lateral deviation of the spine is present in
(*a*) Kyphosis   (*b*) Lordosis
(*c*) Scoliosis   (*d*) Knock kness

41. Navicular Drop is connected with
(*a*) Foots function   (*b*) Eye function
(*c*) Ear function   (*d*) None of these

42. The range of possible movement around a joint is known as
(*a*) Speed   (*b*) Flexibility
(*c*) Agility   (*d*) None of these

43. Goniometer is used for
(*a*) Speed   (*b*) Agility
(*c*) Both   (*d*) None of these

44. Electro goniometer is called as
(*a*) Elgon   (*b*) Leighton
(*c*) Both of these   (*d*) None of these

45. Scott and French test is used to measure
(*a*) Strength
(*b*) Football skill
(*c*) Trunk-Hip Flexibility
(*d*) None of these

46. Cable tension test is used to measure
(*a*) Agility   (*b*) Strength
(*c*) Both   (*d*) None of these

47. Back and leg Dynamometer is used for
(*a*) Vital capacity
(*b*) Strength of back and leg
(*c*) Speed of back and leg
(*d*) None of these

48. A state of decrease in performance capacity is due to
(*a*) Overload   (*b*) Under load
(*c*) Both   (*d*) None of these.

49. The longest training cycle is called
(*a*) Micro cycle   (*b*) Macro cycle
(*c*) Meso cycle   (*d*) None of these

50. The shortest training cycle is called
(*a*) Meso cycle   (*b*) Macro cycle
(*c*) Micro cycle   (*d*) None of these

51. The training cycle which have normal duration of 3-6 weeks is called
(*a*) Macro cycle   (*b*) Micro cycle
(*c*) Meso cycle   (*d*) None of these

52. The training cycle which have normal duration of 3-10 days is called
(*a*) Micro cycle   (*b*) Meso cycle
(*c*) Macro cycle   (*d*) None of these

53. The ability to overcome or to act against maximal resistance is called
(*a*) Explosive strength
(*b*) Maximum strength
(*c*) Strength Endurance
(*d*) None of these

54. The combination of strength and speed ability is called
(*a*) Explosive strength
(*b*) Maximum strength

(*c*) Strength Endurance
(*d*) None of these

55. The ability to overcome resistance or to act against resistance under condition of fatigue is called
(*a*) Explosive strength
(*b*) Maximum strength
(*c*) Strength Endurance
(*d*) None of these

56. Slow continuous, fast continuous, varied pace and Fartlek Method are the variations of
(*a*) Interval method
(*b*) Repetition method
(*c*) Continuous method
(*d*) None of these

57. Wind sprints, acceleration runs are the variations of
(*a*) Interval method
(*b*) Repetition method
(*c*) Continuous method
(*d*) None of these

58. The circuit training was first started, explained and studied by
(*a*) Morgan and Adamson
(*b*) H. Clarke and D. Clarke
(*c*) Scholich
(*d*) None of these

59. Single periodisation has
(*a*) One Transitional period
(*b*) Two transitional period
(*c*) Three transitional period
(*d*) None of these

60. Double periodisation has
(*a*) One Transitional period
(*b*) Two transitional period
(*c*) Three transitional period
(*d*) None of these

61. For the speed work the intensity of load is measured in terms of
(*a*) m/sec. or km.   (*b*) m, km.
(*c*) Both   (*d*) None of these

62. For the endurance work the intensity of load is measured in terms of
(*a*) m/sec. or km.   (*b*) m, km.

(*c*) Both   (*d*) None of these

63. In low resistance work load the percentage of the maximum possible intensity should be
(*a*) 70-80   (*b*) 30-50
(*c*) 80-90   (*d*) None of these

64. In medium resistance work load the percentage of the maximum possible intensity should be
(*a*) 70-80   (*b*) 30-50
(*c*) 80-90   (*d*) None of these

65. In sub-maximum resistance work load the percentage of the maximum possible intensity should be
(*a*) 90-100   (*b*) 75-85
(*c*) 30-50   (*d*) None of these

66. In multiple periodisation the number of the transitional period should be
(*a*) One   (*b*) Two
(*c*) Three   (*d*) None of these

67. In single periodisation the number of preparatory period should be
(*a*) One   (*b*) Two
(*c*) Three   (*d*) None of these

68. Performance deteriorating factors such as insufficient sleep, irregular daily routine, insufficient leisure time, use of alcohol and nicotine are the causes of
(*a*) Underload   (*b*) Over load
(*c*) Both   (*d*) None of these

69. Majors errors in training process such as rapid increase in load without stabilizing the adaptation and rapid increase of load after training breaks are the causes of
(*a*) Overload   (*b*) Underload
(*c*) Both   (*d*) None of these

70. The recovery phase can last for several days. The above statement is
(*a*) True   (*b*) False
(*c*) Partially true   (*d*) Partially false

71. Factors affecting the pace of recovery are
(*a*) Nature of the load
(*b*) Health and physical fitness
(*c*) Sleep
(*d*) None of these

72. When the muscles are stretched first and then made to contract are called
   (*a*) Eccentric – Concentric contraction
   (*b*) Concentric – Eccentric contraction
   (*c*) Both
   (*d*) None of these

73. Iso-kinetic method for the development of strength was first introduced by
   (*a*) Gundlach (1967)
   (*b*) J.J. Perrine (1968)
   (*c*) Hettinger and Muller (1953)
   (*d*) None of these

74. Iso-metric method for the development of static strength was first advocated by
   (*a*) Gundlach (1967)
   (*b*) J.J. Perrine (1968)
   (*c*) Brunner (1967)
   (*d*) Hettinger and Muller (1953)

75. For the development of strength endurance the intensity of work load should be
   (*a*) 80-100%   (*b*) 75-80%
   (*c*) 60-70%   (*d*) 40-60%

76. For the development explosive strength along with maximum strength the intensity should be
   (*a*) 60-70%   (*b*) 25-40%
   (*c*) 30-50%   (*d*) None of these

77. The ability to execute motor actions under given conditions, in minimum possible time is called
   (*a*) Flexibility   (*b*) Agility
   (*c*) Endurance   (*d*) Speed

78. Reaction ability and acceleration ability are the forms of.
   (*a*) Flexibility   (*b*) Agility
   (*c*) Endurance   (*d*) Speed

79. The factor determining the various speed performance are
   (*a*) Explosive strength
   (*b*) Mobility of nervous system
   (*c*) Muscle composition
   (*d*) All of these

80. The ability to maintain the maximum locomotor speed for a long time is called

   (*a*) Acceleration ability
   (*b*) Locomotor ability
   (*c*) Both
   (*d*) None of these

81. The resistance ability against fatigue is called
   (*a*) Strength   (*b*) Endurance
   (*c*) Speed   (*d*) Flexibility

82. The ability to resist fatigue caused by activities done at slow to moderate pace is called
   (*a*) Basic endurance
   (*b*) General endurance
   (*c*) Specific endurance
   (*d*) None of these

83. The ability to resist fatigue caused by any particular sports activity is called
   (*a*) Basic endurance
   (*b*) General endurance
   (*c*) Specific endurance
   (*d*) None of these

84. The ability to resist fatigue satisfactorily caused by various types of activities, may be aerobic or anaerobic or combination of both is called
   (*a*) Basic endurance
   (*b*) General endurance
   (*c*) Specific endurance
   (*d*) None of these

85. Factors determining endurance may be due to
   (*a*) Aerobic capacity
   (*b*) Anaerobic capacity
   (*c*) Various psychological factor
   (*d*) All the above

86. Intensity can be measured in terms of
   (*a*) Speed   (*b*) Distance/height
   (*c*) Speed(tempo)   (*d*) All of these

87. Volume can be measured in terms of
   (*a*) Duration   (*b*) Distance
   (*c*) Frequency   (*d*) All of these

88. A state of decrease in performance capacity can be
   (*a*) Due to overload
   (*b*) Due to underload
   (*c*) Both
   (*d*) None of these

89. Increased excitability, obstinancy, tendency of hysteria, quarrelsome, oversensitive to criticism are the symptoms of overload
(a) True
(b) False
(c) Partially true
(d) partially false

90. The somatic-functional symptoms of overload can be
(a) Loss of sleep
(b) Loss of appetite
(c) Loss of weight
(d) All of these.

91. Intensity and volume of load, nature of load, health and physical fitness, nutrition, sleep, daily routine and total load are the factors affecting the pace of recovery.
(a) True
(b) False
(c) Partially true
(d) Partially false

92. Cinematography and measuring devices are
(a) Bio-mechanical means of training
(b) Psychological means of training
(c) Both
(d) None of these

93. Ideomotor training, Autogenous training and psychotonic training are
(a) Natural means of training
(b) Bio-mechanical means of training
(c) Psychological means of training
(d) None of these

94. Weather conditions and alttitude are
(a) Medical means of training
(b) Natural means of training
(c) Psychological means of training
(d) None of these

95. During conditioning in continuous method
(a) Intensity is kept high
(b) Volume is kept high
(c) Both
(d) None of these

96. Interval training includes
(a) Medium to high intensity
(b) Low to medium volume
(c) Both
(d) None of these

97. In repetition method
(a) Intensity is kept very high
(b) Volume is kept low
(c) Both
(d) None of these

98. Extensive interval training improves
(a) Basic endurance
(b) General endurance
(c) Strength endurance
(d) All of these

99. Intensive interval training improves
(a) Speed endurance
(b) Explosive strength
(c) Maximum strength
(d) All of these

100. Repetition method helps to improve
(a) Speed ability
(b) Maximum strength
(c) Explosive strength
(d) All of these

ANSWERS

1. (a)	2. (c)	3. (a)	4. (a)	5. (d)	6. (a)	7. (b)	8. (a)
9. (c)	10. (b)	11. (b)	12. (c)	13. (b)	14. (b)	15. (a)	16. (a)
17. (a)	18. (b)	19. (a)	20. (a)	21. (a)	22. (c)	23. (b)	24. (d)
25. (a)	26. (b)	27. (b)	28. (a)	29. (d)	30. (a)	31. (c)	32. (a)
33. (b)	34. (a)	35. (a)	36. (a)	37. (a)	38. (b)	39. (c)	40. (a)
41. (b)	42. (d)	43. (a)	44. (c)	45. (b)	46. (b)	47. (c)	48. (b)
49. (c)	50. (c)	51. (c)	52. (b)	53. (a)	54. (c)	55. (c)	56. (a)
57. (a)	58. (b)	59. (a)	60. (a)	61. (b)	62. (a)	63. (b)	64. (b)
65. (a)	66. (b)	67. (a)	68. (a)	69. (b)	70. (a)	71. (b)	72. (d)
73. (d)	74. (d)	75. (d)	76. (d)	77. (d)	78. (b)	79. (b)	80. (b)
81. (c)	82. (a)	83. (a)	84. (d)	85. (d)	86. (c)	87. (a)	88. (d)
89. (a)	90. (a)	91. (c)	92. (b)	93. (b)	94. (a)	95. (a)	96. (c)
97. (a)	98. (a)	99. (a)	100.(a)				

12. HISTORY OF SPORTS AND GAMES

BADMINTON

History : The game Badminton is named after in England called "Badminton''. The game came about, through the combination games "POONA +BATTLEDORE". The English Army officers brought the game to INDIA in A.D. 1860. First time it was played at KARACHI. Badminton assumed popularity in India and some rules were formulated about the game at Karachi in 1877. The International Badminton Federation was formed in 1934. It appeared as demonstration sport in Munich Olympic in 1972. and became part of the Games in Seol Olympic in 1988.

1. Badminton Court: The Badminton playing court is marked as shown in the diagram, and as per the specifications mentioned below.

2. Posts: The posts should be sufficiently firm to the NET tight, and should be placed on the center of the side boundary of lines of the playing court for single and doubles.

Height of the Posts : 159 cm. or 5'-1" from the floor.

Width of the Posts : Not less than 3.8 cm.

3. Net *Length of the NET:* 6.10 m or 20'

Breadth of the NET : 76 cm. or 2'-6"

Height of the NET at posts : 155 cm. or 5'-1"

Height of the NET at the centre : 152 cm. or 5'.

Width of the tap fixed on the NET: 7.05 cm. or 3'. Length and breadth of the meshes 19 × 19 mm. or 3/4" of the NET.

The top of the NET must be edged with a 75 mm. or 3 inch white tape.

4. Shuttle: Weight of the shuttle : 4.73 to 5.50 gram.

No. of feathers: 14 to 16.

Diameter of the cork in which feathers of 2.5 to 2.8 cm. are fixed

Length of the feathers: 6.4 to 7 cm.

Diameter of feathers at the top : 5.4 to 6.4 cm.

5. Games scoring

1. *The men's singles game consist of:* 15 or 10 points in each set.

2. *The Women's singles game consist of:* 11 or 7 points in each set.

(a) In case of "Doubles" Two players shall play the game on each side.

(b) In case of "singles" One player shall play the game on each side.

(c)	Courts Area	Singles	Doubles
(i)	Length of the court	44' or 13.40 m	44' or 13.40 m
(ii)	Breadth of the court	17' or 5.18 m	20' or 6.10 m
(iii)	Distance of post from the End line	22' or 6.70 m	22' or 6.70 m
(iv)	Distance of Short Service Line from the posts	6'.6" or 1.98 m	6-6" or 1.98 m
(v)	Width of the side Gallery	No side Gallery	1'-6" or 46 m
(vi)	Width of the Back Gallery	2'.6" or 76 m	2'-6" or 76 m
(vii)	Distance of long service line from the short service line	13" or 3.96 m	13' or 3.96 m
(viii)	Width of each court	8'-6" or 2.59 m	10' or 3.5 m
(ix)	Length of each court	15'-6" or 4.72 m	13' or 3.96 m

3. ***The Men's Double game consist of :*** 15 or 10 points in each set.

4. ***The Women's double game consist of:*** 11 or 7 point in each set.

5. One game consist of five sets, in which the player or the players who win three sets are declared winner.

6. Side: The side (player) on each having the right to serve shall be called the "IN SIDE" and the opposite side (player) or the receiver of the service side shall be called the "OUT SIDE".

7. Start of the Game: Before the start of the game there shall be toss between the captains of the teams. The captain who wins the toss shall have the following options:

(i) To serve first.

(ii) Not to serve first.

(iii) To choose the END.

8. Single's Play: After the toss the player who has the right too serve, will serve from the right court, and the receiver will receive the service in his right court too. Both the players shall change their service courts after each point they have scored. The point 0-2-4-6-8 (EVEN Numbers) will be served from the right court and the odd numbers like 3-5-**7** will be served from the left court.

9. Doubles Play: Like single play the player who won the right to serving first shall be serving to the opposite player from his right court to the right court of the opponent. A service is considered delivered as soon as the shuttle struck by the server's racket. The shuttle is thereafter "IN PLAY" until it touches the ground or a fault occurs. After the delivery of the service the server and the receiver may take up any position they choose on their side of the net, except any boundary lines. No player may receive two consecutive services in the same game. In all subsequent inning each partner shall have the right to serve and they shall serve consecutively. The winner of a set shall serve first in the next set, but either of the winner will serve and either of the loser will receive the service.

10. Let:

(a). If a player serve out of his turn, or from the wrong service court and he wins the rally it shall be a let, provided that "let" be claimed before the next service.

(b) If the player of the receiving side standing in the wrong court and is ready to receive the service, receives it and wins the rally it shall be a ***"let"*** provided it claimed by the umpire before the next service.

(c) It shall be the duty of an Umpire to call ***"fault"*** or ***"let"*** before the appeal of a player.

(d) If at the time of service or during rally, a shuttle, after passing over the net, is caught in or the NET, it is a ***'let'.***

(e) If a receiver is not within the correct service court, it shall be a let or fault.

(f) If the server commits a fault for service infringement, it shall also be a ***"let".***

(g) When a ***"let"*** or a fault occurs, the play shall not count since the last service and the player who served, shall serve again.

11. Always Remember:

(a) The server cannot serve till his opponent is ready.

(b) If the receiver, attempt to return the service, it means he is ready.

(*c*) The server and the receiver must stand within their respective courts.

(d) A foot on or touching a line in case of either the server or the receiver, shall be treated as out side his service court.

(e) If a player has a chance of striking the shuttle in a downward direction when quite near the net, his opponent must not put up his racket near the net on the expectation that the shuttle rebounding from it. This is a fault.

(f) If the server made a fault, it is the change of service and if the receiver made a fault it is a point in favour of server.

(g) At the time of service if the shuttle, struck higher than waist, it is a fault.

(h) At the time of service if the head of the racket be higher of the server's hand, it is also a fault.

(i) If the served shuttle falls into the wrong service court or falls with in the short service line area, it is a fault.

(j) If shuttle falls outside the boundaries or passes through or under the net or fails (f) to pass the net, it is a fault.

(k) At the time of play, if any player touches the net with racket, bodily or by dress, it is also a violation of rule.

(l) If a shuttle hit twice by the player, it is also a fault.

(m) Server having both feet on the floor in a stationary position inside the service court when the shuttle is struck, if the fault be called against the server, the receiver also found in the same position.

12. Duration of Rest after each set: There is a 5 minutes rest after the completion of each set.

13. Match Officials

Umpire — 1   Service judge — 2
Lines men — 6 to 10   Scorer — 1

14. Racket: The length of the racket's frame should not be more than 680 mm or 27 inch. The width of the racket should not be more then 230 mm or 9 inch.

15. Change of Ends:

(a) At the end of every set.

(b) If the player wins the equal number of sets then they will change their ends on 8 points in a game of 15 and 6 point in a game of 11 and on 4 in a game of 7.

16. Remember at the time of Double's play:

(a) At the start of each set, the service shall be delivered from the right service court.

(b) Only the receiver shall return the service. If the shuttle should be touched or hit by the receiver's partner, the server scores a point.

(c) After the service is returned, the shuttle can be played by either player of serving side or by the receiving side until the shuttle becomes dead.

(d) If the receiving players make a fault, the serving players scores a point and the server serves again.

(e) If the serving player makes a fault then he loses the right to serve again, this time no point will be scored by either side.

(f) The player who receives at the start of any game shall receive in or serve from the right service court when that player's side

has not scored or has scored even number of points in that game and the left service court otherwise.

(g) No player shall serve out of turn or receive two consecutive services in the same set.

(h) Either player of the winning team may serve in the next set, and either player of the losing team may receive.

17. Fault Service:

(a) If the server in attempting to serve misses the shuttle.

(b) If on service the shuttle is caught on the net remains suspended on top or on service after passing over the net.

(c) Lands outside the boundaries of the court.

(d) Passes through or under the net.

(e) Fails to pass the net.

(f) Touching the roof, ceiling or side walls.

(g) Touches the person or the dress of a player.

(h) Fall of shuttle in the short service area.

(i) If the served shuttle falls in to the wrong service court.

(j) If the served shuttle falls in the side galleries.

(k) For correct service the server's racket shall initially hit the base of the shuttle while the whole of shuttle is below the server's waist.

18. Badminton Hall

(a) **Height of the Hall:** The 8 metres height shall be free of all obstructions over the area of the court.

(b) **Space:** There shall be 1.25 mts. clear space surrounding all the boundary lines of the court.

(c) **Colour:** There shall be white or cream colour on the walls. The lines should be marked in white colour of 5 cm., width.

(d) **Light:** There shall be a line of six 150 watt lamps at each side of the court parallel with the side lines, at a height 390 cm, above the floor and 60 cm, outside the NET'S post.

19. Winner : The player or the team who wins **3** sets out of 5 sets will be the winner of the match.

21. Not A Fault: Either the server or the receiver raises any part of the foot of feet, provided that some part of the both feet does maintain contact with the same part of the surface of the court.

22. Set: If the score becomes 13 all or 14 all (9 all or 10 all) (5 all or 6 all).The player who first scored 13 or 14(9 or 10) (5 or 6) shall have the choice of setting or not setting the game to 5 or 3 points. This choice can only be made before the next service is delivered.

If the game is set the score is called "love all" and the side first scoring the set number of point wins the game. The player who wins the game serves first in the next game.

Terminology of Badminton

1. **Backalley :** The area at the back of the court.
2. **Bird :** Another name for the shuttlecork.
3. **Alley :** The 1.5 foot wide extension on both sides of the court used in doubles play.
4. **Carry:** An illegal shot where the shuttle does not rebound immediately off the racket at point of contact.
5. **Throw :** An illegal shot in which the shuttle is carried or thrown by the racket.
6. **Unsight :** Illegal position taken by the server's partner so the receiver cannot see the shuttle as it is hit.
7. **Side-out :** When the individual or team loses serve and becomes the receiver.
8. **Server :** The player who puts the shuttle 'to play.
9. **Receiver :** The player to whom the shuttle is served.
10. **Inning :** The time during which a player or team holds service.
11. **Let :** The stopping of play due to some type of outside interference. The Point is replayed.
12. **Love :** The point which, if won by the server, makes that person the winner of the match.
13. **Rally:** An exchange of shot either in practice or during a match.
14. **Handout :** Term used in doubles to show that one player has lost service.
15. **Game Point :** The point which, if won,

allows the server to win the game.

16. **Forehand :** Any stroke made on the racket side of the body.
17. **Foot fault :** Illegal position or movement of the feet by either the server or receiver.
18. **Drop:** A shot which barely clears the net and immediately drops sharply.
19. **Drive :** A hard driven stroke which just clears the net and does not rise high enough for an opponent to smash.

BASKET BALL

The origin of the game of Basket-Ball dates back to A. D. 1891. It was devised by a clergyman and has the distinction of being the only major competitive sport which began on American soil. It is believed by some sports historians that a game called Pok -Tapok, which was played by ancient South Americans on the Yucatan-Peninsula resembled the game of Basket-Ball. There is a mention of this game having been played in some parts of MEXICO.

Founder: The credit for starting this game and framing its rules goes to JAMES NAISMITH, a Canadian by birth. During his physical education at Spring Field International Y.M.C.A. School, his exceptional sports skill caught the attention of the head of the Athletic department of Mc.Gill University and he retained him as an Instructor after completion of his education. Historians have given him the honour of being the founder of the modern game of Basket-Ball. The game was first played in Y.M.C.A. College of Physical Education, Spring Field- U.S.A.

Game : The game was first practised on suspended peach Basket-Ball. Baskets as it was those Baskets which gave the game its name. The peach baskets were replaced in A.D. 1906, by hoops fixed on a pole or board 10 feet above the ground. The fact that the pole was mostly put in the area necessitating frequent stretching and jumping on the part of the player was considered to be the most useful exercise.

International

I. Federation International de Basket Ball Association. .FIBA...1932

II. Rule Book Published : 1895
III. Demonstration in Olympic :1904 St. Louis.
IV. 1st. International Championship:1932
V.   In Olympic :1936 Berlin.
VI. World Championship :1950

Basket Ball In India

I.   Played for the first time in India: 1930
II. 1st National Championship for MEN :1934 New Delhi
III. Basket-Ball Federation of India :1950

International Tournaments

I.   World Championship
II. Olympic
III. Asia Cup
IV. European Cup

Skills

1. **Player Stance and Ball Entering**
2. **Passing and Receiving**
    (i) One Hand Passes
    (ii) Two Hand Passes
3. **One Hand Passes are:**
    (i)   Over Head Pass
    (ii)   Base Pass
    (iii) Bounce Pass
    (iv)   Side Pass
    (v)   Cross Step and Pass
    (vi)   Back Pass
    (vii) Hook Pass
    (viii) Roll Pass
    (ix)   Round Arm Pass
4. **Two Hand Passes**
    (i)   Over Head Pass
    (ii) Base or shoulder
    (iii) Chest Pass
    (iv) Bounce Pass
    (v)   Side Pass
5. **Dribbling**
    (i) Low Dribble
    (ii) High Dribble
        (a) Standing. (b) Jig-Jag. (c) State Way
6. **Shooting**
    (i) Two Hand Shooting
    (ii) One Hand Shooting
    Two Hand Shooting
    (i) Over Head Shot
    (ii) Base or Shoulder Shot

(iii) Set Shot
(iv) Jump Shot

One Hand Shooting
    (i)   Over Head Shot
    (ii) Base Shot
    (iii) Set Shot
    (iv) Jump Shot
    (v)   Lay up Shot
    (vi) Hook Shot
    (vii) Power Shot or Muscle Shot

7. **Rebound**
    (i) Offensive Rebound
    (ii) Defensive Rebound

8. **Defence and Offence**
    (i) Men to Men Defence
    (ii) Zonal Defence
    (a) Two One two (b) One One One two
    (c) Two Two One

7. **Fake: Faints and Foot Work**
    (i)   Stride Stop
    (ii) Skoot Stop
    (iii) Screening
    (iv) Pivoting

Basic Rules Of Basketball

1. Player's Stance: Feet open as per body weight and erect, knees bend, arms free to hold the ball easily, Strong foot is before the other, e.g., of the body near the mid of the feet.

2. Passing and Receiving

(i) ***Receiving :*** While receiving the ball the speed and technique of the opponent as well as his own partner must be borne in mind. The ball must be received at the chest.

(ii) ***Passes :*** While passing the ball if the passer is not alert the ball may go in opponents hand. The ball should be under full control while passing, the pass must be quick and precise.

While passing or receiving the ball, the player's knee must be bend, fingers well around the ball while passing or receiving the ball with full co-ordination of the body movements and body control.

The passes are of two types : (i) One hand passes; (ii) Two hand passes.

One Hand Passes: In one hand passes, only one hand is used to pass the ball, to the team mate. One hand passes are of **9** types as explained here before.

Two Hand Passes : In two handed passes both the hands are used to pass the ball, to the team mate, these are of five types as mentioned before.

In passes the player stance, and then the eyes on the team mate and then pass. There are four positions at the time of pass, they are: (i) Player Stance (ii) Execution (iii) Release (iv) Follow-through.

In one hand and two hand passes these are the four preliminary positions to make the pass correctly and quickly.

3. Dribbling: While dribbling, few points must be kept in mind:

(i) Body of the player must be leaning forward over the ball.

(ii) The fingers around the ball must keep hold on the ball.

(iii) The body movement must coincide with the dribbling.

(iv) The ball must move forward (forward bounce) and not upward too high in the air.

(v) Keep an eye on opponents movements.

(vi) The ball must be near the body under control.The free arm must guard the ball from opponent.

(viii) All movements of arms, legs and body should help in dribbling.

Dribbling is of two types . (i) Low Dribble; (ii) High Dribble, and these can be used by standing, Jig-jag and flat-way dribble.

4. Shooting: Shooting is of two types:

(i) ***One Hand Shooting:*** In one hand shooting a player must have the shooting power, good practice, and must be able to keep perfect balance, both mentally and bodily and may shoot whenever he gets a chance with ease and confidence. There are seven methods of one hand shooting as written in the main skills.

(ii) ***Two Hand Shooting:*** This is a common technique used by most of the players. Two hand shooting is very easy and precise. One can shoot with confidence and accuracy than one hand shot. The ball is just in front of the chest hence under control. Two hand shooter can withstand resistance and obstructions of the opponents and, at the same time, he can score with perfection.

Shooters are also of two types :

(i) Short Shooters (taking rebounds also);

(ii) Long Shooters (three point shooters).

There are four types of two hand shooting and seven types of one hand shooting as mentioned in the main skills.

5. Rebound : When the ball after striking the board comes down or away from the rings it is known as *Rebound.* While taking Rebound the players must be swift, alert and active. If rebound is taken, two points can be scored which may decide the game. Efforts must be made for a rebound. It is of two types:

(i) *Offensive Rebound:* If an attacker is not able to basket in the first shot, he then jumps up and catches the ball, this is called offensive rebound. Alertness and jumping ability are an asset for a good rebound.

(ii) *Defensive Rebound :* The defensive player when takes the ball after rebound to set the ball in opponent's court it is known as defensive rebound. The defensive player must also possess the same qualities of a rebounded as offender. Lot of practice is required for this to master technique and the skill.

6. Defence and Offence:

There are two types of Defence and Offence: **(i) Blocking; (ii) Tackling.**

(i) ***Blocking :*** Any attacker has to be blocked. A defensive player must block his opponent attacker. The defender while blocking can hit the ball with hands, by spreading his arms forward or sideways. Body is comfortably bending forward, knee flexed and arms spread.

(ii) ***Tackling :*** (i) Trying to get the ball from the opponent without committing fouls is called tackling. While tackling his opponent a player has to be swift, fast, alert, keeping eyes on the anti movements. (ii) He should stop the opponent's movement by blocking him.

Defence

(i) ***Man to Man Defence:*** In the defence every player is responsible for his man (opponent). He has to check his movements, prevent him from making an attack or basket. Checks his all tactics.

(ii) ***Zonal Defence:*** In this technique the players guard their own zone and stop the attackers.

(i) Two one two; (ii) One one two; (iii) Two-two one defence.

7. Fake and Pivot

Fake : Means a dodge or an active action to dodge the opponent with an active body movement only.

Pivot : When a player, while dribbling is stopped by an opponent he has no other alternative except to take pivot and pass the ball to his team mates in any direction convenient to him.

When one foot is firm on the ground (in constant touch with the ground) and movements are made by other foot then it is known as 'PIVOT.

By pivot a player with ball can move in any direction on one foot without lifting his pivot foot from the ground.

Shots through Pivot: (i) Board shot through Pivot (ii) Hook shot through Pivot (iii) Power shot or muscle shot through Pivot.

Shots can be taken by: (i) Low player Stance (ii) High player stance stride stop or skoot stop.

Officials : I. Umpire II. Refree Ill. Scorer IV. Astt. Scorer V. Time keeper VI. 30 sec. Operator.

Light : The lighting of the playing court shall have a minimum of 1500 lux; this level shall be measured **1** mt. above the playing court.

Scorer's Table : The official of the table must be able to see the court clearly. The bench/chairs for substitutes must therefore be lower than the chairs for the officials or alternatively the scorers Table and chairs must be placed on a platform.

Official's Signals: Simultaneously with the whistle being blown by the officials the hand above the head stops the game clock. If a foul is involved the fist with fingers closed above the head is the signal for both the foul and to stop the game clock.

These signals are official. It is poor practice to use an unorthodox signal at any time.

Basket : Ball is played by two teams of five players each. The purpose of each team is to throw the ball into the opponent's basket and to prevent the other team from securing the ball or scoring. The ball may be passed, thrown tapped or dribbled in any direction. Subject to the direction or the restrictions laid down in the rules.

Measurement Of The Play Field & Specification Of Sports Equipment

Court-Dimension : The playing court shall be rectangular 28 m × 15 m flat hard surface free from obstructions.

Boundary Lines: Side lines and end lines spectators should be at last 2 m, away from the lines of 5 cm width.

Centre Circle: Of 1.80 m, radius in the centre of the field.

Centre Line-Front court-Back court: Centre line shall extend 15 cm, beyond each side line.

Three Point Goal Area: Circle of 6.25 m. radius from the centre of the ring, or 1.575 m. from end line.

Restricted Areas: The outer edges being 3 m, from the mid point of the end lines of 5.80 m, length.

Back Board: Made of hard wood 3 cm, thick 1.80 mt., horizontally and 1.05 m, vertically. Rectangle 59 cm × 45 cm, lines marked 5 cm, in width.

Baskets: Ring and Nets: Rings of solid iron 45 cm, in inside diameter painted orange diameter 20 mm, Nets 40 cm, in length.

Ball: Weight 600 to 650 gm, Circumference 75 to 78 cm.

Players Substitutes And Coaches

Teams : Each team consists of ten players. Where more than fine number of matches to be played, then the number of players in each team increases to 12.

Player Leaving Court: A player may not leave the playing court to gain an unfair advantage.

Captain: The captain may address an official on matters of interpretation or to obtain essential information when necessary, if it is done in a courteous manner.

Playing Regulations

Beginning of game : By a jump of the ball in the centre circle.

Jump Ball : A jump ball takes place when the official tosses the ball between two opposing players.

Goal or Basket : When a live ball enters the basket from above and remains within or passes through. A goal from the tiled counts 2- outside 3- point line when it counts 3- A free throw counts **1** point.

Decision of Game: A game shall be decided by the scoring of the greater number of points in the playing time.

Tied score and extra period : 5 minutes.

Dead Ball : The ball become dead when any goal is made or any obstruction occurs.

Substitutions : A substitute before going on the court shall report to the scorer and must be ready to play immediately. A player involved in a jump ball may not be substituted by another player. Substitutions shall be completed as fast as possible.

How ball is played : The ball is played with the hands, it is forbidden to run with the ball, kick it, or strike it with the fist.

Player out of Bounds: A player is out of Bounds when he touches the floor on or outside the boundary lines.

Ball out of Bounds: The ball is out of Bounds when it touches a player who is out of Bounds or any other person.

Pivot: A pivot takes place when a player who is holding the ball steps once or more than once any direction with the same foot.

Dribbling: In a dribble the ball must come in contact with the floor. He may take as many steps as he wishes between bounces.

Player in the act of shooting: A player is in the act of shooting when in the judgement of an official, he makes an attempt to score.

Three second Rule: A player shall not remain for more than three seconds in that part of the opponents restricted area.

Five second Rule: A player who is holding the ball does not pass, shoot, roll or dribble the ball within 5 seconds.

Eight second Rule: A team gains control in its back court must go into its front court within 8 seconds.

24 second Rule: When a team gains control of a live ball on the court a shot for goal must be made within 24 seconds.

Violations: A violation is an infraction of the rules, the Penalty for which is the loss of the ball.

Fouls: A foul is an infraction of the rules involving personal contact with an opponent or unsportsman-like behaviour.

Throw in from out of Bounds: The player who is to throw the ball in from out of bounds shall stand out of bounds at the side line of the place nearest to the point.

Free Throws: A free throw is a privilege given to the player to score one point from an unhindered shot for goal from a position directly behind the free throw line.

Personal Conduct: Basket-Ball is theoretically a no-contact game.

Personal Foul: A personal foul is a player foul which involves contact with an opponent.

Intentional Foul: An intentional foul is a personal foul which, in the opinion of the official, was deliberately committed by a player.

Disqualifying Foul: Any flagrantly unsports-manlike infraction is a disqualifying foul.

Double Foul: A double foul is a situation in which two opponents commit fouls against each other at approximately the same time.

Multiple Foul: A multiple foul is a situation in which two or more team mates commit personal fouls against the same opponent at approximately the same time.

General Provisions

(i) A player who has committed five fouls either personal or technical must automatically leave the game.

(ii) After a team has committed seven team fouls personal or technical in a half (extra periods are considered to the part of the second half) all subsequent players fouls shall be penalized by the one and one rule unless a penalty of greater severity is involved.

(iii) One and One Rule : When a player commits a subsequent personal foul after his team has committed seven player fouls, personal and technical in a half, the one and one rule comes into effect, whereby the player against whom the foul has been committed is given the opportunity to shoot one free throw.

Playing Time : 4 Quarters of 10 minutes each as mentioned below:

I Half : 10 min. Rest : 2 min. II half : 10 min. Half Time : 15 min. III Half : 10 min. Rest : 2 min. IV Half : 10 min.

Extra period = 5 minutes each half.

Goal Time : A team having the ball in possession must try for a goal within 24 seconds otherwise a shot clock violation would take place.

Charged time out : There is a provision of one time out of one minute for each team in the first three quarters and one time out of 2 minutes to each team in the last quarter. In extra period only one time for each team is grated.

8 Second Rule : A team shall move from back court to front court within 8 seconds otherwise it is a violation (foul play).

Terminology Of Basket Ball

1. Assist: Final pass given to shooter of a basket.

2. Free throw : Free shot at basket due to an infringement by the opponent.

3. Hoop : The metal ring of the basket'.

4. Held ball : Called when two opponents have one or two heads so firmly upon the ball that neither can gain possession.

5. Jump ball : method of putting the ball into play whereby the referee tosses it up between two opponents who try to tap it to a teammate.

6. Pick : Action of a player who, without causing contact, delays or prevents an opponent from reaching his desired position.

7. Press : Defensive technique of harassing players into hurried play.

8. Traveling : Running with the ball without bouncing it.

9. Turnover : Loss of possession of the ball by a team before any member has been able to try for a basket.

10. Drive : An aggressive move towards the basket by a player with the ball.

11. Pick : A special type of screen where a player stands so that the defensive player slides to make contact, freeing an offensive teammate for a shot or drive.

12. Charging : Personal contact against the body of an opponent by a players trying to get free a for pass.

13. Switching : A reversal of defensive guarding assignments.

14. Technical Foul : A non contact foul by a player, team or coach for unsportsman like behaviour or failure to abide by rules regarding submission of line ups, uniform numbering and substitution procedures.

15. Travelling : When a player in possession of the ball within bounds progresses illegaly in any direction.

CRICKET

For many enthusiasts cricket today is way of life. Its beginning is obscure. Like all bat-and-ball games, cricket evolved gradually from various sources. It is related to an early Scottish sport known as 'cat-and-dog', a thirteenth century passtime called 'hand-in and hand-out'. The game as is understood and played today has its origin in the south eastern part of England. Various claims have been made (and disputed) regarding the first mention of cricket and its earliest pictorial illustration. According to an expert of sports from Oxford, the game was played in Kent as early as A.D. 1300. The first preserved cricket score and earliest code of laws date back to A.D. 1744. Nevertheless it was not until the second half of the seventeenth century that cricket became a generally adopted sport. It gained popularity among the higher classes, the noble and wealthy, in the following century. The original bat was a primitive club used for attack and defence. Bats greatly varied in shape, length and weight. The earliest bats gave cricket its name. They were just branches taken off the tree and slightly curved.

Terms

Bowled : A batsman is bowled (out) if the ball hits the wicket's and dislodges a ball, even if the ball has come-off his body or bat.

Bump ball : A ball that is hit hard into the ground and rises so fast that, when fielded, it seems like a catch.

Bye(s) : Runs scored when the ball passes the wicket, untouched by bat or person and the batsman runs or the ball crosses the boundary.

Draw : A match in which no decision is reached.

Handled ball : A batsman is out handled ball if he touches the ball with his hand while it is in play. He may, however, touch it if the fielding side gives him the permission to do so.

Hat-trick : A bowler achieves a hat-trick if he dismisses three batsmen with consecutive deliveries either in the same over or at the end of one and the beginning of another over. The wicket must be taken in same match.

Hit wicket: A batsman is out hit wicket if a ball is dislodged by his bat, body or cap while he is in the act of making his stroke.

Leg before wicket (L.B.W.) : A batsman is out L.B.W. if the ball hits the batsman on his pads and in the opinion of the umpire it was pitched on a straight line between the wicket or on the off side and would have hit the wicket.

Maiden over : An over in which no runs are scored by the batsman.

Over the wicket : A method of delivery in which the bowler delivers the ball with the hand nearer the stumps.

Round the wicket : A method of delivery in which the bowler delivers the ball with the hand farther from the stumps.

Technical Terms

Good-Length Ball : A good-length ball is one which presents the batsman with the problem of deciding whether to go forward to play it, or to go back when it pitches. If the batsman tries to hit it from the crease it is quite likely to go into the air.

Full-pitch Ball : A full-pitch ball is one which the batsman can hit from the crease before it pitches.

Off Spin : The off spin bowler aims to pitch the ball on the off side and bring it back into the wicket. The off break is spun in a clockwise direction from left to right, the ball being held between the first two fingers, the two other being curled slightly over the ball, with the thumb on the opposite side.

Leg Breaks : The leg break is spun with the fingers over the ball, and in most of the cases the ball is given in the direction of the spin. The leg break, bowled with the fingers over the ball and in a somewhat downward motion, penetrates the surface of the wicket and turns quickly. It is stock ball. It is suggested that a young bowler interested in leg breaks, should concentrate on the basic bowling action, particularly the high arm and follow through past the left leg.

Grip : The ball is held in the first three fingers, which are spaced comfortably apart. The top joint of the third finger which is under ball, takes most of the pressure of the thumb which has very little part in spinning the ball and naturally rests on the seam. The ball should be held quite firmly. The wrist is bent to almost ninety degrees and the back of the hand is uppermost. On delivery the ball is spun off the third finger by the synchronization of the action plus the flicking and twisting of the wrist in an anticlockwise direction. For better spin, the right arm should be fully extended with a large goal of swing.The back of the right hand must be uppermost throughout the swing, as this will ensure a leg break bowling.

Top-spin : It is a difficult bowling. Right arm straight above your head and wrist bent. Ball is to be held like leg-break. Turn the arm slightly until the seam of the ball points straight down the wicket.

Googly : It is an off break with a leg break action. The grip of the ball is like leg break, with the wrist turned down to ninety degrees. The arm is turned in an anti-clockwise direction with the back of the hand now point out of the back of the hand and generally in an upward direction, but will not hit the pitch quiet so hard and will plop rather than turn or bounce over the third finger.

There is no need to alter the action. Do not drop the left shoulder or point the left foot.

Leg-byes : If the ball, not having been called. "wide" or "no ball", is unintentionally deflected by the striker's dress or person, except a hand holding the bat, and runs are obtained, the umpire shall signal "leg-bye" and the run or runs so scored shall be credited to the batting side. Such leg-byes shall only be scored, if in the opinion of the umpire, the striker has: (a) attempted to play the ball with his bat, or (*b*) tried to avoid being hit by the ball.

Disallowance of leg-byes: In the case of a deflection by the striker's person, other than in leg-byes (a) and (*b*) above, the umpire shall call and signal of "dead ball" as soon as one run has been completed or when it is clear that a run is not being attempted or the ball has reached the boundary. On the call and signal of "dead ball" the batsman shall return to their original ends and no runs shall be allowed.

An appeal "How's that"? shall cover all ways of being out. Answering appeals, the umpire at the bowler's wicket shall answer appeals before the other umpire in all cases, except those arising out of Hit wicket or Stumped or Run out when this occurs at the striker's wicket.

When either umpire has given a batsman not out, the other umpire shall, within this jurisdiction answer the appeal or a further appeal, provided it is made in time in accordance with the Time of Appeals.

Measurement of Cricket Field and Supports Equipment

The Ball : The ball, when new, shall weigh neither less than 155.9 gm nor more than 163 gm. It shall measure not less than the 8.13/16 inches (22.4 cm) nor more than inches (22.9 cm) in circumference, failing which either captain may demand a new ball at the start of each innings. In the event of a ball being lost or becoming unfit for play, the umpires should allow another ball of the similar wear or use. They shall inform the batsman whenever a ball is to be changed.

(a) All cricket ball to be used in first-class matches should be approved before the start of a match by the umpires and captains.

(b) In first-class matches, the captain of the fielding side may demand a new ball after the prescribed number of over has been bowled with the old one. The governing body for cricket in the respective country shall decide the number of over which shall not be less than 75 six ball over or 55 eight ball over. In other classes of cricket, these regulations will not apply unless agreed to before the toss for innings.

(c) Any ball substituted for one lost or becoming unfit for use should have had similar wear or use as that of the one discarded.

NOTES : Specification—The *specification for ball as described above shall apply in top grade balls only The following degrees of technique will be acceptable for other grades of ball.*

(i) *Men's grade* 2-4
   Weight 150 gm. to 165 gm.
   Size 22.0 cm to 23.0 cm.

(ii) *Junior grade*
   Weight 133 gm to 150 gm.
   Size 20.5 cm to 22.0 cm.

(iii) *Women grade*
   Weight 140 gm to 150 gm.
   Size 21.0 cm to 22.5 cm

The bat : The bat shall not exceed 10.8 cms, in the widest part, it shall not be more than 96.5 cm, in length including the handle. The blade of the bat shall be made of wood.

NOTE *: The blade of the bat may be covered with material for protection, strengthening or repair. Such material shall not exceed 1.56 mm in thickness.*

The pitch : The pitch is deemed to be the area of ground between the bowling creases, 1.52 m, in width on either side of the imaginary line joining the centre of the middle stumps of the wickets. Before the toss for innings, the executive of the ground shall be responsible for the selection and preparation of the pitch. Thereafter the umpires shall control its use and maintenance. The pitch shall not be changed during a match unless it becomes unfit for play, and that too with the consent of both the captains.

Length : That of the playing surface to a minimum of 17.68 m.

Width : That of the playing surface to a minimum of 1.83 m.

Terminology of Cricket

1. Beamer: Ball bowled higher than a full toss so endangering the batsman.

2. Bosy/Bosie : Australian name for a googly (named after B.J.T. Bosanquet 1877-1936, an English cricketer).

3. Bouncer: Ball bowled short and fast in order to cause batsman to take evasive action.

4. Chinaman : An off break bowled by a left-hander to a right-handed batsman.

5. Cover : Fielding position midway between infield and outfield in which a good fielder may save a single.

6. Cover Point : Fielding position on the off side and nearer the batsman than the non striker.

7. Fine leg : Fielding position between wicket keeper and square leg but deeper.

8. Googly : Off-break ball bowled with apparent leg-break action.

9. Gully: Fielding position a little wider than the slips.

10. Maiden : An over in which no runs have been scored.

11. Night watchman : An inferior batsman sent in to play out remaining time near the close of day, in order to prevent a better player from being dismissed.

12. Short leg: Fielding position close to the batsman and on the leg side.

13. Slip : Fielding position next to the wicket-keeper.

14. Wicket maiden : Over during which no runs have been scored and a wicket has been taken.

15. Wide : Extra given to batting side due to ball being bowled too wide of the batsman.

16. Yorker: Ball bowled at feet of batsman whether playing back or forward.

FOOT BALL

The origin of foot-ball has been traced to over 5000 years ago in Rome. It is assumed that the first of all this game was played at Sparta and the Roman soldiers brought this game to Britain.

The development of this sport has continually been influenced by changes in the rules. This game became very popular in England in 12th century. Mr. Thring and Dewinton frame new rules in 1862. The revised rules were implemented in 1863. In the same year England Foot-Ball Association was formed. England and Scotland played the first international match. On 21 May 1904 International Foot-Ball Federation was formed. At that time only seven nations were the members of the federation. The first world foot-ball championship was organized at MONTEVIDEO in 1930. British rulers introduced the foot-ball in India. The sport became popular in India due to its being inexpensive sport.

In 1948 at England, India took part first time in Olympic games. In 1956 MELBOURNE Olympics, India played in the semi-final. In 1951 first Asian games held at Delhi, India became the winner of Asian Foot Ball. At the time of opening of the First Asian game Chacha Nehru said *"PLAY THE GAME WITH A SPIRIT OF GAME"*.

Measurement of Foot Ball Play Field & Equipments

Dimension : The foot-ball play field shall be rectangular having

Length = 100 to 110 m

Breadth = 64 to 75 m

Radius of the centre circle at the centre = 9.15 m

Length of each line drawn from goal line 5.50 m. away from the goal posts to draw goal area is = 5.50 m

Distance from one line to other = 18.32 m

Distance of the penalty spot from the centre of the goal line = 11 m

Penalty Area: At a distance of 16.50 m from each goal post two lines shall be drawn at right angles to the goal line, these shall be extend up to 16.50 m, and then joined by a line of 40.32 m This area is called the penalty area and from each penalty spot draw an arc of radius of 9.15 m.

Corner Area: Each corner of the play field draw a quarter circle of radius of 1 m. in the play field.

The Goals : The goal area measuring 7.32 m, in length and 2.44 m in height consist two upright posts.

The width of the upright (hole) = 12.50 to 12.70 cm.

The width of the cross bar = 12.50 to 12.70cm.

Net: Meshes of the Net shall not be more than 10 × 10 cm.

Ball: Ball shall be spherical, outer casing shall be of lather or of the approved material. Circumference of the Ball = 68.5 to 71 cm.

Weight of the Ball = 396 to 453 gram.

Pressure of the air = 1 kg/sq cm at sea level

No. of Players: A match shall be played by two teams having Eleven players in each team one of whom shall be the Goal Keeper. Only two substitutions are allowed in a match.

Rules of Football

Goal-kick: When whole of the ball passes over the goal-line, excluding that portion between the goal posts, either in the air or on the ground, having last been played by one of the attacking team, it shall be kicked directly into play beyond the penalty-area from a point within that half of the goal-area nearest to the point where it crossed the line. A goal keeper shall not receive the bail into his hands from a goal-kick in order that he may thereafter kick it into play. If the ball is not kicked beyond the penalty-area directly into play, the kick shall be retaken. The kicker shall not play the ball a second time until it has touched or been played by another player. A goal shall not be scored directly from such a kick. Players of the opposite team shall remain outside the penalty-area whilst the kick is being taken.

Punishment: If a player is taking a goal-kick, plays the ball second time after it has passed beyond the penalty-area, but before it has touched or been played by another player, an indirect free-kick shall be awarded to the opposing team to be taken from the place where the infringement occurred.

Corner-kick: When the whole of the ball passes over the goal-line, excluding portion between the goal posts, either in the air or on the ground, having last been played by one of the defending team, a member of the attacking team shall take a corner-kick i.e, the whole of the ball shall be placed within the quarter circle at the nearest corner flag-post which must not be moved and it shall be kicked from that position.

A goal may be scored directly from such a kick. Players of the opposite team shall not approach within 10 yards of the ball until it is in play i.e., it has travelled the distance of its own circumference nor shall the kicker play the ball a second time until it has been touched or played by another player.

Throw-In: When the whole of the ball passes over a touch line, either on the ground or in the air, it shall be thrown-in from the point where it crossed the line in any direction, by a player of the team opposite to that of the player who last touched it. The thrower at the moment of delivering the ball must face the field and his each foot shall be either on the touch-line or on the ground outside the touch-line. The thrower shall use both hands and shall deliver the ball from behind and over his head. The ball shall be in play immediately it enters the field of play, but the thrower shall not again play the ball until it has been touched or played by another player. A goal shall not be scored direct from a throw-in.

Punishment: (a) If the ball is improperly thrown-in, throw-in shall be taken by a player of the opposing team.

(b) If the thrower plays the ball a second time before it has been touched or played by another player, an indirect free-kick shall be taken by a player of the opposing team from the place where the infringement occurred.

Off-Side Import

(i) A player is in offside position if he is nearer to his opponents goal line than the ball unless: (a) he is in his own half of the field of play or (*b*) there are at least two of his opponents nearer their own goal line then he is.

(ii) A player shall only be declared off side and penalized for being in off side position. If, at the moment the ball touches or is played by, one of his team, he is, in the opinion of the referee *(a)* interfering with play or with an opponent or (*b*) seeking to gain an advantage by being in that position.

(iii) A player shall not be declared off side by the referee; (a) merely because of his being in an off side position or if he receives the ball, direct from a goal kick, a corner kick, a throw in or dropped by the referee.

(iv) If a player is declared off side, the referee shall award an indirect free kick, which shall be taken, by a player of the opposing team from the place where the infringement occurred unless the offence is committed by a player in his opponents goal area, in which case the free-kick shall be taken from a point anywhere within the half of the goal area in which offence took place.

The Start of Play

(a) At the beginning of the game choice of ends and the kick-off shall be decided by the toss of a coin. The team winning the toss shall have the option of choice of ends or the kick-off.

The referee having given a signal, the game shall be started by a player taking a place-kick: (a kick at the ball while it is stationary on the ground in the center of the field) into his opponents' half of the field. Every player shall be in his own half of the field and every player of the team opposing that of the kicker shall remain not less than 10 yards from the ball until it is kicked-off. The ball shall not be deemed in play until it has travelled the distance of its own circumference. The kicker shall not play the ball second time until it has been touched or played by another player.

(b) After a goal has been scored, the game shall be restarted in a similar manner by a player of the team losing the goal.

(c) After the half-time, ends shall be changed and the kick-off shall be taken.

Ball in and Out of Play

The ball is out of play: (i) When it has wholly crossed the goal line or touch line, whether on the ground or in the air; (ii) when the game has been stopped by the referee.

The ball is in play at all other times from the start of the match to the end including:

(i) if it rebounds from a goal post, crossbar or corner-flag post into the field of play;

(ii) off either the referee or linesmen when they are in the field; or

(iii) in the event of a supposed infringement of the laws until a decision is taken.

Duration of the Game

The duration of the game shall be two equal periods of 45 minutes each unless otherwise mutually agreed upon, subject to the following:

(a) allowance shall be made in either period for all time lost through accident or other causes, as per referee's decision.

(b) Time shall be extended to permit a penalty kick being taken at or after the expiration of the normal period in either half.

Half-time interval shall not exceed five minutes except by consent of the referee.

Technique of Foot Ball Play Game

1. Kicking Technique,
2. Passing Technique
3. Heading Technique,
4. Trapping Technique
5. Throwing Technique,
6. Dribbling Technique

Golden Goal

If a match ended in a draw the team who make goal first in the extra time the goal scored by the team called the Golden Goal.

Methods of Scoring

Except as otherwise provided in these laws, a goal is scored when the whole of the ball has passed over the goal line between the goal posts and under the crossbar, provided it has not been thrown, carried or propelled by hand or arm by a player of the attacking side, except in the case of a goalkeeper who is within his own penalty area.

The team scoring the greater number of goals during a game shall be the winner. If no goals or an equal number of goals are scored, the game shall be termed a draw.

Terminology of Foot Ball

1. Nutmeg : To play the ball between the legs of a defender and run around him to collect it.

2. Wall pass : Pass from one player to another and back to save having to face a defender.

3. Clear : Playing the ball a great distance attempting to move it out of a danger area.

4. Direct free kick : A free kick from which the kicker may immediately score from the initial contact.

5. Half Volley : Contacting the ball just as it hits the ground after being airborne.

6. Square Pass : A pass that is directed toward the side of a player.

7. Trap : The technique used for receiving the ball, bringing it under control.

HOCKEY

Hockey is one of the many sports derived from prehistoric man's delight in stick and ball. Its birth place was Asia and authorities credit Persia with having devised it about 2000 B.C.

It is said that the Greeks and the Romans played Hockey but nothing is known about the nature of the game, that they played. The earliest mention of the present day game dates back only to A.D.1527, when the Galway Statutes included hockey, the horlling of little balls with ... sticks or staves in a list of prohibited games.

Modern Hockey: As created in England it resembles most closely to the game that was once popular in the British Isles and whatnot since, British Hockey's immediate forerunners were the Scottish shinty, the English and Welsh bandy and the Irish hurling. But it is generally assumed that the true ancestor of Hockey was Hurling. Hurling crossed the sea from Iran to England to be assimilated in to the English way of life eventually to become hockey.

The first hockey club was formed in Blackheath in 1861 .The sticks were made of oak and the head position was steamed and then pressed to give it a hooked shape. The ball was a solid cubs of rubber with rounded corners.

Hockey included in a ban, issued by king Edward III in 1365, which is the first definite record of existence of the game in Britain. It was then still called Bandy Ball.

With the passage of time, the game became more refined and civilized. The game was standardised by the Wimbledon Hockey club in 1883. Its regulations adopted in 1886 by the Hockey Association which, thoroughly modernized the sport, making it highly scientific and skillful.

Some Historical Dates : 1st International Hockey match:1895. England's. Ireland

1st time in Olympic: 1908 London

Adopted by women for the first time : 1887. Molesey (England)

Federation of International Hockey: 1924.

1st World Cup Hockey : 1971. Barcelona (spain).

Hockey in India

Hockey became popular in India when the British Indian Regiments played the game.

1st Hockey Club in India: 1885-86. Calcutta. (Bombay + Punjab).

1st Hockey Association in India:1908 (Bengal Hockey Association). IInd:1920 (Sind Hockey Association, Karachi).

With the popularity of the game, associations were formed in different states Bombay, Bihar, Orissa and Delhi.

Types of Hockety

(i)   Ground Hockey; (ii) Ice Hockey.

Skills or Techniques of Hockey

1. Hold: Hold the stick with left hand, apart from the lead, right hand below with firm grip.

2. Hitting The Ball: Put the ball in front of the left feet. Bend the trunk, hold the stick in a firm grip and hit the centre of the ball with the blade of the stick.

3. Stopping The Ball: Hold the stick in a firm grip and the right arm will be in the centre of the stick, Now to stop the Ball make the stick in front of the ball and, stop it.

4. Push: It is a wrist work, and with the help of the blade of the stick roll the ball or push the ball on the ground, the strength used as per the push be reached.

5. Flick: (i) Direct Flick (ii) Reverse Flick. In flick, the stick is at the back of the ball, and play the ball with the help of the wrist. In Reverse flick the use of the stick is when the blade portion of the stick raised and the head of the blade used for the reverse flick, out side left uses it mainly.

6. Scoop: To put the blade part of the stick below the ball and lift it in the air and throw it in the air towards the players is called the scoop.

7. Dribbling: First to control the ball, than to dribble it right and left with the help of the stick using wrist work is called the Dribbling. The left hand on the above and the right hand below it, movement of the Hockey made through the left hand's wrist work.

8. Tackling: To get the Ball from the opponent in control is called Tackling. A long reach from the right side of the opponent player's and try to get the ball in control, tackling from the left side is a foul play.

9. Passing: Taking and giving of the ball to the team mates in a good way is called a passing. At the time of passing it must be in mind that the direction and the speed of the ball be as per the distance.

10. Bully: In bully one and one player of the each team stands near by in a opposite direction with each other and the ball placed between them, the players stricks or touches their sticks two times in the air and at the third time, any one of them pass or make it clear, towards his team mates. At the time of Bully, bend from the trunk, eyes are fixed on the ball so that at the final touch try to get the ball first in control.

11. Push in: In field hockey, this is a method of putting the ball back in play after the opposing team has driven it over the sideline. The player standing outside the sideline pushes or taps the ball into the field of play with his or her stick, where it is played by another player. The player making the push-in may not play the ball or come within playing distance of the ball until another player has played it.

12. Corner: Within 25 yards line if the ball goes out with a touch of defending team a corner hit is awarded. This time a hit is made from the corner. Hold the stick in firm grip and hit the ball at the centre towards the team mates.

13. Penalty Corner

In Attack: When a player push in the ball from the goal line, his team mate will stop the ball using his hand in a quick movement, and the third team mate hits the ball in to the goal. This time the player who is going to hit the ball not to be off-side.

In Defence: At the time of defending the penalty corner the position of the defending players should be: 1. Head of circle; 2. Middle of the circle; 3. Goal mouth.

Right half back goes directly to the shooter.

The Goal keeper comes forward about 5 yards to defend the goal.

Centre Half comes forward to defend the hit of the opponents.

Left Back comes 1 yards towards the hitter.

Left Half comes 4 yards towards the shooter.

Rules

1. Teams and Duration of Play

(a) A game shall be played between two teams. Not more than eleven players of each team, shall be on the field of play at the same time. At no time shall there be on the field more than one goal-keeper in each team.

(b) Each team is permitted to substitute up to two players during the game (*This provision is not mandatory at any level.*)

(c) No player, once substituted, shall be permitted on the field again and no substitute shall be permitted for a suspended player during his suspension.

(d) Substitution of players may only take place with the prior permission of an umpire during any stoppage of play other than for the award of a corner, a penalty corner, or a penalty stroke.

(e) The duration of the game shall be 35-5-35 mm. Unless otherwise agreed before the game.

(f) At the half time the teams shall change ends, and the duration of the interval shall not exceed five minutes if not decided before, but not more than 10 minutes.

(g) The games starts, with bully, with the umpire's whistle.

2. Captains : The captains shall

(a) Toss for choice of ends.

(b) Before the start of play and on any change, indicate its necessary, to each other and to the umpires and their respective goal-keepers.

3. Umpires and Goalkeepers

(a) There shall be two umpires to control the game and to administer the rules. These umpires shall be the sole judges of fair and unfair play during the game.

(b) Unless-otherwise provided, each team shall be responsible for providing one umpire.

(c) (i) Each umpire shall be primarily responsible for decisions in his own half of the field, for the whole of the game without changing ends.

    (ii) Solely responsible for decisions on the push in for the full length of his nearer side line.

    (iii) Shall be responsible for keeping time for the duration of the game.

    (vi) Umpires shall below the whistles at the start and end of the each half.

4. Field of Play

Length 90 m

Width = 52.5 m

Distance of goal line from mid line = 26.25 m

Distance of goal area line from goal line = 22.5 m

Distance of penalty stroke from goal = 6.50 m

Length of goal area = 3.70 m Height of goal area = 2.15 m

5. Goal-posts

(i) Round tubular goal posts and crossbars are not permitted.

(ii) The goal posts and cross bars be made of wood. Painted white.

(iii) Goal posts are correctly placed in relation to the goal line.

6. Ball

Weight of the ball = 5½ to 5¾ ounce.

Diameter of the ball = 8.13/16 to 9¼ inch.

7. Stick

Hockey stick is made of bamboo tree. The weight of hockey stick is 12 to 28 ounce.

8. Players Dress and Equipment

Each player shall bear the dress approved by his Association or club, unless varied to avoid confusion in a particular game. Goal keeper shall bear a colour, different from that of their own team and that of their opponents. Players shall not have dangerous spikes, studs or protruding nails in footwear or wear anything that may be dangerous to other players.

Equipments permitted for Goal keeper:

1. Pads 2. Kickers 3. Gauntlet Gloves 4. Masks.

(a) For any breach of this rule any player concerned shall not be allowed on the field of play until such time as he has compiled with this rule.

(b) Goal keepers are permitted to wear additional equipment for their protection. However, the wearing of such protective equipment does not permit them to conduct themselves in a manner which would not be either possible or safe without such protective equipment.

9. The Bully

(a) A bully shall be played at the centre of the field to start the game, to re-start it after half time and after a goal is scored.

(b) To bully a player of each team shall stand squarely facing the sidelines, each with his own goal line on his right. The ball shall be placed on the ground between the two players.

Each player shall tap with his stick, first the ground between the ball and his own goal line and then with the flat face of his stick, his opponents stick over the ball, three times alternately, after which one of these two players shall play the ball with his stick to put it in to general play.

(c) Until the ball is in general play, all other players shall be nearer to their own goal-line than the ball and shall not stand with in 5 yards of the ball.

(d) A bully is the circle shall not be played within five yards of the goal-line.

For any breach of this rule the bully shall be played again.

(A) Start of the Game

(a) There is a toss for choice of ends or to start the game. The captain who shall have the right to start the game, his teammate shall start the game.

(b) After a goal has been scored by a player of a team, the player of the team against whom the goal has been awarded shall start the game from the centre.

(c) Golden Goal: If the match ended in a draw, the extra time of $7^1/2$ & 7½ minutes shall be given to the teams, if any team scores a goal, the match shall be stopped and the team who scored a goal declared a winner, and this goal called the 'Golden Goal". If there shall be no score in the extra time there is a provision of 5 penalty strockes to each team, it shall continue till the result come.

10. Scoring a Goal

(a) A goal is scored when the ball has passed completely over the goal line between the goal posts, and under the crossbar, the ball, within the circle, having been hit by, or having glanced off the stick of an attacker, except as specially provided for in Rule-is (g). It is immaterial if the ball subsequently touched or played by one or more defenders. If during the game, the goal posts and or the cross bar become displaced, and the ball passes completely over the goal line at a paint which, in the umpire's opinion, be between where the goal posts and/or under where the cross bar respectively, should have been, a goal is scored.

(b) The team scoring the greater number of Goals shall be the winner :
   (i) The lines are part of the circle.
   (ii) The whole ball must cross the goal line before a goal is scored.

After the stoppage of play inside the circle the ball must again be hit from inside the circle by the stick of an attacker, before a goal can be scored.

11. Conduct of Play

(a) A player shall not play the ball with the rounded side of the stick.

(b) Take part in or interfere with the game unless he has his own stick in his hand, or change his stick for the purpose of taking part in the game.

(c) If the ball hits the back of the stick and no advantage result, no offence has taken place.

(d) Hit wildly into an opponent or play or kick the ball in such a way as to be dangerous in itself, or likely to lead to dangerous play.

(e) Stop or deflect the ball on the ground or in the air with any part of the body "To his or his team's advantage.

(f) Use the foot or leg to support the stick in order to resist an opponent.

(g) Kick, pick up throw, carry or propel the ball in any manner or direction except with the stick.

A player may play the ball only with the flat side of his stick which includes that part of the handle above the flat side.

Dangerous Play: This rule is intended to prevent injury to players and umpires should be very firm in penalising dangerous play such as undercutting or rising the ball in any way. A rising ball is dangerous when it causes legitimate evasive action on the part of the player.

Misconduct: Rough or dangerous play, Time wasting or any other behaviour which in the umpire's opinion amounts to misconduct shall not be permitted.

Propelling the Ball

(i) The ball must not be carried forward in any way by the body.

(ii) A player should not be penalised for a rebound when the ball has been propelled straight at him from close quarters by an opponent.

Stick Interference: Hooking and striking at sticks should be strictly penalised.

Should a player slash wildly at the ball and hit an opponent or his stick instead, he should be penalised. A player may not throw his stick at the ball.

12. Penalties Outside the Circle

A foul hit shall be awarded to the opposing team. An umpire shall award a penalty corner for an offence by any defender in his own 25 yards area, when in the umpire's opinion, the offence was deliberate.

Inside the Circle-By (defender). Attacker a free hit shall be awarded to the defending team by Defender.

Penalty corner or stroke shall be awarded to the attacking team.

13. Body Interference and Obstruction : Subject to the advantage rule, umpires should be particularly strict on obstruction and other forms of interference dealt within this rule.

It should be noted that obstruction does not necessarily depend on the distance from the ball of the players concerned.

A player, even if in possession of the ball, may not interpose his body as an obstruction to an opponent. A change of direction by a half turn of the body with this result may amount to obstruction. It should be noted, however that even a complete turn does not constitute a breach unless an opponent has thereby been obstructed in an attempt to play the ball.

Obstruction occurs frequently at push-ins and should be watched for carefully.

A player must not interpose any part of his body or his stick as an obstruction between his opponent and the ball. Watch two for third party interference, i.e., a player interposing himself between his opponent and the ball.

PENALTIES A temporarily suspended player shall remain behind his own goal or in such other places as designated before the start game, until allowed by the umpire by whom he was suspended.

14. Free-Hit

(a) A free hit shall be taken on the spot where the breach occurred except that.

    (i) For a breach by an attacker within the circle it shall be taken.
    Either from any spot within that circle from any spot within 16 yards of the inner edge of the defending team's goal line, on a line drawn through the place where the breach occurred and parallel to the side line.

    (ii) For a breach by an attacker outside the circle but within 16 yards of the defending team's goal line, it shall be taken from any spot within 16 yards of the inner edge of the defending team's

goal line on a line drawn through the place where the breach occurred and parallel to the side line.

(b) The ball shall be stationery and the player shall push the ball along the ground or hit it.

(c) At the moment when the free hit is taken, no player other than the striker shall be within 5 yards of the ball. However, if the umpire consider that a player is standing within 5 yards in order to gain time, the free hit shall not be obliged.

15. Penalty Corner

(a) A player of the attacking team shall push the ball along the ground or hit it from a spot on the goal-line not less than 10 yards from the goal post, on which ever side of the goal the attacking team prefers. The player concerned is not required to be wholly inside or outside the field of play when taking the corner.

(b) At the moment when such push or hit is made no other player shall be within 5 yards of the ball.

The rest of the attacking team shall be in the field of play, with both sticks and feet outside the circle. Not more than six of the defending team shall stand with both sticks and feet behind their own-goal line. The rest of the defending team shall stand beyond the centre line.

(c) Until the ball is pushed or hit no attacker shall enter the circle, nor shall a defender cross the goal-line or the centre line.

(d) No shot at goal shall be made from a penalty corner or from a deflection, unless the ball be stopped on the ground by an attacker to touch the stick or person of a defender.

16. Penalty Stroke

(a) A penalty stroke shall be awarded to the opposing team, if the umpire decided.

    (i) There has been an intentional breach of Rule 12 or 14 inside the circle by a player of the defending team.

    (ii) A goal would probably have been scored had an Unintentional breach of rule 12 inside the circle by a player of the defending team not occurred.

(b) The penalty stroke shall be either a push, flick;

   (i) or scoop stroke taken from a spot 7 yards in front of the centre of the goal by a player of the attacking team and defended by the goal keeper of the opposing team.

   (ii) Whichever stroke is used, the ball may be raised to any height.

(c) (i) During taking of a penalty stroke all the other players of both teams shall stand beyond the immediate 25 yards line.

   (ii) The attacking player shall not take the penalty stroke until the Umpire having satisfied himself that both defender and attackers are ready.

(d) (i) The goal keeper shall stand on the goal line. After the player taking the stroke and the goal-keeper are in position the goal keeper may not leave the goal line or move either of his feet until the ball has been played.

   (ii) Keeper shall be permitted to put on without undue delay protective equipment.

   (iii) If any action by the prior to stricking the ball, induce the goal keeper to move either of his feet or if the stricker pretend at striking the ball, the stroke may be taken again.

   (iii) If there is any unreasonable delay or misconduct by either a defender or an attacker in carrying out any of the provision of this rule, the umpire may treat such action as misconduct and deal with it accordingly.

   (iv) All time taken between the award of a penalty stroke and resumption of play shall be added to the time of play.

KABADDI

History: Kabaddi is essentially an Indian game. Nothing is known about the origin of the game. This game requires both power and skill for its play. It is quite simple and inexpensive game and requires neither a big playing area, nor any playing equipments. This game is popular all over the country. Time to time its rules have been formulated and redefined. It was known by various names, like HU-TU-TU, Kabaddi-kabaddi, HADUDU. Kabaddi is outdoor game having the qualities of wrestling. To catch the raider or escaping from opponent's hold, requires, skill, stamina, agility, courage and presence of mind. In national games, in the year 1952 at Calcutta, it was played for the first time. In Asian games in 1982 at Delhi it was the demonstration game.

Measurement of Play Field and Sports Equipement

1. Ground: The play ground must be leval and soft made of Earth, manure and sawdust. For Men it shall be 12.50 m × 10 m divided by a mid line into two halves measuring 10 m wide and 6.25 m deep. In case of Women it shall be 11 m × 8 m divided by a mid line into two halves each measuring 8 m × 5.50 m.

2. Play Field: 12.50 m × 8 m for men and 11 m × 6 m for women.

3. Lobbies: Each of the strips on the sides of the play field measuring one meter in width are known as lobbies. The area of lobbies can be used for struggle but not for play.

4. Mid Line: The line that divide the play field into two equal halves is known as the MID-LINE

5. Court : Each half of the play field divided by the mid line is known as court.

6. Baulk Line or The Cross Line: Each of the lines in court parallel to MID-LINE are known as the BAULK LINE. The distance of the baulk line from the mid line shall be 3.75 m in case of men and 3 m in case of women.

7. Bonus Line: In each court a line parallel to baulk line is known as Bonus line. The distance of the Bonus line from baulk line is one m in case of both Men & Women also.

8. Lines: All lines will be of 5 cm. width and form the part of the play field.

9. Players: There are 12 players in each side, in which 7 players shall play the game at a time, and the remaining 5 players shall be the reserve players.

10. Time Period of The Game: The duration of a match shall be 20 minutes then 5 minutes rest and again 20 minutes in case of Men and in case of Women it is 15-5-15.

11. Officials:

Chief Referee	1
Umpires	2
Scorer	1
Astt. Scorer	2
Lines Men	2

12. Different signs on score sheet.

Simple points X 2 3 4 5 6 7 8

Lona points 1-2 -3-4-5-6-7-8-9

Bonus Point ↓Δ↑

Time out —

1. Raiding 2. Defence 3. Catching

In catching the sciessor's hold is not allowed.

General Rules Of Kabbadi

1. **Cant :** The clear and continuous sounding word *"Kabaddi- kabbadi"* is called cant. It is not of more than 30 seconds.

2. **Raider :** The player who enters in the court of the opponent with the cant is known as a 'RAIDER'. Cant must be started before entering the opponent's court.

3. **Anti Raider:** Each player of a team in whose court the raid is going on be called the ANTI-RAIDER.

4. **Raid :** When the raider enters in the opponent's court with cant is called Raid.

5. **Successful Raid:** When a raider crosses the baulk line at least one time during the course of a raid and reaches back his own court with cant, is known as a successful raid.

6. **Loosing The Cant :** To stop the continuous and clear sounding cant of the word *kabaddi-kabaddi* known as losing the cant.

7. **Touch :** A contact by raider or anti with the clothing, shoes or any other part of the body, is known as touch.

8. **Anti Raider Out:** If a raider touched an anti-raider or any part of the body of an anti raider touches any part of the body of the raider and then the raider touches his court with cant, the anti-raider is out.

9. **Raider Out:** If an anti or the anties hold the raider and keep the raider in their court and do not allow him to reach his court until he loses his cant, the raider is out.

10. **Bonus Point:** If a raider crosses the bonus line, one point is given for his courage, this point is called the bonus point. It is only given at the time when the opposite team is playing with more than 5 players.

11. **Lona Points :** When all the players of a team are out, the opposite team gets 2 more points, These points are called the LONA points.

12. **Play or Start of Game :** The captain who wins the toss shall have the choice of the court or to raid, After interval when the court shall be changed the opposite team's player will raid and start the match.

13. **Winner :** The team which scores the highest number of points at the end of the game shall be the winner.

14. **Five Raids:** In case of tie, each team shall raid five times. The team which scores highest points shall be the winner.

15. **Sudden Death :** After five raids, if there is again tie, both the teams will raid one by one and as soon as any team scores a point, the match will stop and the team who scored a point declared as a winner.

16. **Time Out :** In each half the captain or the coach of the team shall request for time out. There are two time out in each half of 30 seconds each.

Some Basic Rules

1. If either player of either side goes out of play field during the play, he will be treated as out.

2. Lobby area becomes the play field area during the struggle.

3. Raider must start his raid from his own playing area.

4. Only one player can raid at a time.

5. Player can drink water in the play field but will not be allowed to go out side.

6. Sciessor's hold is not allowed.

7. The out players when become alive they will come in play in the same order in which they were declared out.

8. The play can also be started with five players only, with following terms:

(a) If all the five players are out, the Lona points shall be given to the opposite team.

(b) When the absentees come, they will be allowed to play with the permission of the Referee.

Terminology of Kabaddi

1. **Raid :** When the raider enters the court of the opponent with cant.
2. **Midline :** The line that divides the playfield into two halves.
3. **Lobbies :** Each of the strips on the sides of the playfield measuring one metre in width is known as the lobby.
4. **Baulk Line:** Each of the lines in court parallel to midline is Baulkline.

5. **Anti-Raider:** Every Player of the party in whose court the raid is being made.
6. **Raider :** One who enters the court of the opponent with the cant is known as Raider
7. **Cant :** The continuous clear sounding recitation aloud of the approved world Kabaddi.
8. **Touch :** Contact by raider or opponent with the clothing, shoes or any other outfits on any part of their bodies.

KHO-KHO

History : KHO-KHO is primarily Indian game, Maharashtra is the origin of this game. KHO-KHO is a inexpensive and out-door game. It requires skill, eligibility, stamina, courage, speed and presence of mind. With the passage of time its rules have been formulated and redefined.

Men. Women	Sub Jr. Boys Jr. Boys & Girls	and Girls
(i) End Lines	29 m	25 m
(ii) Side lines	16 m	14 m
(iii) Centre Lane	23.50/30 cm.	19.90 m
(iv) Cross Lanes	16 Mts'2.50 m	14 m
(v) Square	30'30 cm.	30'30 m
(vi) Rectangle Length	16 m	14 m
(vii) Line of post	16'2.50 m	14'2.10 m
(viii) Free zone	16'2.75 m	14'2.55 m
(ix) Strips or the Width of lines	3 to 5 cm.	3 to 5 cm.
(x) Pole to pole distance	23.50 m	19.90 m
(xi) Height of the pole	1.20 to 1.25 m	1.20 to 1.25 m
(xii) Diameter of the pole	9 to 10 cm.	9 to 10 cm.
(xiii) 7 rectangle of	16'2.30 m	14 by 1.90 m
(xiv) Square to square distance	2.30 m	1.90 m

Play Field : The play ground must be level and soft made of earth manure and sawdust. For MEN-WOMEN (seniors and Juniors) End lines having measuring 16 and 14 m and side line 29 and 25 m. There are eight square of 30 × 30 cm on the play field, and a free zone with the line of post, as shown in the diagram.

Play-field for Senior-Juniors

1. Total Length = 2.75 + 2.50 + 30 + 2.30 + 30 + 2.30 + 30 + 2.30 + 30 + 2.30 + 30 + 2.30 + 30 + 2.30 + 30 + 2.50 + 2.75=29 m

Width = 7.85 + 30 + 7.85 = 16 m

Square = 30'30 cm.

Play-field for Sub-Juniors

2. Total length = 2.55 + 2.10 + 30 + 1.90 + 30+1.90+30+1.90+30+1.90+30 + 1.90 + 30 + 1.90 + 30 + 2.10+ 2.55 = 25 m

Width 6.85 + 30 + 6.85 = 14 m

Square = 30'30 cm.

Rules & Regulations of Kho-kho

End Lines and Side Lines :

The lines running parallel to each other and equal in length to the width of the field are known a the END LINES.

Side Lines: The lines running parallel to each other and equal to length to length are known as side lines.

Central Lane: Central lane is 30 cm. broad and 23.50 m long in seniors and 19.90 m in sub juniors, dividing the court in length and breadth into two equal halves.

Cross Lanes: Each rectangles of 30 m in breadth and 16 m length in seniors, and 14 m in sub. juniors play field. Total eight cross lanes are there in the play field.

Squares: 30'30 cm rectangles formed by the intersection of the central lane and by the cross lanes are called the square.

Post: Two smooth and strong wooden poles of specified height and diameter, Fixed firmly in the free zone at tangent to the post line. The posts shall smooth allover.

Post Line: The line which goes through the inner edge of the post up to the side lines and parallel to the end line at a distance of 2.75 in seniors and 2.55 in sub juniors known as post line.

Free Zone: 2.75'16 m and 2.55'14 m area of the play ground in which the posts are fixed firmly is known as the free zone or the area between the end line and post line is known as the FREE ZONE.

Lobby: There must be a lobby around the play field measuring 1 = 0.5 m

Time Period of the Game: One inning will consist of chasing and running turns which shall be of 9 minutes each after one chase or run. Their is a rest of 5 minutes and then 9 minutes play, then after 9 minutes rest and again 9-9 minutes play.

For Seniors: 9-5-9-9-9-5-9 = 55 minutes

For Sub Juniors: 7-3-7-6-7-3-7 = 40 minutes

No. of Players: Each team shall consist 12 players in which only 9 players shall play the game in the beginning. Rest of the three players are called the substitute players.

Chaser: The player's sitting in the squares are called chasers.

Active Chaser: The player who pursues the players of the opposite team with a view to touch them is known as the active chaser.

Runner: The players of the opposite side other than the chaser are called runners.

Defenders: The three runners who are inside the field are known as defenders.

To Give KHO: To give KHO the active chaser touch the chaser by palm of a hand from behind calling the word KHO loudly and clearly. Calling the word KHO and the touching to the chaser shall go together.

Proper Sitting Position of The Chaser: The feet shall be in the square.

Out of Play Field: If a defender loses the contact of his foot with the play field and comes in contact with ground out side play field with his foot he is said to have gone out of field.

Entry: When three runners of a set will be out, the next set of the three runners are said to be entered in the play field as soon as they loses the contact with the ground out side the play field with his foot and comes in contact with the ground inside the play field with his foot.

No. of Runners: There are three sets of runner having three runners in each set. When all the three runners of a set are out, the next set of the three runners shall enter in the play field. This type of entry of runner shall go up to first inning of 9 minutes and so on in the next innings.

No. of Chasers: There are 9 chasers in a team in which 8 chasers shall sit in the squares facing the side line in such a way that no adjacent chaser face the same side line or the cross line. The 9th chaser shall stand near the post in free zone to begin the play.

NOTE: No Attacker and runners shall cross the central lane, i.e., from one pole to another pole having length 23.50 m for seniors and 19.90 m for juniors with the breadth of 30 cm.

Start of The Game: Referee shall call the captains for toss. The winner of the toss will have the choice for running or chasing

Match Officials: Referee: One

Umpires : Two

Time Keeper : One

Scorers : Two

Substitution: (i) Substitution for chasing team is allowed at any time during the match.

(ii) For runners it is only allowed before the start of defence.

Receding: When an active chaser going towards particular direction and comes into contact with the area which he has already covered, it is known as RECEDING.

Winner: The team that scores more points at the end of the match shall be declared as the winner. If the score is equal at the end one more inning shall be played. If again the score is equal an additional inning shall be played, as soon as the first point scored the turn shall be closed, and the time of the turn shall be noted by the referee. Then the opposite team shall chaise, when this team scores a point, the turn shall be closed and the referee will note the time. The team which scored a point in a MINIMUM TIME OR CHASE shall be declared the winner of the match.

LAWN TENNIS

Lawn Tennis is very popular in Europe. Lawn Tennis has its beginning in France. This game was first introduced by Major Wingfield at the Christmas party in Wales in the year 1870. This sport came to be known as tennis in the year 1400 A.D., though the game was played earlier too. England played a decisive role in the development of this sport. Harry Jam, an Englishman established the first tennis club then called 'Limington Club'. The game was earlier known by the name 'Pallota' and 'Lawn Racket'. It was in the 15th century that it began to be called by its present name. This game is played on two types of surfaces namely grass court and hard court. The highest governing body of lawn tennis is the International Tennis Federation, which was established in 1913. Earlier, the game was played by professionals and nonprofessionals but in 1968 this bifurcation was removed. In the year 1900, the first Davis cup was held.

Measurement of Lawn Tennis Court and Sports Equipments

There are two kinds of Tennis Courts. They are Singles Court and Doubles Court. Dimension of the Tennis Courts for Men and Women sections are similar.

1. Single Court: Tennis court for singles game is rectangle in shape. It is 78 feet long and 27 feet in width (23.77 m × 8.23 m). The court is divided into two equal halves. It is divided across the middle by a metal cable attached to the tops of net posts.

All lines marked on the court should not be less than 1 inch (2.5 cm) in width and not more than 2 inches (5 cm) in width. The width of base line is not more than 4 inches (10 cm). All the measurements should be upto the outside of the lines. The lengthwise line of the court are called the side lines and the width-wise lines which bounding the ends and sides of the court are called the base line. From the centre on each side of the net a line is drawn parallel to the centre line at a distance of 21 feet (6.40 m) is called the Service lines. Further, the Service lines and side lines are divided into two equals parts called Service Courts by centre service lines, drawn half way between and parallel with the side lines. Imaginary extension of the centre service line of each base-line shall be bisected to a line 4 inches (10 cm) in length 2 inches (5 cm) in width. It is called as 'Centre mark'. It is drawn inside the court.

2. Doubles Court: Tennis court for doubles game is slightly wider than Singles court but the length remains the same. The court is rectangular in size. The dimensions of the doubles court is 78'0" (23.77 m) in length and 36'0" (10.97 m) in width. The doubles court is 4'6" (1.37 m) wider on each side of the court. Thus, it 9'0" (2.78 m) wider than singles court.

3. Ball: Diameter of the ball is 2.5 to 2.58 inch, the colour of the ball is white or yellow and its weight is between 56.7 to 58.5 gram.

4. Racket: The racket should be uniformly strung. It should have a flat hitting surface and consist of a pattern of crossed nylon strings connected to the frame of the racket. The total length of the frame of the racket should not exceed 32 inches (81.28 cm) and exceed 32 inches (81.28 cm) in length including the handle and 121/2 inch (31.75) in overall width of the racket.

5. Net Posts: Two posts are fixed in the centre of the court. The posts are fixed in the ground that the centre of the posts shall be 3 feet (.0914 m) outside the court on each side. The height of the posts on each side shall be 3 feet 6 inches (1.07 m) above the ground level. The metal cable shall be extended over the post tightly. The thickness of posts should not be more than 6 inches (15 cm) in diameter.

6. Net: Net is fixed tightly to the two posts in the centre of the court. The net is either made by cotton cords mashes or by similar material. The net should have small mashes so that the ball may not pass through it. From the centre the height of the net should not be 3 feet (0.914 m).The net should be held down tight by a white colour strap and not more than 2 inches (5 cm) wide. At the top of the net mash should be a band covering the metal cable which is not be less than 2 inches (5cm) and not more than $2\frac{1}{2}$ inches (6.3 cm) on each side of the net.

Rules & Regulations for Single Game

Lawn Tennis is played in single and double games. The rules followed in single game are:

1. Choice of Service and Ends: This is decided by toss. The player, who is winning toss will decide the ends and service.

2. Service: While making service a player should stand with both feet in a stationery position, behind the base line and in between the imaginary extension of the centre mark and the side line. The service is treated as completed, when the ball strikes the racket.

3. Delivery of the Service: The server should begin his service from the right in every game. The ball delivered in service should pass over the net and hit the ground within the service court.

4. Service Fault: When the striker misses the ball in attempting to strike and if the server does not take the proper position on the court or commits a foot fault or does not deliver the service properly is called service fault.

5. Second Service: If there is fault in the first service, then server is provided another chance.

6. Service Let: If the ball touches the net or strap but crosses the net, in such case the service is a let.

7. Service Order: With the change of game server becomes a receiver and receiver becomes server. This change of order is called service order.

8. Return of Served Ball: The receiver, when returns the ball after its hitting the court is called Return of the Served Ball, provided it not touched the net or the post.

9. Winning a Set: A player, who wins six games wins a set. The winning margin should be of two games. The set may be extended till the margin is achieved.

10. Scoring: In this game scoring consist of four points. On the first game, it is called 15 points, on second 30 points, on the winning the third game it is 40 point and the fourth point won the game. When both players have equal score, it is called deuce and a next point scored by any player is called an advantage for that player.

Rules & Regulations for Double Game

The rules followed in double game are:

1. Serving Order: The pair has to decide, who is going to serve and the opposing pair should decide on the same pattern for second game.

2. Receiving Order: The receiving pair decides, who is going to receive the first service. That partner should continue to receive the first service in every odd game.

3. Service Fault: It is almost same as in the case of single game.

4. Tie Break: When both teams are tied to a point that is position for Tie Break. The player, who is returned to serve for the first point. After that each player should serve in rotation for two points in the same order.

Terminology of Lawn Tennis

1. Ace: When a receiver fails to collect the ball, while receiving a service, the server is said to have served an 'Ace'.

2. Double Fault: If the server delivers two fault services in succession in his turn of serving.

3. Foot Fault: If a player changes his position during walking or running in Serving.

4. Grand Slam: Winning four top tennis tournaments of the world in a year.

5. Volley: Striking a ball, without allowing it to touch the ground is called a volley.

6. Half Volley: Striking a ball immediately after the rebound from the ground is called half-volley shot.

7. Deuce: When two opponents score three equal points in a game (that is 40 all).

8. Chip Shot: A slicing stroke with a forehand or backhand action is called a Chip Shot.

9. A let: Replay of a service or a point is called a Let.

10. Advantage: A player scoring a point after a deuce point is said to have gained an advantage.

TABLE TENNIS

Under the title of 'ping-pong', Table Tennis was a popular parlour game in the late 1890's, but there was little interest in the game between 1906 and 1922. This sport was played in the second half of the 19th century in England. During this period it was known by the name 'Gausima' or 'whip waff. Rubber bats replaced the earlier used wooden bats in the third decade of the 20th century. Since then, it has become popular all over the world. The International Table Tennis Association was set up in 1926 and the first world championship was held in 1927. Between 1930 and 1938 the popularity of the sport increased throughout the world and the world Championship held again in London (for the third time) in 1938, drew large crowds of spectators to the Albert Hall and the Empire Pool and Sports Arena, Wembley. By 1939 the Association had grown to 230 Leagues embracing 4,100 clubs and 75000 individual players, while the world interest is shown by the fact that the International Table Tennis Federation had a membership of 28 countries.

Table Tennis Association of India was formed in 1938. India had hosted world championship three times, i.e., in 1952,1984-85 and 1986-87. It is very popular game not only in world but also in India.

Sport Profile

It is played by two players in a single match and by four players in, a doubles match.

1. Table: The Table Tennis table is rectangular in shape. The size of the table is 2.74 m × 1.52 m. The table is 76 cm high. The playing surface of the table should be smooth and dark in colour. It has normally either dark green and blue top. The table should have a white borderline 2 cm wide marked along each edge. For doubles, a white line 3 cm wide should be drawn at the centre of the table running parallel to the side lines. The playing surface should be horizontal and 76 cm above the floor.

2. Net: The net shall be suspended by a cord and attached at each end to an upright post. The net must extend 6 inches outside each side line. The net should be 1.83 metres in length. The uprights where the net is attached should be 15.25 cm high.

3. Racket: The racket may be of any size, shape, or weight. Its surface shall be dark coloured. The blade shall be of wood, continuous of even thickness, flat and rigid. If the blade is covered on either side, this covering may be either (a) of plain, ordinary pimpled rubber, with pimples outward, of a total thickness of not more than 2 mm or (b) 'sandwich' consisting of a layer of cellular rubber, and which the total thickness includes the height of the pimples and adhesion.

4. Ball: The diameter of the ball is between 37.2 to 38.2 mm and its weight is between 2.4 to 2.53 gram (0.88 ounce). The colour of the ball is either white or yellow. It has standard bounce on the Table Tennis table.

5. Player's Clothes: The player should wear shirt, shorts or skirt by the women players mainly of uniform colour other than white. The collar and sleeves of the shirt may be contrast in colour.

6. Game: A game of table tennis consists of 11 points, but if the score is tied at 10, then the winner is the player that first score 2 points more than the opposing player. If a game is unfinished after 10 minutes, and players have scored 9 points all, the expedite system may be introduced.

7. Choice of Service and Choice of Ends: The player winning the lot should have the right to do service or receive the service first.

8. Change the Service: Change of service in singles game, the server becomes a receiver after every two points until the end of the game. If the score becomes 10 all, the sequence of serving and receiving should remain the same but each players shall deliver only one service in turn upto the end of the game.

9. Change of Ends: At the change of ends, a player that served first in a game should be the first receiver in the following game till the end of the match.

10. Match: The match of table tennis may consist of the best of three games or best of five games.

Terminology of Table Tennis

1. Drop Shot: This is a stroke played for the purpose of returning the ball close to the net on the opponent's side.

2. Back Spin: Backward rotation of the ball in relation to the striker is known as back spin of the ball.

3. Block Stroke: This is a simple stroke of table tennis in which the racket is placed along the line of flight of the oncoming ball in such a way that the ball strikes the racket and rebounds in the direction from which it came or is deflected a little.

4. Chopped Return: This is an under cutting stroke that imparts back spin to the ball.

5. Counter Hitting: It refers to the execution of quick and fast returns by both the opponents.

6. Top Spin: The forward rotation of the ball in relation to the striker is called top spin.

7. Spin: Imparting a movement of rotation in the balls is called spin.

8. Lob: This is a high or lofted return of the ball towards the far end of the table.

9. Push Stroke: Is the basic stroke of table tennis. In this stroke the playing surface of a racket is facing upwards and is inclined backwards to the table. The ball is struck in such a way that the arm holding the bat or racket should move forward, almost straight, without imparting much spin to the ball.

10. Flat Hit: This is a stroke in which the ball is struck in such a way with the racket almost vertical or slightly inclined forward, held in the extended arm, that the ball is driven without any spin or very little spin on it.

VOLLEY BALL

History : Volley Ball is a game played indoors or outdoors by teams whose members seek to score points in the course of hitting a ball back and forth across a net.

Volley Ball according to authoritative sources was invented by William G. Morgan in 1895 when he was the Director for the Y.M.C.A. in Holyoke Mass. His object was a game not too strenuous in nature that would be suitable for men. During world War I & II it was popular among U.S Service men, who helped to make it a famous sport at international level. In 1964 for the first time men's volley ball was as an event of competition in the World Olympic Games (Tokyo-JAPAN).

Measurement of Play Field and Sports Equipments

1. Playing Court: The playing court is a rectangular measuring 18 m × 9 m having rectangular free zone of 3 m in open and 2 m in indoors. The surface must be flat and uniform. All lines are 5 cm in width. For indoors lighting on a court should be 500 to 1500 Luxes measured from 1 m high from the playing surface.

2. Net and Pole: The Net is a mesh 1 m wide and 11 (Eleven) m long vertical placed over the axis of the center line to divide the playing space into two parts. Each mesh measured 10 × 10 cm.

Pole: Two posts (poles) preferably adjustable, round and smooth with a height of 2.55 m, support the net from both ends. They must be fixed on the playing surface at a distance of 1 m, from each side line in the centre.

3. Side Bands: Two tapes of white colour 5 cm wide and 1 m long shall be fastened one's on each side of the end of the centre line both side bands shall be considered as the part of the NET.

4. Antennas: The antennas are two rods made of fiber glass or some flexible material. One m. long and 10 millimeter in diameter. The antennas are marked with the red and white colour with 10 cm bands. Each is fastened on the outer edge of the side Bands. They are considered as the part of the net and mark its side limits.

5. Height of the Net: For Men = 2.43 m (7'.11") For Women = 2.24 m (7.9"). The height of NET shall be measured from the centre of the playing surface.

6. Ball: The ball shall be spherical, made of a flexible leather or similar material.

Circumference	: 65 to 67 cm.
Weight gram.	: 260 to 280
Inside pressure kg /cm^2	: 0.40 to 0.45
Colour	: Uniform and light colour

7. Teams: There are six players in a team, three in front row and three in the back row. Through substitution a team can use up to 12 players in a match.

LIBRO PLAYER = Only One.

8. Serving: The player serving the ball has one chance to serve the ball properly within 8 seconds. If the served ball did not cross the NET or goes out of bound the other team scores one point and have the right to serve. The served ball is allowed to touch the net and to go over the opponent's court.

9. The Match: A match consists of five games (Set) and is played until a team wins three games. Each set of 25 points. If both the teams win two sets each then the last set will be of 15 points. All the points are of rally points. (23-25) (13-15)

10. Technical Time Out: Two Technical time outs in each set of 60 seconds only on 8th and 16th points of score in first 4 sets.

11. Intervals Time: On the completion of each set there are interval of three 3 minutes but the interval time in the last set is of 5 minutes.

12. Change of Courts: On the completion of each set the players shall change their courts. In the last set the change is on the score of 8.

13. Rotation of Players: When the team receiving the serve wins the rally or the opponent commits a fault, it wins the right to serve and its players must rotate one position clock wise. The rotation order as recorded on the score sheet at the beginning of each set must remain the same throughout that set.

14. Match officials

One first Refree: Lines Men

One second Refree: Ball retrievers

One scorer: Floor mappers

15. Volley Ball Skills: (i) Serving; (ii) Passing; (iii) Setting; (iv) Hitting; (v) Blocking (vi) Digging.

(i) Serving : The game starts with the serve. The captain who wins the toss shall have the choice of the court or the service. Service is of three types— (i) Floater Service; (ii) Jump Service; (iii) Top Spin Service.

16. Rally Point Scoring: In Volley ball each rally wins a point. When the receiving team wins a rally, it gains a point and the right to serve, and its players rotate one position clockwise.

The consequence of a fault is a loss of rally, the opponent of the team committing the fault wins the rally with a point.

17. Tie: In the case of a 2-2 tie, the deciding set is played to 15 points with minimum lead of 2 points.

18. The Libro Player: Each team has the option to register ONE specialised player called "LIBRO".

The LIBRO plays as a back row player and is not allowed to play an attack hit from anywhere, LIBRO player cannot serve, block or attempt to block. The substitution of LIBRO player is unlimited. Team Captain shall not be a LIBRO player. He shall be in a different colour of Jersey.

19. Time Outs: In the 5th set there is no technical time out, instead of this, there are two time outs of 30 seconds in each set are allowed.

20. Fixing of Flood Lights: (i) 6 poles of a rigid surface: Three poles on each side at least 12 m in height and 20 m parallel to the side line and 15 m away. Four bulbs of 1000 watts be fixed on each pole of the centre and two bulbs each of 1000 watts be fixed on other four poles.

Terminology of Volley Ball

1. Ace: A point scored on an unreturned serve.

2. Attack: Any method used to return the ball across the net in an attempt to put the opponents at a disadvantage.

3. Block: It occurs when one or more players stop the ball before, or just after, it crosses the net.

4. Craddled Ball: Caught and held and not played cleanly.

5. Deep Dink: A dink that lands in the opponent's back court.

6. Rally: To return the difficult shot.

7. Scoop: A ball lifted in the air with open hands.

8. Set: Contact to set up a spike.

9. Wild: Towards the sideline.

10. Tip: A short shot to an uncovered area; similar to 'dink'.

11. Call Time: As an official, suspend play for signalling a time out.

12. Bump: A forearm pass.

13. Atack Hit: Hit aimed into the opponent's court.

OBJECTIVE QUESTIONS

1. "I get paid to win, not to teach". This statement can be referred to—
   - (*a*) A science teacher
   - (*b*) A physics teacher
   - (*c*) A sports teacher
   - (*d*) A captain

2. If teachers do not live up to their ideals, they will have—
   - (*a*) Strong body
   - (*b*) Poor physique
   - (*c*) Negative influence on their students
   - (*d*) Higher status among students

3. Which among the following is not a aspect of ethical character?
   - (*a*) Justice and equality
   - (*b*) Self respect
   - (*c*) Sense of relative values
   - (*d*) Good sense of business relations

4. Where did the game 'Badminton' originate?
   - (*a*) America
   - (*b*) England
   - (*c*) Ireland
   - (*d*) Mozambique

5. In which year Badminton was introduced in India?
   - (*a*) 1833 A.D.
   - (*b*) 1860 A.D.
   - (*c*) 1866 AD.
   - (*d*) 1874 A.D.

6. In which year Badminton was made part of Olympic games?
   - (*a*) 1972 A.D.
   - (*b*) 1976 A.D.
   - (*c*) 1980 A.D.
   - (*d*) 1988 A.D.

7. How many feathers are there in the badminton shuttle?
   - (*a*) 10-12
   - (*b*) 14-16
   - (*c*) 16-20
   - (*d*) 5-10

8. What is the other name of the shuttle cock?
   - (*a*) Dancing doll
   - (*b*) Bird
   - (*c*) Backalley
   - (*d*) Faire

9. Which among the following term is not associated with Badminton?
   - (*a*) Unsight
   - (*b*) Carry
   - (*c*) Rally
   - (*d*) Duce

10. In which year Basketball first originated in U.S.A?
    - (*a*) 1891 A.D.
    - (b) 1900 A.D.
    - (c) 1904 A.D.
    - (d) 1910 A.D.

11. Who started the game of Basketball?
    - (*a*) Unknown soldier
    - (*b*) James Naismith
    - (*c*) Dereck Underwood
    - (*d*) Dewinton

12. In which year Basketball became the part of Olympic games?
    - (*a*) 1890 A.D.
    - (*b*) 1904 A.D.
    - (*c*) 1936 A.D.
    - (*d*) 1940 A.D.

13. The Basketball Federation of India was founded in the year
    - (*a*) 1930 A.D.
    - (*b*) 1934 A.D
    - (*c*) 1950 A.D.
    - (*d*) 1961 A.D.

14. Which term is not related to Basketball?
    - (*a*) Hoop
    - (*b*) Pick
    - (*c*) Forehand
    - (*d*) Travelling

15. The method of putting the ball into pay where by the referee tosses it up between two opponents, is called
    - (*a*) Hoop
    - (*b*) Jump ball
    - (*c*) Pick
    - (*d*) Charging

16. 'Chinaman' is a term associated with:
    - (*a*) Cricket
    - (*b*) Judo
    - (*c*) Table Tennis
    - (*d*) Marathon

17. Which term is not associated with cricket?
(*a*) Beamer   (*b*) Bosy
(*c*) Googly   (*d*) Hoop

18. What is the normal weight of new cricket ball?
(*a*) 155.9 to 163gm
(*b*) 164.3 to 169gm
(*c*) 160 to l65 gm
(*d*) It is less than 100 gm

19. What could be the maximum width of a cricket bat?
(*a*) 8.2 cm   (*b*) 10.8 cm
(*c*) 13.3 cm   (*d*) 14.1 cm

20. The game of football originated in:
(*a*) England   (*b*) Rome
(*c*) Greece   (*d*) South Africa

21. In which year India send its football team for Olympic games?
(*a*) England,1948   (*b*) Munich, 1924
(*c*) Berlin. 1936   (*d*) Helsinki, 1952

22. The game of Hockey originated probably in:
(*a*) India   (*b*) Persia
(*c*) Greece   (*d*) Rome

23. 'Bandy Ball' is the name given to the sport:
(*a*) Basketball   (*b*) Hockey
(*c*) Lawn Tennis   (*d*) Football

24. In which year first International Hockey Match was played?
(*a*) 1890 A.D.   (*b*) 1895 A.D
(*c*) 1897 AD.   (*d*) 1900 A.D.

25. The first World Cup Hockey was played in the year :
(*a*) 1964 A.D.   (*b*) 1968 A.D.
(*c*) 1971 A.D.   (*d*) 1976 A.D.

26. The first Hockey Federation in India was :
(*a*) Punjab Hockey Federation
(*b*) Bengal Hockey Federation
(*c*) Bombay Hockey Federation
(*d*) Sind Hockey Federation

27. Hockey became the part of Olympic games in the year :
(*a*) 1908 London   (*b*) 1912 Stockholm
(*c*) 1936 Berlin   (*d*) 1964 Tokyo

28. The first Winter Olympic games were held in
(*a*) Chamonix (France)
(*b*) Lake Placid (New York)
(*c*) Sarayevo (Yogoslavia)
(*d*) Turine (Italy)

29. Which equipment is not permitted to a goalkeeper in Hockey?
(*a*) Pads   (*b*) Kickers
(*c*) Masks   (*d*) Thigh pads

30. Kabaddi is essentially of :
(*a*) American origin (*b*) Indian origin
(*c*) African origin (*d*) Australian origin

31. Agha Khan Cup is associated with
(*a*) Hockey   (*b*) Kabaddi
(*c*) Cricket   (*d*) Badminton

32. Shivaji Stadium is located in :
(*a*) Mumbai   (*b*) Nagpur
(*c*) New Delhi   (*d*) Pune

33. In 2004 A.D. Summer Olympic games were held in :
(*a*) Seol (South Korea)
(*b*) Atlanta (U.S.A.)
(*c*) Athens (Greece)
(*d*) Bulin (Germany)

34. Where were 2002 World Cup Football Championship held?
(*a*) Spain
(*b*) Japan and South Korea
(*c*) Mexico and Italy
(*d*) Chile and Brazil

35. Where the 2002 Asian Games were held?
(*a*) Tehran (Iran)
(*b*) Tokyo (Japan)
(*c*) Pusan (South Korea)
(*d*) Bangkok (Thailand)

36. Gurcharan Singh, a famous coach was associated with :
(*a*) Hockey   (*b*) Kabaddi
(*c*) Cricket   (*d*) Wrestling

37. R Gopichand was associated with :
(*a*) TableTennis   (*b*) LawnTennis
(*c*) Badminton   (*d*) Squash

38. Anup Kumar received the award for the year 2003 in which game?
(*a*) Football   (*b*) Hockey
(*c*) Boxing   (*d*) Shooting

39. K.D. Jadhav was a famous :
(*a*) Wrestler   (*b*) Cricketer
(*c*) Chess player   (*d*) Kabaddi player

40. Yadvindra Stadium is located in :
(*a*) Ahmedabad   (*b*) Jaipur
(*c*) Patiala   (*d*) Cuttack

41. 'Murugappa Gold Cup' is associated with :
(*a*) Yatching   (*b*) Hockey
(*c*) Polo   (*d*) Table Tennis

42. Who said that, "the process of education is determined by child nature and his growth and development pattern."—
(*a*) Pestalozzi   (*b*) Rousseau
(*c*) Froebel   (*d*) Kautilya

43. Which period in the history of physical education in India is known as the age of Chivalry?
(*a*) Epic period   (*b*) Historical age
(*c*) Rajput period   (*d*) Nalandine period

44. Emperor Akbar was a famous player of :
(*a*) Hunting   (*b*) Chess
(*c*) Chopar   (*d*) Chaogan

45. Who was the first president of Indian Olympic Association?
(*a*) Mr. H.C. Buck   (*b*) Dr. D.G. Nochern
(*c*) Mr. G.D. Sondhi   (*d*) Mr. DorabjiTata

46. In which year 'Raj Kumari Coaching Scheme' was introduced for games and sports?
(*a*) 1953 A.D.   (*b*) 1956 A.D.
(*c*) 1962 A.D.   (*d*) 1976 A.D.

47. In which year National Rifle Association was setup?
(*a*) 1948 A.D.   (*b*) 1956 A.D.
(*c*) 1958 A.D.   (*d*) 1963 A.D.

48. ReficuloendotheliO tissue is popularly known as :
(*a*) Liver   (*b*) Stomach
(*c*) Lungs   (*d*) Heart

49. What does not result staleness?
(*a*) Pale skin
(*b*) Loss of motivation
(*c*) Anxiety
(*d*) Desire to be on top

50. Who said that the 'essence of mind was conciousness'?
(*a*) Rodolf Geocle
(*b*) Desecrates
(*c*) P. Sengemend Freud
(*d*) J.J. Rousseau

51. The ability to resist fatigue caused by any particular sports activity is called
(*a*) Basic endurance
(*b*) General endurance
(*c*) Specific endurance
(*d*) None of these

52. The ability to resist fatigue satisfactorily caused by various types of activities, may be aerobic or anaerobic or combination of both is called
(*a*) Basic endurance
(*b*) General endurance
(*c*) Specific endurance
(*d*) None of these

53. Factors determining endurance may be due to
(*a*) Aerobic capacity
(*b*) Anaerobic capacity
(*c*) Various psychological factor
(*d*) All the above

54. Intensity can be measured in terms of
(*a*) Speed   (*b*) Distance/height
(*c*) Speed(tempo)   (*d*) All of these

55. Volume can be measured in terms of
(*a*) Duration   (*b*) Distance
(*c*) Frequency   (*d*) All of these

56. A state of decrease in performance capacity can be
(*a*) Due to overload   (*b*) Due to underload
(*c*) Both   (*d*) None of these

57. Increased excitability, obstinancy, tendency of hysteria, quarrelsome, oversensitive to criticism are the symptoms of overload.
(*a*) True   (*b*) False
(*c*) Partially true   (*d*) partially false

58. The somatic-functional symptoms of overload can be.
(*a*) Loss of sleep   (*b*) Loss of appetite
(*c*) Loss of weight   (*d*) All of these

59. Intensity and volume of load, nature of load, health and physical fitness, nutrition, sleep, daily routine and total load are the factors affecting the pace of recovery
(*a*) True   (*b*) False
(*c*) Partially true   (*d*) Partially false

60. Cinematography and measuring devices are:
(*a*) Bio-mechanical means of training
(*b*) Psychological means of training
(*c*) Both
(*d*) None of these

61. Ideomotor training, Autogenous training and psychotonic training are
(*a*) Natural means of training
(*b*) Bio-mechanical means of training
(*c*) Psychological means of training
(*d*) None of these

62. Weather conditions and alttitude are
(*a*) Medical means of training
(*b*) Natural means of training
(*c*) Psychological means of training
(*d*) None of these

63. During conditioning in continuous method
(*a*) Intensity is kept high
(*b*) Volume is kept high
(*c*) Both
(*d*) None of these

64. Interval training includes
(*a*) Medium to high intensity
(*b*) Low to medium volume
(*c*) Both
(*d*) None of these

65. In repetition method.
(*a*) Intensity is kept very high
(*b*) Volume is kept low
(*c*) Both
(*d*) None of these

66. Extensive interval training improves
(*a*) Basic endurance
(*b*) General endurance
(*c*) Strength endurance
(*d*) All of these

67. Intensive interval training improves
(*a*) Speed endurance
(*b*) Explosive strength

(*c*) Maximum strength
(*d*) All of these

68. Repetition method helps to improve
(*a*) Speed ability
(*b*) Maximum strength
(*c*) Explosive strength
(*d*) All of these

69. Factors determining speed are
   I. Mobility of the nervous system
  II. Explosive strength
 III. Technique
 IV. Bio-chemical reserves and metabolic power.
  V. Flexibility
 VI. Psychic factors

The above statement is.
(*a*) True   (*b*) False
(*c*) Partially true   (*d*) Partially false

70. Explosive strength, technique/co-ordination, metabolic power, flexibility are the factors determining.
(*a*) Reaction ability   (*b*) Movement speed
(*c*) Speed endurance   (*d*) None of these

71. Explosive strength, technique/co-ordination, mobility of C.N.S., flexibility are the factors determining.
(*a*) Acceleration ability
(*b*) Reaction ability
(*c*) Locomotor ability
(*d*) None of these

72. Functional capacity of sense organs are the factors determining
(*a*) Reaction ability   (*b*) Movement speed
(*c*) Speed endurance   (*d*) None of these

73. During competition period intensity is kept
(*a*) High   (*b*) Low
(*c*) Both   (*d*) None of these

74. During transitional period the intensity and volume is kept
(*a*) High   (*b*) Low
(*c*) Both   (*d*) None of these

75. Ability to react quickly and effectively to a signal is called
(*a*) Coupling ability
(*b*) Reaction ability

(*c*) Orientation ability

(*d*) None of these

76. The ability to co-ordinate body part movement with one another in relation to definite goal oriented whole body movement is called

(*a*) Reaction ability

(*b*) Orientation ability

(*c*) Coupling ability

(*d*) None of these

77. The ability to perceive the externally given rhythm and to reproduce it in motor action is called

(*a*) Balance ability

(*b*) Rhythm ability

(*c*) Adaptation ability

(*d*) None of these

78. Ballistic method is one of the method of improving

(*a*) Strength (*b*) Endurance

(*c*) Flexibility (*d*) None of these

79. Endurance are classified as

(i) Basic endurance

(ii) General endurance

(iii) Specific endurance according to.

(*a*) Duration of activity

(*b*) Nature of activity

(*c*) Both

(*d*) None of these

80. Endurance are classified as

(i) Speed endurance

(ii) Short time endurance

(iii) Medium time endurance

(iv) Long time endurance

according to

(*a*) Duration of activity

(*b*) Nature of activity

(*c*) Both

(*d*) None of these

81. Co-ordinative ability is mainly affected by coupling ability, rhythm ability, adaptation ability and differentiation ability.

(*a*) True (*b*) False

(*c*) Partially true (*d*) Partially false

82. Anaerobic capacity explosive strength, technique/co-ordination are the factors determining.

(*a*) Movement speed (*b*) Speed endurance

(*c*) Locomotor ability(*d*) None of these

83. If an athlete wishes to run faster, he should

(*a*) Move his arms faster

(*b*) Keep his head bent forward

(*c*) Raise the knew higher

(*d*) Run on toes

84. Fartlek training method improves

(*a*) Endurance (*b*) Speed

(*c*) Strength (*d*) Flexibility

85. Circuit training improves

(*a*) General physical and motor fitness

(*b*) Speed

(*c*) Endurance

(*d*) Strength

86. Ability to release maximum muscular force in the shortest possible time is called

(*a*) Agility

(*b*) Muscular power

(*c*) Muscular strength

(*d*) Muscular endurance

87. Muscle strength is improved by the movement done

(*a*) Against the gravity

(*b*) Assisted by the gravity

(*c*) Both the above

(*d*) None of the above

88. Pushing against the wall is an exercise of

(*a*) Isometric (*b*) Isotonic

(*c*) Isokinetic (*d*) Polymetric

89. Arthur Lydiard's methods of training develops

(*a*) Strength

(*b*) Endurance

(*c*) Agility

(*d*) Flexibility

90. Fartlek is more closely related to

(*a*) Jumpers

(*b*) Throwers

(*c*) Sprinters

(*d*) Middle distance runners

ANSWERS

1. (c)	2. (c)	3. (d)	4. (b)	5. (b)	6. (d)	7. (b)	8. (b)
9. (d)	10. (a)	11. (b)	12. (c)	13. (c)	14. (c)	15. (b)	16. (a)
17. (b)	18. (a)	19. (b)	20. (b)	21. (a)	22. (b)	23. (b)	24. (b)
25. (c)	26. (b)	27. (a)	28. (a)	29. (b)	30. (b)	31. (a)	32. (c)
33. (c)	34. (b)	35. (c)	36. (c)	37. (c)	38. (c)	39. (a)	40. (c)
41. (b)	42. (b)	43. (c)	44. (c)	45. (b)	46. (a)	47. (c)	48. (a)
49. (d)	50. (b)	51. (c)	52. (a)	53. (a)	54. (d)	55. (d)	56. (c)
57. (a)	58. (d)	59. (a)	60. (a)	61. (c)	62. (b)	63. (b)	64. (a)
65. (a)	66. (c)	67. (a)	68. (a)	69. (a)	70. (a)	71. (c)	72. (a)
73. (b)	74. (b)	75. (b)	76. (c)	77. (c)	78. (b)	79. (b)	80. (a)
81. (a)	82. (a)	83. (c)	84. (a)	85. (d)	86. (b)	87. (a)	88. (a)
89. (b)	90. (d)						

13. MISCELLANEOUS FACTS

MAJOR SPORTS AND THE TERMS ASSOCIATED WITH THEM

Badminton: Angled Drive Serve, Backhand Low Serve, Bird, Deuce, Double Drop. Fault, Flick Serve, Forehand Smash, Let, Lob, Love All, Net Shots, Rush, Smash.

Basketball: Ball, Basket, Blocking, Dribbling, Free Throw, Held Ball, Holding, Jump Ball, Multiple Throws, Pivot.

Baseball: Base, Battery, Bunting, Catcher, Diamond, Hitter, Home, Infield, Outfield. pinch, Pitcher Plate, Pullout, Short Stop, Strike.

Billiards: Baulk Line, Break, Bolting, Cannon, cue, hazard, In-off, Jigger, Long Jenney, Pot, Scratch, Screw Back, Short Jenney, Sport Stroke.

Boxing : Auxiliary Point System, Babit Punch, Break, Cut, Defence, Down, Hook, Jab, Lying On, Knock, Seconds Out, Slam, Upper Cut, Weight in, Win by knock-Out.

Bride: Auction, Bid, Chicane, Cut, Declarer, Doubleton, Dummy, Finesse, Grand Slam, Little Slam Notrumps Overtrick, Revoke, Rubber, Ruff, Shuffle, Suit, Vulnerable.

Chess: Bishop, Gambit, Grand Master, king, Knight, Pawn, Capture, Castling, Checkmate, En Passant, Queen, Rook, Stalemate, Under Promoting.

Cricket: Ashes, Banang, Boundary, Bowling, Caught, Chinaman, Cover Drive, Crease, Duck, Duckworth-Lewis Rule, Follow on, Gardening, Googly, Gully, Hat- trick, Hit Wicket, l.b.w., Leg-brack, Leg -by, Maiden Over, No Ball, Off Break, On Drive, Out, Over, Mandatory Over, Pitch, popping Crease, Rubber, Run Down, Run Out, Sixer, Silly Point, Square Leg, Stone Walling, Straight drive, Stumped, Yorker, Wicket.

Croquet: Hoops, Mallet, Peg Out.

Draughts: Huff.

Football: Advantage Clause, Blind Side, Centre Forward, Corner Kick, Dead Ball, Direct Free Kick, Dribble, Goal Kick, Hat- trick, Marking, Off Side, Penalty Kick, Penalty Shootout, Red Card, Striker, Throw In. Tripping.

Golf: Best-ball Foursome, Bogey, Bunker, Caddie, Dormy, fairway, Fourbell, Foursome, Greed Holes, Links, Niblic, Par, Put, Rough, Stymied, Tee, Threesome.

Gymnastics: A- bars, Ariel, Blocks, Come of Swing, Dish, Flairs, Giants, Inlocate, Kip, Planche, Tariff, Tumble Virtuousity, Wrap.

Hockey: Advantage, Back-stick, Bully, Garry, Centre Forward, Corner, Dribble, Flick, Free-hit, Goal Line, Green Card, Halfway Line, Hat-trick, Off-side, Red Card, Roll-in, Scoop, Short Corner, Sixteen-yard Hit, Square pass, Stick, striking Circle, Tackle, Tie-breaker, Zonal Marking.

Horse Racing: Jockery, Punt, Steeplechase, Thorough Bred.

Judo : Ashi-waza, Chui, Dan, Dojo, Gyaku, Hajime, Ippon, Jigotai, Kaeshiwaza, Koka, Makikomi, Nage-waza, O-goshi, Randori, Scarf, Tani-Otoshi, Uchi-komovi, Waki-gatame, Yoshi, Yuko.

Karate : Age Zuki, Ai-uchi, Aka, Chakugan, Dachi, Encho Sen, Fudotachi, Gedan, Geri, Hajime,Ibuki, Jion, Kakato, Koka, Makiwara, Nidan, Obi, Rei Sanbon, Shiro,Tobigeri, Ude, Waza-ari, Yoko-geri, Zanshin, Zen-no.

Polo : Bunker, Chukker, Mallet.

Rowings : Bow, Bucket, Cow, Ergometer, Paddle, Regatta.

Rugby Football : A Trackle, Lines, Scrum, Touch, Try

Shooting Bag : Bull's Eye, Marksmanship, Muzzle, Plug.

Skiing : Tobogganing

Swimming : Breast Stroke, Crawl.

Table Tennis : Anti Loop, Backspin, Chop, Loop, Penhold Grip, Push, Spin, Twiddle.

Tennis: Ace, Backhand Stroke, Deuce, Deep Volley, Deuce, Double Fault, Fault, Ground Stroke, Half Volley, Let, Love, Slice, Smash, Volley.

Volleyball : Acc, Base-line, Blocking, Doubling, Foot Fault, Heave, Holding, Jump Set, Lob Pass, Love All, point, Quick Smash, Scouting, Service, Spike, Tactical Ball, Volley, Windmill, Service,

Wrestling : Half Nelson, Head Lock, Heave, Hold, Rebouts, Scissor

SPORTS MEASUREMENTS

Badminton : 44 ft by 17 ft (singles). 44 ft by 20 ft (doubles)

Baseball : Diamond shaped ground; 90 ft on each side and 127 ft along the diagonals.

Billiards : 10 ft long 5 ft side and 3 ft high.

Basketball : 85 ft. by 46 ft. (maximum dimensions).

Cricket : Ground: Round or oval shaped; Wickets: 22 yds apart; Ball: $8\frac{13}{14}$ to 9 inches in circumference and $5\frac{3}{4}$ oz.in weight, Bat: $4\frac{1}{4}$ inches maximum width and 38 inches maximum lenght Bowling cresaes 8 ft and 8 inches in length; Popping Crease 4 ft from the wicket and deemed unlimited in lenght; Stumps; 27 inches out of the ground.

Derby Coures : $1\frac{1}{2}$ miles (2.4 km)

Football : Lenght 100 yds to 130 yds; breadth 50 yds to 56 yds; Goal with 8 yds, bar 8 ft. from ground; Area 6 yds; from each goal post; Bal; 27 inches to 28 inches in circumference; Duration: 90 minutes maximum

Golf: Hole $4\frac{1}{2}$ inches, ball $1\frac{1}{2}$ oz. in weight.

Hockey : Ground 100 yds by 55 to 60 yds; Duration of game: two periods of 30 minutes each plus extra time in case of draw or suspension of game for some reason; Goal perpendicular posts: 8 yds apart joined together by a horizontal cross bar 7 ft from ground; Ball: $8\frac{13}{14}$ inches circumference, Weight of the ball: $6\frac{3}{4}$ oz .

Polo: Ground : 300 yds by 200 yds.

Marathon Race : 26 miles, 385 yards.

Table Tennis : 9 ft × 6 ft × $2\frac{1}{2}$ ft.

Tennis Court : 78 ft by 28 ft (singles), 78 ft by 36 ft (doubles).

Volleyball Court : rectangular 30 ft by 30 ft.

Water Polo : 30 yds × 20 yds.

NATIONAL SPORTS AND GAMES OF SOME IMPORTANT COUNTRIES

Australia	Cricket
Canada	Ice Bockey
England	Cricket, Rougby Football
India	Hockey
Japan	Ju-Jitsu
Russia	Chees
Scotland	Rugby Football
Spain	Bull Fighting
USA	Baseball

NUMBER OF PLAYERS IN SOME POPULAR SPORTS/GAMES

The number of players on each side (each team) in various sports and games are mentioned below:

1.	Badminton	1 or 2 (Single & Doubles Respectively)
2.	Baseball	9
3.	Basketball	5
4.	Billiards (Snooker)	1
5.	Boxing	1
6.	Bridge	2
7.	Chess	1
8.	Cricket	11
9.	Croquet	13 or 15
10.	Football (Soccer)	11
11.	Golf	Several individuals compete simultaneously
12.	Gymnastics	Several individuals compete simultaneously
13.	Hockey	11
14.	Lacrosse	12
15.	Net Ball	7
16.	Polo	4
17.	Table Tennis	1 or 2 (Single & Doubles respectively)
18.	Tennis Court	1 or 2 (Single & Doubles respectively)
19.	Rugby Football	15
20.	Volleyball	6
21.	Water Polo	7

IMPORTANT PLACES
(Associated with Sports and Games)

Athletics : Commowealth Stadium (Canada), StadiumAustralia (Sydney).

Baseball : Brooklyn (USA), Dodger Stadium (USA), Qualcomm Stadium (USA), Veterans Stadium (USA).

Basketball : Alamodome (Texas), Charlotte Coliseum (USA).

Boat Rowing : Putney (England).

Boxing : Madison Square Garden (USA),Yankee Stadium (USA).

Cricket : Asgiriya Stadium (Kandy), Arbalniaz Stadium (Peshawar), Bangabandhu National Stadium (Dhaka), Barabati Stadium (Cuttack), Brabourne Stadium (Mumbai), Chepauk Ground (Chennai), Chinnaswamy Stadium (Bagalore), Eden Gardens (Kolkata), Eden Park (Auckland), Ferozeshah Kotla Ground (Delhi), Gaddafi Stadium (Lahore), Green park (Kanpur), Indira Priyadarshini Stadium (Visakhapatnam), Iqbal Stadium (Faisalabad), Jinnah Stadium (Gujranwala), Khettarama Stadium (Colombo), Lal Bahadur Stadium (Hyderabad), Leeds (London, England), Lord's (London, England), M.A. Chidambaram Stadium (Chennai), Melbourne (Australia), National Stadium (Karachi), Nehru Stadium (Pune), Nehru Stadium (Chennia), Nehru Stadium (New Delhi), Nehru Stadium (Goa), Old Trafford (Manchester, England),Oval (London, England) Pindi Stadium (Rawalpindi), Sabina Park (West Indies), Sawai Man Singh Stadium (Jaipur), Sinhalese Sports Club Stadium (Colombo), Trent bridge (England), Wankhede Stadium (Mumbai), Wanderers (South Africa).

Football : Ambedkar Stadium (New Delhi), Athens Olympic Stadium (Greece), Brookland (England), Corporation Stadium (Kolkata), Fed Ex Field (USA), Millennium Stadium (UK), Nehru Stadium (New Delhi), Oita Big Eye Stadium (Japan), Pontiac Silverdome (USA), Salt lake Stadium (Kolkata), San Januario Stadium (Brazil), Veterans Stadium (USA), Wembley (London), Yokohama International Stadium (Japan).

Golf : Augusta National Club (USA), Lyon Golf Club (France), Metroplitan Club (Melbourne), Sendy Lodge (Scotland), Yangon Club (Myanmar).

Greyhound Racing : white City (England).

Hockey : Dhyan Chand Stadium (Lucknow), Lal Bahadur Stadium (Hyderabad), Merdeka Stadium (Kuala Lumpur), Major Dhyan Chand Stadium (formerly National Stadium) (New Delhi), Nehru Stadium (New Delhi), Sawai Man Singh Stadium (Jaipur), Shivaji Stadium (New Delhi), Wagener Stadium (The Netherlands).

Horse Racing: Aintree (England), Doncaster (England), Epsom (England), Flemington (Melbourne).

Lawn Tennis : DLTA Grounds (New Delhi), Wimbledon (England), Forese Hill (USA).

Polo : Hurlington (England), Jaipur Pologrounds.

Rugby Football : Blackheath, Twickenham (England), Millennium Stadium (Cardiff, UK).

Shooting : Bisley (England).

Snooker : Blackpool (England)

Swimming : Subhas Sarovar (Kolkata), Talkatora Swimming Pool (New Delhi).

Swimming and Rowing : Cape Griz Zen Putney-Mort- Lake (England), Sleen Sports Complex (Australia).

Table Tennis : NDMC Indoor Stadium (New Delhi)

Tennis : Foro Italico Stadium (Rome), Rolland Garros Stadium (Paris)

CUPS AND TROPHIES
(Associated with Sports and Games)

Archery: Federation Cup.

Atheletics : Charminar Trophy, Federation Cup World Cup.

Air Racing : Jawaharlal Challenge Trophy King's Cup schneider Cup (sea planes race in UK)

Badminton : Agarwal Cup, Amrit Diwan Cup, Asia Cup, Australia Cup, Chadha Cup, European Cup, Harilela Cup, Konica Cup, Ibrahim Rahimatollah Challenge Cup, Narang Cup, Sophia Kitiakara Cup, S. R. Ruia Cup, Thomas Cup, Tunku Abdul Rahman Cup, Uþer Cup, World Cup, Yonex Cup,

Basketball : Basalat Jha Trophy, B. C. Gupta Trophy, Federation Cup, S.M. Arjuna Raja Trophy, Todd Memorial Trophy, William Jones Cup.

Billiards: Arhur Walker Trophy, Thomas Cup.

Boat Rowing : American Cup (Yacht racing), wellington Trophy (India)

Boxing : Aspy adjahia trophy, Federation Cup Val baker Tropy.

Bridge : Basalat Jha Trophy, Holkar Trophy, Ruia Gold Cup, Singhania Trophy.

Chess: Naidu Trophy, Khaitan Trophy, Limca Trophy, Linakes city Trophy, world Cup.

Cricket : Anthony D' Mellow Trophy, Ashes, Asia Cup, Benson and Hedges Cup, Bose Trophy Champions Trophy, Charminar challenge Cup, C. K. Nayudu Trophy, Coochbehar Trophy, Deodhar Trophy, Duleep Trophy, Gavaskar-Border Trophy, G. D. Birla Trophy, Gillette Cup, Ghulam Ahmad Trophy, Hakumat Rai Trophy, ICC World Cup, Interface Cup, Irani Trophy, Jawaharlal Nehru Cup, Lombard World Challenge Cup, Mc Dowells challenge Cup, Vijay Merchant Trophy, Prudential Cup (World Cup), Rani Jhansi Trophy, Ranji trophy, Rohinton Baria Trophy, Rothamans Cup, Sahara Cup, Sharjah Cup, Sheesh Mahal Trophy, Sheffield shield, Singer Cup, Texaco Cup, Titan cup Vijay Hazare Trophy, Vijay merchant Trophy, Vizzy Trophy, Wisden Tropy, Wills Trophy, World Series Cup, Worrel Trophy.

Football : African Nations Cups, Airlines Cup, America Cup, Asia Cup, Asian Women's Cup, Bandodkar Trophy. B.C. Roy trophy, Begum hazrat mahal Cup, Bicentennial Gold Cup, BILT Cup, Bordoloi Trophy, Colombo Cup, Confedersations Cup, DCM Cup, Durand Cup, European Cup, FA Cup, Federation Cup, G. V. Raja Memorial Trophy, Gold Cup, Governor's Cup, Greek Cup, Great Wall Cup, IFA Shield, Independence Day Cup, Indira Gandhi Trophy, Inter-Continental Cup, Jawaharlal Nehru Gold Cup, Jules Rimet Trophy Kalinga Cup, Kirin Cup, Lal Bahadur Shastri Trophy, McDowell Cup, Merdeka Cup, Nagjee Trophy, Naidunia Trophy, Nations Cup, NFL Trophy, Nehru Gold Cup, Nizam Gold Cup, Raghbir Singh Memorial Cup, Rajiv Gandhi Trophy, Rovers Cup, Sanjay Gold Cup, Santosh Trophy, Scissors Cup, Sir Ashutosh Mukherjee Trophy, Stafford Cup, Subroto Cup, Supercup Throphy, Todd Memorial Trophy, UEFA Cup, Vittal Trophy, Winner's Cup, World Cup.

Golf : Canada Cup, Eisenhower Trophy, Inter-Continental Cup, Mackyung LG Fashion Open

Trophy, Muthiah Gold Cup, Nomura Trophy, Paralamdi Trophy, President's Trophy, Prince of Wales Cup, Ryder Cup, Solheim Cups, Topolino Trophy, Walker Cup, Waterford Crystal Trophy, World Cup.

Hockey : Agha Khan Cup, Allwyn Asia Cup, Azlan Shah Cup, Beighton Cup, Bhim Sain Trophy, BMW Trophy, Bombay Gold Cup, Champions Trophy, Clarke trophy, Dhyan Chand Trophy, Esands Champions Cup, European Nations Cup, Gyanvati devi Trophy, Gurmeet Trophy, Guru Nanak Cup, Indira Gandhi Gold Cup, Intercontinental Cup, Khan Abdul Gaffar Khan Cup, Kuppuswamy Naidu Cup, Lady Rattan Tata Cup (women), Lal Bahadur Shastri Cup, Maharaja Ranjit Singh Gold Cup, Modi Gold Cup, Murugappa Gold Cup, Nehru Trophy, Obaidullah Gold Cup, Prime Minister's Gold Cup, RangaSwami Cup, Ranjit Singh Gold Cup, Rene Frank Trophy, Sanjay Gandhi Trophy, Scindia Gold Cup, Shriram Trophy, Tunku Abdul Razak Cup, Wellington Cup, World Cup, Yadavindra Cup.

Horse Racing : Beresford Cup, Blue Riband, Derby, Grand National Cup.

Kabaddi: Federation Cup.

Kho-Kho : Federation Cup.

Netball : Anantrao Pawar Trophy.

Polo : Ezar Cup, Gold Cup, King's Cup, President Cup, Prithi Singh Cup, Radha Mohan Cup, Winchester Cup.

Rowing : Ecefeater's Gin.

Rugby : Bledisloe Cup, Calcutta Cup, Webb Ellis Trophy.

Shooting : North Wales Cup, Wales Grand Prix.

Snooker : Team Tournament Asean Cup.

Table Tennis : Asian Cup, Berna Bellack Cup, Corbillion Cup, (women), Electra Gold Cup, Gasper-Giest Prize, Grand Prix, Jayalaxmi Cup (women), Kamala Ramanunjan Cup, Marcel Corbillon Cup, Pithapuram Cup (men), Swaythling Cup (men), Travancore Cup (women), U Thant Cup, World Cup,

Tennis : Amber Solaire Cup, AT & T Cup, Champions Cup, ATP President's Cup, Davis Cup, Dr. Rajendra Prasad Cup, Edgbsston Cup, Evett

Cup, Federation Cup, Ghafar Cup, Grand Prix, Grand Slam Cup, Hamlet Cup, Lipton Trophy, Mercedes Cup, Nations' Cup, Watson's Water Trophy, Wightman Cup, Wimbledon Trophy, World Cup, World Team Cup.

Volleyball : Centennial Cup, Federation Cup, Indira Pradhan Trophy, Shivanthi Gold Cup, World Cup, World Leage Cup.

Wrestling : Bharat Kesari, Burdwan Shield, World Cup.

Weightlifting : World Cup

Yacht Racing : America Cup.

SPORTS TERMS EXPLAINED

CRICKET

Ashes, The. The mythical trophy (being the ashes of the wicket and ball used in the first series of matches played in 1881 between England and Australia). Australia won the rubber, and it took away the Ashes. Since then it is colloquially said 'England and Australia play for the Ashes'.

Bodyline Bowling or Bumper Bowling. It denotes bumper bowling wherein the bowler aims at making the ball rise high enough so as to hit the batsman's body; first put in practice by Larwood, English fast bowler, in a series of Tests against Australia. Its main object is to intimidate the batsman.

Bowling. When the bowler throws the ball to the batsman in the proper manner, it is called bowling.

Bye and Leg Bye. Runs obtained are categorised as 'bye' when the ball passes the batsman without touching his bat or person; in case the ball touches any part of the batsman (except his hands) the runs obtained are categories 'leg-bye'.

Chucher. Fast bowler who throws the ball at the wicket instead of bowling with a straightened arm with a view to intimating the batsman.

Cover Point. It is a position given by the bowler to a fielder on the offside in front of the wicket.

Creases. These are two lines, which specify the position of batsman and the bowler.

Drive. When a batsman hits a ball in such a way as it catches the same direction from where it was bowled and rolls long the ground, it is called a 'drive'.

Duck. When a batsman is out without having scored a single run.

Follow on. When a team is asked to continue the second innings after the close of its first, it is given a 'follow on'. The other team must be leading by at least 200 runs.

Googly. An off-breaking ball with an apparent leg-break action on the part of the bowler and conversery a leg-breaking ball with an apparent off-break action on the part of the bowler.

Hat Trick. When the bowler bowls out three batsmen with three successive balls in the same over, it is used in hockey or football, when the same player scores three successive goals.

Hit Wicket. While playing at the ball, when the batsman hits down his own wicket with his bat or any part of his person or clothes, it is called 'Hit Wicket', and the batsman is declared out.

l.b.w. If the batsman intercepts the ball with any part of his person (except his hands) between the wickets which otherwise would have hit the stumps, he is declared to be l.b.w. (leg before wicket).

Maiden Over. The over in wihch the batsman does not add any run in his account, is called a 'maiden over'.

No Ball. The ball is declared 'No Ball' by the umpire (a) when the bowler puts both his legs inside the pitch, while bowling (b) when the ball is thrown in an improper way.

Over. When a bowler-bowls six balls in succession, one 'over' is said to be completed. Bowling then starts at the other end. In Australia, eight balls in succession, one 'over' is said to be completed. Bowling then starts at the other end. In Australia, eight balls constitute an 'over'.

Run Out. when the batsman tries to take a run, and he is out of the creases, but the fielder hits the wicket with the ball, he is declared 'run-out'.

FOOTBALL

Corner Kicks. If the ball passes over the goal line (excluding the portion between the goal-posts) having last been played by one of the defending team, a member of the attacking team shall take a kick from within the quarter circle nearest to the corner flag post.

Dribble. To kick forward the ball little by little; this term is also used in hockey as well as basketball.

Offside. A player is declared off-side by the referee, if he is nearer his opponent's goal line and there are fewer than two players of the opposite team at that time, when the ball is played from behind. This term is also used in hockey.

HOCKEY

Bully. When the game starts or there is goal, we have a 'bully' at the centre, or when the ball goes out, we have a 'bully' at the assigned point.

Dribble. Carrying the ball on the blade of the hockey stick, and moving with it.

Off side. See above.

Roll in. When the ball passes over the side-line, it is required to be rolled into the field by hand.

Undercutting and Scoop. None of the players is allowed to undercut the ball intentionally; but the scoop (sweeping) stroke which raises the ball from the ground is permissible.

TENNIS

Backhand. When you make a shot by hitting from the other side of your normal playing hand.

Deuce. A term that shows that each side has scored equal points (forty each) at the game point; the term is also used in badminton.

Fault. A failure by the server to drive the ball into the proper part of opponent's court.

Half Volley. It is return stroke, when one strikes the ball, just as it touches or rises from the ground.

Let. First service, if not correct, is called 'let'.

Volley. this is hard stroke, generally made close to the net, before the ball touches the ground.

MISCELLANEOUS TERMS

Cue (Billiards). The long stick for striking the balls.

Cannons (Billiards). When the player's ball touches two other balls.

Dead Heat (Athletics). When the participants in a race reach the winning point at the same time.

Gambit (Chess). A mode of opening the game.

Little Slam (Bridge). When the player makes 12 tricks.

Mallet (Croquet, polo). Hammer for striking the ball.

Tee (Gold). The small conical support on which the ball is placed before it is struck by the club.

SOME BALL GAMES EXPLAINED

Baseball. It is the national game of U.S.A. played with a white ball (weight 5 ozs.) and a bat (heavy Indian Club). Runs have to be scored and to score one run, one has to complete the circuit of the three bases (distance between each base from the batter is 30 yards); and the game consists of nine innings, each being completed, when three playes are out.

Basket Ball. The ball resembling an Association Football is played only with hands, the goal consists of posts with iron rings at the top through which the ball must be thrown, and blackboards are fixed at the top of the posts to aid the ball to fall through the ring. The game originated in the U.S.A.

Net Ball. It is similar to basket ball except that the posts have no blackboads.

Croquet. The game is played with balls coloured blue, black, yellow and red; four mallets, six hoops and a peg for striking the ball. Dimensions of the ground are 35 yards by 25 yards.

Golf. It consists of using clubs to play a small, hard white ball over a cross country of 18 holes. The course is two miles in length, and each hole is a distance of several hundred yards, the object of the game is to throw the ball in each hole, and eventually to play the entire course in as few strokes as possible.

Lacrosse. (12 players each side). It is the simplest of all field games. The main object is the scoring of goals propelling the balls (4.5 to 5 ozs.) through the goal posts with a cross. The distance between the goal posts is 90 to 100 yards; there are no fixed dimensions of the boundary of the field: the play can take place even behind the goal posts at a considerable distance.

Rugby and Association Football. In the former there are 15 players on each side, the ball is oval-shaped, and it can be played with the hands as well; whereas in the latter there are 11 players on each side; ball is rounded and it cannot be touched with the hand.

NUMBER OF PLAYERS ON EACH SIDE IN IMPORTANT GAMES

Baseball	9
Net Ball	7
Hockey	11
Water Polo	7
Lacrosse	12
Polo	4
Volleyball	6
Basket ball	5
Cricket	11
Association Football	11
Rugby Football	15
Croquet	13 or 15
Badminton, Tennis	1 or 2
Table Tennis	1 or 2

Rajkumari Sports Coaching Scheme. In September, 1953, a new scheme was introduced in India to give proper training to the athletes and sportsmen. Besides, assistance was given to sports federations to modernise sports equipments and to enable them to participate in international sports tournaments. Professionals were invited every year from various countries to impart coaching. It was named after Rajkumari Amrit Kaur. This scheme has now been taken over by the National Institute of Sports at Patiala.

Arjuna Awards. Instituted for the first time in 1961, awarded to the sportsmen in recognition of their outstanding contribution to sports. They are awarded to the best sportsmen of the year. Dronacharya awards are given to the best coaches.

CRICKET

It is played by two teams of 11 men (or women) each on a level grass field (or cement-based matted stretch). Each eleven normally has two innings, taken alternately. In the centre of the field, a "wicket" is sited-3 stumps of wood about 1.5 inches in diameter and 27 inches high are "set" vertically into the ground-in a line so that they stretch across 8 inches. On top of the stumps are placed two wooden "bails" or crosspieces. In a direct line opposite and 22 yards from these stumps a similar wicket or trio of topped stumps is placed. A white line 8 feet 8 inches long is drawn sideways through each of these wickets-4 feet to the left and 4 feet to the right in line with the stumps. These lines are called the "bowling crease" beyond which the bowler must not pass when delivering the ball towards the batsman at the other end of the wicket. In front of the stumps 4 feet from them and parallel with them another white line is drawn: this is the "popping crease" which delineates the batsman's domain.

The bat used must not be longer than 38 inches nor wider than 4.5 inches. It has a flat surface compared to a base ball bat. The ball, a core of cork built up with string and cased with polished red/white leather, is 3 inches in diameter and weight 5.5 to 5.75 ounces.

A Batsman is "out" (1) if he fails to defend the wicket and the bowled ball knocks off the bails (he is said to be "bowled" at this event); (2) if a fielder catch his batted ball on the fly (he is "caught"); (3) if he fails to have his bat or any part of his person within the popping crease (after a run) before his wicket is thrown down with the ball either by a fielder or the wicket keeper (he is "run out"); (4) if he steps out of his popping crease to hit a ball, missed it, and the wicket keeper throws his wicket down before he can step back (he is "stumped"); (5) if he interfered with a straight ball with a part of his body not his arm below the elbow, or his bat, and the umpire decides it would otherwise have hit the wicket (this is called "leg before wicket"); (6) if he knock down the wicket himself in playing at the ball ("hit wicket"); (7) or if he wilfully obstructs the fielders.

FIELD HOCKEY

The field of turf is 100 yards long and 55 to 60 yards wide with netted goals 12 feet wide and 7 feet high set on the centre of the end lines. There is a large arc in front of each goal known as the striking circle. Twenty-five yard lines are marked on the field and a centre line, which divides the field in half, has a circle at its mid-point. Played by

11 men (or women) on each side, the purpose of the game is to hit a ball with long sticks curved at the end, through opposite goals. There are 5 forwards on each team. 3 halfbacks, 2 fullbacks and a goalkeeper. The game is divided into 2 halves of 30 minutes each, the teams changing sides at the end of each half. Substitutions are made only for injury and only during the 5-minute half-time."

The ball has a cork centre wound with twine and covered with white leather. It weights between 5.5 and 5.75 ounces, and has a circumference of 8.75 to 9.25 inches.

A hockey stick, weighing not more than 28 ounces, has a flat face on its left side and is rounded on the right. The ball may only be struck with the left side. The stick's curved blade is about 3 feet long.

SOCCER

The modern soccer field's playing area is 100 to 120 yards long, 55 to 75 yards wide, with 120 × 75 the preferred dimensions. In the middle of each end (goal line) is a goal which stands 8 feet high and 24 feet wide, usually backed with netting. There is a 6 × 20 yards goal area in front of each goal and this, in turn, is enclosed by a larger 18 × 44 yard penalty area. A halfway line, parallel to the goal lines, bisects the field, and in the exact centre of the field three is a circle with a radius of 10 yards.

Soccer is played with an inflated round leather ball that must be not less than 27 inches in circumference and not more than 28. It must be between 14 and 16 ounces dry weight.

The game of soccer is played in two periods of 45 minutes, the teams changing sides. At the start of the game, the goal to be defended is decided by the toss of a coin. At the kickoff circle, the centre forward starts the game by kicking the ball to another teammate. When the ball has travelled 27 inches the players may cross the half way line on the field and the game is on. The object of the game is to move the ball down the field and past the defending goalie into the opposing team's goal for a score.

BASKET BALL

The regulation basketball court is a rectangle with certain maximum and minimum dimensions. The largest court may be 94 feet long by 50 feet wide, which is used by players of college age and older. A court 84 feet by 50 feet is used for high school players, and the smallest court, 74 feet long by 42 feet wide is permissible for players of early high school age or younger. For girls' basket Ball, the court sizes are the same. In the middle of each end of the playing area are the basket and backboards.

The backboard behind the basket is made of wood, glass, plastic, or metal. There are two basic types-a square type, 6 feet wide and 4 feet high, and a fan-shaped backboard. The baskets are white cord nets, open at both ends, suspended from a metal ring 18 inches in diameter and hung on the backboard 10 feet from the floor.

The ball weights between 20 and 22 ounces, and holds from 7 to 9 pounds of air. It may not be less than 29 inches in circumference and not more than 30.

Five men form a basket Ball team-a centre, two forwards and two guards. A women's team has six players-two offensive, two defensive and two roving.

TABLE TENNIS

Table tennis is a fast-moving indoor game similar to lawn tennis. The regulation table is 9 feet long and 5 feet wide, its non-reflecting surface 30 inches from the floor. The net is 6 feet long, extending 6 inches beyond each side of the table. A white line ¾ of an inch side outlines the table and a 1/8 inch centre line (important only in doubles play) divides the table into right and left quarters. The minimum floor space requirements are 10 feet at each end of the table, 5 feet long either side and an overhead clearance of 8 feet.

A representative racket is made of laminated wood, covered first with a thin layer of sponge rubber. An outer layer of stippled rubber serves to control the ball and impart spin in chop and drive strokes.

The white celluloid, hollow ball with a circumference of 4.5 to 4.75 inches weights between 37 and 39 grains (US).

A game is completed when one player scores 21 points, provided he is at least 2 points ahead at the time. At score 20-all, service alternates after each point and the winner must score two points more than his opponent.

TENNIS

The area or court on which tennis is played may be either indoors or outdoors. In a single game, the playing court is 78 feet long and 27 feet wide. In a doubles game, played by partners, the playing area is widened by 4.5 feet on each side. Those added side strips are called "alleys".

The side boundary lines are called "base lines".

Across the middle of the court, stretched between two posts, is a net trailing on the ground, but 3 feet 6 inches high at the posts and its top edge 3 feet high in the middle.

On each side of the net, parallel to it and 21 feet from it, are the "service lines," and the short line bisecting the exact middle of the baseline is known as the "centre mark." Thus, the court is divided into 6 areas-4 service courts and 2 back courts.

Basic equipment for playing tennis consists of a racket and a few balls. The racket, which has a wooden or metal frame strung with gut, nylon, or silk cords, is about 27 inches long, about 9 inches wide and weighs from 12 to 16 ounces. The regulation tennis ball is made of inflated rubber, covered with whitish coloured felt. It is 2.5 to 2.3/6 inches in diameter and weighs about 2 to 21/16 ounces.

VOLLEYBALL

The volleyball court is a rectangle 60 feet by 30 feet marked by boundary lines 2 inches wide. This area is divided into two equal courts by a centre line. A net, 3 feet in height, is suspended across the centre line with its upper edge 8 feet from the floor. Each half of the court has a restraining line 7.5 feet from and parallel to the middle of the centre line.

The regulation volleyball weights between 9 and 10 ounces and has air pressure of not less than 7 nor more than 8 points. Its circumferences is between 26 and 27 inches.

There are 6 men in a volleyball team, and each man is responsible for covering the ground in his court area. Three men stand in the front half of the court and three in the rear. These positions are designated left forward, centre forward, right forward, right back, centre back, and left back.

Only the serving team can score. If the opposing team commits an error or foul, the serving team receives one point. But if the serving team commits an error or foul, it loses the service. Whenever a team takes over the service, every player of that team rotates one position in a clockwise direction, as they face the net. The player who moves into the service area serves until his team loses the service. The team which loses the service remain in position.

There are 8 minutes of playing time in a game. If a team scores 15 points before the 8 minutes have expired and has a 2-point advantage, the team wins and the game is ended. If neither team scores 15 points during the game period, the team with at least a 2-point advantage wins. If after the end of 8 minutes the score is tied or one team does not have a 2-point advantage, play continues until one team gains the 2-point advantage.

IMPORTANT TROPHIES AND CUPS (International)

Name	Associated Sport
American Cup	Yacht Racing
Ashes	Cricket (Australia-England)
Canada Cup	Golf (World Championship)
Colombo Cup	Football (India, Pakistan, Sri Lanka and Myanmar)
Corbillion Cup	World Table Tennis (women)
Davis Cup	Tennis
Derby	Horse Racing
Holker	Bridge
Jules Rimet Trophy	World Football (Soccer)
Merdeka	Football (Asian Cup)
Ryder Cup	Golf
Reliance Cup	Cricket
Swaythling Cup	World Table Tennis (men)
Tunku Abdul Rahman Cup	Asian Badminton
U. Thant Cup	Lawn Tennis
Uber Cup	World Badminton (women)
Yonex Cup	Badminton
Walker Cup	Golf
William Cup	Basketball
Wimbledon Trophy	Tennis
World Cup	Cricket (Prudential/Reliance Cup)
Todd Memorial Trophy	Basket Ball
Thomas Cup	World Badminton (Men)

IMPORTANT TROPHIES AND CUPS (National)

Name	Associated Sport
Aga Khan Cup	Hockey
Ranjit Singh Gold Cup	Hockey
Guru Nanak Championship	Hockey (all India women)
Barna-Bellack Cup	Table Tennis (men)
Beighton Cup	Hockey
Dhyan Chand Trophy	Hockey
Dr B. C. Roy Trophy	Football (National junior)
Duleep Trophy	Cricket
Durand Cup	Football
EZAR Cup	Polo
Irani Trophy	Cricket
Lady Ratan Tata Trophy	Hockey (women)
Murugappa Gold Cup	Hockey
Nehru Trophy	Hockey
Nizam Gold Cup	Football
Rangaswami Cup	Hockey (National championship)
Ranji Trophy	Cricket (National championship)
Rovers Cup	Football
Santosh Trophy	Football
Sanjay Gold Cup	Football
Sheesh Mahal Trophy	Cricket
Subroto Mukherjee Cup	Football
Todd Memorial Trophy	Football
Vittal Trophy	Football
Vizzy Trophy	Cricket
Yadvindra Cup	Hockey

IMPORTANT NATIONAL SPORTS

Country	National Sports
Australia	Tennis and Cricket
Canada	Lacrosse
China	Table Tennis (Ping Pong)
England	Cricket, Football
India	Hockey, Kabaddi
Japan	Judo
Malaysia	Badminton
Scotland	Rugby
Spain	Bull Fighting
U.S.	Baseball

SPORTS STADIUMS IN INDIA

Name	Location
Netaji Indoor Stadium	Kolkata
Wankhede Stadium	Mumbai
Nehru (Chepauk) Stadium	Chennai
National Stadium	New Delhi
Vallabhbha Patel Stadium	Ahmedabad
Keenan Stadium	Jamshedpur
Brabourne Stadium	Mumbai
Yadvindra Stadium	Patiala
Ranjit Stadium	Kolkata
Barahati Stadium	Cuttak
Eden Gardens	Kolkata
Green Park Stadium	Kanpur
Sawai Mansingh Stadium	Jaipur
Shivaji Stadium	New Delhi
Jawaharlal Nehru Stadium	New Delhi
Yuba Bharati Stadium* (Salt Lake Stadium)	Kolkata
Indira Gandhi Indoor Stadium**	New Delhi

* It is India's largest stadium which can accommodate 1,20,000 people, and it spreads over an area of 30.75 hectares. It is also the largest covered stadium in the world.

** It is India's largest indoor stadium, which can accommodate 25,000 people, having a diameter of 150m:

OLYMPIC GAMES (Summer)

S.No.	Year	Place	Country
1.	1896	Athens	Greece
2.	1900	Paris	France
3.	1904*	St. Luis	U.S.A.
4.	1906	Athens	Greece
5.	1908	London	England
6.	1912	Stockholm	Sweden
7.	1920	Antwerp	Belgium
8.	1924	Paris	France
9.	1928	Amsterdam	Netherland
10.	1932	Los Angels	U.S.A.
11.	1936	Berlin	Germany
12.	1948	London	England
13.	1952	Helsinki	Finland
14.	1956	Melbourne	Italy
15.	1960	Rome	France
16.	1964	Tokyo	Japan
17.	1968	Mexico City	Mexico
18.	1972	Munich	Germany
19.	1976	Montreal	Canada
20.	1980	Moscow	Russia
21.	1984	Los Angeles	U.S.A.
22.	1988	Seoul	South Korea
23.	1992	Barcelona	France
24.	1996	Atlanta	U.S.A.
25.	2000	Sydney	Australia
26.	2004	Athens	Greece
27.	2008	Beijing	China
28.	2012	London	United Kingdom
29.	2016	Rio de Janeiro	Brazil
30.	2020	Tokyo	Japan (Proposed)

*Games weren't held in the years 1916, 1940 & 1944 due to world wars.
*Games weren't recognized by International Olympic Committee.

OLYMPIC GAMES (Winter)

S.No.	Year	Place	Country
1.	1924	Chamonix	France
2.	1928	St. Moritz	Switzerland
3.	1932	Lake Placid	New York
4.	1936	Garmisch-Partenkirchen	Germany
5.	1948	St. Moriz	Switzerland
6.	1952	Oslo	Norway
7.	1956	Cortina d'Anpezzo	Italy
8.	1960	Sqvaw Valley	California (USA)
9.	1964	Innsbruck	Austria
10.	1968	Grenble	France
11.	1972	Sapporo	Japan
12.	1976	Innsbruck	Austria

13.	1980	Lake Placid	New York
14.	1984	Sarajevo	Yugoslavia
15.	1988	Calgary	Alberta
16.	1992	Albertville	France
17.	1994	Lillehammer	Norway
18.	1998	Nagono	Japan
19.	2002	Salt Lake City	U.S.A.
20.	2006	Turine	Italy
21.	2010	Vancouver	Canada
22.	2014	London	United Kingdom
23.	2018	Pyeongchang	South Korea
24.	2022	Beijing	China (Proposed)

VENUE OF COMMONWEALTH GAMES

S.No.	Venue	Country	Year	No. of Countries
1.	Hamilton	Canada	1930	11
2.	London	U.K.	1934	16
3.	Sydney	Australia	1938	15
4.	Auckland	New Zealand	1950	12
5.	Vancouver	Canada	1954	24
6.	Cardiff	U.K.	1958	35
7.	Perth	Australia	1962	35
8.	Jamaica	West Indies	1966	34
9.	Edinburgh	U.K.	1970	42
10.	Christchurch	New Zealand	1974	38
11.	Edmonton	Canada	1978	48
12.	Brisbane	Australia	1982	47
13.	Edinburgh	U.K.	1986	26
14.	Auckland	New Zealand	1990	55
15.	Victoria	Canada	1994	64
16.	Kuala Lumpur	Malaysia	1998	70
17.	Manchester	U.K.	2002	72
18.	Melbourne	Australia	2006	71
19.	New Delhi	India	2010	71
20.	Glasgow	Scotland	2014	71
21.	Gold Coast	Australia	2018	(Proposed)

VENUE OF ASIAN GAMES

S.No.	Year	Venue	Country
1.	1951	New Delhi	India
2.	1954	Manila	Philippines
3.	1958	Tokyo	Japan
4.	1962	Jakarta	Indonesia
5.	1966	Bangkok	Thailand
6.	1970	Bangkok	Thailand
7.	1974	Tehran	Iran
8.	1978	Bangkok	Thailand
9.	1982	New Delhi	India

10.	1986	Seoul	South Korea
11.	1990	Beijing	China
12.	1994	Hiroshima	Japan
13.	1998	Bangkok	Thailand
14.	2002	Pusan	South Korea
15.	2006	Doha	Qatar
16.	2010	Guangzhou	China
17.	2014	Incheon	South Korea
18.	2018	Jakarta-Palembang	Indonesia (Proposed)

WORLD CUP FOOTBALL CHAMPIONSHIP

S.No.	Year	Place	Winner	Runners-up	Score
1.	1930	Uruguay	Uruguay	Argentina	4-2
2.	1934	Italy	Italy	Chechoslovakia	2-1
3.	1938	France	Italy	Hungary	4-2
4.	1950	Brazil	Uruguay	Brazil	2-1
5.	1954	Switzerland	W. Germany	Hungary	3-2
6.	1958	Sweden	Brazil	Sweden	5-2
7.	1962	Chile	Brazil	Czechoslovakia	3-1
8.	1966	England	England	W. Germany	4-2
9.	1970	Mexico	Brazil	Italy	4-1
10.	1974	W. Germany	W. Germany	Netherlands	2-1
11.	1978	Argentina	Argentina	Netherlands	3-1
12.	1982	Spain	Italy	W. Germany	3-1
13.	1986	Mexico	Argentina	W. Germany	3-2
14.	1990	Italy	W. Germany	Argentina	1-0
15.	1994	U.S.A.	Brazil	Italy	3-2
16.	1998	France	France	Brazil	3-0
17.	2002	Japan & South Korea	Brazil	Germany	2-0
18.	2006	Germany	Italy	France	2-0
19.	2010	South Africa	Spain	Netherlands	1-0
20.	2014	Brazil	Germany	Argentina	1-0
21.	2018	Russia (Proposed)	–	–	–

In 1942 & 1946 matches weren't played.

PRESIDENT OF INTERNATIONAL FOOTBALL ASSOCIATION

S.No.	Name	Tenure
1.	Robert Guerin	1904-1906
2.	Daniel Burley	1906-1918
3.	Jules rimet	1921-1954
4.	Rudolf William Seldreyars	1954-1955
5.	Arghur Drevy	1955-1961
6.	Sir Stanley Rose	1961-1974
7.	Joe Haveyonge	1974-1998
8.	Sepp Blatter	1998-2015
9.	Issa Hayatou (Acting)	2015-2016
10.	Gianni Infantino	2016-till date

OBJECTIVE QUESTIONS

1. Which of the following(s) is/are the best example of competitive exercises?
   (*a*) Training with heavy discus
   (*b*) Long jump with weight jackets
   (*c*) Both the above
   (*d*) None of the above

2. The literal meaning of the word 'Isotonic' is—
   (*a*) Rapid tension
   (*b*) Constant tension
   (*c*) Increasing tension
   (*d*) Decreasing tension

3. Keeping Isotonic method in mind, choose the correct statement
   (*a*) Since Isotonic method involves movement, it enhances coordination
   (*b*) This method is worst for improving techniques
   (*c*) It is less effective for developing speed of movement and endurance
   (*d*) Strength developed through this method cannot be maintained for longer period.

4. Among the following choose the correct statement(s) regarding disadvantages of Isotonic method:
   (*a*) The contraction of muscle is not systematic and objective.
   (*b*) The time for which contraction is maintained is short.
   (*c*) Distribution of energy is much greater because movement is repeated several times.
   (*d*) All the above

5. In which of the following methods muscles injuries are more frequent?
   (*a*) Isometric method
   (*b*) Isotonic method
   (*c*) Both the above
   (*d*) None of the above

6. Choose the correct literal meaning of the word 'Isometric':
   (*a*) Increased length (*b*) Decreased length
   (*c*) Constant length (*d*) Variable length

7. Regarding benefits of Isometric method choose the correct statement(s):
   (*a*) Muscle can be contracted more systematically and objectively
   (*b*) The duration of contraction is longer
   (*c*) Need for energy requirement is less and due to this sports person does not get tired
   (*d*) All the above

8. Choose the correct disadvantage(s) of Isometric method:
   (*a*) Since this method does not involve movement, it is bad for the development of coordination and skill
   (*b*) Strength developed using this method is not maintained for long time
   (*c*) It does not contribute to development of speed of movement
   (*d*) All the above

9. Among the following, in which type of muscle contraction, the muscle shortens with varying tension while lifting a constant load?
   (*a*) Isotonic contraction
   (*b*) Isometric contraction
   (*c*) Eccentric contraction
   (*d*) Iso Kinetic contraction

10. In which type of muscle contraction, contraction tension is developed in the muscle working against resistance but there is no change in the length of the muscle?
    (*a*) Isotonic contraction
    (*b*) Isometric contraction
    (*c*) Eccentric contraction
    (*d*) Iso Kinetic contraction

11. In which of the following muscle contraction both the origin and insertion of the muscle move away while the muscle is contrating?
    (*a*) Isotonic contraction
    (*b*) Isometric contraction
    (*c*) Eccentric contraction
    (*d*) Iso Kinetic contraction

12. Which of the following contractions can be best explained with the example of elbow flexion against resistance?
    (*a*) Isotonic contraction
    (*b*) Isometric contraction
    (*c*) Eccentric contraction
    (*d*) Iso Kinetic contraction

13. In which year, the concept of Isokinetic contraction method was introduced?
    (*a*) 1954   (*b*) 1964
    (*c*) 1968   (*d*) 1978

14. Which of the following involves development of maximum tension in the muscle which shortens at constant speed at all angles over the full range of motion?
    (*a*) Isotonic contraction
    (*b*) Isometric contraction
    (*c*) Eccentric contraction
    (*d*) Iso Kinetic contraction

15. Among the followings which is the most modern concept of exercises?
    (*a*) Isotonic contraction
    (*b*) Isometric contraction
    (*c*) Eccentric contraction
    (*d*) 1so Kinetic contraction

16. Iso Kinetic contraction method was introduced by
    (*a*) J.J. Perrine
    (*b*) W.B. Shelly
    (*c*) William Huntington
    (*d*) Winston D. Belly

17. Arm stroke in butterfly style swimming is an example of—
    (*a*) Isotonic contraction
    (*b*) Isometric contraction
    (*c*) Eccentric contraction
    (*d*) Iso Kinetic contraction

18. Which of the following method is considered to be the best for improving muscular strength and endurance for sports?
    (*a*) Isotonic contraction
    (*b*) Isometric contraction
    (*c*) Eccentric contraction
    (*d*) Iso Kinetic contraction

19. Which of the following pair is concentric?
    (*a*) Isometric and Isotonic contraction
    (*b*) Isotonic and Iso Kinetic contraction
    (*c*) Eccentric and Iso Kinetic contraction
    (*d*) Isotonic and Eccentric contraction

20. Which training enables an individual to use the PRT most effectively. Here PRT stands for—
    (*a*) Passive Resistance Technique
    (*b*) Progressive Resistance Technique
    (*c*) Passive Resistance Treatment
    (*d*) Progressive Resistance Treatment

21. Variations are made in which of the followings so that different forms of strength can be trained?
    (*a*) Intensity and repetition
    (*b*) Number of sets
    (*c*) Recovery between sets and series
    (*d*) All the above

22. For developing maximum strength—
    (*a*) Intensity is low and repetitions are less performed
    (*b*) Intensity is high and repetitions are less performed
    (*c*) Intensity is high and repetitions are maximum performed
    (*d*) Intensity is low and repetitions are maximum performed

23. Among the following strength training methods which is not suited for developing strength endurance?
    (*a*) Super set method
    (*b*) Combination method
    (*c*) Simple method
    (*d*) Pyramid method

24. Which one of the following methods is recommended for the beginners?
    (*a*) Super set method
    (*b*) Combination method
    (*c*) Simple method
    (*d*) Pyramid method

25. In which of the following strength training method, between a set for developing flexor and a set for developing extensor muscles, no recovery is provided?
    (*a*) Super set method
    (*b*) Combination method

(*c*) Simple method

(*d*) Pyramid method

26. Circuit training is an effective method of developing—

(*a*) Progressive resistance

(*b*) Passive resistance

(*c*) Strength endurance

(*d*) None of the above

27. Which of the following exercise(s) come under Plyometric jumps?

(*a*) Hopping   (*b*) Bounding

(*c*) Depth jumps   (*d*) All of the above

28. Which of the following exercise involves alternate hopping and stepping?

(*a*) Hopping   (*b*) Bounding

(*c*) Depth jumps   (*d*) All of the above

29. Barbell training, specially which has a direct impact on the vertibral column of the child is not recommended below the age of—

(*a*) 14 years   (*b*) 10 years

(*c*) 12 years   (*d*) 16 years

30. Administration of load and recovery is done in—

(*a*) Three ways   (*b*) Five ways

(*c*) Two ways   (*d*) Four ways

31. Which of the following loading procedure involves progressive increase of resistance and decreasing repetitions in the first half and gradually decreasing resistance and increasing repetitions in the second half?

(*a*) Progressive System

(*b*) Progressive Regressive System

(*c*) Reducing Resistance and Fixed Repetitions

(*d*) Contrast Method

32. Since strength has direct relevance to performance in sports, which of the following suggestion can be given for developing strength among children?

(*a*) The exercises should be done with high intensity

(*b*) Lesser stress should be laid on general exercises

(*c*) In the initial stages, isometric exercises should be avoided

(*d*) Variations of exercises should be avoided

33. Which of the following changes is/are brought about in the body composition of women during strength training?

(*a*) Little or no change in total body weight

(*b*) Significant gain in lean body weight

(*c*) Both the above

(*d*) None of the above

34. The ability to do sports movements with the desired quality and speed, under condition of fatique is called

(*a*) Endurance   (*b*) Agility

(*c*) Power   (*d*) Speed

35. Regarding benefits of endurance, choose the correct statement(s):

(*a*) It enables sports person to successfully complete training schedules of high loads

(*b*) It facilitates maintenance of pace and tempo of an activity during training and competition

(*c*) It helps in delaying the onset of fatigue and to recover quickly from fatigue during completion and training

(*d*) All of above

36. On the basis of nature of the activity the endurance can be classified into—

(*a*) Three types   (*b*) Four types

(*c*) Five types   (*d*) Two types

37. Keeping in mind the nature of the activity which one of the following is not a type of endurance?

(*a*) Basic endurance

(*b*) Speed endurance

(*c*) Contant endurance

(*d*) Sprint endurance

38. On the basis of the duration of different games and sports, endurance can be classified into—

(*a*) Three types   (*b*) Four types

(*c*) Five types   (*d*) Two types

39. Keeping in mind the duration of different games and sports, which one of the following is not a type of endurance?

(*a*) Short time endurance

(*b*) Middle time endurance

(*c*) Long time endurance

(*d*) None of the above

40. Endurance ability depends upon—
(*a*) Aerobic capacity
(*b*) Anaerobic capacity
(*c*) Economy of movement
(*d*) All the above

41. Which of the following psychological factor(s) is/are also important in enabling a sports person to continue activity for a prolonged period?
(*a*) Motivation
(*b*) Will power
(*c*) Ability to tolerate pain and discomforts
(*d*) All the above

42. Which of the following load methods involves application of uninterrupted loads but with change of speed?
(*a*) Slow constant method
(*b*) Fast constant method
(*c*) Varied pace method
(*d*) None of the above

43. Which of the following load method is a system of training which demands hard but untired efforts?
(*a*) Constant method
(*b*) Alternating method
(*c*) Fartlek
(*d*) Interval running method

44. Among the following which one was developed in Scandinavia to provide an alternative to constant running?
(*a*) Interval running method
(*b*) Repetition training method
(*c*) Competition and test method
(*d*) Fartlek

45. Which of the following load method is used to describe cross country runs where the steady speed of ordinary cross country running is changed into a mixture of faster and slower phases, each covering a different distance over natural terrain according to the individual approach of the sports person?
(*a*) Fartlek
(*b*) Contant method
(*c*) Alternating method
(*d*) None of the above

46. Which of the following load method is very useful for athletes who run of the track events?
(*a*) Interval running method

(*b*) Fartlek
(*c*) Constant method
(*d*) None of the above

47. The effects of interval training method is determined by—
(*a*) Intensity and density of stimulus
(*b*) Duration and frequency of stimulus
(*c*) Mode of recovery
(*d*) All the above

48. Which one of the followings is considered as the best method for developing speed endurance and pace judgement?
(*a*) Competition and test method
(*b*) Repetition training method
(*c*) Interval running method
(*d*) None of the above

49. The problem of speed barrier can be dealt with—
(*a*) Delaying of speed barrier
(*b*) Tacking of speed barrier
(*c*) Both the above
(*d*) None of the above

50. Sprinting speed can be developed directly using—
(*a*) the Acceleration runs
(*b*) the Ins and outs
(*c*) the Differential races
(*d*) All the above

51. The term 'Butterfly' in sports is associated with—
(*a*) Basketball   (*b*) Swimming
(*c*) Rowing   (*d*) Golf

52. The term 'Dribbling' is not associated with—
(*a*) Hockey   (*b*) Football
(*c*) Basketball   (*d*) Baseball

53. The term 'Jump Ball' in sports is associated with—
(*a*) Lawn Tennis   (*b*) Badminton
(*c*) Basketball   (*d*) Hockey

54. The term 'Bogey' is associated with—
(*a*) Tennis   (*b*) Golf
(*c*) Baseball   (*d*) Chess

55. The place 'Epsom' is associated with—
(*a*) Polo   (*b*) Water polo
(*c*) Table tennis   (*d*) Horse Racing

56. The term 'Pivot' is associated with which of the following games?
(a) Hockey   (b) Basketball
(c) Golf   (d) Tennis

57. The term 'Deuce' is common in which of the following two games?
(a) Basketball and Badminton
(b) Badminton and Tennis
(c) Volleyball and Tennis
(d) Cricket and Football

58. The term 'rook 'is associated with which game?
(a) Golf   (b) Chess
(c) Bridge   (d) Billiards

59. The term 'stone walling' is associated with—
(a) Tennis   (b) Badminton
(c) Hockey   (d) Cricket

60. Which of the following pairs is not correct?
(a) Anthony D'Mello Trophy : Hockey
(b) Stafford Cup: Football
(c) Corbillion Cup :Table Tennis
(d) Irani Cup : Cricket

61. How many players take part in each team in a volleyball match played under international rules?
(a) 7   (b) 11
(c) 6   (d) 8

62. How many players are there in each side in Baseball match?
(a) 11   (b) 7
(c) 5   (d) 9

63. The duration of a normal one half of a Hockey match is—
(a) 45 mm   (b) 40 mm
(c) 35 mm   (d) 30 mm

64. What is the duration of each period before and after the ten minute break in a basketball game?
(a) 30 mm   (b) 25 mm
(c) 35 mm   (d) 45 mm

65. When and where was the game of Volleyball invented?
(a) England, 1904   (b) USA, 1895
(c) Canada, 1894   (d) Australia, 1890

66. The normal length of a Football ground must be—
(a) 110-120 m   (b) 90-120 m
(c) 90-100 m   (d) 120-130 m

67. How many players are there in a Football team?
(a) 10   (b) 11
(c) 12   (d) 6

68. How many players are there on each side in a women's Basketball game?
(a) 5   (b) 6
(c) 7   (d) 10

69. U Thant Cup is associated with the game of—
(a) LawnTennis   (b) TableTennis
(c) Hockey   (d) Golf

70. Who among the following is associated with Badminton?
(a) AnupBasak
(b) Prakash Padukone
(c) Diana Edulji
(d) Manuel Aaron

71. Dhyan Chand 's name is associated with which game?
(a) Football   (b) Hockey
(c) Badminton   (d) Tennis

72. 'Play the game in the spirit of game' was said by—
(a) Samaranch   (b) Coubertin
(c) Pt. Nehru   (d) None of these

73. Who among the following was named as 'Wisden's Cricketer'?
(a) Vinod Kambli   (b) Gavaskar
(c) Subash Gupta   (d) Vijay Manjrekar

74. Sports goods are mainly manufactured in—
(a) Mumbai   (b) Lucknow
(c) Jalandhar   (d) Chennai

75. Who among the following players was the first to win Wimbledon Singles title five times in a row?
(a) Pete Sampras   (b) John McEnroe
(c) Boris Becker   (d) Biorn Borg

76. Football (soccer) is said to have originated in—
(a) Russia   (b) England
(c) China   (d) Australia

77. Lawn tennis is said to have originated in—
(a) England   (b) France
(c) Australia   (d) USA

78. In 1984 Olympics, P.T. Usha lost the bronze medal by 1/1000 of a second in—
(*a*) 800 m hurdles   (*b*) 400 m hurdles
(*c*) 100 m relay   (*d*) 200 m relay

79. With which sport is the term 'Chinaman' associated
(*a*) Boxing   (*b*) Yachting
(*c*) Judo   (*d*) Cricket

80. Who among the following is not a spin bowler?
(*a*) Richie Benaud
(*b*) Dennis Lillee
(*c*) B. S. Bedi
(*d*) B. S. Chandrashekar

81. 'The Wisden Trophy' is associated with cricket matches played between?
(*a*) Australia and West Indies
(*b*) India and England
(*c*) England and West Indies
(*d*) New Zealand and Sri Lanka

82. Who was elected 'Champion of Champions' by an international jury of sports writers in Paris in 1989?
(*a*) Florence Griffith Joyner
(*b*) Stefan Edberg
(*c*) Carl Lewis
(*d*) Steffi Graf

83. Who had the distinction of competing in five Olympic games by participating in the 1988 Seoul Olympics?
(*a*) Don Budge
(*b*) Pietro Mennea
(*c*) Maureen Connolly
(*d*) Gelindo Bordin

84. Which sport returned to Olympics in 1988 after 64 years?
(*a*) Judo   (*b*) Tennis
(*c*) Croquet   (*d*) Canoeing

85. Which of the following sports was introduced in the 1988 Seoul Olympic games?
(*a*) Tennis   (*b*) Badminton
(*c*) Table Tennis (*d*) Rowing

86. Which one of the following sports and country of their origin is correctly matched ?
(*a*) Hockey-USA   (*b*) Baseball-Canada
(*c*) Polo-India   (*d*) Cricket-Australia

87. Santosh Trophy is associated with
(*a*) Fotball   (*b*) Hockey
(*c*) Weight Lifting (*d*) Tennis

88. The length of the pitch in the cricket is
(*a*) 22 metres   (*b*) 25 yards
(*c*) 50 feet   (*d*) 22 yards

89. Who is the first Indian to win the Grand Master's Title in Chess
(*a*) D.V. Prasad
(*b*) S.V. Natrajan
(*c*) Vishwanathan Anand
(*d*) R. Ramanathan

90. Which of the following pair is not correct
(*a*) Rangaswami Cup-Hockey
(*b*) Rovers Cup-Football
(*c*) Federation Cup-Badminton
(*d*) Deodhar Trophy-Cricket

ANSWERS

1. (*c*)	2. (*b*)	3. (*a*)	4. (*d*)	5. (*b*)	6. (*c*)	7. (*d*)	8. (*d*)
9. (*a*)	10. (*b*)	11. (*c*)	12. (*c*)	13. (*c*)	14. (*d*)	15. (*d*)	16. (*a*)
17. (*d*)	18. (*b*)	19. (*b*)	20. (*b*)	21. (*d*)	22. (*b*)	23. (*b*)	24. (*c*)
25. (*a*)	26. (*c*)	27. (*d*)	28. (*b*)	29. (*a*)	30. (*c*)	31. (*b*)	32. (*c*)
33. (*c*)	34. (*a*)	35. (*d*)	36. (*b*)	37. (*c*)	38. (*a*)	39. (*d*)	40. (*d*)
41. (*d*)	42. (*c*)	43. (*c*)	44. (*d*)	45. (*a*)	46. (*a*)	47. (*d*)	48. (*b*)
49. (*c*)	50. (*d*)	51. (*b*)	52. (*d*)	53. (*c*)	54. (*b*)	55. (*d*)	56. (*b*)
57. (*b*)	58. (*b*)	59. (*d*)	60. (*a*)	61. (*c*)	62. (*d*)	63. (*c*)	64. (*b*)
65. (*b*)	66. (*b*)	67. (*b*)	68. (*b*)	69. (*b*)	70. (*b*)	71. (*b*)	72. (*c*)
73. (*b*)	74. (*c*)	75. (*d*)	76. (*c*)	77. (*b*)	78. (*b*)	79. (*d*)	80. (*b*)
81. (*c*)	82. (*a*)	83. (*b*)	84. (*b*)	85. (*c*)	86. (*d*)	87. (*a*)	88. (*d*)
89. (*c*)	90. (*c*)						

PRACTICE TEST PAPERS

PAPER SET-1

1. The size of the pool for Water Polo is:
   (a) 30 × 20 yds   (b) 50 × 30 yds
   (c) 25 × 20 yds   (d) 20 × 15 yds

2. What was 'polo' known as, in the ancient times?
   (a) Poona   (b) Ghurasawari
   (c) Chaugan   (d) Chaupar

3. 'Mango Cup" is associated with which game?
   (a) Athletics   (b) Hockey
   (c) Basketball   (d) Football

4. In which International Championship. "Thomas Cup" is given
   (a) Football   (b) Cricket
   (c) Badminton   (d) Tennis

5. 'Gambit' is related to which among the following sports?
   (a) Carrom   (b) Bridge
   (c) Chess   (d) Billiards

6. "Dead Ball" is associated with-
   (a) Football   (b) Handball
   (c) Hockey   (d) Cricket

7. Which of the following is the oldest sport in India?
   (a) Wrestling   (b) Judo
   (c) Boxing   (d) Atya patya

8. The term 'Punter' is associated with the game of:
   (a) Golf   (b) Polo
   (c) Chess   (d) Horse Racing

9. "Bodhidharma", the Buddhist monk is associated with which of the following?
   (a) Yoga   (b) Malkhamb
   (c) Karate   (d) Judo.

10. What is the name of Chinese form of Karate?
    (a) Fu-Jitsu   (b) Kung fu
    (c) Kempo   (d) Paleastra

11. Which sport is known as Payattu in Kerala?
    (a) Kung-fu   (b) Tae-kwando
    (c) Judo   (d) Karate

12. Word "Kho" in the game of "Kho-kho" is from
    (a) Haryanvi language
    (b) Bengali language
    (c) Sindhi language
    (d) Marathi language

13. Word "Kho" in the game of "Kho-kho" means-
    (a) Come and catch
    (b) Go and chase
    (c) Jump
    (d) Run

14. Which ancient game was the forerunner of the modern game of chess?
    (a) Chaturanga   (b) Chaupar
    (c) Kai-danda   (d) Ludo

15. The term 'Grandmaster' is used in which of these games?
    (a) Chess   (b) Judo
    (c) Bridge   (d) Karate

16. The term "Derby" is related with which of the following?
    (a) Polo   (b) Horse Racing
    (c) Racing   (d) Swimming

17. When was the "All India council of Sports" formed?
    (a) 1952   (b) 1953
    (c) 1954   (d) 1955

18. When was the 'National Discipline Scheme' started?
(*a*) 1952   (*b*) 1953
(*c*) 1954   (*d*) 1955

19. When was "School Games Federation of India" formed?
(*a*) 1953   (*b*) 1954
(*c*) 1955   (*d*) 1956

20. Oldest recognised "Polo" club in the world is -
(*a*) The Kolkata Polo Club
(*b*) The Bangalore Polo Club
(*c*) The Delhi Polo Club
(*d*) The Chennai Polo Club

21. What is the ancient name of 'Polo' and who gave it?
(*a*) 'Chaupar' by Rajputs
(*b*) 'Chaugan' by Mughals
(*c*) 'Chaturanga' by Marathas
(*d*) None of the above

22. Which of the following international games originated in India?
(*a*) Volleyball and Kho-Kho
(*b*) Snooker and Badminton
(*c*) Tae-kwando and Judo
(*d*) Judo and Karate

23. Where is the world's highest cricket ground situated?
(*a*) Lords (England)   (*b*) Chail (India)
(*c*) Oval (England)   (*d*) Kolkata (India)

24. Where was the 'School Games Federation of India' (SGFI) formed?
(*a*) Karnataka   (*b*) Mumbai
(*c*) Chennai   (*d*) Kolkata

25. 'Ruud Gullit' is associated with which sports-
(*a*) Volleyball   (*b*) Football
(*c*) Athletics   (*d*) Basketball

26. Karnam Malleshwari weight lifter belongs to which state?
(*a*) Andhra pradesh
(*b*) Arunanchal Pradesh
(*c*) Karnataka
(*d*) Kerala

27. In which state is the 'Britania Amritraj Tennis Academy' situated?
(*a*) Kerala   (*b*) Chennai
(*c*) Karnataka   (*d*) Pondicherry

28. 'Pugilists' are also known as-
(*a*) Athletics   (*b*) Chess Players
(*c*) Boxers   (*d*) Archers

29. Word "Tee off" is associated with which game?
(*a*) Polo   (*b*) Snooker
(*c*) Golf   (*d*) Billiards

30. Which of the following games has the largest playing area?
(*a*) Football   (*b*) Polo
(*c*) Basketball   (*d*) Hockey

31. In which of the following countries is the headquarters of "World Physical Education Congress" located?
(*a*) Japan   (*b*) USA
(*c*) England   (*d*) Germany

32. In the game of Volleyball, the number of players on each side is
(*a*) Eight   (*b*) Five
(*c*) Seven   (*d*) Six

33. 'Mens sana in copore Sano' means-
(*a*) Sound mind in a sound body
(*b*) I think therefore I am
(*c*) Higher, stronger, faster
(*d*) None of the above.

34. India participated in Olympics Games for the first time in
(*a*) 1896   (*b*) 1900
(*c*) 1904   (*d*) 1924

35. 'Sweathling Cup' is associated with which game?
(*a*) Athletics   (*b*) Basketball
(*c*) Table Tennis   (*d*) Badminton

36. With which sport is the 'Oval' stadium associated?
(*a*) Basketball   (*b*) Cricket
(*c*) Hockey   (*d*) Football

37. 'Wembley' Stadium is associated with-
(*a*) Rugby
(*b*) Association Football
(*c*) Hockey
(*d*) Equestrian

38. Which of the following stadiums is associated with boxing?
(*a*) Juba Bharti Kridangam
(*b*) Nehru Stadium
(*c*) National Stadium
(*d*) Yankee Stadium

39. 'Agha Khan' Cup is associated with the game of -
(*a*) Hockey   (*b*) Baseball
(*c*) Basket ball (*d*) Football

40. 'Dr. B. C. Roy' trophy is associated with the game of -
(*a*) Kho-Kho   (*b*) Hockey
(*c*) Kabaddi   (*d*) Football

41. 'Lady Ratan Tata' trophy is associated with the game of -
(*a*) Kho-Kho   (*b*) Volleyball
(*c*) Hockey   (*d*) Football

42. 'Rovers Cup' is associated with the game of-
(*a*) Football   (*b*) Volleyball
(*c*) Hockey   (*d*) Kabaddi

43. "Scindia Gold Cup" is associated with the game-
(*a*) Hockey   (*b*) Basketball
(*c*) Kho-kho   (*d*) Cricket

44. 'Thomas cup' is associated with-
(*a*) Badminton (men)
(*b*) Badminton (women)
(*c*) Table Tennis (men)
(*d*) Table Tennis (women)

45. 'Uber Cup' is associated with-
(*a*) Table Tennis (men)
(*b*) Table Tennis (women)
(*c*) Badminton (men)
(*d*) Badminton (women)

46. 'Arthur Ashe' was associated with which sport?
(*a*) Badminton   (*b*) Tennis
(*c*) Athletics   (*d*) Basketball

47. The "Cagers" are
(*a*) Hockey players
(*b*) Basketball players
(*c*) Football players
(*d*) Volleyball players

48. 'Antenna' is used in -
(*a*) Football   (*b*) Basketball
(*c*) Handball   (*d*) Volleyball

49. The term "Yorker" is used in-
(*a*) Football   (*b*) Table Tennis
(*c*) Tennis   (*d*) Cricket

50. The name of "Tiger Woods" is associated with-
(*a*) Tennis   (*b*) Boxing
(*c*) Hockey   (*d*) Golf

ANSWERS

1. (*a*)	2. (*c*)	3. (*b*)	4. (*c*)	5. (*c*)	6. (*d*)	7. (*a*)	8. (*d*)
9. (*c*)	10. (*c*)	11. (*d*)	12. (*b*)	13. (*b*)	14. (*a*)	15. (*a*)	16. (*b*)
17. (*c*)	18. (*c*)	19. (*b*)	20. (*a*)	21. (*b*)	22. (*b*)	23. (*b*)	24. (*b*)
25. (*b*)	26. (*a*)	27. (*b*)	28. (*c*)	29. (*c*)	30. (*b*)	31. (*b*)	32. (*d*)
33. (*a*)	34. (*b*)	35. (*c*)	36. (*b*)	37. (*b*)	38. (*d*)	39. (*a*)	40. (*d*)
41. (*c*)	42. (*a*)	43. (*a*)	44. (*a*)	45. (*d*)	46. (*b*)	47. (*b*)	48. (*d*)
49. (*d*)	50. (*d*)						

PAPER SET-2

1. Match List-I (Trophies) with List-II (Sports) and select the correct answer using the codes given below the Lists:

List-I (Trophies)	*List-II (Sports)*
A. Swathling Cup	1. Basketball
B. Obaidullah Gold Cup	2. Football
C. Merdeka Cup	3. Hockey
D. S.M. Arjuna Roya Trophy	4. Table Tennis

Codes:

	(A)	(B)	(C)	(D)
(a)	4	1	2	3
(b)	1	4	3	2
(c)	3	4	1	2
(d)	4	3	2	1

2. During training the sensation of vomiting is caused due to
(a) Carbon dioxide
(b) Adrenaline
(c) More Oxygen intake
(d) Accumulation of Lactic acid

3. The first member of International Olympic Committee from India was
(a) Sir Dorabji Tata
(b) Raja Bhalinder Singh
(c) G.D. Sondhi
(d) P.M. Joseph

4. Viswanathan Anand's name is associated with:
(a) Cricket
(b) Chess
(c) Football
(d) Tennis

5. When were the modern Olympic Games first held?
(a) 1876
(b) 1887
(c) 1895
(d) 1896

6. With which game is Geet Sethi Associated?
(a) Basketball
(b) Snooker
(c) Chess
(d) Tennis

7. Name of the German game on which the modern basketball has been based is-
(a) Handball
(b) Korfball
(c) Hockey
(d) Volleyball

8. Which of the following stadium was known as Irwin Amphitheater?
(a) National Stadium, Delhi
(b) Yuba Bharti Kridangam, Kolkata
(c) Jawahar Lal Nehru Stadium, Delhi
(d) None of the above

9. Sports Authority of India was formed in-
(a) 1983
(b) 1984
(c) 1985
(d) 1986

10. 'Michael Ferriera' is associated with the game of -
(a) Snooker
(b) Billiards
(c) Golf
(d) Equestrian

11. 'Ranga Swami Cup' is associated with the game of-
(a) Hockey
(b) Football
(c) Volleyball
(d) Kho-Kho

12. 'Cue' is associated with the game of-
(a) Bridge
(b) Hockey
(c) Billiards
(d) Golf

13. Which style of Kabaddi is officially recognized?
(a) National
(b) Samvahini
(c) Sanjeevani
(d) Circle

14. The term 'caddy' is associated with-
(a) Golf
(b) Billiards
(c) Bridge
(d) Snooker

15. Who among the following became the first Indian to win a grand slam title?
(a) Leander Paes
(b) Mahesh Bhupati
(c) Both (a) and (b)
(d) None of the above

16. The First Olympic Games were held in Olympia (Greece) in the year:
(a) 300 BC
(b) 872 BC
(c) 776 BC
(d) 205 AD

17. How many players are there in each side in the game of Netball?
(a) 7
(b) 6
(c) 9
(d) 11

18. Yonex Cup is associated with
(a) Basket ball
(b) Volleyball
(c) Lawn Tennis
(d) Badminton

19. 'Martina Hingis' belongs to
(*a*) Canada   (*b*) USA
(*c*) England   (*d*) Switzerland

20. 'Uber Cup' is associated with which of the following:
(*a*) Tennis   (*b*) Badminton
(*c*) Chess   (*d*) Cricket

21. Who was the captain of the Indian team which played its first official Cricket Test Series against England in 1932?
(*a*) The Maharaja of Porbandar
(*b*) Ranjit Singhji
(*c*) The Yuvraj of Patiala
(*d*) The Raja of Baroda

22. Number of players on each side of Volleyball, Basketball and Baseball game are respectively.
(*a*) 5, 6, 9   (*b*) 6, 9, 5
(*c*) 6, 5, 9   (*d*) 6, 5, 7

23. Arjuna Award has been instituted for outstanding contribution in the field of
(*a*) social service
(*b*) literature
(*c*) games and sports
(*d*) art and music

24. Weight training method was started by German gymnastic coach in the year
(*a*) 1810   (*b*) 1812
(*c*) 1820   (*d*) 1816

25. Olympic symbol represents
(*a*) Sporting friendship of all people
(*b*) The five continents only
(*c*) Both (a) & (b) are true
(*d*) None of these

26. In the word 'Judo', 'Ju' and 'do' means-
(*a*) Gentle and giving the way
(*b*) Japan and giving the way
(*c*) Let go and easy
(*d*) None of the above

27. What is the motto of Judo-
(*a*) Maximum effort
(*b*) Minimum effort
(*c*) Maximum efficiency with minimum effort
(*d*) None of the above.

28. Which of the following hosted the first Afro-Asian Games in 2001?
(*a*) New Delhi   (*b*) Kathmandu
(*c*) Paris   (*d*) Mumbai

29. The Olympic Motto is
(*a*) Health is wealth
(*b*) Promote Universal brotherhood
(*c*) Faster, higher, stronger
(*d*) Excellence is the goal

30. The first woman in the history of US Open Championship to have played 100 matches, is:
(*a*) Martina Navaratilova
(*b*) Chris Evert
(*c*) Steffi Graf
(*d*) Helena Sukova

31. After how many years Thomas Cup and Uber Cup tournaments in Badminton held?
(*a*) Bi annually   (*b*) Tri annually
(*c*) Annually   (*d*) Quarterly

32. Which Indian was the first to win world title in Badminton?
(*a*) Prakash Padukon (*b*) Syed Modi
(*c*) Aparna Popat (*d*) P. Gopichand

33. Which of the following universities won the MAKA trophy for maximum number of times?
(*a*) Punjab University
(*b*) Delhi University
(*c*) Guru Nanak Dev University
(*d*) Calicut University

34. Which of the following is the highest award in sports in the world?
(*a*) Arjuna Award
(*b*) Olympic order
(*c*) Padma shree
(*d*) Jesse Owens Award.

35. In the olympic events, the gold medal awarded for the first place has the following ratio of gold.
(*a*) Silver gilt with 8 grams of fine gold
(*b*) Silver gilt with 6 grams of fine gold
(*c*) Silver gilt with 7 grams of fine gold
(*d*) Silver gilt with 10 grams of fine gold

36. Which of the following grand slam tournament starts on the first day of every new year?
  (*a*) French Open (*b*) Australian Open
  (*c*) US Open (*d*) Wimbledon

37. Name the first Indian (male) to swim across the English Channel?
  (*a*) Thomas Cook (*b*) Khazan Singh
  (*c*) Mihir Sen (*d*) None

38. Who was the first Indian women to swim across he English Channel?
  (*a*) P. T. Usha (*b*) Shiny Wilson
  (*c*) Arti Shah (*d*) Bhanu Sachdeva

39. 'FINA' is associated with?
  (*a*) Chess (*b*) Volleyball
  (*c*) Swimming (*d*) Billiards

40. Who was the first Indian male Athlete to win the Arjuna Award?
  (*a*) V. S. Chauhan (*b*) Milkha Singh
  (*c*) G. S. Randhawa (*d*) Gulab Chand

41. What is the ladies equivalent to Davis Cup?
  (*a*) Mardeka Cup (*b*) Chancellor's Cup
  (*c*) Federation Cup (*d*) Wills Cup

42. Who was the first black player to have won Wimbeldon singles title?
  (*a*) Tiger woods (*b*) Michael Johnson
  (*c*) Arthur Ashe (*d*) None of the above

43. Who made it to the Wimbeldon semi finals twice in 1960?
  (*a*) Ramesh Krishnan
  (*b*) Ramanathan Krishnan
  (*c*) Vijay Amritraj
  (*d*) Ajay Amritraj

44. IBF (International Badminton Federation) was found in the year
  (*a*) 1934 (*b*) 1937

  (*c*) 1936 (*d*) 1935

45. Who among the following was the first Indian to win the Wimbeldon and French open Junior Championships-
  (*a*) Ramesh Krishnan
  (*b*) Ramanathan Krishnan
  (*c*) Vijay Amritraj
  (*d*) Mahesh Bhupati

46. Who among the following was Steffi Graf's coach when she was young?
  (*a*) Her father (*b*) Her mother
  (*c*) Her sister (*d*) None

47. What is the official name of Davis Cup?
  (*a*) International Lawn Tennis Challenge Trophy
  (*b*) Mardeka Cup
  (*c*) Uber Cup
  (*d*) Federation Cup.

48. Who among the following was the first unseeded player to win Wimbledon?
  (*a*) Pat Cash (*b*) Pete Sampras
  (*c*) Boris Becker (*d*) Ivan Lendle

49. When did India make her debut in Davis Cup?
  (*a*) 1918 (*b*) 1919
  (*c*) 1920 (*d*) 1921

50. Which of the following constitutes a Grand Slam?
  (*a*) US Open, French Open, Wimbledon, Australian Open
  (*b*) Italian Open, US Open, Wimbledon, Australian Open
  (*c*) Italian Open, US Open, Grand Slam Cup, Australian Open
  (*d*) Italian Open, US Open, Grand Slam Cup and Federation Cup.

ANSWERS

1. (*d*)	2. (*d*)	3. (*a*)	4. (*b*)	5. (*d*)	6. (*b*)	7. (*b*)	8. (*a*)
9. (*a*)	10. (*b*)	11. (*a*)	12. (*c*)	13. (*c*)	14. (*a*)	15. (*b*)	16. (*c*)
17. (*a*)	18. (*d*)	19. (*d*)	20. (*b*)	21. (*a*)	22. (*c*)	23. (*c*)	24. (*b*)
25. (*c*)	26. (*a*)	27. (*c*)	28. (*a*)	29. (*c*)	30. (*b*)	31. (*b*)	32. (*a*)
33. (*c*)	34. (*b*)	35. (*b*)	36. (*b*)	37. (*c*)	38. (*c*)	39. (*c*)	40. (*c*)
41. (*c*)	42. (*c*)	43. (*b*)	44. (*a*)	45. (*a*)	46. (*a*)	47. (*a*)	48. (*c*)
49. (*d*)	50. (*a*)						

PAPER SET-3

1. Which two teams compete for the Raghuramaiah Trophy?
   - (a) Actors and politicians
   - (b) Lok Sabha and Rajya Sabha
   - (c) Cricketers and Actors
   - (d) Veterans and current players

2. Which bowler has the First World Cup hat trick?
   - (a) Srinath
   - (b) Kapil Dev
   - (c) Chetan Sharma
   - (d) Manoj Prabhakar

3. When and where was the first World Cup Cricket tournament held?
   - (a) 1979, England
   - (b) 1975, England
   - (c) 1983, England
   - (d) None of the above

4. What was the name of the first World Cup?
   - (a) Wills World Cup
   - (b) Pepsi World Cup
   - (c) ICC Trophy
   - (d) Prudential Cup

5. Which Indian sportsman is known as Hockey Wizard throughout the world?
   - (a) A.B. Subbaiah
   - (b) Jude Felix
   - (c) Dhyan Chand
   - (d) Ajitpal Singh

6. All India Council of Sport was formed in
   - (a) 1954
   - (b) 1953
   - (c) 1952
   - (d) 1951

7. Who was the first Indian to make a test century in Indian cricket?
   - (a) Binu Mankad
   - (b) C.K. Naidu
   - (c) Lala Amarnath
   - (d) Mansoor Ali Padaudi

8. Aim of sports training is
   - (a) improvement of physical fitness
   - (b) imrovement of technical skills
   - (c) improvement of tactical efficiency
   - (d) improvement of sports performance

9. In which year the Olympic Games were revived at Athens?
   - (a) 1905
   - (b) 1856
   - (c) 1801
   - (d) 1896

10. Sport is a shortened form of "disport" originated from "des-porto". What does 'des-proto' mean literally?
    - (a) Carry on
    - (b) Carry away
    - (c) Support
    - (d) Get along

11. 'Baseball' is the national game of-
    - (a) Canada
    - (b) France
    - (c) USA
    - (d) England

12. In which country is the Sumo wrestling generally practiced?
    - (a) China
    - (b) Japan
    - (c) South Korea
    - (d) North Korea

13. Which game was once known as 'ping pong'?
    - (a) Tennis
    - (b) Volleyball
    - (c) Table Tennis
    - (d) Basketball

14. Which of the following is the international volleyball controlling authority ?
    - (a) VFI
    - (b) FIVB
    - (c) FILA
    - (d) FITA

15. Baron Pierre de Coubertin father of the modern Olympic Games, belongs to:
    - (a) Greece
    - (b) USA
    - (c) Italy
    - (d) France

16. Which of the following is the Indoor Stadium for swimming in Delhi?
    - (a) National Stadium
    - (b) Indira Gandhi Stadium
    - (c) Talkatora Stadium
    - (d) Ambedkar Stadium

17. For excellence in which sport is the 'Eklavya' award given?
    - (a) Malkhamb
    - (b) Kabaddi
    - (c) Wrestling
    - (d) Kho-kho

18. 'Rani Laxmi Award' is given for outstanding performance in the sport of-
    - (a) Judo
    - (b) Kabaddi
    - (c) Kho-kho
    - (d) Tae-kwando

19. In which of the following sport is the largest trophy presented in the world?
    (*a*) Car racing   (*b*) Chess
    (*c*) Polo   (*d*) Equestrian

20. "Googly" is associated with:
    (*a*) Cricket   (*b*) Table-Tennis
    (*c*) Hockey   (*d*) Billiards

21. B. L. Gupta Trophy is associated with-
    (*a*) Inter University championships
    (*b*) International championships
    (*c*) National championships
    (*d*) S. A. F. Games.

22. Which of the following is the highest award in field of sports
    (*a*) Maharaja Ranjit Singh Award
    (*b*) Arjuna Award
    (*c*) Eklavya Award
    (*d*) Vishwamitra Award

23. The name 'Asian Games' to 'Asiatic Games' was proposed by-
    (*a*) Dr. B. R. Ambedkar
    (*b*) Pt. J. L. Nehru
    (*c*) G. D. Sondhi
    (*d*) Maharaja Patiala

24. In which game is the term 'bully' used?
    (*a*) Football   (*b*) Hockey
    (*c*) Volleyball   (*d*) Cricket

25. Which of the following is the highest sports award given by Punjab state-
    (*a*) Eklavya Award
    (*b*) Maharaja Patiala Award
    (*c*) Maharaja Ranjit Singh Award
    (*d*) Guru Govind Singh Award

26. With which game are the terms bull's eye, muzzle and plug associated?
    (*a*) Shooting   (*b*) Solitaire
    (*c*) Billiards   (*d*) Rowing

27. Cricket was an Olympic event at which of the following Olympics?
    (*a*) London, 1908   (*b*) Amsterdam, 1928
    (*c*) Paris, 1900   (*d*) Melbourne, 1956

28. The top All-India soccer tournament for schools is known as -
    (*a*) Subroto Mukharjee Cup
    (*b*) Durand Cup
    (*c*) Federation Cup
    (*d*) Santosh Trophy

29. Who was the driving force behind Commonwealth Games?
    (*a*) G. D. Sondhi
    (*b*) Bobby Robinson
    (*c*) Juan Antonio Samaranch
    (*d*) Mark Robinson

30. In which year were the first Common Wealth Games held?
    (*a*) 1929   (*b*) 1930
    (*c*) 1931   (*d*) 1932

31. The modern olympics were hold outside United States and Europe for the first time in
    (*a*) 1950   (*b*) 1940
    (*c*) 1956   (*d*) 1944

32. Which is the America's highest Athletics Award?
    (*a*) Jesse Ownes Award
    (*b*) Michael Johnson Award
    (*c*) Carl Lewis Award
    (*d*) None of the above

33. Who is the first Indian to take a hat trick in an international test?
    (*a*) Kapil Dev
    (*b*) Jasu Patel
    (*c*) Harbhajan Singh
    (*d*) B.S. Chandrashekhar

34. What is the amount of money that is given to the winner of Arjuna Award-
    (*a*) ₹ 5,00,000   (*b*) ₹ 50,000
    (*c*) ₹ 2,00,000   (*d*) None of the above

35. What is the amount of money that is given to winner of Dronacharya Award-
    (*a*) $ 75,000   (*b*) ₹ 2,50,000
    (*c*) ₹ 80,000   (*d*) ₹ 5,00,000

36. In which year was the 'Rajiv Gandhi Khel Ratna' award instituted?
    (*a*) 1990-91   (*b*) 1991-92
    (*c*) 1992-93   (*d*) 1993-94

37. Dronacharya Award was constituted in the year-
    (*a*) 1983   (*b*) 1984
    (*c*) 1985   (*d*) 1986

38. The final recommendation for Arjuna Awards is given by-
- (*a*)   Ministry of H. R. D.
- (*b*)   The Prime Minister of India
- (*c*)   State Government
- (*d*)   The President of India

39. How many countries participated in the first Asian Games held in Delhi-
- (*a*)   10
- (*b*)   11
- (*c*)   12
- (*d*)   13

40. Who was the first Asian to become member of I.O.C.
- (*a*)   Pt. Jawahar Lal Nehru
- (*b*)   Dr. Rajendra Prasad
- (*c*)   Jigaro Kano
- (*d*)   Smt. Benazir Bhutto

41. Who was declared by wisden as "The Best Indian Bowler of the Century" (20th Century)
- (*a*)   Kapil Dev
- (*b*)   B.S. Chandrashekhar
- (*c*)   B.S. Bedi
- (*d*)   Subhash V. Gupte

42. What was the old name of Commonwealth Games?
- (*a*)   The Empire games
- (*b*)   The British Empire games
- (*c*)   The British games
- (*d*)   None of the above

43. In which of the following events in the first Commonwealth Games, were women allowed to participate?
- (*a*)   Gymnastics
- (*b*)   Bowling
- (*c*)   Swimming
- (*d*)   Table Tennis

44. Who inaugurated the first Asian Games?
- (*a*)   Dr. Rajendra Prasad
- (*b*)   Maharaja Patiala
- (*c*)   G. D. Sondhi
- (*d*)   Pt. Jawaharlal Nehru

45. Which country is coined as the cradle of chess?
- (*a*)   Japan
- (*b*)   Malaysia
- (*c*)   China
- (*d*)   India

46. The term 'Third Eye' is associated with:
- (*a*)   Billiards
- (*b*)   Shooting
- (*c*)   Archery
- (*d*)   Cricket

47. "Jab" and "Parry" are terms used in which sport?
- (*a*)   Wrestling
- (*b*)   Boxing
- (*c*)   Billiards
- (*d*)   Weightlifting

48. The term "deuce" is associated with which of the following two games?
- (*a*)   Basketball and Badminton
- (*b*)   Badminton and Tennis
- (*c*)   Volleyball and Tennis
- (*d*)   Cricket and Badminton

49. When was the MAKA Trophy instituted?
- (*a*)   1958-59
- (*b*)   1959-60
- (*c*)   1960-61
- (*d*)   1956-57

50. Who among the following is not a recipient of Arjun and Dronachary awards both?
- (*a*)   Syed Naimiddin
- (*b*)   A. Ramana Rao
- (*c*)   M. Shyam Sunder Rao
- (*d*)   Milkha Singh

ANSWERS

1. (*b*)	2. (*c*)	3. (*b*)	4. (*d*)	5. (*c*)	6. (*a*)	7. (*a*)	8. (*d*)
9. (*d*)	10. (*b*)	11. (*c*)	12. (*b*)	13. (*c*)	14. (*b*)	15. (*d*)	16. (*c*)
17. (*d*)	18. (*c*)	19. (*c*)	20. (*a*)	21. (*a*)	22. (*b*)	23. (*b*)	24. (*b*)
25. (*c*)	26. (*a*)	27. (*d*)	28. (*a*)	29. (*b*)	30. (*b*)	31. (*c*)	32. (*a*)
33. (*c*)	34. (*a*)	35. (*d*)	36. (*d*)	37. (*c*)	38. (*d*)	39. (*b*)	40. (*c*)
41. (*a*)	42. (*b*)	43. (*c*)	44. (*d*)	45. (*b*)	46. (*d*)	47. (*b*)	48. (*b*)
49. (*d*)	50. (*d*)						

PAPER SET-4

1. Who among the following is the first women Asian Gold medalist in athletics?
   (*a*) M. D. Valasamma
   (*b*) Rosa Kutti
   (*c*) Kamaljeet Sandhu
   (*d*) P. T. Usha

2. Where were the first SAF games held?
   (*a*) Kathmandu   (*b*) Malaysia
   (*c*) Delhi   (*d*) Pakistan

3. Which city hosted the first National Games?
   (*a*) Kolkata   (*b*) New Delhi
   (*c*) Chennai   (*d*) Karnataka

4. In the game of Baseball, distance between each base in a Diamond shaped ground is:
   (*a*) 56 ft   (*b*) 80 ft
   (*c*) 72 ft   (*d*) 90 ft

5. 'Helms' award was confirmed on-
   (*a*) K. D. Singh 'Babu'
   (*b*) Balbir Singh
   (*c*) Roop Singh
   (*d*) L. Claudius

6. The trophy awarded to men's team in National Hockey Champion is named as-
   (*a*) Nehru Trophy
   (*b*) Rangaswami Cup
   (*c*) Ramaswami Cup
   (*d*) Dhyan Chand Trophy

7. The term Spot-Stroke is used in-
   (*a*) Golf   (*b*) Hockey
   (*c*) Billiards   (*d*) Swimming

8. Term "Free Throw" is used in -
   (*a*) Wrestling   (*b*) Soccer
   (*c*) Volleyball   (*d*) Basketball

9. The term 'Nine penal offences' is associated with-
   (*a*) Hockey   (*b*) Soccer
   (*c*) Judo   (*d*) Tae kwon do

10. When was the game of Football included in the Olympics?
   (*a*) 1928   (*b*) 1900
   (*c*) 1932   (*d*) 1996

11. When and where was FIFA formed?
   (*a*) 1900 in USA   (*b*) 1900 in UK
   (*c*) 1904 in Paris   (*d*) 1904 in Rome

12. When did India first participate as a Football team in the Olympics?
   (*a*) 1948   (*b*) 1952
   (*c*) 1956   (*d*) 1928

13. Free hand exercises done generally in group are called
   (*a*) Circuit training
   (*b*) Callisthenics
   (*c*) Drill and marching
   (*d*) Weight training

14. India's national game is:
   (*a*) Football   (*b*) Cricket
   (*c*) Tennis   (*d*) Hockey

15. Where was the first World Cup Football held?
   (*a*) Uruguay   (*b*) France
   (*c*) Canada   (*d*) Brazil

16. Which of the following is against the principles of organization?
   (*a*) Delegation of power
   (*b*) Proper decentralization
   (*c*) Overlapping of authority
   (*d*) Proper communication

17. In which of the following World Cup Soccer tournaments did maximum number of nations participate?
   (*a*) Uruguay 1930   (*b*) France 98
   (*c*) Both (*a*) and (*b*)   (*d*) None of the above

18. Getting the right facts to the right people at the right time in the right way is called
   (*a*) Game management
   (*b*) Leadership in sport
   (*c*) Motivation in sport
   (*d*) Public relations in sport

19. Davis Cup is associated with the sport of
   (*a*) Tennis   (*b*) Football
   (*c*) Cricket   (*d*) Hockey

20. Which country won the first World Cup Football tournament held at Uruguay?
(*a*) Argentina   (*b*) Brazil
(*c*) Germany   (*d*) France

21. In which game pressure training method was first used?
(*a*) Hockey   (*b*) Football
(*c*) Volleyball   (*d*) Basketball

22. The term 'breast stroke' is associated with:
(*a*) Skating   (*b*) Croquet
(*c*) Swimming   (*d*) Rifle Shooting

23. In which Olympics was the women's Football included for the first time?
(*a*) 1988, Seoul   (*b*) 1992, Barcelona
(*c*) 1996, Atlanta   (*d*) 1984, Los Angles

24. With which game is Jehangir Khan associated:
(*a*) Boxing   (*b*) Squash
(*c*) Hockey   (*d*) Cricket

25. The term 'Bogey' is associated with
(*a*) Tennis   (*b*) Golf
(*c*) Baseball   (*d*) Chess

26. India's first National Cricket Academy has been established in:
(*a*) Hyderabad   (*b*) Pune
(*c*) Bangalore   (*d*) None of these

27. What is the National Game of the USA?
(*a*) Cricket   (*b*) Baseball
(*c*) Soccer   (*d*) Billiards

28. Who introduced the game of football in India?
(*a*) British   (*b*) Germans
(*c*) Americans   (*d*) Greek

29. Who among the following has not received the Arjuna Award in football?
(*a*) Jarnail Singh
(*b*) Shyam Sunder Rao
(*c*) Manjit Singh
(*d*) Arung Gosh

30. Which of the following cups/ trophies is not related to Football?
(*a*) Subroto Cup   (*b*) World Cup
(*c*) Durand Cup   (*d*) Wills Cup

31. India was the winner of Olympic Gold Medal in Hockey from-
(*a*) 1920-1948   (*b*) 1928-1956
(*c*) 1896-1928   (*d*) 1956-1964

32. India regained top position in Hockey in which Olympics?
(*a*) 1996   (*b*) 1958
(*c*) 1964   (*d*) 1928

33. What was 'Dhyanchand's' rank in the Army?
(*a*) Major   (*b*) Lieutenant
(*c*) Captain   (*d*) Lance Naik

34. At what position 'Dhyanchand' used to play?
(*a*) Center half
(*b*) Center forward
(*c*) Full back
(*d*) Goal Keeper

35. What was the nickname of Indian legend hockey player 'Dhyanchand'?
(*a*) 'Hockey wizard'
(*b*) 'Hockey Man'
(*c*) 'Little Master'
(*d*) 'Hockey Jockey'

36. In which year was the first World Cup Hockey tournament held?
(*a*) 1970   (*b*) 1971
(*c*) 1972   (*d*) 1973

37. At the time of inception, the World cup Hockey tournament used to take place-
(*a*) Once in three years
(*b*) Once in two years
(*c*) Twice a year
(*d*) Once in four years

38. Which of the following international tennis tournaments is held on grass court?
(*a*) US Open   (*b*) Wimbledon
(*c*) French Open   (*d*) Australian Open

39. Which country is the birth place of Modern Hockey?
(*a*) India   (*b*) China
(*c*) USA   (*d*) England

40. Goran Ivanisevic is associated with:
(*a*) Hockey   (*b*) Lawn Tennis
(*c*) Golf   (*d*) Badminton

41. In which year was Hockey introduced in the Olympics?
 (*a*) 1908, London (*b*) 1920, Antwerp
 (*c*) 1936, Berlin (*d*) 1956, Melbourne

42. When was Hockey introduced in the Asian Games?
 (*a*) 1951, Delhi (*b*) 1954, Manila
 (*c*) 1958, Tokyo (*d*) 1962, Jakarta

43. 'Merdeka Cup' is associated with..............
 (*a*) Golf (*b*) Football
 (*c*) Squash (*d*) Hockey

44. The "Dronacharya Award" is associated with:
 (*a*) Eminent Surgeons
 (*b*) Sport Coaches
 (*c*) Famous Artists
 (*d*) Expert Engineers

45. Which village in Punjab is called the Nursery of Hockey?
 (*a*) Rajpura (*b*) Patiala
 (*c*) Gurdaspur (*d*) Sansarpur

46. Who among the following is not a recipient of Arjuna Award in Hockey?
 (*a*) Mukesh Kumar
 (*b*) Rupa Saini
 (*c*) Om Prakash
 (*d*) Dhanraj Pillay

47. Which Cricketer nicknamed "Jumbo"?
 (*a*) Venkatesh Prasad
 (*b*) Anil Kumble
 (*c*) Gleen McGrath
 (*d*) Shane Warne

48. Who among the following has become the first woman in the world to swim across seven seas?
 (*a*) Shikha Tandon
 (*b*) Bula Chowdhury
 (*c*) Amanda Beard
 (*d*) Arti Saha

49. Which country won the first World Cup Hockey tournament?
 (*a*) India (*b*) Pakistan
 (*c*) Holland (*d*) Germany

50. What is the diameter of a golf hole?
 (*a*) 5.5" (*b*) 4.5"
 (*c*) 3.5" (*d*) 7.5"

ANSWERS

1. (*c*)	2. (*c*)	3. (*b*)	4. (*d*)	5. (*a*)	6. (*b*)	7. (*c*)	8. (*d*)
9. (*b*)	10. (*b*)	11. (*c*)	12. (*a*)	13. (*b*)	14. (*d*)	15. (*a*)	16. (*c*)
17. (*b*)	18. (*b*)	19. (*a*)	20. (*c*)	21. (*b*)	22. (*c*)	23. (*c*)	24. (*b*)
25. (*b*)	26. (*c*)	27. (*b*)	28. (*a*)	29. (*b*)	30. (*b*)	31. (*b*)	32. (*c*)
33. (*a*)	34. (*b*)	35. (*a*)	36. (*b*)	37. (*b*)	38. (*b*)	39. (*d*)	40. (*b*)
41. (*a*)	42. (*c*)	43. (*b*)	44. (*b*)	45. (*d*)	46. (*c*)	47. (*c*)	48. (*b*)
49. (*b*)	50. (*b*)						

PAPER SET-5

1. The term "Diamond" is associated with the game of:
   (a) Bridge   (b) Baseball
   (c) Basketball   (d) Billiards

2. The term 'athwart' in sailing means:
   (a) in with the wind
   (b) into the breeze
   (c) across
   (d) downward

3. What is the distance of running in a marathon race?
   (a) 26 miles
   (b) 26 miles 405 yeards
   (c) 26 miles 385 yards
   (d) 26 miles 180 yards

4. Sportsmen and the sports in which they attained worldwide distinction are listed below. Which one of the following pairs is not correct?
   (a) KD Singh – Hockey
   (b) Don Brademan – Cricket
   (c) Billie Jean King – Tennis
   (d) Pele – Chess

5. Prince of Wales Cup is associated with the game of :
   (a) Volleyball   (b) Basketball
   (c) Polo   (d) Golf

6. The weight of the cricket ball is approximately:
   (a) 3 oz   (b) 4 oz
   (c) 5 oz   (d) 6 oz

7. Dick Fosbury, who invented the 'Fosbury Flop' style in high jump event belongs to-
   (a) USA   (b) England
   (c) Russia   (d) Ukraine

8. 'Synthetic track' in athletic was used for the first time in-
   (a) 1968 (Mexico Olympics)
   (b) 1948 (London Olympics)
   (c) 1896 (Athens Olympics)
   (d) 1996 (Atlanta Olympics)

9. First World Cup Athletics Championships was held at -
   (a) Pusan   (b) Helsinki
   (c) Kathamandu   (d) Stuttguart

10. National sport of Australia is:
    (a) Football   (b) Cricket
    (c) Hockey   (d) Tennis

11. What is the length of a cricket pitch?
    (a) 22 feet   (b) 34 feet
    (c) 22 yards   (d) 54 feet

12. I.A.A.F. stands for -
    (a) International Amateur Athletics Federation
    (b) Indian Amateur Athletics Federation
    (c) Indian Association of Athletics and Field events
    (d) None of the above

13. I.A.A.F. was formed in -
    (a) 1911   (b) 1912
    (c) 1913   (d) 1914

14. Who was the first athlete to be awarded Padamshree Award?
    (a) P. T. Usha
    (b) Milkha Singh
    (c) G. S. Randhawa
    (d) V. S. Chauhan

15. Who among the following was the first Indian women athlete to represent India in the Olympics?
    (a) P. T. Usha
    (b) Mary D'souza
    (c) M. D. Valasamma
    (d) Shiny Wilson

16. Who was the first women athlete to be awarded the Arjuna Award?
    (a) Mary D'Souza   (b) Stephie D'Souza
    (c) P. T. Usha   (d) Shiny Wilson

17. What is the national sport of Japan?
    (a) Ju-Jitsu   (b) Mikado
    (c) Karate   (d) Sumo

18. When was the A.A.F.I. formed?
(*a*) 1943   (*b*) 1945
(*c*) 1946   (*d*) 1947

19. 'Baulk' term is associated with:
(*a*) Golf   (*b*) Boxing
(*c*) Basketball   (*d*) Billiard

20. Which of the following Indian women athlete was the first to reach the finals of Olympic Games?
(*a*) P. T. Usha   (*b*) Shiny Wilson
(*c*) M. D. Wilson   (*d*) Rosa Kutty

21. 'Eagle' is a term used in:
(*a*) Golf
(*b*) Tennis
(*c*) Billiards
(*d*) Volleyball

22. To which village in Kerala does P. T. Usha belong-
(*a*) Trivandrum   (*b*) Payyoli
(*c*) Guntur   (*d*) None of the above

23. Sullivan Trophy is awarded to-
(*a*) The best Amateur Athlete of America
(*b*) The best Amateur Athlete of England
(*c*) The best Amateur Athlete of Canada
(*d*) The best Amateur Athlete of Greece

24. In which Olympics did India sent its athletes for the first time?
(*a*) 1924, Paris   (*b*) 1948, London
(*c*) 1952, Helsinki   (*d*) 1920, Antwerp

25. Who was the first Indian women athlete to win a gold medal in the Asian Games?
(*a*) Shiny Wilson
(*b*) Kamaljit Sandhu
(*c*) P. T. Usha
(*d*) Rosa Kutty

26. Whose athletic autobiography is named 'Inside Track'?
(*a*) Jesse Owens   (*b*) Carl Lewis
(*c*) Merlene Ottey   (*d*) P. T. Usha

27. 'Queensberry Rules' is the name given to the rules in:
(*a*) Cricket   (*b*) Tennis
(*c*) Boxing   (*d*) Hockey

28. In which year was the first World Track and Field Championship held?
(*a*) 1981   (*b*) 1982
(*c*) 1983   (*d*) 1984

29. India's National Cricket Championship is:
(*a*) Ranji Trophy
(*b*) Duleep Trophy
(*c*) Irani Trophy
(*d*) Sheesh Mahal Trophy

30. What is the association between 'Scissor' and 'A Half Nelson'?
(*a*) They are both terms used in wrestling
(*b*) They are the vital tools of a dressmaker
(*c*) Scissors are used to execute a standard trick in magic shows-A Half Nelson
(*d*) They are famous shops near Trafalgar Square

31. In which sport do you have bails?
(*a*) Squash   (*b*) Cricket
(*c*) Ice hockey   (*d*) Polo

32. When were the earliest written laws of cricket made?
(*a*) 1556   (*b*) 1700
(*c*) 1744   (*d*) 1771

33. In which country did the game of Volleyball originate?
(*a*) USA   (*b*) Japan
(*c*) Russia   (*d*) Australia

34. In which year was the game of volleyball invented?
(*a*) 1895   (*b*) 1896
(*c*) 1897   (*d*) 1898

35. Who invented the game of volleyball?
(*a*) William Morgan
(*b*) C. A. Bucher
(*c*) J. f. Williams
(*d*) James Nai Smith

36. Who among the following is not an Arjuna Awardee in volleyball?
(*a*) Shyam Sunder Rao
(*b*) Ramana Rao
(*c*) Dalel Singh
(*d*) Shakti Singh

37. Which of the following cups/ trophies is not associated with the game of Volleyball?
    (*a*) Super Challenge Cup
    (*b*) Federation Cup
    (*c*) World Cup
    (*d*) European Cup

38. 'Smashing' in volleyball is also known as
    (*a*) Lifting   (*b*) Spiking
    (*c*) Servicing   (*d*) Blocking

39. Subroto Cup is related to:
    (*a*) Badminton   (*b*) Hockey
    (*c*) Football   (*d*) Polo

40. Mohun Began is associated with–
    (*a*) Cricket   (*b*) Hockey
    (*c*) Soccer   (*d*) Racing

41. In which country did the game of Basketball originate?
    (*a*) Russia   (*b*) Japan
    (*c*) USA   (*d*) Canada

42. In which year did the game of Basketball originate?
    (*a*) 1896   (*b*) 1928
    (*c*) 1892   (*d*) 1891

43. Who invented the game of Basketball?
    (*a*) James Nai Smith
    (*b*) W. A. Morgan
    (*c*) C. A. Bucher
    (*d*) Orbeteuffer

44. What is the name of trophy awarded to the winners of National Men's Championship in Basketball?
    (*a*) B. L. Gupta Trophy
    (*b*) Sulivan Cup
    (*c*) Todd Memorial Trophy
    (*d*) None of the above

45. Which trophy is awarded to Women's National Basketball Champion?
    (*a*) Uber Cup
    (*b*) Thomas Cup
    (*c*) Sulivan Cup
    (*d*) Basalat Jab Trophy

46. What is 'triangle and two' in Basketball?
    (*a*) A team defence
    (*b*) A combination offence
    (*c*) One to one defence
    (*d*) Zone offence

47. Who was the first female Basketball player to receive Arjuna Award?
    (*a*) P. T. Usha   (*b*) Suman Sharma
    (*c*) Vandana Rao   (*d*) Gurmeet Kaur

48. National game of Canada is:
    (*a*) Cricket   (*b*) Football
    (*c*) Ice Hockey   (*d*) Tennis

49. F. I. F. A. was formed in the year-
    (*a*) 1931   (*b*) 1932
    (*c*) 1933   (*d*) 1934

50. In which year was the game of Basketball included in the Olympics?
    (*a*) 1936, Berlin   (*b*) 1948, London
    (*c*) 1920, Antwerp   (*d*) 1924, Los Angles

ANSWERS

1. (*b*)	2. (*c*)	3. (*c*)	4. (*d*)	5. (*d*)	6. (*c*)	7. (*a*)	8. (*a*)
9. (*b*)	10. (*b*)	11. (*c*)	12. (*a*)	13. (*c*)	14. (*b*)	15. (*b*)	16. (*b*)
17. (*a*)	18. (*c*)	19. (*d*)	20. (*a*)	21. (*a*)	22. (*b*)	23. (*a*)	24. (*d*)
25. (*d*)	26. (*b*)	27. (*c*)	28. (*c*)	29. (*a*)	30. (*a*)	31. (*b*)	32. (*c*)
33. (*a*)	34. (*a*)	35. (*a*)	36. (*d*)	37. (*d*)	38. (*b*)	39. (*c*)	40. (*c*)
41. (*c*)	42. (*d*)	43. (*a*)	44. (*c*)	45. (*d*)	46. (*b*)	47. (*b*)	48. (*c*)
49. (*a*)	50. (*a*)						

www.ingramcontent.com/pod-product-compliance
Lightning Source LLC
LaVergne TN
LVHW062201190726
843495LV00009B/1508